Preparing the E Counselor Educ

Preparing the Educator in Counselor Education is a comprehensive skill development resource for counselor educators looking to engage students, develop curriculum, and provide effective feedback. Chapters fully aligned with the 2016 CACREP standards and grounded in current research discuss topics including pedagogy, identity development, classroom diversity, student engagement, teaching strategies, ethical and legal issues, gatekeeping, and mentoring. The book is replete with guided practice exercises, descriptive commentary, illustrative case studies, and examples from seasoned professionals that provide context, humor, and encouragement.

Laura R. Haddock, PhD, is full-time clinical faculty at Southern New Hampshire University and has more than two decades of experience as a clinician and a counselor educator.

Joy S. Whitman, PhD, is a core faculty member of Counseling@Northwestern at the Family Institute at Northwestern University and has over two decades of experience as a counselor and counselor educator.

Preparing the Educator in Counselor Education

A Comprehensive Guide to Building Knowledge and Developing Skills

Edited by
Laura R. Haddock
Joy S. Whitman

NEW YORK AND LONDON

First published 2019
by Routledge
711 Third Avenue, New York, NY 10017

and by Routledge
2 Park Square, Milton Park, Abingdon, Oxon, OX14 4RN

Routledge is an imprint of the Taylor & Francis Group, an informa business

© 2019 Laura R. Haddock and Joy S. Whitman

The right of Laura R. Haddock and Joy S. Whitman to be identified as the authors of the editorial material, and of the authors for their individual chapters, has been asserted in accordance with sections 77 and 78 of the Copyright, Designs and Patents Act 1988.

All rights reserved. No part of this book may be reprinted or reproduced or utilised in any form or by any electronic, mechanical, or other means, now known or hereafter invented, including photocopying and recording, or in any information storage or retrieval system, without permission in writing from the publishers.

Trademark notice: Product or corporate names may be trademarks or registered trademarks, and are used only for identification and explanation without intent to infringe.

Library of Congress Cataloging-in-Publication Data
Names: Haddock, Laura R., editor. | Whitman, Joy S., editor.
Title: Preparing the educator in counselor education : a comprehensive guide to building knowledge and developing skills/ edited by Laura R. Haddock, Joy S. Whitman.
Description: New York, NY : Routledge, 2018. | Includes bibliographical references and index.
Identifiers: LCCN 2018009638 (print) | LCCN 2018012114 (ebook) | ISBN 9781315521695 (eBook) | ISBN 9781138684843 (hardback) | ISBN 9781138684850 (pbk.)
Subjects: LCSH: Counseling—Study and teaching. | Counseling psychology—Study and teaching.
Classification: LCC BF636.65 (ebook) | LCC BF636.65. P74 2018 (print) | DDC 158.3071—dc23
LC record available at https://lccn.loc.gov/2018009638

ISBN: 978-1-138-68484-3 (hbk)
ISBN: 978-1-138-68485-0 (pbk)
ISBN: 978-1-315-52169-5 (ebk)

Typeset in Galliard
by Apex CoVantage, LLC

Contents

List of Contributors	vii
Preface	xi
Acknowledgments	xii

1 Establishing an Identity as a Counselor Educator   1
LAURA R. HADDOCK

2 Developing a Personal Philosophy of Teaching   14
JOY S. WHITMAN AND ERIC T. BEESON

3 Ethical and Legal Issues for Counselor Educators   35
THEODORE P. REMLEY, JR. AND CASSANDRA G. PUSATERI

4 Multicultural and Social Justice Leadership and Learning in the Classroom   59
ANNELIESE A. SINGH

5 Classroom Engagement and Evidence-Based Teaching Strategies With Adult Learners   78
MELISSA OCKERMAN AND BREANNA ADAMS

6 Acquisition of Knowledge and Skills   101
MICHAEL P. CHANEY AND JENNIFER J. MATTHEWS

7 Curriculum Development   120
J. KELLY COKER AND SAVITRI DIXON-SAXON

8 Evaluation of Student Learning: Instructor Feedback and Developmental Assessment   145
KRISTI CANNON

9	The Role of Gatekeeping in Counselor Education JANET L. MUSE-BURKE, AMANDA S. HANKO, AND JENNIFER S. BARNA	168
10	Teaching Across Settings CORINNE BRIDGES AND WALTER L. FRAZIER	190
11	The Role of Mentoring in Counselor Education CIRECIE A. WEST-OLATUNJI, KATHRYN WILLIAMS, AND CHRISTIAN D. CHAN	213
12	Voices From the Classroom	231
	Index	240

Contributors

Breanna Adams, MEd, LPC, teaches child/adolescent development and social/emotional learning at DePaul University as Adjunct Professor in the counselor and teacher education programs; she was a school counselor in Chicago for five years and currently manages a tutoring business, creates and delivers school-based interventions, and researches systemic barriers that contribute to inequitable education for her podcast, *Relatus*.

Jennifer S. Barna, PhD, NCC, ACS, is Associate Professor and Coordinator of the Counseling Program at Marywood University. Dr. Barna earned her PhD in Counselor Education and Supervision from Virginia Tech (CACREP-accredited). Dr. Barna has authored four publications in the area of school counseling and has presented on the topic of clinical supervision at professional conferences. She is an approved clinical supervisor (ACS) and has provided individual and group supervision to graduate students and site supervisors for nine years.

Eric T. Beeson, PhD, is a Core Faculty member with The Family Institute at Northwestern University and serves as an Associate Editor of the *Journal of Mental Health Counseling*. Eric is a long-time advocate for digital learning and bolsters a diverse research agenda focusing on sense of community in higher education, neuroscience in counseling, and ally training programs in higher education.

Corinne Bridges, EdD, LPC, NCC, is currently a full-time member of the Counselor Education and Supervision PhD program faculty at Walden University. Dr. Bridges serves as a qualitative research expert and mentors doctoral candidates throughout the dissertation process. Her research interests include treatment of mental health disorders and chronic pain; ecological counseling; women's issues; multicultural and LGBTQ counseling; and online education, gender, and relationship building.

Kristi Cannon received an MA in Community Counseling and a PhD in Counselor Education & Supervision from St. Mary's University. She is a licensed Professional Counselor, nationally certified counselor, and serves as Clinical Faculty for Southern New Hampshire University. Dr. Cannon regularly presents research at the state and national levels and publishes scholarly writings for professional counseling journals and textbooks. Her research interests include counselor development, Relational-Cultural Theory, and assessment practices in higher education.

Christian D. Chan, PhD, NCC, is Assistant Professor of Counseling at Idaho State University. His interests revolve around intersectionality of cultural and social identity; multiculturalism in counseling, supervision, and counselor education; social justice; career development; critical research methods; acculturative stress; intergenerational conflict; and cultural factors in identity development and socialization. He is particularly dedicated to mentorship for current and future professionals and leaders in counseling and counselor education.

Michael P. Chaney, PhD, LPC, NCC, ACS, is Associate Professor in the Department of Counseling at Oakland University. He is Past-President of the Association of LGBT Issues in Counseling, and currently serves as Editor-in-Chief for the *Journal of LGBT Issues in Counseling*. He has numerous publications in prestigious professional journals in the areas of substance use disorders, sexual compulsivity, sexual orientation, male body image, social justice, and advocacy in counseling.

J. Kelly Coker, PhD, is Associate Professor in the Department of Counseling at Palo Alto University. She has been a professional counselor since 1992 and a counselor educator in CACREP accredited programs since 1998. Dr. Coker is a licensed professional counselor in North Carolina, and she has worked in school, private practice, and tele-behavioral health settings with children, adolescents, adults, and couples. Dr. Coker has multiple professional publications and presentations, and she recently served as the Chair of the CACREP Board.

Savitri Dixon-Saxon, Dean of the School of Counseling and the Barbara Solomon School of Social Work and Human Services at Walden University, is a counselor educator and licensed professional counselor in the state of North Carolina and a national certified counselor. Dr. Dixon-Saxon has served in higher education for over 28 years. She understands that effective teaching is essential to the success of any counseling program and she is committed to the development of counselor educators.

Walter L. Frazier, PhD, LPC-S, NCC, is a Core Faculty Member for Walden University's PhD in Counselor Education and Supervision Program. He is a Licensed Professional Counselor, Board Qualified Supervisor, and a National Certified Counselor. Walter served from 2012 to 2017 as a member of the Mississippi State Board of Examiners for Licensed Professional Counselors, where he was the Board Chair from 2015 to 2017. Walter is an Ordained United Methodist Minister and is married to Terri Cowart Frazier.

Laura R. Haddock, PhD, LPC-S, NCC, ACS, currently serves as a full-time member of the Clinical Faculty for the Clinical Mental Health Program at Southern New Hampshire University. Laura routinely presents and publishes scholarly works and was the recipient of the 2017 Association of Counselor Education and Supervision Distinguished Service Award–Counselor Educator. Her research interests include counselor wellness and secondary trauma, graduate student development and remediation, cultural diversity, and supervision.

Amanda S. Hanko, PsyD, is a licensed Psychologist currently serving a geriatric population in Connecticut. Dr. Hanko earned her doctorate of clinical psychology from Marywood University in 2015. Her research has focused on gatekeeping procedures in supervision leading to the development of a measure of characterological traits of psychotherapists. Additionally, she has given presentations at state and international conferences. Dr. Hanko has provided individual supervision to master's and doctoral students for 2 years.

Jennifer J. Matthews is Assistant Professor in the Department of Counseling at Oakland University in Rochester, Michigan. She earned her PhD in Counselor Education and Supervision from the University of Central Florida. Dr. Matthews is a Licensed Professional Counselor, certified School Counselor, National Certified Counselor and Approved Clinical Supervisor. Her clinical experience and research interests include grief and loss, multicultural counseling, and counselor education and supervision.

Janet L. Muse-Burke, PhD, LPC, is Associate Professor at Marywood University and maintains a private practice. Dr. Muse-Burke earned her PhD in Counseling Psychology from Lehigh University (APA-accredited). She has co-authored six publications and two measures in clinical supervision. Further, she frequently presents at state, national, and international conferences. Dr. Muse-Burke trained for three years in clinical supervision and has provided individual and group supervision to students and mental health professionals for 17 years.

Melissa Ockerman is Associate Professor in the Counseling Program at DePaul University. Melissa has established a strong research agenda focusing on school counselor leadership, the efficacy of school counseling interventions, and systemic anti-bullying and school safety strategies. In 2012, she was named the *Illinois Counselor Educator of the Year*. Melissa is the co-author of the text *101 Solutions for School Counselors and Leaders in Challenging Times*.

Cassandra G. Pusateri is Director of Field Instruction within the Department of Counseling and Human Services at East Tennessee State University in Johnson City. She earned a PhD in Counselor Education and Supervision from Old Dominion University in Norfolk, Virginia. Cassandra has experience working with grant-funded programs and in clinical mental health agencies. Her research interests include the provision of counseling services in rural communities and Appalachia.

Theodore P. Remley, Jr., LPC, NCC, is Professor of Counseling at the University of Holy Cross in New Orleans, Louisiana. He holds a PhD in Counselor Education from the University of Florida and a JD from Catholic University in Washington, DC. Dr. Remley is the author and co-author of a number of articles, books, and book chapters related to legal and ethical issues in counseling.

Anneliese A. Singh, PhD, is Professor and Associate Dean for Diversity Equity, and Inclusion at the University of Georgia. Dr. Singh has worked on many counseling competencies (ACA *Multicultural and Social Justice Counseling Competencies*, ACA *Transgender Competencies*) and co-authored *Social Justice*

Counseling in Group Work, Affirmative Counseling and Psychological Practice with Transgender and Gender Nonconforming Clients, the *Queer and Trans Resilience Workbook,* and the upcoming *Healing from Racism Workbook.* She is Past-President of the Association of LGBT Issues in Counseling and SACES.

Cirecie A. West-Olatunji is Associate Professor and Director of the Center for Traumatic Stress Research at Xavier University of Louisiana. She is also Past President of the American Counseling Association (ACA). Dr. West-Olatunji's research projects focus on the relationship between traumatic stress and systemic oppression.

Joy S. Whitman, PhD, is a Core Faculty member with The Family Institute at Northwestern University. Prior to this position, she was Core Faculty at Walden University, Associate Professor at DePaul University, and Associate Professor at Purdue University Calumet. Her research focus is on LGBTQ counseling issues, specifically on training counselors to provide affirmative therapeutic treatment. Joy is a Licensed Clinical Professional Counselor in Illinois and a Licensed Professional Counselor in Missouri.

Kathryn "Kate" Williams, LMFT, is a Doctoral student in Counselor Education at the University of Florida. She is a past president of the Florida Counseling Association and is passionate about mentoring future counselors and counselor leaders. Her research and writing interests include: clinical supervision, leadership, advocacy, social justice, organizational culture, and competency development.

Preface

When we first developed the idea for this book, we were working fairly exclusively with doctoral students seeking a PhD in Counselor Education and Supervision. We were particularly passionate about being good teachers and trying to ensure that our students fully understood both the privilege and the responsibility that comes with becoming a counselor educator and training the future generations of counselors. We both spent hours searching for resources to help students gain both academic understanding of the practicalities of teaching, such as lesson planning, rubrics, and learning outcomes, as well tools to foster the development of a personal philosophy and style of teaching. What we found were texts that spoke to teachers and those in education and very few resources that address the specific needs of the education identity of a counselor educator. Those resources were available in various forms of well researched articles and in one text from the Association for Counselor Education and Supervision. We wondered why the dearth of comprehensive texts exists since one of the major responsibilities and roles for this career in counselor education and supervision is teaching. However, there still seemed to be lacking a comprehensive volume, and we found ourselves collaborating with colleagues and mentors to develop inclusive resources to support our students. We spent a considerable amount of time reflecting on our own past experiences of clinical training, supervision, and mentoring, our education as educators, and our experiences as counselor educators. We persistently looked towards the future trying to consider what would be needed in an educational landscape where words matter and Twitter is often a lens through which the world is viewed. Ultimately this editorial collaboration, born of a love of teaching, led to the development and co-editing of this book. It is our hope that you will find it both useful and inspiring.

Laura R. Haddock and Joy S. Whitman

Acknowledgments

It is with great thanks and appreciation that I wish to acknowledge the unwavering support I have received with this project. To my husband, Sean, thank you for your patience on the days when my answer to everything was "I can't, I have to work on the book." To my children, Austin and Anna, thank you for the endless supply of encouragement, hugs, and laughter! To hear you say you are proud of me feels good *every* time! To all my friends, colleagues, and students—both current and previous—who offered praise, suggestions, assistance, and support, I am humbled by the bounty of your presence in my life. And to my co-editor, Joy, thank you for your wisdom, your sense of humor, and especially your friendship!

Laura R. Haddock

I want to thank you, Laura, for your initial idea that we should edit a book on teaching future counselor educators. It has been quite a ride, and I am thankful to be on this professional and personal journey with you. I also want to thank my graduate assistant, Danica Rodriguez, a master's student in the Counseling@ Northwestern program, for her unfailing assistance and eagerness to help and to do so with professionalism and humor. Finally, I want to thank my partner, Liz McVay, who lost me when I spent hours and days working on the book. Though I was busy, you understood and kept us going.

Joy S. Whitman

1 Establishing an Identity as a Counselor Educator

Laura R. Haddock

The choice to teach the art and science of professional counseling is complex. If you have made the choice to become a counselor educator, you may anticipate an exceptionally rewarding and simultaneously challenging opportunity! As an educator, watching students' insight crystalize or understanding emerge like a buried treasure brings indescribable joy. But in other moments, the classroom can feel lifeless, and a teacher can feel powerless to make a difference. The clinical skills and professional dispositions required of counselors are not a good fit for all who express a desire to become a helping professional. Thus, you are not only charged with teaching counselors-in-training how to do the work, but you must also serve as a gatekeeper for the profession and the community at large. So where do you begin? While the focus of this chapter is establishing an identity as a counselor educator, remember teaching is about helping students learn and not about our own achievements as professors. Embrace the realization that students learn in diverse and wondrous ways, including learning that is a product of autonomous effort beyond the classroom or the instructor! But regardless of the setting—traditional face-to-face classrooms or synchronous and asynchronous online formats—good counselor educators possess the power to create conditions that can help counselors-in-training learn a great deal or become a barrier, leaving students learning nothing at all. Counselor educators are challenged to create those conditions, and to do so requires that we understand what makes up the professional identity of a counselor educator as well as the act of teaching.

Learning Objectives

After reading this chapter, you will have the information to:

1. Understand the role your professional identity plays in your work as a counselor educator.
2. Identify three primary roles of counselor educators.
3. Discuss the reciprocal relationship between teaching and the other primary roles of a counselor educator.
4. Describe the characteristics of effective teachers of adult learners.
5. Conceptualize the skills and dispositions needed as a counselor educator.

Relevant CACREP Standards

The relevant Council for Accreditation of Counseling and Related Programs (CACREP) standards addressed in this chapter are doctoral standards from Section 6, including the following:

a. Roles and responsibilities related to educating counselors
b. Pedagogy and teaching methods relevant to counselor education
f. Screening, remediation, and gatekeeping functions relevant to teaching

In addition, you will be oriented to the counselor education faculty role and responsibilities that align with Section 1 (The Environment; Faculty and Staff), including:

1. X Core counselor education program faculty identify with the counseling profession (1) through sustained memberships in professional counseling organizations, (2) through the maintenance of certifications and/or licenses related to their counseling specialty area(s), and (3) by showing evidence of sustained (a) professional development and renewal activities related to counseling, (b) professional service and advocacy in counseling, and (c) research and scholarly activity in counseling commensurate with their faculty role.

Counseling Professional as Educator

Let's talk more about creating a classroom environment that facilitates learning. In the weeks immediately prior to developing this chapter, I launched a new academic term teaching students who are pursuing a master's degree in clinical mental health counseling. I am five years into my second decade of work as a counselor educator and continue to feel grateful for another chance to teach as it engages my soul in a meaningful way. I was teaching two courses in a clinical mental health program of study and by the third week into the new term, I was, once again, challenged in my role as educator. The students in the first course section were virtually mute. I felt like I had essentially begged them to engage with me and with each other with little response. This left me convinced that I must truly be the most boring professor that has ever lived. In the second section, the students were engaged, which was terrific! Alas, some of the exchanges included a disrespectful battle between opposing positions. I did not display my frustration with the unprofessional behavior and instead used it as a teachable moment to demonstrate cultural sensitivity and openness to diverse views. While great discussions are often a product of opposing conversation, I was left fearing the consequences of the toxic residue of the student dialogue and an awkward classroom climate going forward. I have an arsenal of teaching strategies in my toolbox of creative teaching practices, but the launch of any new course has the potential to trigger feeling like I am starting over and can leave me feeling like an imposter—a novice who will be judged incompetent at any moment. I offer this story to simply say that no matter the years of experience, the techniques you will master can serve you well, but they are not enough. When you are in the role of counselor educator and it is your students and you—whether face to face or in an online exchange—the resources at your solid command are your identity, your education, and your experience as counselor educator and clinician. So, in your journey to become a counselor educator and create an environment that facilitates learning, I encourage you to consider that good teaching may not be based on technique and knowledge alone but be enriched by your experience and identity as a counseling professional.

Professional Identity as a Counselor Educator

Kottler (1991) observed that "we are the sum of all the teachers and mentors we have worked with, all the classes and workshops we have attended, and all the books we have read, movies we have watched, and experiences we have lived" (p. 41). In every class you teach, your ability to connect with your students and to connect with the subject may depend less on the methods you use than on the degree to which you know and trust your identity as a counseling professional and your willingness to make it available to students in the service of learning. Research has offered this same idea regarding clinical practice. If studies have shown we may help clients gain insight, improvement, and a decrease in dysfunction in spite of the chosen clinical intervention but with greater emphasis on the therapeutic relationship (Regas, Kostick, Bakaly, & Doonan, 2017), what might this say for the power of a strong sense of professional identity being shared with students in an educational setting?

> **Guided Practice Exercise 1.1**
>
> Take a moment to consider Kottler's (1991) assertion that "we are the sum of all the teachers and mentors we have worked with, all the classes and workshops we have attended, and all the books we have read, movies we have watched, and experiences we have lived" (p. 41). With consideration for that thought, reflect on each item—teachers and mentors—classes and workshops—books you have read—movies you have watched—experiences you have lived—one at a time. Write one adjective to represent your greatest take-away for each concept. For example, for teachers and mentors, you might say "creative." For life experiences, you might say "cynical." After you generate the list, consider each description as one part of your professional identity. Do you view those descriptions as strengths or areas for growth?

The process of professional identity development is defined as the "successful integration of personal attributes and professional training in the context of a professional community" (Gibson, Dollarhide, & Moss, 2010, pp. 23–24). If a counselor educator's classroom is part of their "professional community," this suggests that the role of professional identity is important for effective teaching. Goltz and Smith (2014) emphasize that professional identity is something that we are responsible for developing, not something that automatically happens.

I would argue that is absolutely true of our identity as a counselor educator. You must be intentional in developing your identity as an educator and supervisor. What sort of teacher do you want to be? What learning theory do you embrace? What model of supervision is the best fit for you? I have spent countless hours talking with students and colleagues, reading published studies, and reflecting on what I viewed as moments of success in the classroom as I have investigated what qualities define a "good" counselor educator. While the answers varied, and a number of themes emerged, one common thread in excellent teaching was a fully developed, confident professional identity that was transparently shared with students.

The Roles of Counselor Educators

Before we explore the topic of teaching in greater depth, it is important to recognize that counselor educators typically have responsibilities beyond instruction. Some primary roles of an academic faculty position include teaching and supervision, scholarship, and service (Green, 2008). Of course, every position is slightly different and the program that you work for will assign your responsibilities and define the expectations of the job. However, in general, counselor educators will participate in any or all of these roles on any given day. Thus, the development of a strong professional identity certainly has implications beyond the classroom. There is an interactive dynamic among and between all of the responsibilities of a counselor educator. The roles are not static and even tasks beyond that of instructor can, at times, have a teaching component. Let's take a look at the roles of teaching, scholarship, and service and consider how each one relates to the role of instructor.

Teaching and Supervision

Teaching and supervision are core activities for the counselor educator, and all faculty members are expected to achieve excellence in this role (Barrio Minton, Watcher Morris, & Yaites, 2013; Green, 2008). Teaching includes not just classroom instruction in which students gain knowledge about the core content in a counselor education program but also supervision of practicum and internship masters students and doctoral teaching assistants. It occurs not just in a face-to-face environment but in blended and purely online platforms. Faculty members are generally expected to teach courses within the program of study as part of their required workload. Mentoring, which you will explore in more detail in Chapter 11, is an extension of teaching and is an important component of teaching. It includes activities such as the supervision of student research and faculty advising (Baltrinic, Jencius, & McGlothlin, 2016; Murdock, Stipanovic, & Lucas, 2013). Program accreditation may also have requirements that dictate workloads related to teaching and supervision as well as informing how many course assignments are made. For example, CACREP (2016) maintains guidelines that require a strict faculty-student ratio that full time students should not exceed full time faculty by more than 12:1 (Section 1.T) and that students are taught primarily by full time faculty (Section 1.S). Additionally, faculty members at some universities may be expected to engage in academic advisement of students, though that is not the case in all settings.

Because the focus of this entire text is on the role of teaching for counselor educators, it is important to emphasize that faculty members are expected to engage regularly in activities designed to enhance the effectiveness of their own teaching (Choudhuri, 1999; Malik & Bashir, 2015). Building a broad repertoire of teaching strategies and knowing when and how to use the strategies is a critical skill for a counselor educator. You will be introduced to information that will assist you in developing your own teaching philosophy in Chapter 2, skills to use with students in Chapter 5, and strategies for maximizing your effectiveness in Chapter 8.

Scholarship

Boyer, Moser, Ream, and Braxton (2015) wrote, "All faculty, throughout their careers, should themselves, remain students. As scholars, they should continue to learn and be seriously and continuously engaged in the expanding intellectual world" (p. 36). For many faculty members, scholarship is often equated with conducting research and creative activities like professional presentations. However, it is fair to say that scholarship is nuanced and multidimensional. Nicholls (2004) conducted a qualitative inquiry and interviewed 25 academicians across disciplines, age, and position in an effort to define what faculty perceive as the responsibilities of scholarship. The outcome of the inquiry included three primary components to scholarship (p. 38):

1. Critical thinking and problem solving
2. Production, conceptualization, and understanding of new knowledge
3. Dissemination of knowledge to various audiences

These three principles hold true for counselor educators, who are frequently engaged in conducting scholarly investigations and adding empirical research to the professional counseling knowledge base. And, from a practical perspective, it is likely that your employment as a counselor educator will include expectation to publish original research and present at professional conferences. As mentioned earlier, the program or university that you work for will set the expectations for the type and amount of scholarship activity you are expected to produce. In accordance with the Carnegie Classifications of Institutions of Higher Learning, Research I schools give high priority to research (http://carnegieclassifications.iu.edu/classification_descriptions/basic.php). Thus, the expectations for publishing in scholarly peer reviewed journals are likely higher for faculty members at programs at Research I schools. Delivering professional presentations, on the other hand, is a common scholarship activity for counselor educators regardless of academic setting (Carlson, Portman, & Bartlett, 2006). Professional conferences, community advocacy, and continuing education are just a few of the venues that provide opportunities for counselor educators to disseminate professional information. The three principles of scholarship mentioned above include skills that an instructor would use in a classroom. For example, because as instructors we tend to use empirical evidence in teaching students, we are not only an active participant in generating new knowledge, but we are also an active participant in interpreting this knowledge. This implies a reciprocal relationship between scholarship and teaching, and in our teaching role, we use scholarship to draw the strands of the field together in a way that provides both coherence and meaning.

Service

Service is defined as activities in which faculty members offer professional knowledge, skills, and advice to their university, professional, and local communities (O'Meara, Kuvaeva, & Nyunt, 2017). Service activities draw on professional expertise, relate to the teaching and research missions of the University, and often imply a connection to the University and the profession (Carlson et al., 2006; O'Meara et al., 2017).

Faculty expectations for service vary depending upon the type of institution, the discipline, and the policies and practices of a particular program and department. It is critical for counselor educators to serve the department, college, profession, and community in ways that demonstrate a clear commitment to students, programs, the university, and the professional community (Meyers, 2014). Activities that contribute in a substantial manner to the important work of the institution for which you teach are an integral part of work as a faculty member. This may consist of serving in leadership roles, on committees, or as a mentors and advisors (Green, 2008; La Lopa, 2013; Meyers, 2014). This frequently involves developing courses, curriculum, and programs, and pursuit or maintenance of accreditation (Green, 2008; Meyers, 2014). Other duties could include reviewing proposals for funding or manuscripts authored by colleagues for presenting or publishing (Green, 2008). In addition, the obligation of service often extends to the profession and the local community through special assignments and initiatives, membership and offices in organizations, and sharing of expertise, such as serving on Health Advisory Boards or Crisis Response Teams, which is also routine practice for many counselor educators. As if service at the university and community level are not enough, faculty members are often expected to contribute their disciplinary expertise to address issues of importance in the region, state, and nation (Green, 2008). New counselor educators tend to become increasingly active in service, assuming increased responsibilities over the course of their careers. It is important to note that activities in which faculty engage that do not involve their professional expertise but instead center on family, political party, or social justice actions are commendable as being the normal commitments of citizenship, but they are not components of the workload of a member of the faculty.

Regardless of what stage of your career you are in or which service options you choose, every service selection tends to overlap with the role of teaching. For example, leadership on a committee models for students how as counselors their roles in the profession expand beyond the direct service to a client. Helping students get engaged, make coherent decisions about their education, understand course material, or plan future endeavors is all service to students that requires the ability to accurately inform students and facilitate understanding of the options. For the students, participation in community and professional organizations or boards deepens their experiences, so again, counselor educators are charged with helping students gain insight into the importance of the activities and acquire the knowledge needed to be successful in their efforts to carry out the activities they choose.

Guided Practice Exercise 1.2

After learning more about common roles of counselor educators, generate a list of your interests for each area. For Teaching/Supervision, list the subjects you think you would be interested in teaching. Describe why those are of interest to you. Next list what subjects you think that you would prefer not to teach and describe why you would prefer not to teach those topics. Now, consider scholarship. Are you interested in conducting research and publishing your findings in the professional counseling literature? Why or why not? If yes, what topics might you want to research? Would you like to present your research at a professional counseling conference? Finally, consider service. What service opportunities are of interest to you at the university level? Are there particular faculty committees you think you would be interested in? Service to the profession? Do you aspire to have a leadership position in a professional counseling organization? Service to the community? After you have generated your list for all three areas, consider what implications your choices have for your professional identity as a counselor educator and supervisor. Finally, reflect on your current skills, knowledge, and own dispositions that prepare you engage in each of these roles.

Counselor as Teacher

As I have reviewed roles common to counselor educators and emphasized the importance of the teaching role, it seems important to stop for a moment and consider that counselor educators may or may not have any background whatsoever in education or instruction. The American Counseling Association (ACA) Code of Ethics (2014) clearly states in standard F.7.a. that "Counselor educators . . . are skilled as teachers and practitioners" (p. 14). This standard aligns with the CACREP (2016) standards for a doctorate in Counselor Education and Supervision, which emphasize teaching as one of the five core areas. However, the skills needed to be an educator are not necessarily congruent with those of a counselor. While it seems obvious that teachers may benefit from counselor-related skills such as active listening or reflection, clinical skills do not necessarily prepare an educator to impart vast amounts of information, attend to various learning styles, meet learning objectives, or assess a student's work and return individualized feedback. Another example of how characteristics of clinical counselors may not naturally translate to the teaching role is that in clinical work, you can view a client as intrinsically valuable while doing the best they can, even if that is not terribly productive or healthy and progress is extraordinarily slow. On the other hand, you may not apply the same approach to working with students in terms of a dedication to positive regard without regard for program success or gatekeeping. You have a responsibility to protect and serve the student counselor's future clients, so you must learn to balance affirmation with accountability. In addition, while you may have very clear understanding of what to do in your clinical role, it doesn't mean that you know how teach someone else how to do it. Realistically, all who are great clinicians are not automatically great teachers. Learning to be an educator requires a dedicated effort and a commitment to lifelong learning. Albert Einstein taught throughout his career, and has been credited with a quote that underscores the importance of being prepared: "If you can't explain it simply, you don't understand it well enough" (Klein, 2017, para. 8).

The Act of Teaching

Now that we have examined the primary roles of counselor educators and recognized that the transition from clinician to educator does not occur naturally for all, let's take a deeper dive into establishing an identity as a counselor educator. Parker (2017) writes, "Bad teachers distance themselves from the subjects they are teaching—and in the process, from their students. Good teachers join self and subject and students in the fabric of life" (p. 11). So, what might this look like for a counselor educator? First let's pause to consider that counselor educators are instructing adult learners.

Adults as Learners

Before we consider characteristics that are commonly emphasized when educating adult learners, let's first consider the potential life circumstances of the students. Adults tend to attend or return to school for a variety of reasons (Bohonos, 2014). Understanding the context of an adult's participation in graduate school is important when anticipating student needs. Stein, Wanstreet, and Trinko (2011) reported that professional image and increased career opportunities were among the most common predictors of adult enrollment and persistence. This makes sense for counselors-in-training as a master's degree in counseling is necessary to seek licensure as a counseling professional. While many students enter a counseling training program with no background in the helping professions, others may have worked in a helping profession field in other capacities. Regardless of their background, your potential students are adults who have successfully completed a bachelor's degree and who are generally seeking advanced training or credentialing eligibility as a professional counselor. You will be introduced to models of teaching adult learners in Chapter 2 and Chapter 5. But based on your current thoughts, consider how might you approach teaching a diverse group of adult students? Consider the teaching scenario in Guided Practice Exercise 1.3.

Guided Practice Exercise 1.3

You have just entered your first week of class teaching an Introduction to the Counseling Profession. Your students are all newly admitted to a master's level counseling program, and you are looking to learn more about your students to help you prepare for course instruction. First, based on what you know thus far about adult learners, what do you feel would be your number one objective to set the tone for the course? What do you feel is important for you to learn about your students to help you with your course planning? What do you feel is most critical in terms of the student's first impressions?

Remember that there is not one way to teach. The key is to find your own voice, your own style, and your own approach that allows you to highlight what you have to offer while simultaneously honoring the life experiences and knowledge that the students bring to the process. I think it is fair to say that your teaching style and approach is likely to adapt and adjust in response to the particular group of learners that you are working with. Every student will have many powerful influences in their lives, namely the depth and breadth of their experiences, their family situations (caring for children or parents, for example), their obligations and responsibilities, and their ages. Sometimes you may feel similarities to students within your class and experience a generational connection with your students; for example, you may share memories of notable events, you may like the same music, or your children may be the same age. Learning this information about your students enables you to make personal connections with them and potentially heighten their engagement in the learning process. You may also find that with strong relational connections, your students often demonstrate increased interest in your professional or personal experiences, allowing you to create rich examples and context for students that enrich the learning process. Barnett (2008) contended that in an academic setting, graduate students are expected to "ultimately become colleagues and peers to faculty" (p. 9). This has certainly proven true in the field of counselor education. In Chapter 5, you will take a more detailed look at teaching strategies for use with adult learners. But it is important to recognize that you must develop a personal teaching style that not only allows you to share your professional identity but also honors the adult learner and facilitates the student-teacher connection. Before you begin reading the next section, complete Guided Practice Exercise 1.4.

Guided Practice Exercise 1.4

Take a moment to reflect on the instructors you have worked with along your academic journey. Choose one teacher from your post-secondary education who stands out for you as your least favorite and one who stands out for you as your most favorite. For each one, identify three characteristics that inform your selection for favorite and least favorite. Describe what makes that professor stand out for you.

Characteristics of Effective Teachers

In reviewing literature related to teaching excellence, there are many sources that examine characteristics of good teachers, although interestingly, few that were focused specifically on counselor education (Bryant, Druyos, & Strabavy, 2013; Korthagen, 2004; Malik & Bashir, 2015; Stein, Fujisaki, & Davis, 2011; Tang, Chou, & Chiang, 2005; Walker, 2008). Importantly, in-depth content knowledge and expert use of instructional methods were repeatedly included as part of the critical foundation of any good educator (Malik & Bashir, 2015; Tang et al., 2005; Walker, 2008). Please note this list is not intended to be exhaustive but merely a sample of qualities that emerged as common in outstanding faculty instructors regardless of the academic discipline (Bryant et al., 2013; Malik & Bashir, 2015; Stein et al., 2011; Tang et al., 2005; Walker, 2008).

Enjoy Their Work

Great instructors not only love their subject, but they love to share that joy with students. Faculty members identified as strong by students find joy in teaching because of their talent for relating to students over a particular topic. An important part of greatness is the match between the educator's skills and interests and the needs of the students. Counselor educators that share case examples or relevant clinical experiences with students can demonstrate not only joy in their teaching but also joy in the experience of clinical work that the students are preparing to do!

Offer Supportive Encouragement While Gatekeeping

While challenging, it is important to strive for a balance between promoting accountability and encouraging student success. Teaching, like counseling, is a humanistic profession, requiring compassion and genuine caring. Strong counselor educators orient their students to the role of gatekeeping from the very beginning of the program with transparency, and they respect and honor their students and the profession by holding them accountable for necessary skill development and professional dispositions.

Are Creative/Respond to Student Learning Styles

A great teacher can adjust and be flexible when a plan isn't working. They assess their teaching throughout the course and find new ways to present material to make sure that every student understands the key concepts. Strong counselor educators have no fear of learning new teaching strategies or incorporating new technologies into lessons.

Have a Willingness to Reflect

Asking yourself why things went the way they did, both on good days and bad days, is an important element of a dedication to growth and improvement. This means you have to be able to accept responsibility when the reasons it went bad were because of what you did or did not do, versus only considering the students' role in the problem. Also important is the understanding that often things go right because of what your students brought to the table, not because of your contribution. Effective teaching requires a willingness to cast a critical eye on the process and your own role in that process. We talk about how education should be transformative for students, but if you expect students to be changed by their interaction with you, ideally it will be a two-way street.

Understand the Content and Teach to the Developmental Level of the Student

Great professors keep in mind that every student and every class is unique, and what worked perfectly well with one class can miss the mark with another group of people. Individualizing instruction and honoring the learning styles and preferences of your students is critical, as is meeting your students where they are. Teachers that teach below the academic level of their students leave their students bored, and those who teach over the heads of their students are not facilitating learning. Strong professors always ask questions, listen to their students, and pay a lot of attention to their responses in order to adjust and meet the needs of the students.

Draw Upon Their Clinical Experience

Interestingly, there was little research identified which examined the role of clinical experience in strengthening the teaching excellence of counselor educators. Because clinical skill development is a significant facet of the counseling profession, it is critical for students to be presented with opportunities to connect theory to practice. Having professional counseling experience is invaluable for putting learning into context. Imparting knowledge is a key attribute to teaching, so having clinical experience and staying current in professional counseling literature are certainly activities that could strengthen a counselor educator's work with students.

Evaluating Your Effectiveness as a Teacher

Regardless of whether you are preparing to teach your very first course or whether you have been teaching for years, we all share the same goal of excellence in teaching. Counselor educators are expected to be engaged with a broad cross-section of students in a variety of different learning circumstances and to make substantial contributions to the counseling program. Now you will prepare to move into Chapter 2 and begin the process of building the skills and dispositions to be a quality teacher.

Summary

Choosing to be a counselor educator allows you the opportunity to participate in a variety of professional responsibilities. We have explored the roles common for counselor educators and investigated the reciprocal relationships among teaching, scholarship, and service. The task of educator is arguably one of the most critical components of a counselor educator's job description. Learning to be an instructor for adult learners requires a dedication to understanding your students and taking responsibility for growing the skills and professional dispositions that contribute to teaching excellence. For you to build a personal relationship with your chosen occupation, you must be intentional about building a professional identity as a counselor educator. Excellence in the classroom may be nourished through sharing your professional identity with your students in an authentic and transparent way. Your next step for building the foundation of your professional identity as a counselor educator is constructing a teaching philosophy which clarifies and distinguishes your profession from other similar vocations or roles such as clinician or supervisor. Now it's time for you to move ahead to Chapter 2, where you will be provided a roadmap for the development of your own personal philosophy of teaching.

References

American Counseling Association. (2014). *ACA code of ethics*. Alexandria, VA: Author.

Baltrinic, E., Jencius, M., & McGlothlin, J. (2016). Coteaching in counselor education: Preparing doctoral students for future teaching. *Counselor Education and Supervision, 55*(1), 31–45.

Barnett, J. E. (2008). Mentoring, boundaries, and multiple relationships: Opportunities and challenges. *Mentoring and Tutoring: Partnership in Learning, 16*, 3–16. doi:10/1080//13611260701800900

Barrio Minton, C. A., Watcher Morris, C. A., & Yaites, L. D. (2013). Pedagogy in counselor education: A 10-year content analysis of journals. *Counselor Education & Supervision, 53*, 162–177. doi:10.1002/j.1556-6978.2014.00055.x

Bohonos, J. (2014). Understanding career context as a key to best serving adult students. *Sage Journals, 25*(1), 28–30. Retrieved from http://journals.sagepub.com/doi/abs/10.1177/1045159513510144?journalCode=alxa

Boyer, E., Moser, D., Ream, R., & Braxton, J. (2015). *Scholarship Reconsidered: Priorities of the Professoriate* (2nd ed.). San Fransisco, CA: Jossey-Bass.

Bryant, J., Druyos, M., & Strabavy, D. (2013). Gatekeeping in counselor education programs: An examination of current trends. *Vistas Online*. Retrieved from www.counseling.org/docs/default-source/vistas/gatekeeping-in-counselor-education-programs.pdf?sfvrsn=7f6e77b5_13

Carlson, L., Portman, T., & Bartlett, L. (2006). Self-management of career development: Intentionality for counselor educators in training. *Journal of Humanistic Counseling, Education and Development, 45*, 126–137.

Choudhuri, D. (1999, October). *Navigating the role of counselor educator: The counselor as teacher*. Paper presented at the Association of Counselor Education and Supervision, New Orleans, LA.

Council for Accreditation of Counseling and Related Programs. (2016). *2016 CACREP Standards*. Retrieved from www.cacrep.org/wp-content/uploads/2017/07/2016-Standards-with-Glossary-7.2017.pdf

Gibson, D., Dollarhide, C., & Moss, J. (2010). Professional identity development: A grounded theory of transformational tasks of new counselors. *Counselor Education and Supervision, 50*, 21–38.

Goltz, H., & Smith, M. (2014). Forming and developing your professional identity: Easy as PI. *Health Promotion Practice, 15*(6), 785–789. doi:10.1177/1524839914541279

Green, R. (2008). Tenure and promotion decisions: The relative importance of teaching, scholarship, and service. *The Journal of Social Work Education, 44*(2), 117–127.

Klein, P. (2017). *Those who can't do, teach? Think again*. Retrieved from www.theglobeandmail.com/globe-debate/those-who-can-learn-certainly-do-teach/article24818663/

Korthagen, F. A. (2004). In search of the essence of a good teacher: Towards a more holistic approach in teacher education. *Teaching and Teacher Education, 20*(1), 77–97.

Kottler, J. A. (1991). *The complete therapist.* San Francisco, CA: Jossey-Bass.

La Lopa, J. (2013). The scholarship of teaching. *Journal of Culinary Science and Technology, 11,* 183–202. doi:10.1080/15428052.2013.783292

Malik, A., & Bashir, S. (2015). Good teacher: Student's perception about top qualities in health sciences. *The Professional Medical Journal, 22*(5), 670–673. doi:10/1080. 1356251032000155812

Meyers, C. (2014). Public philosophy and tenure/promotion: Rethinking "Teaching, Scholarship, and Service." *Philosophy, 15*(1), Article 5. doi:10.7710/1526-0569.1489

Murdock, J., Stipanovic, N., & Lucas, K. (2013). Fostering connections between graduate students and strengthening professional identity through co-mentoring. *British Journal of Guidance and Counselling, 41*(5), 487–503. doi:10.1080/0306 9885.2012.756972

Nicholls, G. (2004). Scholarship in teaching as a core professional value: What does this mean to the academic? *Teaching in Higher Education, 9*(1), 29–42.

O'Meara, K., Kuvaeva, A., & Nyunt, G. (2017). Constrained choices: A view of campus service inequality from annual faculty reports. *The Journal of Higher Education, 88*(5), 672–700. doi:10.1080/00221546.2016.1257312

Parker, P. J. (2017). *The courage to teach. Exploring the inner landscape of a teachers life.* San Francisco, CA: Jossey Bass

Regas, S., Kostick, K., Bakaly, J., & Doonan, R. (2017). Including the self of the therapist in clinical training. *Couple and Family Psychology: Research and Practice, 6*(1), 18–31. doi:10.1037/cfp0000073

Stein, S. M., Fujisaki, B. S., & Davis, S. E. (2011). What does effective teaching look like? Profession-centric perceptions of effective teaching in pharmacy and nursing education. *Health Interprofessional Practice, 1*(1), 1–14.

Stein, D. S., Wanstreet, C., & Trinko, L. A. (2011). From consideration to commitment factors in adults' decisions to enroll in a higher education degree program. *The Journal of Continuing Higher Education, 39,* 61–76.

Tang, F., Chou, S., & Chiang, H. (2005). Students' perceptions of effective and ineffective clinical instructors. *Journal of Nursing Education, 44*(4), 187–192.

Walker, R. (2008). Twelve characteristics of an effective teacher: A longitudinal, qualitative, quasi-research study on in-service and pre-service teachers' opinions. *Educational Horizons, 87*(1), 61–68. Retrieved from http://eric.ed.gov/PDFS/EJ815372.pdf

2 Developing a Personal Philosophy of Teaching

Joy S. Whitman and Eric T. Beeson

Close your eyes, take a deep breath, and when you are ready, imagine you are applying for your first position as a counselor educator, either as an adjunct or full time faculty. You notice the search committees commonly request a written statement of your teaching philosophy, a request that is present in over half of online job postings (Meizlish & Kaplan, 2008). How do you articulate what you think about teaching and learning? How do you understand the processes of learning and the related functions of teaching? How do you assess learning outcomes, and how do you address the diversity of adult learners? What role does the teacher-student relationship serve and what importance do you place on that relationship? These questions are simply a sample of the kinds of questions you must address as you develop your philosophy of teaching. For some, creating a personal philosophy of teaching can lead to anxiety and maybe even fear, especially when a potential faculty appointment is on the line. However, feel free to relax because this chapter will help you think through your beliefs about teaching and learning, review existing theories of education, and provide you with the opportunity to construct a personal philosophy of teaching.

In Chapter 1 you learned the importance of a strong professional identity, and the process of creating a personal philosophy of teaching begins to establish that identity as a counselor educator. How you understand your role as a counselor educator and articulate your beliefs about the process of learning and teaching is as central as is your ability to articulate your theoretical orientation and understanding of the counseling process as a counselor. This understanding becomes your personal philosophy of teaching that guides your practice as an educator. From foundational suppositions of constructivism to the modern approaches of transformational teaching and emerging neuroscience insights, the existing scholarship of teaching and learning provides a standard against which to compare your personal thoughts about teaching and learning (Hegarty, 2015; Schussler et al., 2011). As you explore your personal epistemology and pull from your past experiences as a student and from the existing literature, you will embark on a journey of self-discovery. This journey will arrive at a sound personal philosophy of teaching that incorporates current theories of learning, best practices of teaching and evidence-based practices of counseling, as well as ethical and national standards (Barrio Minton, Morris, & Yaites, 2014; Schönwetter, Sokal, Friesen, & Taylor, 2002).

Articulating your personal philosophy of teaching, much like a foundational theory of counseling, is a hallmark of ethical and effective practice as well as a process that can tap into your creative spirit. Much like your quest for a personal theory of counseling began with an exploration of your personal assumptions about the process of counseling, human nature, and the role of the therapeutic relationship, so too will the journey to create a personal philosophy of teaching. Before reading any further, take a moment to complete Guided Practice Exercise 2.1 to explore what you believe about teaching and learning. As you read the rest of this chapter, compare the information with your responses to Guided Practice Exercise 2.1. In doing so, your teaching philosophy will begin to evolve.

> **Guided Practice Exercise 2.1**
>
> If you have not yet done so, create a document that articulates your counseling theoretical orientation. Include in this document your understanding of human nature, how you believe people change, guiding principles and key concepts, development of the healthy personality and psychopathology, the influence of social development and identities, the impact of neurobiology, the significance of the therapeutic relationship, and key indicators of client change. Please use whatever outline best suits your ability to comprehensively state your theoretical orientation.
>
> Now, use this document to connect to the theories of learning that fit best to your theoretical orientation. It might be helpful to at first simply note next to each theoretical statement what theory of learning most aligns and then develop your own connection between them. Keep doing so until you have a clear understanding of the theory or theories of learning that are consistent with your theoretical orientation.

Learning Objectives

After reading this chapter, you will be able to:

1. Understand the difference between pedagogy and andragogy.
2. Identify current theories of learning and teaching for adult learners and strategies for learning and teaching.
3. Discuss the importance of neuroscience in teaching and learning.
4. Articulate the roles of teacher and learner and the relationship between them.
5. Develop a personal philosophy of teaching and learning.

CACREP Standards

The relevant CACREP teaching standards addressed in the chapter are related to those doctoral standards in Section 6.B.3. These standards primarily address teaching and overlap with those addressed in other chapters of this book. Section 6.B.3 includes the following:

a. Roles and responsibilities related to educating counselors
b. Pedagogy and teaching methods relevant to counselor education

c. Models of adult development and learning
d. Instructional and curriculum design, delivery, and evaluation methods relevant to counselor education
e. Effective approaches for online instruction
f. Screening, remediation, and gatekeeping functions relevant to teaching
g. Assessment of learning
h. Ethical and culturally relevant strategies used in counselor preparation
i. The role of mentoring in counselor education

Pedagogy Versus Andragogy

Pedagogy is a term you have likely heard in higher education. This term broadly describes the study of teaching and is a mainstay in higher education. The importance of pedagogy is outlined in the 2016 CACREP Standards (2015, 6.B.3.b) and these principles are discussed throughout this text. Given the broad definition of pedagogy, there is little empirical evaluation of pedagogy as a specific instructional method. Rather, specific forms of pedagogy (e.g., constructivist, critical) have emerged that provide operationalized assumptions and techniques that can be empirically tested. Despite the development of various forms of pedagogy, some have criticized the use of this term in higher education given its root emphasis on the education of children (e.g., Knowles, 1980).

Knowles, Holton, and Swanson (2005) described pedagogy as a model of instruction that is:

> designed for teaching children, assigns to the teacher full responsibility for all decision making about the learning content, method, timing, and evaluation . . . [while] learners play a submissive role in the educational dynamics.
> (p. 72)

Pedagogy has been described as a hierarchical system in which the teacher assumes full responsibility for what will be taught and how it will be taught as well as a system in which the learner has little autonomy, their prior experience has little meaning to the current educational endeavor, and the learner is dependent on the teacher for their learning (Taylor & Kroth, 2009b). Given the differences in the way people learn across the lifespan, alternative perspectives such as andragogy have emerged to address the teaching and learning of adults.

Andragogy is defined as the "art and science of helping adults learn" (Knowles, 1980, p. 43). Andragogy gained popularity in the 1960s due to the work of Malcolm Knowles, an American educator, but it was originally conceptualized by Alexander Knapp, a German educator in the early 1800s (Taylor & Kroth, 2009a). As will be discussed in Chapter 6, adult learners engage differently with knowledge than do children; therefore, how we understand and resultantly how we create learning experiences for adult learners will inform our philosophy of teaching. Below we offer a brief discussion of the major concepts, principles, and processes of andragogy as they are important concepts to consider when creating your philosophy of teaching.

The Importance of Andragogy in Developing a Teaching Philosophy

Andragogy as a model of instruction is grounded in the belief that adults:

> need to know why they need to learn something . . . maintain the concept of responsibility for their own decisions and life . . . enter the educational activity with a greater volume and more varied experiences than do children . . . have a readiness to learn those things that they need to know in order to cope effectively with real-life situations . . . are life-centered in their orientation to learning . . . and are more responsive to internal motivators than external motivators.
>
> (Knowles et al., 2005, p. 72)

These characteristics of adult learners differ from those of children for whom traditional pedagogic theories and strategies for learning were based. As such, it is important to keep in mind these core assumptions of adults learners: (a) why and how I need to learn must be communicated, (b) my previous life experiences must be integrated and valued in my learning process, (c) my self-concept as independent and autonomous must be respected, (d) instruction must be relevant to my developmental tasks to foster my readiness to learn, (e) real world scenarios of personal importance are integral to the orientation I take toward learning, and (f) I am internally motivated by goal attainment and problem resolution (Gom, 2009; Knowles et al., 2005). These assumptions guide the creation of a learning environment where (a) the teacher is a co-constructor of experiences that focus on student self-directedness and autonomy, (b) instructional methods are primarily experiential (such as problem- and case-based learning, role-playing, and simulations) and based on real world scenarios, and (c) learning and contexts are scaffolded to address desired learning outcomes and current developmental level.

The development of cognitive complexity and self-directed learning skills is key to an andragogical approach, and the evaluation of student learning outcomes is best assessed when using multiple strategies, such as case presentations, role-playing, and clinical scenario exams. Instructional practices using the principles of andragogy follow an eight-step process recommended by Knowles et al. (2005):

> (1) preparing the learner, (2) establishing a climate conducive to learning, (3) creating a mechanism for mutual planning, (4) diagnosing the needs for learning, (5) formulating program objectives (which is content) that will satisfy these needs, (6) designing a pattern of learning experiences, (7) conducting these learning experiences with suitable techniques and materials, and (8) evaluating the learning outcomes and rediagnosing learning needs.
> (p. 115)

How adults learn and their expectations of instructors and the learning environment are processes integral to consider as you review the modern theories of learning and teaching discussed in the next section. These key assumptions of adult learning must find their way into your teaching philosophy to reflect current research and knowledge about how adults learn and therefore how we design educational experiences.

As you are thinking about your personal philosophy of teaching, what do you think about the differences between pedagogy and andragogy? Which of the assumptions do you think you align with most? If you are interested in further evaluating your instructional methods, consider using the Teaching Methodology Instrument (Taylor & Kroth, 2009b) to explore whether your practices are more aligned with a pedagogical or andragogical approach.

Theories of Teaching and Learning

As you consider your personal philosophy of teaching, it is important to consider theories of teaching and learning. Much like counseling theory informs your clinical practice, theories of teaching and learning provide guidance for the instructional methods you choose. Although Chapters 5 and 6 will review learning theory in more detail, we provide you an introduction to some of the most frequently used theories in education and strategies for teaching suggested by each theory. The purpose of this chapter is to review seminal works rather than provide an exhaustive review and current literature. Theories continue to evolve as do their evidence, so remember to continue to review up-to-date literature on each of the topics. As you read the following sections, compare your responses to Guided Practice Exercise 2.1 with the thoughts of other theorists described below. You can consider how these theories also connect to your counseling theoretical orientation as a means to seamlessly integrate and articulate your teaching philosophy with your theoretical perspective. Table 2.1 offers you an overview of each of the theories discussed below.

Constructivism

A major principle of this theory is the belief that learners are active in building knowledge from their experiences (Kumari, 2014; McAuliffe & Eriksen, 2010). That students create meaning from what they learn and how they use their subjective experiences to do so is significant to this approach (Brooks & Brooks, 2005; McAuliffe & Eriksen, 2010; McCaughan, Binkley, Wilde, Parmanand, & Allen, 2013). You are instrumental in helping students understand that learning is a process of creating meaning from experiences without there being one interpretation of that experience (McCaughan et al., 2013; Nelson & Neufeldt, 1998). Students solve problems by using their own skills, and you as their teacher provide an environment conducive to the application of those skills to these problems. In essence, you are the guide to student learning whereby meaningful discussions of life problems are understood within their social contexts (Kumari, 2014; Eriksen & McAuliffe, 2001).

Through dialogue, you and your students establish that there exists no absolute truth and students' life experiences are appreciated as instrumental to their active learning (Brooks & Brooks, 2005; McCaughan et al., 2013). Students are viewed as the experts of their own learning and learning is self-reflective (Nelson & Neufeldt, 1998). These principles of constructivist pedagogy align with

Table 2.1 Learning Theories Chart

Theory	Major Principles	Role of Student	Role of Teacher	Strategies
Constructivist	Learning is co-constructed with no one meaning or absolute truth to experiences. Students are expert to their own learning.	Co-creator of and active in building knowledge. Students use their own experiences to become reflective learners.	Guide and facilitator. Provide an environment conducive to exploration.	Engage in dialogue, reflective learning and teaching, and foster student-driven approaches and lessons.
Critical Pedagogy	Concerned with power, oppression, justice, and society and how education can create opportunities where there is economic, cultural, and political equality. Highlights the healing and enriching power of education as well as well-being, self-actualization, and empowerment in both students and teachers.	Critically analyze social conditions and work toward changing their consciousness leading to social change. Learn through their experiences and those of others while taking ownership of the learning process.	De-emphasize your power and status and learn side by side with students. Encourage students' questioning and their voices in the classroom.	Create student-centered learning environments. Pose current social problems to students who use their experiences and critical thinking to raise their consciousness.
Transformative	Learning is understood as a process of changing students' frames of references through critical reflection. How students think, act, and feel shapes their views of the world and causes them to act in ways that may include assumptions of others that will be challenged and transformed through the educational process.	Students are responsible for their learning and are invited to challenge their assumptions and distortions of the world. They are placed at the center of the learning process and encouraged to be autonomous thinkers.	Create a learning environment that supports a learner-centered approach and that invites students to critically reflect on their frame of reference.	Take a learner-centered approach. Students are tasked with contributing to the creation of the learning environment, assignments, etc. Students are respected and encouraged to take an open stance toward others.

the humanistic approach to counseling (Rudes & Guterman, 2007) and can lead to a seamless alignment with your theoretical orientation.

If you are interested in taking a more in-depth look at a constructivist approach to teaching, Brooks and Brooks (2005) offer guidance in terms of constructivist teaching behaviors, such as encouraging student autonomy, students' engagement with each other and the professor, fostering student-driven lessons, and nurturing student curiosity (please see Brooks and Brooks, 2005, for a complete list of identified behaviors). McAuliffe and Eriksen (2010) guide counselor educators in the application of constructivist theory to the instruction of counselors. Their work applies a constructivist approach to the varied courses in a counselor education program, offering theory and application as well as example activities. Using a reflective learning approach, Tobin, Willow, Bastow, and Ratkowski (2009) explored how this practice is included in a community counseling program. They offer unique learning activities that operationalize the concepts of constructivist learning within a counselor education curriculum.

Critical Pedagogy

Critical pedagogy (CP) is concerned with power, oppression, justice, and society and how education can create opportunities where there is economic, cultural, and political equality (Freire, 1970). The focus of CP is on creating awareness of those conditions that oppress and marginalize people and rejecting those systems that discriminate and disempower. This leads to changing educational systems, such that people are transformed "from being objects of education to subjects of their own autonomy and emancipation" (Aliakbari & Faraji, 2011, p. 77). The end goal of CP is for students to become critical thinkers who are empowered to improve their lives and those of others (Aliakbari & Faraji, 2011; Freire, 1970).

Strategies for teaching include altering the conviction that you as the teacher are the keeper of knowledge and students are passive receivers of that knowledge (Freire, 1970), and instead creating a learning environment that is student-centered with a de-emphasis on the power and status of you as the teacher (Foley, 2007). To do so, you would focus on posing problems to students to inspire their critical thinking and foster the development of their knowledge (Aliakbari & Faraji, 2011; Kabilan, 2000; Nixon-Ponder, 1995). Students rewrite their experiences and perceptions (Degener, 2001; Giroux, 2004) and, in so doing, raise their consciousness and develop a critical perspective of the world that can lead to transformation of oppressive societal conditions (Aliakbari & Faraji, 2011; Elias, 1976). These strategies support the belief that students have a right to question and to be heard (Aliakbari & Faraji, 2011; Freire, 1970; Nixon-Ponder, 1995).

Critical pedagogy can also be viewed as a broad classification of theories that align with similar assumptions. For instance, feminist pedagogy has the same assumptions as critical pedagogy, but might place a higher focus on inequalities and oppression related to gender roles (Enns & Forrest, 2005). Additionally, engaged pedagogy (Hooks, 1994) extends the assumptions of critical pedagogy by highlighting the healing and enriching power of education as well as well-being, self-actualization, and empowerment in both students and teachers.

Transformative Learning

Transformative learning theory was created by Mezirow (1978) and proposes that learning occurs through the process of changing our frame of reference. By this he meant that adults create a frame of reference based on cumulative values, assumptions, feelings, associations, and concepts resulting from our perceptions of life experiences. There are two dimensions of the frame of reference, and these include what he calls habits of mind and points of view (Kitchenham, 2008; Mezirow, 2012). Both consist of ways we think, act, and feel that over time shape how we view the world, with habits of mind having greater stability over time than points of view. Systems around us, for example culture, politics, and education, influence our habits of mind and help to create a set of codes, which are then articulated via our point of view. For a more detailed discussion of the theoretical concepts, please refer to Mezirow's work (1978, 2012), Kitchenham (2008), and Taylor and Cranton (2012).

In terms of how transformative learning is understood as an educational process, the emphasis is on critical reflection of the assumptions we make about the world in the service of changing our frames of reference and updating our perceptions (Kitchenham, 2008; Mezirow, 2012). Critical thinking is key to the process as we are vulnerable to integrating stereotypes and distortions of the world based on unexamined past experiences. Learners must question their assumptions and perspectives, which are based on dominant views, and move beyond them to create social change (Hoggan, Mälkki, & Finnegan, 2017).

How is learning guided, and what are the roles of learner and you as teacher in transformational learning? Similar to constructivist and critical pedagogies, transformational learning takes a learner-centered approach (Weimer, 2012). For example, students take responsibility for their learning tasks and choice of assignments, for contributing to classroom policies, and for setting due dates. The simple act of placing students in the center of learning and as directors of the process is transformative in that it causes learners to critically question assumptions about education. Your role as teacher is to create a learning environment that supports a learner-centered approach and which invites students to critically reflect on their frame of reference. This is accomplished through dialogue and in a learning environment that encourages autonomous and critical thinking, respects and encourages empathic expression of thoughts and feelings, and maintains an open stance toward others (Mezirow, 2012). These strategies are similar to those you may use as a counselor, and you can model these attitudes and principles of the theory by how you set up your classroom, engage your students to foster autonomy, and value their diverse backgrounds.

Congruence Between Theory and Practice

Many of the theories described above share similar characteristics. As you think about your personal theory of teaching, it is important to articulate these beliefs as well as describe how you put those beliefs into action. It is essential that your practice match the beliefs that you espouse in your teaching philosophy. For instance, consider an educator who claims to have a constructivist pedagogical stance but describes their favorite instructional method as requiring students to memorize the key findings of the educator's own publications and assessing their acquisition of these "facts" via multiple choice exams. Although this is an extreme example, this person's teaching philosophy does not match their instructional methods, and this is not uncommon. Therefore, remain congruent with who you are as a person and an educator, both on paper and in person. Here is a chart summarizing the theories, major tenets, and strategies described above. Using this chart, consider how you might address the following case as well.

Case Illustration 2.1

Danica is a student in your doctoral course on teaching in counselor education. She has come to you because the theories she is learning so far all resonate with her. She is not sure which ones really fit for her style as an educator. You are attempting to help her narrow her focus in terms of those theories of learning that most resonate with her. Using the chart above and what you have learned from the material on learning theories, how can you help her find those theories that best fit? What kinds of questions and assignments might you create with her to help her deepen her learning? How can you help her parse out the differences among the various learning theories and strategies so she can begin to integrate those learning theories that resonate with her counseling theoretical perspective?

Theory in Action

Given the importance of aligning personal philosophy and instructional methods, we propose one approach, problem-based learning (PBL), that shows the theoretical assumptions outlined in this chapter in action. Its key features include: (a) learning is student-centered, (b) learning uses small student groups, (c) the role of the teacher is that of facilitator or guide, (d) learning is organized and stimulated by the introduction of problems, (e) clinical and problem-solving skills are developed through the use of problems, and (f) self-direction drives integration of new information, which promotes future implementation (see Barrows, 1983; Davis & Harden, 1999; Savery, 2006). PBL is grounded in a sequence of learning that begins with the creation of student groups and concludes with the application of learning to new situations.

PBL is best understood as a continuum based upon the degree to which the learning environment is organized around an ill-structured problem-scenario (Harden & Davis, 1998). For instance, traditional lecture-based methods assume the existence of objective "right" answers that establish the content as the organizing structure for learning experiences. This content is then presented to students and followed by problem-scenarios that allow the students to apply the previous content to the problem-scenarios. In PBL, the presentation sequence is reversed; the problem-scenario is presented before the content. Student groups, normally between five and 10 members, define the problem-scenario, activate pre-existing knowledge, identify gaps in learning, develop learning outcomes, engage in independent study, present their findings, re-hypothesize as needed, and apply learning to new scenarios (Harden & Davis, 1998; Savery, 2006).

Although many models exist regarding the steps in the PBL sequence (see Davis & Harden, 1999; Hmelo-Silver, 2004), the PBL sequence can be synthesized into seven steps: (a) group formation, (b) presentation of the problem-scenario, (c) problem-definition, (d) identification of learning goals, (e) independent inquiry, (f) present findings and re-conceptualize problem-scenario and potential solutions, and (g) synthesize new learning and generalize to additional scenarios. It should also be noted that formative evaluation continues throughout the entire process.

Several instructional practices are helpful to facilitate the PBL sequence. Hmelo-Silver (2004) describe the use of a PBL whiteboard that includes four columns labeled *facts, ideas, learning issues,* and *action plan* (p. 243). The PBL whiteboard is similar to traditional educational tools such as the KWL chart (Ogle, 1986). KWL charts can be used to identify what students know, what they want to know, and finally what they have learned.

What About the Brain?

Any discussion of modern teaching philosophy would be incomplete without mention of emerging neuroscience findings. From cognitive to educational psychology and beyond, neuroscientists are exploring the process of learning. Around 2013, the Association of Counselor Education and Supervision (ACES) established the Neuroscience Interest Network to vision about the future of neuroscience in the practice of counselor education (Beeson & Field, 2017). However, at the time of this writing, the empirical discourse about neuroscience in counselor education has been absent. In fact, the 2016 ACES Teaching Task Force Report failed to mention neuroscience in its review of best practices. So, the question remains, how does neuroscience research inform counselor education?

While educators in general are often interested in neuroscience concepts and how they inform their course design and teaching methods, there is often difficulty translating these findings to educational practice (Pickering & Howard-Jones, 2007). When creating a teaching philosophy, it is important to consider how neuroscience research informs your beliefs about student development, the learning process, course design, instructional methods, and outcome evaluation. As neuroscience and the biological bases of human functioning are appearing more and more in what we teach (CACREP, 2015) and how we practice (Beeson & Field, 2017), it is important to explore the impact of neuroscience research on how we teach. We believe that neuroscience-informed teaching could be considered a meta-framework that explains and extends existing theories of teaching and learning in counselor education.

Considerations for the infusion of neuroscience in counselor education can be informed by the existing literature surrounding brain-based teaching approaches (BBTA), initially outlined by Caine and Caine (1990) and expanded upon and evaluated by many others (e.g., Gözüyeşí & Díkíc, 2014; Thomas & Swamy, 2014). Caine and Caine (1990) introduced twelve principles of brain-based learning that encompass many brain processes (e.g., parallel processing, physiological elements, etc.) as well as strategies for educators to create meaningful learning environments that speak to the unique and inherent functions of the brain (e.g., experiential and collaborative learning). They recommend that brain-based learning promote relaxed alertness and challenge (relaxed alertness), immerse students in the material connected to multiple senses and contexts (orchestrated immersion), and engage in active processing and self-reflection (active processing). BBTA incorporates techniques such as breathwork, music, and environmental manipulation (Thomas & Swamy, 2014) as well as regular assessment to promote the belief that growth is possible, the use of positive/encouraging feedback, and a review of main points at the end of class sessions to consolidate learning (Oghyanous, 2017),

Tafti and Kadkhodaie (2017) further expanded on the process of BBTA by describing the education sequence as follows: activating the brain by explaining the importance of the concepts to daily living, introducing novel scenarios, challenging through experiential expression and the connection between topics and personal life in order to make meaning of the new information, using problem solving tasks to create multiple solutions, delivering feedback interactively, and closing with small group review to promote retention. In addition to techniques, neuroscience research is highlighting important characteristics of teachers that seem to be linked to educational outcomes. One study indicated that qualities such as vivacity, humor, creativity, inquisitiveness, concentration, cautiousness, and dynamism were key features of excellent educators (Inocian, 2016).

The outcomes of BBTA show promise. BBTA has shown statistically significant benefits in learning and retention of social skills (Tafti & Kadkhodaie, 2017), self-efficacy (Oghyanous, 2017), as well as academic achievement and stress reduction (Thomas & Swamy, 2014). Additionally, Gözüyesi and Dikici (2014) conducted a meta-analysis of studies comparing brain-based learning to traditional instructional methods from various countries around the world. In 35 of the 42 studies, results suggested that brain-based learning had a medium effect size in promoting student achievement. There were no significant differences according to subject matter or educational level. It should also be noted that a major limitation in the BBTA research is the focus on primary and secondary, rather than post-secondary, education.

Owens and Tanner (2017) share a compelling description of the neurobiological basis of several teaching strategies (e.g., concept mapping, active homework, problem-based learning, culturally relevant examples, and think-pair-share). In sum, they focus on the ability to stimulate synaptic connections to foster memory retrieval, release neurotransmitters necessary in memory formation, and prevent the release of stress hormones (e.g., cortisol) that impair learning. In doing so, these authors suggest, learning is more sustained and more easily applied in the completion of exams and future professional tasks.

Despite the excitement and importance surrounding the neuroscience and neurocounseling movement, counselor educators should exercise caution. There is a risk for neuroscience findings to be overstated or overgeneralized. When presented with a list of statements about neuroscience and education, both true and false, Dekker, Lee, Howard-Jones, and Jolles (2012) found that educators believed 49% of the presented myths about neuroscience and education. These findings underscore our ethical obligation to critique emerging research, ground our practices in the best science possible, and continually evaluate our practices with a high degree of empiricism.

Developing a Personal Philosophy of Teaching

What, then, comprises a personal philosophy of teaching? There are many examples of how to construct a teaching philosophy, and most agree on key aspects for inclusion (Hegarty, 2015; Kearns & Sullivan, 2011; O'Neal, Meizlish, & Kaplan, 2007). It is up to you and your personal preference as to what you include and how. If you consider Lang's (2010) belief that a teaching philosophy is a form of "creative nonfiction" (p. 62), ensuring that you do more than discuss the components but also include specific examples and narratives supporting those sections, your philosophy will result in a personal and idiosyncratic representation of your beliefs and strategies for learning and teaching. For a narrative and personal example of a teaching philosophy, see Licklider (2004).

Pragmatically, a teaching philosophy at a minimum should include the following sections: (a) how students learn and their role in the process, (b) how instructors teach and their role in the learning process, (c) methods of instruction, (d) goals of learning and teaching, (e) assessment of learning and teaching, and (f) attention to diverse learners and learning styles (Kearns & Sullivan, 2011; Lang, 2010; O'Neal et al., 2007). Each of these components is more fully addressed in the chapters of this book, and we recommend reviewing those chapters to inform your philosophy.

We also recommend grounding your philosophy in evidence-based teaching (EBT). Malott, Hall, Sheely-Moore, Krell, and Cardaciotto (2014) explored EBT in higher education and applied their findings to counselor education. They found three foci for best practices, which include how you create an effective learning environment, how you structure intentional learning experiences, and how you assess for effective teaching. Additionally, Felicilda-Reynaldo and Utley (2015) studied the inclusion of evidence-based practice (EBP) in the teaching philosophies of nurse educators and found that integration of EBP was included. We suggest including some discussion of EBT and EBP, both in terms of clinical practice and andragogical approach.

Now that you have a general idea of the various components of a philosophy of teaching, how do you put it all together? Lang (2010) suggests starting with the end and offers a pragmatic approach to the construction. He recommends envisioning how your students are different because of your course and including both general and specific beliefs about how they became different. For example, you may offer general strategies of how you teach counseling students and add an example of one specific strategy you find effective and why. In addition, there are key questions you can ask yourself to guide you.

Guided Practice Exercise 2.2

Using the following guiding questions, create your teaching philosophy. We suggest you start with the document you created in Guided Practice Exercise 2.1 and build from there. It is important to integrate your theoretical orientation, personal style, and understanding of learning and teaching with reference to the most current research. Additional chapters in the text can also offer you information to include in terms of learning objectives, ethics, assessment, and multicultural and social justice.

Before addressing the questions below, reflect on this question: Why do I teach and what value do I find in teaching? From that reflection, address the following to inform and create your teaching philosophy.

Learning Goals

1. What do you want students to learn about counseling?
2. How is the acquisition of knowledge, skills, and dispositions connected to learning counseling as a practice?
3. If a student were to recommend your class to another student, what would you want the student to say in regard to what they learned in your classes?
4. How are specific issues of ethics, diversity, and advocacy weaved through student learning?

Teaching Methods and Enactment of Goals

1. What are the roles and responsibilities of students and teachers in the process of learning?
2. What theories of learning and counseling inform your beliefs about how students learn and the methods you use to teach?
3. How do your methods help adult learners reach your goals of learning?
4. What about who you are as person, including your values and beliefs, informs what methods of instruction you incorporate in your teaching?
5. How do the methods vary along online and face-to-face platforms and how are they similar?

Learning Environment

1. What kind of learning environment do I want to create for adult learners?
2. How does the creation of this learning environment connect to my beliefs and values and to my theoretical orientation and convictions about learning and teaching?
3. How do I create an inclusive environment that addresses the various styles of student learning and diversity of student identities? How do I create this both in online and face-to-face platforms?
4. What is my approach to managing the learning environment so that all students feel included while modeling the values of the counseling profession?

Assessment of Learning Goals

1. How do I know students are learning?

2. What assessments of student learning do I use that are consistent with my understanding of learning and counseling?
3. How are the goals of learning assessed formatively and summatively?
4. How do students know they are learning? What have I developed to help them self-assess their own progress toward learning goals? How are those processes integrated with my philosophy of learning and theoretical orientation of counseling?
5. How do I understand and enact my roles as gatekeeper in the counseling profession via assessment of student learning and dispositional development?

Assessment of Teaching

1. How do I know my teaching methods are effective and assess what I intend to assess?
2. How do I use teaching evaluations to strengthen and transform my approach and philosophy of student learning?
3. What are my strengths as a teacher, and how are those strengths connected to my identity as a counselor and counselor educator?
4. How do I enact my role as reflective practitioner to improve my teaching and continue to develop?

These questions are adapted from various sources (Hannon, 2014; Kearns & Sullivan, 2011; O'Neal et al., 2007; Schönwetter et al., 2002) and include the integration of your counseling perspective. For example, when addressing how students learn, if you are a humanistic counselor, integrating humanistic theoretical concepts into how you believe students learn is an effective way to additionally showcase your counseling perspective as it pertains to student learning.

When crafting your statement, keep in mind the findings by Meizlish and Kaplan (2008). They found search committees did not favorably receive teaching philosophy statements using boilerplates. Instead, they discovered search committees valued the following components and approaches to the articulation of a philosophy of teaching: (a) evidence of practice, (b) reflectiveness, (c) how and that teaching is valued, (d) student- or learner-centered teaching with attention to diversity of student learning and backgrounds, and (e) a document that is well written. Lang (2010) also recommended being specific and concrete and citing sources that inform your statement. In doing so, use examples from your own teaching to illustrate goals, methods, and assessments. We recommend using these suggestions while integrating your own creativity to guide you as you create philosophical statements about teaching.

We are including a teaching philosophy created by one of the authors to illustrate one way you can approach the development of your philosophy. It is creative and less traditional than other statements you may encounter, and it offers an example of how to make the statement personal while also professional. There are ample examples to pattern yours after, and the resources below offer some ideas. Of most importance is to be true to your counseling and theoretical orientation and to those theories of learning that are compatible with your values and beliefs and to clearly articulate how they are integrated into your philosophy of teaching. Finally, as you consider what a teaching philosophy for a counselor educator might include, return to the values of the counseling profession (ACA, 2014). In doing so, ask yourself, why do I teach? What value is there in teaching? How do I model the values of the counseling profession through my philosophical statement of teaching?

Example Teaching Philosophy

Imagine that there was a person **(teacher)** who was planning to host a bonfire **(course/curriculum)** for a few colleagues **(students)**. Creative invitations **(engaging course descriptions)** were distributed, and recipe books **(accreditation standards)** were explored to identify some popular bonfire treats **(student learning outcomes [SLOs])**. While looking at the recipes, it was discovered that the host already had many of the ingredients **(prior knowledge, experience, and expertise)** needed to make the treats but required a few more from the local grocery **(current literature and other resources)**. While at the grocery store, the host purchased the remaining ingredients as well as a few additional items to spice up the recipes **(innovation and personal style)**. With all the ingredients in hand, the host returned home and made sure the seating around the fire pit was in order **(learning environment)**.

When the colleagues arrived, the host realized that the trip to the grocery store was not needed because each person brought their own ingredients **(diversity in past experiences)**. There were so many options that some colleagues were unable to pick the treats that they wanted, so they asked the host, "What should I do?" **(dualistic thinking)**. The host shared the recipe book with them, and they explored the ingredients together **(synergy)** until everyone chose a treat of their own **(self-directed learning)**. Afterwards, everyone gathered around the fire pit and arranged the seats **(individualized learning environment)** to their liking **(responsive to learning styles and diversity)**, but the fire was not going. Although not everyone knew how to build a fire, they worked together **(social learning)** and searched **(self-directed learning)** for the necessary materials **(learning resources)**. They found ample kindling and logs that were thrown into the fire pit **(conceptualization)**, but it was clear that the kindling and logs had to be rebuilt **(reconceptualization)**. Once the fire structure was stable, they realized that they still needed something to light the fire. Luckily, the host gave them a lighter **(presentation of the curricular activity)**, and they were so excited for their campfire treats **(intrinsic motivation)** that they immediately lit the fire **(discovery)**.

After gathering the ingredients and cooking the treats **(demonstration of SLOs)**, it was clear that more treats were created than the host had ever planned; some made s'mores while others made campfire pies, and some even made Italian sausages **(transcends prescribed SLOs)**. After the treats were made, everyone gathered around the fire pit to enjoy their snacks **(benefits of SLOs)** and share their experiences **(self-reflection and group processing)**. During this process, the host observed the colleagues having a good time **(subjective assessment of SLOs)** and asked them about their experiences before they left **(self-assessment of SLOs)**. Most of the colleagues expressed their enjoyment with the experience and reported that they hoped to do it again soon **(transfer of SLOs to new situations)**.

So, what does cooking treats have to do with my instructional philosophy? In addition to its novelty, this metaphor demonstrates the principles of *andragogy*, which I believe best represent my instructional philosophy. Out of this philosophy grows my primary instructional method of problem-based learning (PBL). PBL differs from traditional instructional methods because it reverses the presentation order of theory and application. In traditional models of education, content, rules, and theory are presented to students, followed by various forms of problems designed to assess remembering, understanding, and application; however, this has been suggested to promote conformity over creativity and stifle clinical reasoning. Therefore, PBL flips this process by providing students with the problems first, and it is through their interaction with these problems that the content, rules, and theory emerge and new knowledge is created.

Each PBL sequence is structured similarly to the metaphor above. It begins with the instructor's identification of the desired SLOs and creation of an ill-structured problem. After students select tutorial groups, they are presented with a scenario that is designed to direct them to the desired SLOs. The presentation of the problem scenario activates students' prior knowledge and experiences as well as situational interest. Then, students work together to conceptualize the problem and construct their own learning outcomes. Next, strategies are selected to obtain resources that are needed to demonstrate their learning outcomes. The self-directed search for these resources can take place in groups or individually, but after it is completed, the students analyze and synthesize each other's resources before asking for more information, re-conceptualizing the problem, or implementing their solution. The final step of this sequence involves transferring this knowledge to new situations and assessing SLOs. At this point it is very important to ensure that the minimum standards have been met; however, one benefit of PBL is that students are encouraged to construct knowledge beyond the desired learning outcomes of the instructor, which might not be possible with more traditional models of education.

While metaphors provide an outlet for my creative zeal, the best description of my instructional philosophy comes from students' evaluations of my courses and teaching. Quantitatively, my teaching evaluations are consistently ranked in the upper quartile. Qualitatively, students identified several learning outcomes from my courses that include: increased self-direction, increased critical thinking, increased lifelong learning skills, and improvements to the person and professional. In regard to my instructional methods, students have complimented my ability to facilitate lively discussions, engaging role-plays, and engaging presentations but have questions about the amount of work required in my courses and the purpose of portfolios.

Although outcomes and methods are important, I believe that a large portion of learning outcomes, much like therapeutic outcomes, are related to the relationships that I forge with students. I believe evidence for these relationships are best demonstrated by students' descriptions of my characteristics as an educator. These characteristics include the following: great, gifted, excellent, climate changer, caring, encouraging, ready to listen, supportive and challenging, goes above and beyond, personable, fun, enthusiastic, kind, funny, knowledgeable, and communicates high expectations. These comments are the result of my person-first philosophy that guides my intentional communication of the value that I have for students as people, in addition to their role as a student.

In closing, my instructional philosophy is grounded in social constructivism and the tenets of andragogy proposed by Malcolm Knowles. I believe that it is impossible to dispense knowledge to students. Instead, I believe learning is about providing an experience through which students can activate their previous experience and expertise, enhance their self-concept, develop autonomous learning skills, find a reason to learn, build intrinsic motivation, and actively reflect on the process. There is one quote that encapsulates the development of my instructional philosophy. One student, while holding her head on the desk, stated, "Don't stop what you are doing . . . no matter how much we complain, we know it is well worth it."

Despite the challenges and rewards that have presented themselves during the early stages of my career, I believe this quote provides reinforcement for my decision to become a Counselor Educator and to set high expectations that are balanced with personal and professional support. With that being said, my instructional philosophy is firm but flexible and in a constant state of evolution based upon the ongoing scholarship regarding innovative methods of counselor education. In fact, it is my hope to contribute to this body of knowledge with my ongoing research projects related to PBL that focus on its implementation in counselor education activities, courses, and entire programs.

Summary

There will be many opportunities throughout your career as a counselor educator to develop a teaching philosophy that evolves as you do. This chapter provided you with a starting point and invited you to address the why and how of teaching. We also suggested incorporating the who of you and your identity as a counselor with your identity as a counselor educator. Developing a teaching philosophy is akin to developing a cogent theoretical orientation statement, and they both start with knowing who you are, what your values are, and how they are operationalized through the activity of teaching.

Know that this process evolves as you learn from your experiences, students, clients, colleagues, literature, and life events. Using the information from this chapter, including learning theories to ground your teaching, and ensuring that your teaching philosophy encapsulates the various components often required and expected will provide you with a roadmap that develops over time. WE are excited you have begun this journey to be a counselor educator and hope this chapter has helped you begin crafting a personal philosophy of teaching that will enhance your practice, the lives of your students, and the clients they will serve.

The following websites provide additional information relating to the chapter topics.

Useful Websites

Austin, R. N. (2006). Writing the teaching statement. Retrieved from http://www.sciencemag.org/careers/2006/04/writing-teaching-statement

Centre for Educational Neuroscience. www.educationalneuroscience.org.uk/

Edutopia Brain-Based Learning. www.edutopia.org/blogs/beat/brain-based-learning

Edutopia Resources on Learning and the Brain. https://www.edutopia.org/article/brain-based-learning-resources

Grundman, H. G. (2006). Writing a teaching philosophy statement. Retrieved from www.ams.org/notices/200611/comm-grundman.pdf

Interdisciplinary Journal of Problem-Based Learning. http://docs.lib.purdue.edu/ijpbl/

Jensen Learning. www.jensenlearning.com/

Journal of Problem-Based Learning. www.ejpbl.org/

Journal of Problem Based Learning in Higher Education. https://journals.aau.dk/index.ph/pbl/index

McMaster University's Department of Chemical Engineering Program. www.eng.mcmaster.ca/chemeng/problem-based-learning-pbl#What-is-PBL-

Montell, G. (2003). How to write a statement of teaching philosophy. Retrieved from www.chronicle.com/article/How-to-Write-a-Statement-of/45133

Additional Resources

The following resources provide additional information relating to the chapter topics.

Hannon, N. P. (2014). *Writing a teaching philosophy statement*. Retrieved from http://teachingcenter.wustl.edu/About/ProgramsforGraduateStudentsandPostdocs/resources/Pages/Writing-a-Teaching-Philosophy-Statement.aspx

Merriam, S. B., Caffarella, R. S., & Baumgartner, L. M. (2007). *Learning in adulthood: A comprehensive guide* (3rd ed.). San Francisco, CA: Jossey-Bass.

Palmer, P. J. (2017). *The courage to teach: Exploring the inner landscape of a teacher's life* (20th ed.). San Francisco, CA: Jossey-Bass.

References

Aliakbari, M., & Faraji, E. (2011). Basic principles of critical pedagogy. *2nd International Conference on Humanities, Historical and Social Sciences, 17*, 77–83. Retrieved from www.ipedr.com/vol17/14-CHHSS%202011-H00057.pdf

American Counseling Association. (2014). *ACA code of ethics*. Alexandria, VA: Author.

Barrio Minton, C. A., Wachter Morris, C. A., & Yaites, L. D. (2014). Pedagogy in counselor education: A 10-year content analysis of journals. *Counselor Education & Supervision, 53*(3), 162–177. doi:10.1002/j.1556-6978.2014.00055.x

Barrows, H. S. (1983). Problem-based, self-directed learning. *Journal of the American Medical Association, 250*(22), 3077–3080.

Beeson, E. T., & Field, T. A. (2017). Neurocounseling: A new section of the Journal of Mental Health Counseling. *Journal of Mental Health Counseling, 39*(1), 71–83. doi:10.17744/mehc.39.1.06

Brooks, J. G., & Brooks, M. G. (2005). *In search of understanding: The case for constructivist classrooms*. Alexandria, VA: Association for Supervision and Curriculum Development.

Caine, R. N., & Caine, G. (1990). Understanding a brain-based approach to learning and teaching. *Educational Leadership, 48*(2), 66–70.

Council for Accreditation of Counseling and Related Educational Programs (CACREP). (2015). *2016 CACREP standards*. Retrieved from www.cacrep.org

Davis, M. H., & Harden, R. M. (1999). Problem-based learning: A practical guide. *Medical Teacher, 21*(2), 130–140. doi:10.1080/01421599979743

Degener, S. C. (2001). Making sense of critical pedagogy in adult literacy education. Retrieved November 16, 2017, from www.ncsall.net/?id=562

Dekker, S., Lee, N. C., Howard-Jones, P., & Jolles, J. (2012). Neuromyths in education: Prevalence and predictors of misconceptions among teachers. *Frontiers in Psychology, 3*(429), 1–8. doi:10.3389/fpsyg.2012.00429

Elias, J. L. (1976). *Conscientization and deschooling: Freire's and Illich's proposals for reshaping society*. Philadelphia, PA: Westminster Press.

Enns, C. Z., & Forrest, L. M. (2005). Toward defining and integrating multicultural and feminist pedagogies. In C. Z. Enns & A. L. Sinacore (Eds.), *Teaching and social justice: Integrating multicultural and feminist theories in the classroom* (pp. 3–23). Washington, DC: American Psychological Association.

Eriksen, K., & McAuliffe, G. (2001). *Teaching counselors and therapists: Constructivist and developmental course design*. Westport, CT: Bergin & Garvey.

Felicilda-Reynaldo, R. F. D., & Utley, R. (2015). Reflections of evidence-based practice in nurse educators' teaching philosophy statements. *Nursing Education Perspectives (National League for Nursing), 36*(2), 89–95. doi:10.5480/13-1176

Foley, P. (2007). A case "for" and "of" critical pedagogy: Meeting the challenge of liberatory education at Gallaudet University. *American Communication Journal, 9*(4), 1–21.

Freire, P. (1970). *Pedagogy of the oppressed*. New York, NY: The Seabury Press.

Giroux, H. (2004). Critical pedagogy and the postmodern/modern divide: Towards a pedagogy of democratization. *Teacher Education Quarterly, 31*(1), 31–47.

Gom, O. (2009). Motivation and adult learning. *Contemporary PNG Studies: DWU Research Journal, 10*, 17–25.

Gözüyeşí, E., & Dikici, A. (2014). The effect of brain based learning on academic achievement: A meta-analytical study. *Education Sciences: Theory & Practice, 14*(2), 642–648. doi:10.12738/estp.2014.2.2103

Hannon, N. P. (2014). *Writing a teaching philosophy statement*. Retrieved from http://teachingcenter.wustl.edu/About/ProgramsforGraduateStudentsandPostdocs/resources/Pages/Writing-a-Teaching-Philosophy-Statement.aspx

Harden, R. M., & Davis, M. H. (1998). The continuum of problem-based learning. *Medical Teacher, 20*(4), 317–322.

Hegarty, N. (2015). The growing importance of teaching philosophy statements and what they mean for the future: Why teaching philosophy statements will affect you. *Journal of Adult Education, 44*(2), 28–30.

Hmelo-Silver, C. E. (2004). Problem-based learning: What and how do students learn? *Educational Psychology Review, 16*(3), 235–266. doi:1040–726X/04/0900–0235/0

Hoggan, C., Mälkki, K., & Finnegan, F. (2017). Developing the theory of perspective transformation. *Adult Education Quarterly, 67*(1), 48–64. doi:10.1177/0741713616674076

Hooks, B. (1994). *Teaching to transgress: Education as the practice of freedom*. New York, NY: Routledge.

Inocian, R. (2016). Outcomes-based teaching for brain-based learning vis-á-vis pedagogical content knowledge. *Asia Pacific Journal of Multidisciplinary Research, 4*(2), 65–75.

Kabilan, M. M. (2000). Creative and critical thinking in language classrooms. *The Internet TESL Journal, 6*(6). Retrieved from http://iteslj.org/Techniques/Kabilan-CriticalThinking.html

Kearns, K. D., & Sullivan, C. S. (2011). Resources and practices to help graduate students and postdoctoral fellows write statements of teaching philosophy. *Advances in Physiology Education, 35*(2), 136–145. doi:10.1152/advan.00123.2010

Kitchenham, A. (2008). The evolution of John Mezirow's transformative learning theory. *Journal of Transformative Education, 6*(2), 104–123. doi:10.1177/1541344608322678

Knowles, M. S. (1980). *The modern practice of adult education: From pedagogy to andragogy*. New York, NY: Cambridge.

Knowles, M. S., Holton, III, E. F., & Swanson, R. A. (2005). *Adult learner: The definitive classic in adult education and human resources development* (6th ed.). Burlington, MA: Elsevier.

Kumari, V. (2014). Constructivist approach to teacher education: An integrative model for reflective teaching. *Journal of Educational Psychology, 7*(4), 31–40.

Lang, J. M. (2010, September 3). 5 Steps to a memorable teaching philosophy. *Chronicle of Higher Education*, A61–A62.

Licklider, B. (2004). An eloquent, insightful teaching philosophy statement. *Teaching Professor, 18*(10), 1.

Malott, K. M., Hall, K. H., Sheely-Moore, A., Krell, M. M., & Cardaciotto, L. (2014). Evidence-based teaching in higher education: Application to counselor education. *Counselor Education and Supervision, 53*, 294–305. doi:10.1002/j.1556-6978.2014.00064.x

McAuliffe, G., & Eriksen, K. (2010). *Handbook of counselor preparation: Constructivist, developmental, and experiential approaches*. Thousand Oaks, CA: Sage.

McCaughan, A. M., Binkley, E. E., Wilde, B. J., Parmanand, S. P., & Allen, V. B. (2013). Observing the development of constructivist pedagogy in one counselor education doctoral cohort: A single case design. *Practitioner Scholar: Journal of Counseling & Professional Psychology, 2*(1), 95–107.

Meizlish, D., & Kaplan, M. (2008). Valuing and evaluating teaching in academic hiring: A multidisciplinary, cross-institutional study. *Journal of Higher Education, 79*(5), 489–512.

Mezirow, J. (1978). *Education for perspective transformation: Women's re-entry programs in community colleges*. New York, NY: Teacher's College, Columbia.

Mezirow, J. (2012). Learning to think like an adult: Core concepts of transformation theory. In E. W. Taylor & P. Cranton (Eds.), *The handbook of transformative learning: Theory, research, and practice* (pp. 73–95). Thousand Oaks, CA: Jossey-Bass.

Nixon-Ponder, S. (1995). Using problem-posing dialogue. *Adult Learning*, 7(2), 10–12. doi:10.1177/104515959500700206

Oghyanous, P. A. (2017). The effect of brain-based teaching on young EFL learners' self efficacy. *English Language Teaching*, 10(5), 158–166. doi:10.5539/elt.v10n5p158

Ogle, D. M. (1986). K-W-L: A teaching model that develops active reading of expository text. *Reading Teacher*, 39, 564–570.

O'Neal, C., Meizlish, D., & Kaplan, M. (2007). *Writing a statement of teaching philosophy for the academic job search.* (Scholarly Project, University of Michigan). Retrieved from www.crlt.umich.edu/sites/default/files/resource_files/CRLT_no23.pdf

Owens, M. T., & Tanner, K. D. (2017). Teaching as brain changing: Exploring connections between neuroscience and innovative teaching. *CBE: Life Sciences Education*, 16(2), 1–9. doi:10.1187/cbe.17-01-0005

Pickering, S. J., & Howard-Jones, P. (2007). Educators' views on the role of neuroscience in education: Findings from a study of UK and international perspectives. *Mind, Brain, & Education*, 1(3), 109–113.

Rudes, J., & Guterman, J. T. (2007). The value of social constructionism for the counseling profession: A reply to Hansen. *Journal of Counseling & Development*, 85, 387–392.

Savery, J. R. (2006). Overview of problem-based learning: Definitions and distinctions. *International Journal of Problem-based Learning*, 1(1), 9–20. doi:10.7771/1541-5015.1002

Schönwetter, D. J., Sokal, L., Friesen, M., & Taylor, K. L. (2002). Teaching philosophies reconsidered: A conceptual model for the development and evaluation of teaching philosophy statements. *International Journal for Academic Development*, 7(1), 83–97. doi:10.1080/13601440210156501

Schussler, E. E., Rowland, F. E., Distel, C. A., Bauman, J. M., Keppler, M. L., Kawarasaki, Y., . . . Salem, H. (2011). Promoting the development of graduate students' teaching philosophy statements. *Journal of College Science Teaching*, 40(3), 32–35.

Tafti, M. A., & Kadkhodaie, M. S. (2017). The effects of brain-based training on the learning and retention of life skills in adolescents. *International Journal of Behavioral Science*, 10(4), 140–144.

Taylor, B., & Kroth, M. (2009a). Andragogy's transition into the future: Meta-analysis of andragogy and its search for a measurable instrument. *Journal of Adult Education*, 38(1), 1–11.

Taylor, B., & Kroth, M. (2009b). A single conversation with a wise man is better than ten years of study: A model for testing methodologies for pedagogy or andragogy. *Journal of the Scholarship of Teaching and Learning*, 9(2), 42–56.

Taylor, E. W., & Cranton, P. (Eds.). (2012). *The handbook of transformative learning: Theory, research, and practice.* Thousand Oaks, CA: Jossey-Bass.

Thomas, B. M., & Swamy, S. S. (2014). Brain based teaching approach: A new paradigm of teaching. *International Journal of Education and Psychological Research*, 3(2), 62–65.

Tobin, D. J., Willow, R. A., Bastow, E. K., & Ratkowski, E. M. (2009). Reflective learning within a counselor education curriculum. *The Journal of Counselor Preparation and Supervision*, 1(1), 3–9. doi:10.7729/11.0104

Weimer, M. (2012). Learner-centered teaching and transformative learning. In E. W. Taylor & P. Cranton (Eds.), *The handbook of transformative learning: Theory, research, and practice* (pp. 439–454). Thousand Oaks, CA: Jossey-Bass.

3 Ethical and Legal Issues for Counselor Educators

Theodore P. Remley, Jr. and Cassandra G. Pusateri

A primary role of a counselor educator is that of teacher. You teach when you deliver assigned formal courses in the classroom, supervise practicum and internship students, serve on master's thesis or doctoral dissertation committees, and mentor future counselors, counseling leaders, or counselor educators. In all teacher role activities, you hold positions of authority and power over your students. Power can be abused, and as a result, there are a number of ethical standards and legal requirements that are designed to protect students. Students are vulnerable because entry into the profession depends upon first earning a graduate degree. Once they graduate, students remain vulnerable in that they often rely on the counselor educators who taught them and the clinical supervisors who supervised them to help them gain certification or licensure credentials by providing endorsements and to find employment by providing recommendations. By reviewing the ethical and legal guidelines that are related to the teacher role, you can heighten awareness of the power you hold and can make sure you do not unknowingly engage in unethical or illegal practices when you are teaching. Most counselor educators are well intended and want to practice in an appropriate manner, but sometimes activities such as overzealous gatekeeping or holding students to unreasonable standards of performance can lead to problems.

Even the most novice counselor educators understand that the roles of teacher and clinical supervisor are much different from the role of counselor that they have assumed in the past. All counselor educators have been counselors. The counselor-client relationship has some similarities to the counselor educator-student relationship, but the differences overshadow the similarities. In both, the counselor or counselor educator has a position of power, and clients or students are therefore vulnerable. Teachers are responsible for transferring knowledge to students in a fair and reasonable manner. Counselors promise clients confidentiality and assume responsibility for the well-being of clients. Teachers do not have the same high level of confidentiality duties to students. Counselors do not require behaviors from clients, but teachers regularly make appropriate performance demands of students. There is a growing body of literature on effective teaching in counselor education (Barrio Minton, Wachter Morris, & Yaites, 2014). You are advised to teach in an intentional manner and to use literature to guide you toward teacher effectiveness (Malott, Hall, Sheely-Moore, Krell, & Cardaciotto, 2014).

Throughout this chapter, the American Counseling Association (ACA) *Code of Ethics* (2014), the graduate program accreditation standards of the Council on Accreditation of Counseling and Related Educational Programs (CACREP, 2016), and various sources of law will be referenced. Ethical requirements for counselor educators are included in the ACA *Code of Ethics* (2014). Even though ethical standards are aspirational and somewhat idealistic, they are meant to guide the practice of counselor educators, and you should make every attempt to adhere to ethical standards. The graduate program accreditation standards of the CACREP (2016) provide a foundation of what is considered by the counseling profession to be best practice in delivering counseling graduate programs. As a result, the CACREP standards have both ethical and legal implications for counselor educators. An ethics panel or a court of law might look to the CACREP standards when determining whether a counselor educator's or a counseling program's actions were either ethical or legal. Even though there are a few federal and state statutes that are related to the teacher role of counselor educators, most legal requirements of counselor educators are based on the United States Constitution, the principles of tort and contract law, and state and federal cases that have interpreted legal requirements.

In considering the ethical and legal obligations of counselor educators, it is important to understand the differences among the concepts of *legal standards*, *ethical standards*, and *best practice*. *Legal standards* represent the minimum behavior that society will tolerate from a professional; *ethical standards* occupy a middle ground, suggesting the behavior the profession demands from its members; and *best practice* is the best behavior a professional might be capable of achieving, but is not required by ethical or legal standards (Remley & Herlihy, 2016). You should aspire to best practice; however, you should be careful not to misconstrue your actions or the actions of other counselor educators that are less than best practice as automatically either illegal or unethical.

Learning Objectives

After reading this chapter, you will have a better understanding of the following:

- Legal and ethical requirements of counselor educators.
- Current best practices related to multiple areas of counselor education.
- The delicate and intricate nature of professor-student relationships.
- Multicultural considerations related to multiple areas of counselor education.
- Problematic student behaviors and dispositions and remediation.

CACREP Standards

The following sections of the 2016 CACREP accreditation standards are reviewed in this chapter. Section 1: The Learning Environment includes standards specific to the institution, academic unit, and faculty and staff (pp. 5–8). Section 2: Professional Counseling Identity includes the foundation and counseling curriculum of entry and doctoral level counseling programs (pp. 9–13). Section 3: Professional Practice includes standards related to practicum and internship as well as qualifications of supervisors (pp. 14–16). Section 4: Evaluation in the Program includes information specific to evaluation of the program, faculty, and supervisors as well as assessment of student learning (pp. 17–18).

The Counselor Educator as Teacher

There are several responsibilities for counselor educators within each of the three pillars of academia—teaching, scholarship, and service. In this section, the ethical considerations for counselor educators as teachers are discussed and relevant CACREP standards are identified. You will be provided suggestions related to admissions, program orientations and handbooks, teaching, assessments, and practicum and internship, among others.

Student Admissions

The ACA *Code of Ethics* (2014) does not include ethical standards related to admitting applicants to counseling graduate programs. However, Section 1.L.1–4 of the CACREP (2016) accreditation standards indicates that counselor educators must include the following considerations when making admissions decisions: each applicant's relevance of career goals to the graduate counseling program; aptitude for graduate study; potential for success in forming counseling relationships; and respect for cultural differences. You should take the admissions process seriously and follow CACREP requirements in screening applicants (Swank & Smith-Adcock, 2014).

The primary legal consideration in admissions decisions is that applicants to public institutions cannot be discriminated against on the basis of their status if that status is protected by the U.S. Constitution or federal or statutes. Protected categories include race, color, religion, national origin, age, sex, pregnancy, citizenship, familial status, and disability status (U.S. Constitution; Civil Rights Act of 1964; Age Discrimination in Employment Act of 1967; Equal Pay Act of 1963; Pregnancy Discrimination Act; Immigration Reform and Control Act; Civil Rights Act of 1968; Rehabilitation Act of 1973). State laws may prohibit discrimination based on additional areas. Public universities may utilize affirmative action in their admissions decisions, giving preference to minority race candidates in some instances (*Fisher v. University of Texas at Austin*, No. 14–981, 579 U.S., 2016).

You can use a variety of methods for screening applicants. For example, personal or goal statements, individual and/or group interviews, and resumes or curriculum vitae could be used to determine the relevance of a candidate's career goals. An indicator of graduate-level academic ability might be a candidate's undergraduate grade point average, standardized aptitude test scores, and letters of recommendation. Most counseling graduate programs assess an applicant's ability to form effective counseling relationships and respect for cultural differences through individual and/or group interviews and experiential activities (Swank & Smith-Adcock, 2014; Ziomek-Daigle & Christensen, 2010).

Counselor educators sometimes admit candidates for a probationary period followed by formal admission to the program if established criteria are met

(Swank & Smith-Adcock, 2014). Although some counselor educators may think about reviewing postings of applicants on social media to learn more about the applicants, Brew, Cervantes, and Shepard (2013) have warned that investigating candidates through common social media outlets could create bias among faculty as admission recommendations are made. It would be wise to establish policies that prohibit faculty investigation of program applicants through social media outlets. When developing policies and procedures related to program admissions, you are encouraged to consult with legal representatives at your institution regarding any legal consequences of screening protocols (Swank & Smith-Adcock, 2014).

Orientation to the Program

After admission decisions are made, you are responsible for sharing information with students about the program and profession. According to the ACA *Code of Ethics* (2014), orientation continues throughout the preparation program (F.8.a). Section 1.M of the CACREP (2016) standards state that during the program orientation, "a student handbook is disseminated and discussed, students' ethical and professional obligations and personal growth expectations as counselors-in-training are explained, and eligibility for licensure/certification is reviewed." Pease-Carter and Barrio Minton (2012) found that students desired information about expectations for self-disclosure and reflection, academic requirements including general and specific information about courses, specific information about the program, the impact of counselor training on relationships, student rights, and post-graduation considerations. You can inform students of their obligations verbally as well in writing through program handbooks, handouts, and student-informed guides (Pease-Carter & Barrio Minton, 2012; Protivnak & Foss, 2009).

Regarding the development of program handbooks, CACREP (2016) has indicated that the following information should be included:

> The student handbook includes (1) the mission statement of the academic unit and program objectives, (2) information about professional counseling organizations, opportunities for professional involvement, and activities appropriate for students, (3) matriculation requirements, (4) expectations of students, (5) academic appeal policy, (6) written endorsement of policy explaining the procedures for recommending students for credentialing and employment, and (7) policy for student retention, remediation, and dismissal from the program.
>
> (CACREP, 2016, Section 1.N)

As indicated by CACREP (2016), you should include specific expectations of students in the program handbook. Doing so promotes transparency within the program, provides students with due process, and aids with gatekeeping responsibilities. Faculty expectations of students could include among others professional behaviors (i.e., understand and comply with ethical guidelines and legal requirements), interpersonal behaviors (i.e., ability to establish and maintain appropriate interpersonal relationships), and intrapersonal behaviors (i.e., receptivity to examination of self; Duba, Paez, & Kindsvatter, 2010; Homrich, DeLorenzi, Bloom, & Godbee, 2014).

You should articulate the potential consequences for failing to meet the program's expectations as well as due process steps available for students to take in the event of disciplinary action (Brown, 2013; Brown-Rice & Furr, 2013; Dugger & Francis, 2014; Foster & McAdams, 2009). The 2016 CACREP standards state, "Counselor education programs have and follow a policy of student retention, remediation, and dismissal from the program consistent with institutional due process policies and with the counseling profession's ethical codes and standards of practice" (CACREP, 2016, Section 1.O). The policy you develop should include information about the assessment of student performance post admission, the development of remediation plans and associated documentation, and the determination of a successful, unsuccessful, or neutral outcome of remediation (Ziomek-Daigle & Christensen, 2010).

When developing and discussing retention, remediation, and dismissal policies and procedures, you should view the process from an assistive rather than punitive perspective (Foster & McAdams, 2009). You should conduct periodic reviews of existing policies and procedures to ensure they are consistent with current standards of practice and consult with the university's legal representatives prior to finalizing policies (Brown, 2013; Dugger & Francis, 2014; Hutchens, Block, & Young, 2013). However, once established, it is important that you adhere closely to these policies and procedures you have adopted (Dugger & Francis, 2014; Hutchens et al., 2013). Although it is important that information about retention, remediation, and dismissal is available through a program handbook, you should also consider providing these policies and procedures electronically (e.g., through the department's website; Brown, 2013; Dugger & Francis, 2014). Finally, you should develop a method for documenting the delivery and student acknowledgement of this information. For example, students could be asked to sign an acknowledgments page to communicate their understanding of the information provided (Hutchens et al., 2013; Pease-Carter & Barrio Minton, 2012).

Teaching and Assessment

The ACA *Code of Ethics* (2014) and 2016 CACREP standards call for counselor educators to "provide instruction within their areas of knowledge and competence" (ACA, 2014, F.7.b) and to "have relevant preparation and experience in relation to the courses they teach" (CACREP, 2016, Section 1.BB). Therefore, when engaging in discussions about faculty course assignment, you are expected to be honest with yourself and your colleagues about your areas of competence. Take a moment to consider Case Illustration 3.1 related to evaluating one's competence to teach. Additionally, you are encouraged to have or secure appropriate training that will help you develop the skills needed for effective classroom management, the creation of course materials, and the development of a teaching philosophy (Hunt & Gilmore, 2011). (See in this text Chapter 2: Developing a Personal Philosophy of Teaching and Chapter 5: Classroom Engagement and Evidence-Based Teaching Strategies for Adult Learners.) You may also find yourself teaching in a variety of settings (e.g., online, hybrid, or face-to-face) and are expected to demonstrate competence using the available technology (ACA, 2014, F.7.b). (See in this text Chapter 10: Teaching Across Settings.)

Case Illustration 3.1

Evaluating Competence to Teach

Shortly after defending his dissertation, Antonio accepted an offer to join the faculty at a large university in an urban area. A few weeks after signing the contract, Antonio received an email message from the department chair asking which classes he would like to teach during the upcoming semester. Antonio responded with a list of four courses for which he believes he currently has the expertise and training to teach—social and cultural diversity, counseling theories, assessment, and practicum. A few weeks later, Antonio received another email message, this time from the program coordinator, with the semester schedule attached. Much to his surprise, Antonio had been scheduled to teach career counseling, a course he does not feel prepared to teach and a subject area with which Antonio has very little experience. Antonio is hesitant to bring his concerns to the attention of the department chair and program coordinator given the potential impact on his career and future in the program. Imagine that Antonio consults with you, his colleague and friend. What ideas might you share with him? What are the implications of bringing his concerns to the department chair and program coordinator? What are the implications of remaining silent?

As you prepare to teach a course, often one of the first tasks is the formation of the course syllabus. Even though course syllabi (ACA, 2016) and graduate program handbooks may not meet the technical legal standards to be considered a binding contract (Kauffman, 2014), it is very important that such documents be written so that students understand what is expected of them. In addition, faculty members and counseling graduate programs are expected to adhere to materials published in course syllabi and program handbooks. The 2016 CACREP standards provide specific information that should be included in each syllabus: "(1) content areas, (2) knowledge and skills outcomes, (3) methods of instruction, (4) required text(s) and/or readings, (5) student performance evaluation criteria and procedures, and (6) a disability accommodation policy and procedure statement" (Section 2.D). In addition to including this information, you should develop approaches that allow diverse cultural perspectives to be included in the course curriculum. By ensuring that diversity is recognized and valued within each course, you demonstrate respect for culturally diverse students and colleagues (Haskins et al., 2013). (See in this text Chapter 6: Acquisition of Knowledge and Skills and Chapter 7: Curriculum Development.)

While teaching counselor preparation courses, you are responsible for the appropriate and fair assessment of student learning and dispositions. Objectivity can be particularly difficult given the subjective nature inherent to many student assessments. Earlier in this section, it was recommended that expectations of students be included in the program handbook. According to the 2016 CACREP standards, key dispositions should not only be identified but also assessed at various points over time (Section 4.G). You are required by CACREP to identify "key performance indicators of student learning" which should be assessed "via multiple measures and over multiple points in time" (Section 4.F). According to Section F.9.a of the ACA *Code of Ethics* (2014), students should be informed of these evaluations through "ongoing feedback regarding their performance throughout the training program." Finally, it is expected that there will be a clear connection between the assessment of student learning and dispositions and the program's policies and procedures for retention, remediation, and dismissal (CACREP, 2016, Section 4.H). (See in this text Chapter 8: Evaluation of Student Learning.)

The role of assessment, however, does not conclude with evaluations of student learning and dispositions. Students must also be given the opportunity to regularly evaluate instructors and supervisors and provide feedback regarding their experiences in each course (Sections 4.I, 4.J, and 4.K of the 2016 CACREP standards). The feedback provided by students is valuable information and should be used to inform self-development and ongoing curriculum changes. Additionally, programs are expected to have policies and procedures in place to respond to student complaints. Finally, you should perform regular evaluations of your program by collecting and reviewing data from relevant stakeholders to inform program modifications. Evaluation results should be available on the program's website (Section 4.A, 4.B, 4.C., 4.D, and 4.E of the 2016 CACREP standards). Although program evaluation is not an ethical requirement, it is required by the 2016 CACREP standards.

Practicum and Internship

Practicum and internship courses and related field experiences are integral components of counselor preparation. In fact, research has shown that initial, direct experiences with counseling clients can effectively increase self-efficacy among graduate students in counseling programs (Ikonomopoulos, Vela, Smith, & Dell'Aquila, 2016). You play an important role in providing guidance related to the selection of field placements and ensuring that appropriate supervision is provided to facilitate the training of students and ensure the welfare of clients. Specific information regarding practicum and internship are provided in Section 3 of the 2016 CACREP standards. Additionally, it is an ethical mandate that counselor educators "develop clear policies and provide direct assistance within their training programs regarding appropriate field placement and other clinical experiences" (ACA, 2014, F.7.i). When developing policies related to practicum and internship, you are encouraged to consult with legal representatives at your institution as well as professional associations (Hutchens et al., 2013).

As you prepare students for practicum and internship, you should also consider the influence of technology on the profession. There are ethical and legal requirements in settings in which electronic medical records are maintained or electronic communication is used to communicate with clientele (see ACA, 2014, H.5.a). You should pay particular attention to educating students regarding the confidentiality of recorded sessions when students are using personal devices such as smart phones, tablets, laptops. Additionally, with the rise of social media, students need to be aware of the ethical and legal ramifications of knowingly or unknowingly sharing personal information through these outlets with clientele (see ACA, 2014, A.5.e). Brew et al. (2013), Lawley (2012), and Wilkinson and Reinhardt (2015) have suggested that counselor educators incorporate recent technological shifts within policies and procedures related to practicum and internship as well as throughout the counseling program curriculum.

Requiring Counseling for Students

The question of whether or not it is appropriate to require students to engage in counseling for personal growth and development is one that has been pondered by counselor educators for some time. The ACA *Code of Ethics* (2014) states that "Counselor educators may require students to address any personal concerns that have the potential to affect professional competency" (F.8.d). Although the ethical code does not explicitly require that students engage in personal counseling for themselves, you can suggest it to students. Both Section F.9.c of the ACA *Code of Ethics* (2014) and Section 1.H. of the 2016 CACREP standards state that counselor educators should be prepared to provide information about appropriate counseling services offered in the community. Additionally, Prosek, Holm, and Daly (2013) found that students required to attend personal counseling reported decreases in anxiety, depression, and overall problems, thereby indicating that personal counseling might be a method for prevention of problematic student concerns in the future. However, before policies requiring personal counseling for students are developed, you should consult with the legal representatives of your university.

Mentoring

Mentoring provided by both peers and faculty has been determined to be a helpful experience for students in counselor preparation programs (Hunt & Gilmore, 2011; Protivnak & Foss, 2009). The selection of students to mentor, existing power dynamics, potential for misuse of power, and the distribution of opportunities should be considered. Additionally, you should take care to acknowledge and thoughtfully address the impact of cultural differences, oppression, and privilege on the mentor-mentee relationship (Borders et al., 2012; Henfield, Woo, & Washington, 2013). (See in this text Chapter 11: The Role of Mentoring in Counselor Education.)

Legal Requirements and Considerations

A number of legal requirements of counselor educators when they are in the role of teacher are reviewed in this section. Suggestions for best practice in dealing with difficult legal issues are provided.

Requiring Students to Counsel Diverse Clients

The contemporary legal issue that is the most challenging is the position the American Counseling Association (ACA) has taken, and most counseling graduate programs have adopted as well, that counseling graduate students must be willing to accept as counseling clients individuals whose identities, cultures, values, beliefs, etc. are in conflict with a counselor's personal religious or moral values. Whether counseling students or practicing counselors who hold religious beliefs that any sexual orientation other than heterosexual is morally wrong or is a sin can be required by graduate programs or employers to accept as clients and provide counseling services to individuals who are lesbian, gay, bisexual, transgender, queer, intersex, and questioning (LGBTQIQ) is being debated within the counseling profession (Dugger & Francis, 2014; Herlihy, Hermann, & Greden, 2014; Hutchens et al., 2013; Kaplan, 2014) and litigated in the courts (*Keeton v. Anderson-Wiley*, 2010; *Ward v. Wilbanks*, 2011). A survey of counselor educators found that while most believed ACA had taken the proper position regarding the *Ward v. Wilbanks* (2011) case, a number disagreed and some thought the situation with *Ward* should have been handled differently (Burkholder, Hall, & Burkholder, 2014). Tennessee has passed Senate Bill 1556 which says that counselors with "sincerely held principles" can reject gay, lesbian, or transgender clients. According to Almasy (2016), there have been 100 bills introduced in legislatures across the United States that would allow professionals to invoke religion as a basis for refusing to serve gay individuals. ACA (2016, June 14) cancelled contracts to hold the 2017 annual conference in Nashville, Tennessee, and relocated the conference to San Francisco, California, saying that the law passed in Tennessee "denies services to those most in need, targets the counseling profession, and is a violation of ACA's *Code of Ethics*."

The most recent ACA *Code of Ethics* that was adopted in 2014 addressed this issue directly. Section A.4.b of the code states,

> Counselors are aware of—and avoid imposing—their own values, attitudes, beliefs, and behaviors. Counselors respect the diversity of clients, trainees, and research participants and seek training in areas in which they are at risk of imposing their values onto clients, especially when the counselor's values are inconsistent with the client's goals or are discriminatory in nature.

Section A.11.b prohibits counselors from "referring prospective and current clients based solely on the counselor's personally held values, attitudes, beliefs, and behaviors" and again requires counselors to seek training to avoid imposing their values onto clients. In addition, section C.5 of the code prohibits counselors from discriminating against prospective or current clients on the basis of "age, culture, disability, ethnicity, race, religion/spirituality, gender, gender identity, sexual orientation, marital/partnership status, language preference, socioeconomic status, immigration status, or any basis proscribed by law." Section F.6.b of the code states that supervisors "recommend dismissal . . . when supervisees are unable to demonstrate that they can provide competent professional services to a range of diverse clients."

In two federal court cases, counseling graduate students were dismissed from programs when they refused to counsel a gay client (*Keeton v. Anderson-Wiley*,

2010; *Ward v. Wilbanks*, 2011). In two other court cases, practicing counselors sued after they were dismissed from their jobs after refusing to counsel a gay client (*Bruff v. North Mississippi Health Services, Inc.*, 2001; *Walden v. Centers for Disease Control and Prevention*, 2010).

Despite ACA's position on the issue and in spite of clear standards within the ACA *Code of Ethics* (2014) that prohibit counselors from refusing to counsel clients if they are not heterosexual, the debate within the counseling profession and American society as to whether this position is appropriate will continue in the future. An example of the continuing debate occurred when Smith and Okech (2016) suggested that CACREP should not accredit counseling preparation programs in universities that do not support individuals with sexual minority identities. In response, Sells and Hagedorn (2016) said, "We believe that it is possible for conservative Christian students to provide professional and competent services to sexual minorities without violating their own principles of conscience and ethics" (p. 266). Weighing in on the debate, CACREP issued an open letter stating that CACREP "expects accredited programs to 'adopt and adhere to' the ACA *Code of Ethics*" and believes that faith-based institutions can "provide the training necessary to prepare students to serve multicultural populations" (Parsons & Bobby, 2016).

Establishing and Following Procedures

Counselor educators are required to establish formal procedures that allow students to appeal grades or negative actions taken against them such as dismissal from a graduate program. The legal principles of procedural due process require that before a benefit or right an American citizen has can be taken from him or her by a governmental entity, the individual must be given an opportunity to appeal (Black's Law Dictionary, 2016). Because the idea of due process is so ingrained in American society, non-governmental entities also have adopted the concept that adverse actions against students must include an opportunity for appeal. In addition, CACREP (2016) and university regional accrediting agencies that belong to the Council for Higher Education Accreditation (CHEA, 2016) require that counseling graduate programs establish and then follow formal appeals processes for students who believe grades were awarded to them unfairly or who have adverse actions taken against them. Generally, neither the legal principle of procedural due process nor accrediting agencies specify the procedural steps that must be followed. Section 1.N.5 of the CACREP Standards (2016) requires accredited programs to have an academic appeal policy but gives no details regarding what that policy must include. Also, the ACA *Code of Ethics* (2014) in Section F.9.b requires counselor educators to dismiss students when necessary and to provide due process, but again does not specify the procedures to be followed. As a result, you must establish written procedures for appeals that are fair and reasonable. But, more importantly, once such procedures are established, they must be followed when students file appeals. In determining whether a university has provided an adequate appeals procedure, generally a court will evaluate the written appeals process to determine whether it is fair, and then will evaluate whether the process was followed. If an appeals policy is determined to be fair, then academic dismissals will be upheld by courts if the written procedures developed by the university are followed. Rust, Raskin, and

Hill (2013) and Goodrich and Shin (2013) have developed guidelines to assist counselor education programs in developing policies and procedures for handling situations in which graduate students are not able to demonstrate professional competence. Take a moment to engage in Guided Practice Exercise 3.1, which provides an opportunity for you to consider the academic appeals policy of your current graduate program.

Guided Practice Exercise 3.1

Evaluating a Student Appeals Policy

Locate the academic appeals policy of the counseling graduate program at the university where you are currently a student or where you are affiliated. If you are not currently affiliated with a university, look up the policy at any university that has a counseling graduate program. In some cases, the appeals process might be related specifically to grade appeals, but would most likely be used as well if a student were dismissed from a program.

Next, put yourself in the position of a faculty member in the program who must go through the procedural steps when a student appeals a dismissal. Do you believe the existing policy is fair and reasonable from the perspective of students? Why or why not? What are the strengths of the policy? What are some possible problems with the policy? Are there any steps in the policy that you believe faculty members might fail to take? Can you suggest changes in the policy to make it more likely that faculty members will follow all of the steps?

Gatekeeping

The process in which counselor educators or supervisors exercise their authority and take actions that result in an individual not being admitted to the counseling profession is known as *gatekeeping*. Gatekeeping can be exercised by denying an applicant admission to a counseling graduate program, assigning an unacceptable grade to a student in a required course, or dismissing a student from a program. Brown-Rice and Furr (2015), after finding that most counselor educators are aware of problems of professional competency within the ranks of counselor educators, have suggested that counselor educators should be gatekeeping themselves as well. (See in this text Chapter 9: The Role of Gatekeeping in Counselor Education.)

Most procedures counselor educators develop for removing students from their counseling graduate programs require that once a student has been identified as being deficient in skills or proficiency, efforts must be made to help the student improve, which is known as *remediation*. To practice ethically, you must make sincere efforts to help a student improve and not simply go through the motions waiting for the time when you can dismiss the student. The attitude you have toward remediation is not something that can easily be evaluated by a court, so it truly is an ethical principle that requires you to attempt to help a student who is having problems improve.

Gatekeeping is a very important ethical and legal issue in counselor education. You must be careful not to abuse the power you hold over students. Making subjective judgments about a student's appropriateness for the counseling profession leaves room for you to be emotional and unfair. On the other hand, both the ACA *Code of Ethics* (2014) and the accreditation standards of CACREP (2016) require that counselor educators engage in *gatekeeping* for the counseling profession.

Section 4.F of the CACREP (2016) accreditation standards requires that counselor educators systematically assess each student's progress throughout the program. Determining what constitutes a particular student's inappropriateness for a counseling graduate program is a difficult task and is subjective in nature (Brown, 2013). A number of provisions of the ACA *Code of Ethics* (2014) address the gatekeeping function of counselor educators. Section F.5 of the ACA code makes it clear that students and supervisees must follow the code's requirements. Section F.5.b requires that students who become impaired because of physical, mental, or emotional problems "limit, suspend, or terminate their professional responsibilities" until the impairment has been successfully resolved. As was discussed above, Section F.6.b requires that counselor educators recommend dismissal of students who "are unable to demonstrate that they can provide competent services to a range of diverse clients." Section F.8.d allows counselor educators to require students to address their personal concerns if those concerns might affect their professional competency. In Section F.9.b of the code, counselor educators are required to be "aware of and address the inability of some students to achieve counseling competencies." You are required to assist students who are experiencing problems developing competencies, to seek consultation and document decisions to dismiss students, and to provide due process procedures for students who are dismissed.

Generally, courts defer to university professors in setting and evaluating standards for clinical performance and do not interfere when universities dismiss students who fail to meet the standards faculty members have established (*Connelly v. University of Vermont*, 1965). The U.S. Supreme Court in *Horowitz v. Board of Curators of the University of Missouri* (1978) held that courts should not substitute their own standards for those of faculty members and in that particular case upheld the dismissal of a medical student who had excellent grades but was determined to be deficient in clinical performance, peer and patient relations, and personal hygiene. The holding in the *Horowitz* (1978) case appears to have laid a foundation for supporting faculty members in counselor education programs reviewing students for their fitness for the counseling profession, and in dismissing students if they fail to meet standards of professional behavior set by the faculty.

Dealing With Student Cheating or Plagiarism

Cheating is not morally acceptable in our society and in academic settings cheating can be the basis for severe sanctions or even dismissal from a university. Section G.5.b of the ACA *Code of Ethics* (2014) makes the simple statement that counselors do not plagiarize, which is defined as presenting another's work as their own.

What constitutes cheating or plagiarism is not always clear to students (Remley & Herlihy, 2016). You should specifically define the behaviors that constitute cheating or plagiarizing in course syllabi and student handbooks. In addition, best practice would include listing possible sanctions for cheating or plagiarizing. Initial incidents of cheating or plagiarizing should be seen as opportunities to educate students about what constitutes such offenses and that such practices are unacceptable, rather than immediately punishing offenders. Additionally, universities have policies and procedures related to academic integrity. Therefore, you must be aware of and follow any policies adopted by your employing university related to student cheating or plagiarizing.

Endorsements and Recommendations

CACREP (2016) Section 1.N.6 requires that counseling graduate programs have a written policy that sets forth the procedures faculty follow for recommending students for credentialing and employment. If you are unable to provide an endorsement or recommendation for a student or graduate because the student is unqualified, the best practice would be to inform the student that you are unable to provide a positive endorsement or recommendation. Specific reasons for declining should be provided to the student. You have the right to give your professional opinions regarding students' or graduates' performance as long as your opinions are based on objective evaluations. You could be held accountable to students if you were to express opinions that are not well founded. If students could prove that you were biased against them, and as a result of your negative opinions, students were denied credentials, jobs, or professional opportunities, you could be held accountable.

Malpractice Insurance Requirement for Students

Section 3.A of the CACREP (2016) accreditation standards requires that students have individual professional liability insurance policies while enrolled in practicum or internship. Professional malpractice insurance will provide legal representation for students who are sued while completing their practicum and internship. Such insurance would also pay any judgments or monetary settlements related to such potential lawsuits.

Privacy of Students and Clients of Students

The Family Educational Rights and Privacy Act (FERPA, 1974; West 1997) requires that public universities and those that receive federal funds (which includes almost all universities) keep confidential any private information about students. Since this act was passed in 1974, contemporary faculty members are well aware that they may not release private information to others without the written permission of students. Faculty members also are aware that FERPA requires that students have access to their educational records. You need to be aware that discussions regarding the performance of students in the program are private and should not be disclosed outside of formal faculty meetings. In addition, anything written about a student that is not kept in the sole possession of the maker is an educational record and students can demand copies.

The confidentiality of clients must be ensured when students are providing counseling services in a campus laboratory or at practicum or internship sites. It is important to operate counselor education laboratories in which clients are seen in a professional manner (Lauka & McCarthy, 2013; Mobley & Myers, 2010).

It is unclear whether counseling graduate programs that operate counseling laboratories in which community clients are seen by graduate students are required to follow the Health Insurance Portability and Accountability Act of 1996 (HIPAA, 2013) or the Health Information Technology for Economic and Clinical Health (HITECH, 2009) Act of 2009. These federal laws require health care entities to protect the privacy of consumers when using technology. Provisions of the laws have been summarized by several scholars (Lawley, 2012; Wheeler & Bertram, 2012; Wilkinson & Reinhardt, 2015). Most university counselor educators comply with FERPA, but do not believe they are *covered entities* that must comply with HIPAA or HITECH. If you are unsure whether you must comply with HIPAA and HITECH, you should request clarification from attorneys who advise your university. Wilkinson and Reinhardt (2015) have suggested that even though counselor education programs may not be required to follow HIPAA and HITECH standards, they should follow the standards in order to achieve *best practice*. The *Technical Competencies for Counselor Education* (Jencius, Poynton, & Patrick, 2007) were developed to assist you in using technology appropriately.

Professor-Student Relationships

Counselor educators are expected to groom counseling graduate students to assume positions as professionals within the counseling profession. While you are mentoring students, socializing with them at professional gatherings and conferences, and perhaps collaborating with them on scholarly projects, you also have a responsibility to maintain a professional distance from students. You must avoid meeting your personal and social needs through relationships with students or using the power you have over students in any way that might be harmful. The burden of maintaining appropriate boundaries with students is solely your responsibility because students often try to push the boundaries in order to receive special attention from their professors. Take a moment to consider Case Illustration 3.2 related to establishing and maintaining professional boundaries with students.

Case Illustration 3.2

Establishing and Maintaining Professional Boundaries With Students

Cora is an educator in a master's-level counseling program at a private university in a small, suburban community. Over the previous semester, she has been the primary instructor for the counseling theories course.

> One of the students, Benjamin, has made a positive impression on Cora by the initiative and diligence he has demonstrated through class activities, discussions, and assignments. Benjamin seems to be equally impressed with Cora and has occasionally sought advisement from her regarding his academic pursuits and professional goals. Cora feels that she is a mentor to Benjamin, a relationship that Cora hopes to nurture in the future. On the last day of class, Benjamin invites Cora to meet him and some other students at a local bar for some drinks to celebrate the conclusion of the semester. Cora feels torn. She worries that, by declining Benjamin's offer, she will compromise the burgeoning mentor-mentee relationship. However, she also worries that, by accepting the offer, she will compromise her professional boundaries, especially given that alcohol is involved. Consider this situation for a moment. What is the best course of action? What are the consequences of the course of action you chose?

Section F.10.d of the ACA *Code of Ethics* (2014) specifically prohibits counselor educators from engaging in sexual or romantic relationships with students who are currently enrolled in a program when the professors have power or authority over the students. Section F.10.d of the code says "Counselor educators avoid nonacademic relationships with students in which there is a risk of potential harm to the student or which may compromise the training experience or grades assigned." Further the ACA *Code of Ethics* (2014) in Section F.10.c appears to allow counselor educators to have "social, sexual, or other intimate relationships" with former students as long as the counselor educators "are aware of the power differential" and discuss potential risks with their former students. The ACA *Code of Ethics* (2014) provisions include language that might suggest that counselor educators can engage in nonacademic relationships with students under some circumstances; and further may have sexual or intimate relationships with former students. However, because the power differential between professors and counseling graduate students does not end when students graduate (they continue to request endorsements and recommendations, for example), best practice is for counselor educators to maintain professional boundaries with both current and former students.

Counselor educators who teach doctoral students in counselor education and supervision programs often interact differently with their doctoral students than they do with their master's students. The dissertation process is very individualized and faculty members meet often with students whose dissertation committees they chair and the process can sometimes be intense and stressful. In addition, doctoral students might serve as teaching assistants in courses counselor educators teach, might engage in joint research projects, or might plan and present programs at refereed professional conferences. In the course of supervising master's students, doctoral students must evaluate other students' performance under the supervision of their professors. Doctoral graduate students who serve as graduate assistants often are privy to conversations among faculty members that might include private information about other students or they might observe conflicts among professors. Instead of loosening boundaries because of the intensity of work of doctoral students, in keeping with the ACA *Code of Ethics* (2014), Sections F.3 and F.10, it is wise for you to maintain professional boundaries to ensure doctoral students are not put in compromising situations because of any nonacademic relationships they might have with you.

An additional area of concern with professor and student relationships occurs when professors engage in joint research projects with students, apply for grants together, coauthor manuscripts for publication, or submit proposals for presentations to refereed conferences and later make presentations together. In all of these scholarly activities, the potential exists for students to be harmed or taken advantage of because of the power differential that exists between professors and students. When peers who are colleagues engage in scholarly activities, a negotiation process occurs in which decisions are made regarding the degree of credit each faculty member will receive for the scholarly product. Because students are vulnerable to the power professors have over them, students do not have the same status as peers or colleagues and therefore might feel as if they have to accept assignment of credit for scholarly products as dictated by a faculty member.

Section G.5.c of the ACA *Code of Ethics* (2014) says that counselors give recognition to previous work on a research topic and give full credit to those who deserve the credit. According to code section G.5.d, counselor educators must give credit through "joint authorship, acknowledgment, footnote statements, or other appropriate means to those who have contributed significantly." The degree of credit given must be in accordance with the contributions of others. Moore and Griffin (2007) and Brand, Allen, Altman, Hlava, and Scott (2015) have developed guidelines for determining the order and types of acknowledgment to be given when more than one person has contributed to research. Section G.5.d of the ACA *Code of Ethics* (2014) says that the principal contributor is listed first and that lesser contributions are acknowledged in notes or introductory statements. Section G.5.f of the code specifies that a student is listed as the principal author on an article that is substantially based on the student's course paper, project, dissertation, or thesis. Excellent advice for avoiding problems when engaged in scholarly activities is provided in Section G.5.e of the ACA *Code of Ethics* (2014), which indicates that counselor educators who engage in scholarly activities with colleagues, students, or supervisees should establish agreements in advance regarding each individual's tasks, publication credit, and types of acknowledgement for completing the project.

Multicultural Considerations

You are expected to demonstrate multicultural competence when recruiting, retaining, and preparing counselor trainees. In fact, this expectation is communicated several times throughout the ACA *Code of Ethics* (2014) and the 2016 CACREP accreditation standards (ACA, 2014, F.11.b; CACREP, 2016, Section 1.K). As you contemplate ways to actively recruit and retain culturally diverse students, you should also consider how the interaction between a student's cultural identity and the counseling program might affect the student's overall experience (Protivnak & Foss, 2009). For example, feelings of isolation, exclusion, and tokenization as well as cultural misunderstanding, a lack of support, and overall disrespect among culturally diverse students have been reported (Haskins et al., 2013; Henfield et al., 2013). These factors can impact a student's satisfaction with a counseling program.

You should seek to understand the experiences of students within your programs and address any factors that might contribute to a hostile learning environment and perpetuate institutional oppression (Goodrich & Shin, 2013; Henfield, Owens, & Witherspoon, 2011; Henfield et al., 2013). Additionally, you should be sensitive to the needs of culturally diverse students and provide information and support as needed and requested (e.g., information about culturally specific communities or programs on campus and within the local area; Henfield et al., 2011). Efforts to increase the diversity of counselor preparation programs should be continuous and include the consistent review of the current demographics among students and faculty as well as any changes or shifts (Goodrich & Shin, 2013).

When preparing to teach courses, you should also consider how you will "infuse material related to multiculturalism/diversity" (ACA, 2014, F.7.c) in order to "actively train students to gain awareness, knowledge, and skills in the competencies of multicultural practice" (ACA, 2014, F.11.c). The 2016 CACREP standards echo this responsibility by including "Social and Cultural Diversity" as one of the eight common core areas required for instruction of all counseling students (Section 2.F.2). You should consider how you can represent diverse cultural perspectives in each class to ensure that counseling trainees are prepared to provide culturally competent services to diverse clientele. Additionally, you should consider the intersection between their cultural identities and the cultural identities of the students in their classes. (See in this text Chapter 4: Multicultural and Social Justice Leadership and Learning in the Classroom.)

You should also be familiar with three important pieces of legislation that relate to the education of people with disabilities. The Americans with Disabilities Act (ADA) protects the rights of people with disabilities by ensuring that they are not discriminated against due to a disability (U.S. Department of Justice-Civil Rights Division, 2016). The ADA requires equal opportunity for people with disabilities to participate in and receive a variety of programs and services, including public education (U.S. Department of Justice-Civil Rights Division, 2009). Likewise, Section 504 of the Rehabilitation Act of 1973 protects individuals with disabilities who participate in programs that receive funding from the U.S. Department of Education from discrimination (U.S. Department of Education, 2016). Finally, the Individuals with Disabilities Education Act (IDEA) ensures that equal opportunities to receive public education are provided to children with disabilities. IDEA requires that all eligible children with disabilities are provided special education or related services (U.S. Department of Labor-Office of Disability Employment Policy, 2016). You should be sensitive to the needs of students with disabilities and must follow university procedures for granting accommodations to students who request them.

Problematic Student Behaviors and Dispositions

Problematic student behaviors and dispositions can disrupt the institutional learning environment as well as practicum and internship sites and ultimately affect peers, faculty, and supervisors (Brown-Rice & Furr, 2013). Clinical incompetence, unprofessional behavior, inadequate interpersonal skills, multicultural incompetence, unresolved mental health and substance abuse issues, inadequate academic skills, difficulty regulating emotions, reluctance to receive feedback, and lack of initiative and conscientiousness have been identified in the counseling literature as problematic student behaviors (Brown-Rice & Furr, 2013; Brown-Rice & Furr, 2016; Parker et al., 2014; Kress & Protivnak, 2009). When behaviors and dispositions such as these are identified, there is little debate about your responsibility as a gatekeeper for the profession. Unfortunately, a lack of consensus regarding what is deemed problematic, limited information about effectively addressing these issues, inadequate support from colleagues and administrators, and fear of negative consequences can create barriers to successfully fulfilling the role of gatekeeper (Brown-Rice & Furr, 2016; Rust et al., 2013). You should consider how you can clarify expectations regarding student behaviors and dispositions as well as effectively communicate remediation and dismissal policies and procedures to both students and faculty.

Kress and Protivnak (2009) provided suggestions for developing a professional development plan, a remediation plan focused on modifying student behavior. The development of the plan involves identifying the problematic behavior, determining remediation actions, regularly meeting with and providing feedback to the student, identifying the faculty to be involved in the process, securing signatures from all involved, determining deadlines and discussing consequences, notifying the student of her or his right to appeal, and providing circumstances for which immediate dismissal is warranted (Kress & Protivnak, 2009). Plans such as the one proposed by Kress and Protivnak (2009) might provide you with a systematic and structured method for addressing problematic student behaviors and dispositions. Regardless of the method chosen, it is important that you adequately and appropriately document each step in the process (Hutchens et al., 2013). Take a moment to complete Guided Practice Exercise 3.2, which provides you an opportunity to learn more about student remediation from the perspective of a current counselor educator.

Guided Practice Exercise 3.2

Student Remediation

According to the ACA *Code of Ethics* (2014), counselor educators and supervisors have an obligation to protect the welfare of clientele by monitoring the provision of services by counseling trainees (F.1.a). Additionally, the 2016 CACREP standards call for counselor educators to serve a gatekeeping capacity by assessing the professional performance of trainees and implementing remediation plans when needed. As a result, many counseling programs have remediation policies and procedures. To gain a better understanding, you are encouraged to speak with a counselor educator about her or his program's approach to remediation. As you listen, consider the following questions:

- Are students informed of the required competencies and student expectations prior to and while enrolled in the program?
- Does the remediation policy and procedure demonstrate due process (i.e., notification of charges, opportunity to be heard, and provision of remediation plan and opportunity to respond prior to dismissal)?
- Does the remediation process seem to be fair in relation to accessibility, adaptability, and consistency with accepted practice?
- Is the remediation process well documented (i.e., documentation of the deficiency and any student rebuttal, documentation of the remediation plan, and documentation of faculty support and oversight)?
- Does the remediation process seem to convey an interest in correcting the student behavior or disposition rather than penalizing the student?

Counselor educators may not be the only individuals to identify and seek to address concerns about students; counseling students might be the first to identify problematic student behaviors. Therefore, you should thoughtfully consider how you will respond to student reports about the problematic behaviors and dispositions of their peers (Parker et al., 2014). You should consider creating a formal method by which reports of problematic behavior and dispositions can be made by counseling students including limits to confidentiality and procedures to follow once faculty members are notified (Brown-Rice & Furr, 2013; Parker et al., 2014).

You should demonstrate awareness of how cultural and environmental factors might influence student behaviors and dispositions as well as the educators' perceptions regarding what is and is not problematic (Goodrich & Shin, 2013; Henfield et al., 2013). Although assessing for and addressing problematic behaviors and dispositions applies to all students, you should demonstrate heightened sensitivity to the power differential that may be present when interacting with culturally diverse students and work to ensure that respect for cultural differences is conveyed throughout the process (Goodrich & Shin, 2013). By viewing the situation from a holistic, systemic perspective, you can both value the diverse perspectives involved while also fulfilling your gatekeeping responsibilities. (See in this text Chapter 9: The Role of Gatekeeping in Counselor Education.)

Summary

This chapter highlights a number of ethical and legal challenges you may face when functioning in the role of teacher. Legal principles drawn from the U.S. Constitution, federal and state statutes, and tort law have been reviewed. Ethical guidelines provided by the ACA *Code of Ethics* (2014) and the accreditation standards of CACREP (2016) have been summarized in relation to the teaching responsibilities of counselor educators. Differences among ethical standards, legal standards, and best practice were discussed.

As a teacher in a counseling graduate program, you must be aware of your ethical and legal responsibilities from the time you advertise your program to potential applicants until you provide endorsements or recommendations for graduates. Areas that are particularly stressful for counselor educators were reviewed in this chapter, including gatekeeping for the counseling profession, requiring remediation for students who fail to meet performance standards, dealing with cheating or plagiarism by students, and managing relationship boundaries with students while teaching, supervising, and mentoring them.

You must be constantly mindful of the power you hold over students and treat students with respect. In addition, when in the role of teacher, you must grade the performance of students, assign grades, and dismiss students who are not able to meet minimum standards of professional performance.

Useful Websites

The following websites provide additional information relating to the chapter topics.

American Counseling Association. www.counseling.org
Americans with Disabilities Act. www.ada.gov
Association for Counselor Education and Supervision. www.acesonline.net
Council on Accreditation of Counseling and Related Educational Programs (CACREP). www.cacrep.org
Individuals with Disabilities Education Act (IDEA). www.disability.gov/individuals-disabilities-education-act-idea/
Section 504 of the Rehabilitation Act of 1973. http://www2.ed.gov/about/offices/list/ocr/504faq.html
Syllabus Clearinghouse. www.counseling.org/knowledge-center/clearinghouses/syllabus-clearinghouse

Additional Resources

The following resources provide additional information relating to the chapter topics.

Best Practices in Clinical Supervision. www.acesonline.net/sites/default/files/ACES-Best-Practices-in-clinical-supervision-document-FINAL.pdf
Developing and Maintaining Counselor Education Laboratories (2nd ed.) by A. Keith Mobley and Jane E. Myers. www.acesonline.net/sites/default/files/mobley_myers.pdf
In-House Training Clinic: An Ideal Setting for Training Doctoral Students in Supervision by L. DiAnne Borders. www.acesonline.net/sites/default/files/17.%20Borders%20copy.pdf
Standards for Counseling Supervisors. www.acesonline.net/sites/default/files/aces_stds_for_counseling_supervisors_jcdv69n1-1.pdf
Technical Competencies for Counselor Education: Recommended Guidelines for Program Development by Marty Jencius, Tim Poynton, and Pamela Patrick. www.acesonline.net/sites/default/files/2007_aces_technology_competencies.pdf

References

Almasy, S. (2016, April 27). *Tennessee governor signs "therapist bill" into law.* Retrieved from www.cnn.com/2016/04/27/politics/tennessee-therapist-bill

American Counseling Association. (2014). *ACA code of ethics.* Retrieved from www.counseling.org

American Counseling Association. (2016, June 14). *ACA 2017 conference & expo will be held in San Francisco.* Retrieved from www.counseling.org/my-voice

American Counseling Association. (2016). *Syllabus clearinghouse.* Retrieved from www.counseling.org/knowledge-center/clearinghouses/syllabus-clearinghouse

Barrio Minton, C. A., Wachter Morris, C. A., & Yaites, L. D. (2014). Pedagogy in counselor education: A 10-year content analysis of journals. *Counselor Education and Supervision, 53,* 162–177. doi:10.1002/j.1556-6978.2014.00055.x

Black's Law Dictionary. (2016). *Black's law dictionary free online legal dictionary* (2nd ed.). Retrieved from www.thelawdictionary.org

Borders, L. D., Wester, K. L., Granello, D. H., Chang, C. Y., Hays, D. G., Pepperell, J., & Spurgeon, S. (2012). Association for counselor education and supervision guidelines for research mentorship: Development and implementation. *Counselor Education and Supervision, 51,* 162–175. doi:10.1002/j.1556-6978.2012.00012.x

Brand, A., Allen, L., Altman, M., Hlava, M., & Scott, J. (2015). Beyond authorship: Attribution, contribution, collaboration, and credit. *Learned Publishing, 28,* 151–155. doi:10.1087/20150211

Brew, L., Cervantes, J. M., & Shepard, D. (2013). Millennial counselors and the ethical use of Facebook. *The Professional Counselor, 3,* 93–104. doi:10.15241/lbb.3.2.93

Brown, M. (2013). A content analysis of problematic behavior in counselor education programs. *Counselor Education and Supervision, 52,* 179–192. doi:10.1002/j.1556-6978.2013.00036.x

Brown-Rice, K., & Furr, S. (2013). Preservice counselors' knowledge of classmates' problems of professional competency. *Journal of Counseling & Development, 91,* 224–233. doi:10.1002/j.1556-6676.2013.00089.x

Brown-Rice, K., & Furr, S. (2015). Gatekeeping ourselves: Counselor educators' knowledge of colleagues' problematic behaviors. *Counselor Education and Supervision, 54,* 176–188. doi:10.1002/ceas.12012

Brown-Rice, K., & Furr, S. (2016). Counselor educators and students with problems of professional competence: A survey and discussion. *The Professional Counselor, 6,* 134–146. doi:10.15241/kbr.6.2.134

Bruff v. North Mississippi Health Services, 244 F.3d 495. (5th Cir. 2001).

Burkholder, D., Hall, S. F., & Burkholder, J. (2014). Ward v. Wilbanks: Counselor educators respond. *Counselor Education and Supervision, 53,* 267–283. doi:10.1002/j.1556-6978.2014.00062.x

Council for Higher Education Accreditation. (2016). Retrieved from www.chea.org

Counseling for Accreditation of Counseling and Related Educational Programs. (2016). *Standards.* Retrieved from www.cacrep.org

Duba, J. D., Paez, S. B., & Kindsvatter, A. (2010). Criteria of nonacademic characteristics used to evaluate and retain community counseling students. *Journal of Counseling & Development, 88,* 154–162. doi:10.1002/j.1556-6678.2010.tb00004.x

Dugger, S. M., & Francis, P. C. (2014). Surviving a lawsuit against a counseling program: Lessons learned from Ward v. Wilbanks. *Journal of Counseling & Development, 92,* 135–141. doi:10.1002/j.1556-6676.2014.00139.x

Family Educational Rights and Privacy Act of 1974, 20 U.S.C.A. §1232g (West, 1997).

Foster, V. A., & McAdams, C. R. (2009). A framework for creating a climate of transparency for professional performance assessment: Fostering student investment in gatekeeping. *Counselor Education and Supervision, 48*, 271–284. doi:10.1002/j.1556-6978.2009.tb00080.x

Goodrich, K. M., & Shin, R. Q. (2013). A culturally responsive intervention for addressing problematic behaviors in counseling students. *Counselor Education and Supervision, 52*, 43–55. doi:10.1002/j.1556-6978.2013.00027.x

Haskins, N., Whitfield-Williams, M., Shillingford, M. A., Singh, A., Moxley, R., & Ofauni, C. (2013). The experiences of Black master's counseling students: A phenomenological inquiry. *Counselor Education and Supervision, 52*, 162–178. doi:10.1002/j.1556-6978.2013.00035.x

Hays, D. G., Wood, C., & Smith, J. E. (2012). Advocacy and leadership through research best practices. In C. Y. Chang, C. A. Barrio Minton, A. L. Dixon, J. E. Myers, & T. J. Sweeney (Eds.), *Professional counseling excellence through leadership and advocacy* (pp. 227–243). New York, NY: Taylor & Francis.

Health Information Technology for Economic and Clinical Health (HITECH) Act, Title XIII §13001 of Division A of the American Recovery and Reinvestment Act of 2009 (AARA), Pub. L. No. 111-5 (2009).

Health Insurance Portability and Accountability Act (HIPAA), 45 CFR §§160, 162, & 164. (2013). Retrieved from www.gpo.gov/fdsys/pkg/CFR-2013-title45-vol1/pdf/CFR-2013-title45-vol1-chapA-subchapC.pdf

Henfield, M. S., Owens, D., & Witherspoon, S. (2011). African American students in counselor education programs: Perceptions of their experiences. *Counselor Education and Supervision, 50*, 226–242. doi:10.1002/j.1556-6978.2011.tb00121.x

Henfield, M. S., Woo, H., & Washington, A. (2013). A phenomenological investigation of African American counselor education students' challenging experiences. *Counselor Education and Supervision, 52*, 122–136. doi:10.1002/j.1556-6978.2013.00033.x

Herlihy, B. J., Hermann, M. A., & Greden, L. R. (2014). Legal and ethical implications of using religious beliefs as the basis for refusing to counsel certain clients. *Journal of Counseling & Development, 92*, 148–153. doi:10.1002/j.1556-6676.2014.00142.x

Homrich, A. M., DeLorenzi, L. D., Bloom, Z. D., & Godbee, B. (2014). Making the case for standards of conduct in clinical training. *Counselor Education and Supervision, 53*, 126–144. doi:10.1002/j.1556-6978.2014.00053.x

Hunt, B., & Gilmore, G. W. (2011). Learning to teach: Teaching internships in counselor education and supervision. *The Professional Counselor, 1*, 143–151. doi:10.15241/bhh.1.2.143

Hutchens, N., Block, J., & Young, M. (2013). Counselor educators' gatekeeping responsibilities and students' First Amendment rights. *Counselor Education and Supervision, 52*, 82–95. doi:10.1002/j.1556-6978.2013.00030.x

Ikonomopoulos, J., Vela, J. C., Smith, W. D., & Dell'Aquila, J. (2016). Examining the practicum experience to increase counseling students' self-efficacy. *The Professional Counselor, 6*, 161–173. doi:10.15241/ji.6.2.161

Jencius, M., Poynton, T., & Patrick, P. (2007). *Technical competencies for counselor education: Recommended guidelines for program development*. Alexandria, VA: Association for Counselor Education and Supervision. Retrieved from www.acesonline.net/sites/default/files/2007_aces_technology_competencies.pdf

Kaplan, D. M. (2014). Ethical implications of a critical legal case for the counseling profession: Ward v. Wilbanks. *Journal of Counseling & Development, 92*, 142–146. doi:10.1002/j.1556-6676.2014.00140.x

Kauffman, K. D. (March 26, 2014). *Is your syllabus a contract? A comparison of the SoTL literature and "the law."* SoTL Commons Conference. Paper 89. Retrieved from http://digitalcommons.georgiasouthern.edu/sotlcommons/SoTL/2014/89

Keeton v. Anderson-Wiley, No. 1:10-CV-00099-JRH-WLB, 733 F. Supp. 2d 1368. (S.D.Ga., Aug. 20, 2010).

Kress, V. E., & Protivnak, J. J. (2009). Professional development plans to remedy problematic counseling student behaviors. *Counselor Education and Supervision, 48,* 154–166. doi:10.1002/j.1556-6978.2009.tb00071.x

Lauka, J. D., & McCarthy, A. K. (2013). Proposed guidelines for operating counselor education and supervision training clinics. *Counselor Education and Supervision, 52,* 109–121. doi:10.1002/j.1556-6978.2013.00032.x

Lawley, J. S. (2012). HIPAA, HITECH, and the practicing counselor: Electronic records and practice guidelines. *The Professional Counselor, 2*(3), 192–200. doi:10.15241/jsl.2.3.192

Malott, K. M., Hall, K. H., Sheely-Moore, A., Krell, M. M., & Cardaciotto, L. (2014). Evidence-based teaching in higher education: Application to counselor education. *Counselor Education and Supervision, 53,* 294–305. doi:10.1002/j.1556-6978.2014.00064.x

Mobley, A. K., & Myers, J. E. (Eds.). (2010). *Developing and maintaining counselor education laboratories* (2nd ed.). Alexandria, VA: Association for Counselor Education and Supervision. Retrieved from www.acesonline.net/sites/default/files/mobley_myers.pdf

Moore, M. T., & Griffin, B. W. (2007). Identification of factors that influence authorship name placement and decisions to collaborate in peer-reviewed, education-related publications. *Studies in Educational Evaluation, 32,* 125–135.

Parker, L. K., Chang, C. Y., Corthell, K. K., Walsh, M. E., Brack, G., & Grubbs, N. K. (2014). A grounded theory of counseling students who report problematic peers. *Counselor Education and Supervision, 53,* 111–125. doi:10.1002/j.1556-6978.2014.00052.x

Parsons, J., & Bobby, C. L. (2016, July 15). *CACREP response letter to JCD articles.* Retrieved from www.cacrep.org/wp-content/uploads/2016/07/CACREP-response-letter-to-JCD-articles-7-15-16-2.pdf

Pease-Carter, C., & Barrio Minton, C. A. (2012). Counseling programs' informed consent practices: A survey of student preferences. *Counselor Education and Supervision, 51,* 308–319. doi:10.1002/j.1556-6978.2012.00023.x

Prosek, E. A., Holm, J. M., & Daly, C. M. (2013). Benefits of required counseling for counseling students. *Counselor Education and Supervision, 52,* 242–254. doi:10.1002/j.1556-6978.2013.00040.x

Protivnak, J. J., & Foss, L. L. (2009). An exploration of themes that influence the counselor education doctoral student experience. *Counselor Education and Supervision, 48,* 239–256. doi:10.1002/j.1556-6978.2009.tb00078.x

Remley, T. P., Jr., & Herlihy, B. (2016). *Ethical, legal, and professional issues in counseling* (5th ed.). Boston, MA: Pearson.

Rust, J. P., Raskin, J. D., & Hill. M. S. (2013). Problems of professional competence among counselor trainees: Programmatic issues and guidelines. *Counselor Education and Supervision, 52,* 3042. doi:10.1002/j.1556-6978.2013.00026.x

Sells, J. N., & Hagedorn, W. B. (2016). CACREP accreditation, ethics, and the affirmation of both religious and sexual identities: A response to Smith and Okech. *Journal of Counseling and Development, 94,* 265–279. doi:10.1002/jcad.12083

Smith, L. C., & Okech, J. E. A. (2016). Ethical issues raised by CACREP accreditation of programs within institutions that disaffirm or disallow diverse sexual orientations. *Journal of Counseling & Development, 94*, 252–264. doi:10.1002/jcad.12082

Swank, J. M., & Smith-Adcock, S. (2014). Gatekeeping during admissions: A survey of counselor education programs. *Counselor Education and Supervision, 53*, 47–61. doi:10.1002/j.1556-6978.2014.00048.x

U.S. Department of Education. (2016). *Office of civil rights: Protecting students with disabilities*. Retrieved from http://www2.ed.gov/about/offices/list/ocr/504faq.html

U.S. Department of Justice-Civil Rights Division. (2009). *A guide to disability rights laws: Americans with Disabilities Act (ADA)*. Retrieved from www.ada.gov/cguide.htm

U.S. Department of Justice-Civil Rights Division. (2016). *Introduction to the ADA*. Retrieved from www.ada.gov/ada_intro.htm

U.S. Department of Labor-Office of Disability Employment Policy. (2016). *Individuals with Disabilities Education Act (IDEA)*. Retrieved from www.disability.gov/individuals-disabilities-education-act-idea/

Walden v. Centers for Disease Control and Prevention. No. 1:08-cv-02278-JEC. (U.S. District Court for the Northern District of Georgia, March 18, 2010).

Ward v. Wilbanks, No. 10–2100, Doc. 006110869854. (6th Cir. Court of Appeals, Feb. 11, 2011). Retrieved from www.counseling.org/resources/pdfs/EMUamicusbrief.pdf

Wheeler, A. M. N., & Bertram, B. (2012). *The counselor and the law: A guide to legal and ethical practice* (6th ed.). Alexandria, VA: American Counseling Association.

Wilkinson, T., & Reinhardt, R. (2015). Technology in counselor education: HIPAA and HITECH as best practice. *The Professional Counselor, 5*(3), 407–418. doi:10.15241/tw.5.3.407

Ziomek-Daigle, J., & Christensen, T. M. (2010). An emergent theory of gatekeeping practices in counselor education. *Journal of Counseling & Development, 88*, 407–415. doi:10.1002/j.1556-6678.2010.tb00040.x

4 Multicultural and Social Justice Leadership and Learning in the Classroom

Anneliese A. Singh

Diversity has been a hallmark of the counseling profession for several decades, and the ways that diversity has been presented within counselor education have evolved over this time (Arredondo et al., 1996; Ratts, Singh, Nasser-McMillan, Butler, & McCullough, 2016). In this chapter, issues related to diversity in the counselor education classroom are discussed as they relate to both the social identities of the instructor and student. In addition, the connection of diversity to issues of multiculturalism, advocacy, and social justice are described so you understand how these interrelationships guide all of your work as a counselor educator. You will read case illustrations and guided practices related to integrating diversity within counselor education that can be useful for these explorations in your classroom, as well as considerations for working with students who might be resistant to diversity explorations.

Learning Objectives

After reading this chapter, you will be able to:

1. Describe the difference between diversity, multiculturalism, advocacy, and social justice.
2. Understand how to use a privilege and oppression framework within diversity work in counselor education.
3. Know the relevant professional documents within counseling related to diversity (e.g., ACA Multicultural Competencies, CACREP Standards).
4. Identify pedagogical strategies for integrating diversity within counselor education.
5. Understand the emotional impact of diversity explorations on various social identity groups (e.g., students of color, LGBTQ+ students).
6. Critique the field of counselor education from a diversity perspective.
7. Integrate an interdisciplinary perspective on diversity work within counselor education.
8. Identify strategies for working with students who are resistant to diversity work.

CACREP Standards Guiding Integration of Diversity Into Counselor Education

There is a specific section within the CACREP Standards (2016) in Section 2 (Professional Practice), titled "Social and Cultural Diversity," that has eight standards guiding the integration of diversity within counselor education:

Social and Cultural Diversity

a. multicultural and pluralistic characteristics within and among diverse groups nationally and internationally
b. theories and models of multicultural counseling, cultural identity development, and social justice and advocacy
c. multicultural counseling competencies
d. the impact of heritage, attitudes, beliefs, understandings, and acculturative experiences on an individual's views of others
e. the effects of power and privilege for counselors and clients
f. help-seeking behaviors of diverse clients
g. the impact of spiritual beliefs on clients' and counselors' worldviews
h. strategies for identifying and eliminating barriers, prejudices, and processes of intentional and unintentional oppression and discrimination

Notice that within this list is also an integration of multiculturalism, social justice, and advocacy, which I will discuss later in the chapter. In addition to these core areas of professional practice listed above, Section 2B (Professional Counseling Identity Foundation) asserts the importance of counselor program objectives that "reflect current knowledge and projected needs concerning counseling practice in a multicultural and pluralistic society" (p. 9). Essentially, CACREP-accreditation helps us ensure that we are striving to integrate the most current and relevant training that supports our students in becoming future counselors who understand the important areas of diversity, multiculturalism, social justice, and advocacy.

Diversity Within Counselor Education: History and Competency Development

There are numerous historical and competency development landmarks within the counseling profession that inform counselor educator attention to diversity. Diversity is a term that has a range of definitions and meanings for many people, which makes the term even more relevant for counselor educators to understand. In the 1980s, the term came into common use within the profession to bring attention to issues related to people of color within counseling—specifically related to African Americans (Parham & Clauss-Ehlers, 2016). Subsequently, as the diversity conversation continued within the profession, I have observed that the discussion shifted from a focus on White-Black discussions around race/ethnicity to a larger exploration of racial/ethnic identities, including Native American/First Nations, Asian American/Pacific Islanders, and Latino/a/x Americans.

As this discussion expanded, attention to issues related to racial/ethnic privilege expanded in a parallel process.

Within this context and focus on racial/ethnic concerns, many counselor educators and counseling psychologists began to work on shifting the counseling field from scholarship and practice discussions related to diversity to a more formal call for the development of multicultural competencies (Xie, 2014). Whereas the word "diversity" had been an umbrella term used to highlight mostly issues related to race/ethnicity, I have the observed the word "multicultural" became an umbrella term to encompass more social identities, such as class, disability, gender, sexual orientation, and other identities.

The formal call for development of multicultural competencies resulted in the significant document—the *Association of Multicultural Counseling and Development (AMCD) Multicultural Counseling Competencies* (Sue, Arredondo, & McDavis, 1992). This was a landmark document, as for the first time "diversity" had become an institutionalized component of the counseling profession with important implications for counselor education (Roysircar, 2010). Three domains were lauded as foundational components of multicultural competence: (a) counselor awareness or attitudes, (b) counselor knowledge, and (c) counselor skills. These domains were foundational in that the onus for the development of multicultural competency was positioned as a counselor responsibility and an ethical concern and are discussed further below.

Counselor Awareness and Attitudes

This domain is considered the starting point for counselor educators to work on the development of multicultural competence with counselor trainees, as counselor awareness entails self-reflection and acknowledgement of potential biases related to various social identities. For instance, a White counselor—who identifies as a man—may begin to "wake up" to his White and male privilege and stereotyped notions of race/ethnicity and Whiteness as he self-reflects on his own gender and race/ethnicity.

A significant component of counselor awareness is also being aware of one's limits related to social identity groups, as awareness of the multicultural knowledge that is needed is key to further developing multicultural competence. In this example, as a counselor educator, you have the responsibility to develop your own ways of engaging in ongoing self-awareness related to your identities and others, as well as biases related to diversity. This self-exploration is critical in helping you recognize the implications of how your cultural worldview and biases become a personal lens to interpret the world. This self-exploration then assists you in understanding diversity issues that are embedded within the counselor education classroom, interactions with students, grading, and design of course assignments, among other counselor educator activities.

Counselor Knowledge

Knowledge refers to the information that counseling trainees may or may not have about various multicultural groups. For example, a counselor who does not have a disability may not know much about how to work with clients who have a range of ability statuses. Development of multicultural competency would include, therefore, the counselor acquiring the knowledge of how to work with people living with disabilities—as well as seeking knowledge of how the mental health of people with disabilities is influenced by society. Counselor knowledge lays the groundwork for and leads to the development of skills in working with people with disabilities.

Counselor Skills

Once counselor self-awareness and counselor knowledge are acquired related to working with a specific social identity group, then the development of skills becomes critical to placing multicultural competency into action. *Skills* refers to the counselor's ability to use culturally responsive and empowering counseling interventions with a specific group. For instance, a counselor who is a citizen of the United States (U.S.) who is working with people who have refugee status from Syria would need to acquire the skills in developing counseling interventions with Syrian individuals and communities. Developing these multicultural skills would also entail a continuous self-reflection on counselor awareness and counselor knowledge as skills are developed further.

In the late 1990s, counselor educators and counseling psychologists began connecting the need for multicultural competence with advocacy. Advocacy is defined as the work that counselors can do in two domains related to social change: (a) advocacy *with* clients and (b) advocacy *on behalf of* clients. These two domains became the central foci of the ACA Advocacy Competencies (Lewis, Arnold, House, & Toporek, 2003), which were grounded in a socioecological model of micro (client/student empowerment and client/student advocacy), meso (community collaboration and systems advocacy), and macro (public information and social/political advocacy) levels.

After the AMCD Multicultural Counseling Competencies and Advocacy Competencies were adopted by ACA, soon after calls began to be issued from various groups within ACA that who continued to experience marginalization within the profession despite the new competencies. One of these groups began advocating for attention to sexual orientation within the counseling profession—and much later also entailed a call for multicultural competency development with transgender clients—and so subsequent competencies were developed for lesbian, gay, and bisexual (LGB) clients, then transgender clients (ACA, 2010), and later competencies that replaced the original LGB competencies (Competencies for Counseling Lesbian, Gay, Bisexual, Queer, Questioning, Intersex, and Ally Individuals, 2013). Several other competency documents related to diversity have proliferated within ACA divisions, such as the Association for Spiritual, Ethical, and Religious Values in Counseling (ASERVIC) Competencies for Addressing Spiritual and Religious Issues in Counseling (2011).

From 2000 on, calls for an increased focus on social justice change were issued (Ratts, Arredondo, & D'Andrea, 2005) and counselor educators called for attention to how counselors could not only develop multicultural competence, but also engage in social justice change. Many scholars called this emphasis a "return" to the roots of social justice in counseling. For instance, Singh and Salazar (2010) pointed out that the origins of group work related to Jane Hull's work as a feminist with immigrants living with medical concerns in the Hull House as rooted in social justice concerns. Over this time, conceptual and empirical work additionally began calling for the integration of multicultural and social justice competency development together.

Responding to these calls, in 2015 the ACA endorsed the *Multicultural and Social Justice Competencies* (Ratts et al., 2016). This document was a revision of the original 1992 *Multicultural Counseling Competencies*, and addressed some of the growing edges of the original competencies. One issue was that the original competencies did not address issues of when a counselor with a marginalized identity (e.g., counselor of color, LGBTQ+ counselor) was working with a client with privilege (e.g., White client, heterosexual, or cisgender client). In addition, the new competencies added a fourth domain of "action" to the counselor awareness, knowledge, and skills, and also integrated attention to socioecological levels of counselor intervention (e.g., intrapersonal, interpersonal, institutional, community, public policy, international and global affairs). The revised competencies were organized in four quadrants to develop a focus on the multiple dyads that could occur within the counseling relationship (see Figure 4.1 for these quadrants).

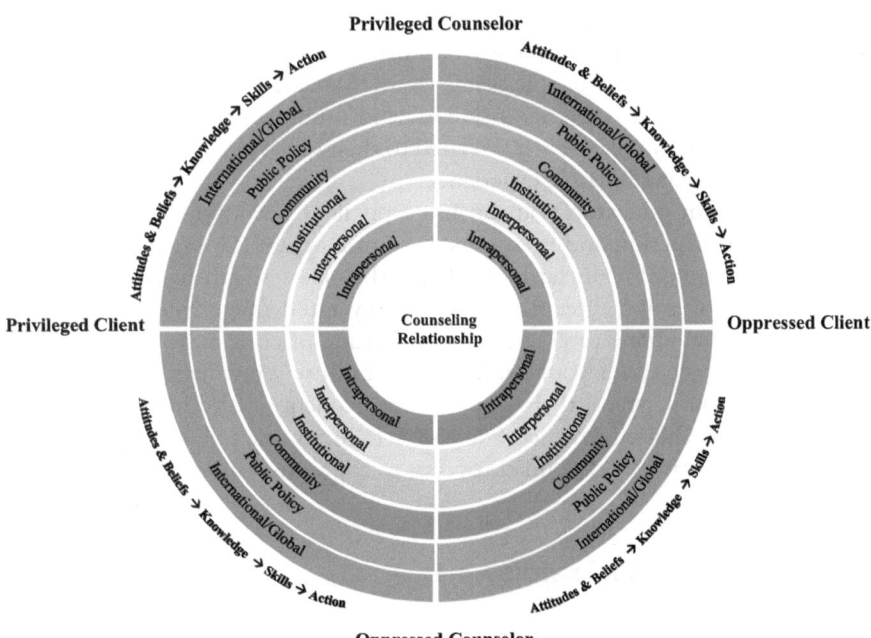

Figure 4.1 Multicultural and Social Justice Counseling Competencies Conceptual Framework

In addition to these various competencies, you should be familiar with the focus on diversity contained within the CACREP standards. These multiple calls for attention to diversity, multicultural, social justice, and advocacy issues within the field led to the integration of these core areas of training being included within the CACREP standards. Over the many revisions of the CACREP standards, this focus has similarly moved from a brief note of the importance of diversity to a more integrated attention to diversity issues within counselor education as an ethical imperative and competency benchmark across courses within the CACREP core.

Using a Privilege and Oppression Framework in Counselor Education

As you can see from the history of diversity within the counseling profession, over time attention to issues of privilege and oppression increased significantly. This increase was influenced by attention to issues of privilege and oppression explored in other disciplines, especially women's studies. For example, Peggy McIntosh's famous exploration of White privilege in her 1988 article entitled *White Privilege and Male Privilege: A Personal Account of Coming to See Correspondences through Work in Women's Studies* had a significant impact on diversity discussions across disciplines. She defined privilege as unearned advantages that people with White and male privilege could rely on as they moved through various institutions within society, such as schools and workplaces. Scholars have defined oppression as the absence of these unearned advantages (Adams, 2015) that also situate clients with marginalized statuses as experiencing microaggressions (Sue, 2010) and minority stress (Meyer, 2003). Microaggressions refer to the everyday injuries that people with historically marginalized identities experience, such as transgender people being asked, "What is your *real* name?" Minority stress refers to the chronic, insidious, and multiplicative stress that people with minority identities experience related to their social identity that is on top of everyday stress that all people experience.

As a counselor educator, you can use a privilege and oppression framework throughout instruction and even outside of instruction (Smith & Shin, 2008). For instance, counselor educators can begin their classes with an exploration and establishment of group agreements that identify and define privilege and oppression as they may influence class learning. Outside of class, as you receive information or contact about your students, you can use a privilege and oppression framework to understand their students and student-faculty interactions more holistically. See Guided Practice Exercise 4.1 for an example of using privilege and oppression frameworks outside of class to conceptualize student interactions.

Guided Practice Exercise 4.1

Dr. Williams Receives a Text

Dr. Williams is a White American counselor educator. She received a text from a student who has missed two subsequent Counseling Theory

> classes. The student, Dara, is a Latina American who identifies as a woman, who is also the primary financial provider for her extended family. Dr. Williams reached out to Dara via email to inquire about her absences. After the second missed class, Dr. Williams received a text from Dara asking to speak with her. Dr. Williams had provided her phone number to students in cases of emergencies. In her text, Dara shares that she was fired from her job the week before and has had to immediately begin a job search and is temporarily working in a department store where she does not have control over her hours. Discuss the following:
>
> - What are the issues of privilege and oppression arising in this interaction?
> - How can Dr. Williams interact with Dara in a way that recognizes these various issues of privilege and oppression and also upholds her responsibilities as a counselor educator?
> - How can the various competencies related to multiculturalism and social justice guide Dr. Williams in this student-faculty interaction?

Pedagogical strategies related to diversity work in the counselor education classroom are discussed further below; however, the "Action Continuum" (see Table 4.1) proposed by Adams et al. (2015) is a helpful tool in both establishing an accountability measure for the establishment of and exploration of a privilege and oppression framework. This Action Continuum can help both you, as the instructor, and students assess where you all are related to the acquisition of counselor awareness, knowledge, and skills around particular diversity issues, and then connect these three domains with where you are in terms of "action" on these same diversity issues. For example, a Native American/First Nations, cisgender, heterosexual man who is a counselor educator might want to assess where he is in his awareness, knowledge, and skills related to disability issues in counselor education. Consulting the Action Continuum in Table 4.1, he can then track where he is in taking action to further strengthen his growing edges in this diversity area.

Pedagogical Strategies for Integrating Diversity

Once you are grounded in the various multicultural and social justice competencies within the counseling field and have a strong understanding of privilege and oppression, there are numerous pedagogical strategies for integrating diversity that you may use (Goodman et al., 2015). Some strategies relate to timing of diversity discussions, such as the development of a learning environment that is conducive and supportive of diversity explorations. Other pedagogical strategies relate to increasing the depth of diversity discussion, which can often be tied to knowledge and skills of group work. For instance, in the earlier parts of class, you may decide that icebreaker activities are more appropriate than long discussions that intensely interrogate diversity concerns.

Table 4.1 Using an Action Continuum to Frame Diversity Explorations

Actively Participate	Denying and Ignoring	Recognize, No Action	Recognize, Action	Educating Self	Educating Others	Support, Encourage	Initiating, Preventing
• Derogatory jokes • Put-downs • Verbal or physical harassment • Discrimination	• Enabling thru denial • Collusion through inaction	• Aware but no action • Fear • Lack of info • Confusion • Experiences discomfort and contradiction between awareness and action	• Aware • Recognizes oppressive actions by self and others • Takes action to stop	• Learn more about oppression and privilege • Read • Workshops • Cultural events • Discussions • Join anti-discrimination organizations	• Questions and dialogue with others • Share with others why you object to oppressive comments and actions	• Back up others who speak out • Form an allies group • Join a coalition group	• Work to change individual and institutional actions and policies • Plan educational programs or events • Make sure members of marginalized groups are full participants

Other considerations you should be mindful of include the social identity composition of the students (Ober, Granello, & Henfield, 2009). Some counselor educators work in settings where students have social identities that are predominantly privileged (e.g., White, heterosexual, Christian, middle to upper class), whereas other counselor training settings are more diverse in some identities (e.g., students of color) but not others (e.g., students with disabilities). Pedagogical interventions can vary across these settings, as in mostly privileged settings, and you may need to bring in various media and Internet resources to explore issues of diversity, while also ensuring that the class environment does not turn to students in the minority (e.g., a class of 24 White students and 2 students of color) to educate the students who hold the majority social identity. Pedagogical strategies are explored more below.

Setting the Container of the Class

Just like counselors must intentionally develop a safe space for the client in the counseling environment, you as a counselor educator are responsible for doing the same for diversity issues. In this regard, there are several pedagogical strategies that counselor educators may employ. When beginning the first class, you can develop a "full value contract" or "group agreements" that set foundational expectations for diversity discussions that are a supplement to the syllabus. For instance, the following prompts can be used in these discussions:

- What expectations do you have of one another?
- What expectations do you have of yourself?
- What expectations do you have of me?
- What expectations do I have of you?

As students respond to these prompts, you can ensure that attention to issues of diversity are included. Common group agreements supporting diversity discussions might include the following:

- Respect
- Curiosity
- Assume best intentions
- Use "I" statements
- Listen to others to learn, not to prepare to speak your point

Once a "group agreements" list is brainstormed by the class, the instructor can review the overall list of group agreements with the class. Then, instructors can ask students if there are any additions they would like to add that would facilitate dialogues around diversity issues.

Other ways you might begin class might also include diversity icebreakers. For instance, I facilitate an icebreaker at the beginning of each of my courses that I call the "Cultural Name Game." In this exercise, students introduce themselves with the history and origins of their name. As they introduce themselves, there will be many cultural identities and influences (e.g., religion, gender, race/ethnicity) that arise—and there will also be students who do not know a lot about their name or do not have access to the history of their name. This can result in a rich beginning exploration of diversity. Another common starting point in counseling classes is to begin with the prompt of "I am _____," and ask students to fill in the blank with as many identifiers as they can in a timed one minute. Typically, students with privilege will not name their privileges (e.g., cisgender, heterosexual), whereas people without privilege will name their social identities (e.g., queer, Black woman). Processing questions can peak students' curiosity about the obliviousness of privilege and the salience of oppression in everyday experiences of their own identities.

Continuing Diversity Discussions

A common misstep in diversity explorations in the classroom can be leaving diversity discussions unexamined or at the surface level (Pack-Brown, Coulter, & Fuller, 2012). Therefore, you have an important role as a counselor educator to ensure that diversity discussions are not relegated only to diversity classes and that once students have had time to get to know one another that the diversity explorations deepen. There are several strategies to do this, starting with syllabus assignments that are informed by various multicultural and social justice competencies and provide space to explore counseling trainee social identities. An example might be a self-exploration paper (Xie, 2014) of family upbringing and biases that influence how the counseling trainee views constructs such as counseling, healing, and help-seeking. Another example might be developing class discussions around case conceptualizations with diversity components embedded in them or inviting students to consider what social identities would be important if they were the client and connecting these to the multicultural and social justice competencies.

Group Dynamics and Diversity

Group dynamics certainly come into play any time there are diversity discussions, so counselor educators should feel well grounded in group worker skills and dynamics as an instructor (Singh & Salazar, 2014). As previously noted, classes are a microcosm of a group, so beginning diversity discussions should be thoughtfully planned out and integrated into classroom learning. You should also expect that there will be a "storm" of some type—whether this storm is related to diversity conversations or not (often the two are connected!). Your role is to support the class through the storm and sharing their authentic selves, which often involves having courageous conversations (discussed in the next section). These courageous conversations are essential, as they help provide a transition to the class as a group to be able to move on to the working stage—and ultimately to termination of the class as a group.

It is important to be mindful that all of the counseling competencies related to diversity should not be limited to the multicultural counseling course. Rather, these competencies can be used as a training lens for all courses within counselor education. For instance, the Association for Specialists in Group Work (ASGW) *Multicultural and Social Justice Competence Principles for Group* ASGW multicultural and social justice principles (Singh, Merchant, Skuryzk, & Ingene, 2012) can provide considerations for the timing of diversity discussions and how to plan and process these diversity concerns. Therefore, as a counselor educator, you will want to develop skills of integrating diversity throughout courses that do not have the words *diversity, multicultural, social justice,* or *advocacy* within the title.

Because diversity discussions and group dynamics can be intricately linked, it can be helpful to consult the ASGW multicultural and social justice principles (Singh et al., 2012). These principles are organized across three domains: (a) awareness of self and group members, (b) strategies and skills in group worker planning and group workers performing and processing, and (c) social justice advocacy. Counselor educators can benefit from reading the principles, as these guidelines can help tailor pedagogical strategies. For example, let's take the situation where you are teaching an assessment or appraisal class and would like to integrate attention to diversity issues related to measurement. You can use diversity competencies to help them integrate diversity into case studies, examinations, and class discussion, as well as how diversity influences what we know and do not know in terms of appraisal with various communities. Then, you as a counselor educator are helping your students gain knowledge that is helpful for them to be more culturally responsive and stronger advocates, as well as ensuring that you are meeting baselines CACREP diversity standards of integration throughout course content. See Guided Practice Exercise 4.2 for an example of how you might use Section I of the ASGW *Multicultural and Social Justice Competence Principles for Group Workers* (Singh et al., 2012).

Guided Practice Exercise 4.2

Domain I of the ASGW Multicultural and Social Justice Competence Principles for Group Workers (Singh et al., 2012)

You are a counselor educator teaching a Research Methods course. Name three ways that you might use Domain I of the *ASGW Multicultural and Social Justice Competence Principles for Group Workers* to shape how you will engage the students who are in your class on diversity concerns in counselor education and research methods.

I. Awareness of Self and Group Members: As Group Workers Move Towards Multicultural and Social Justice Advocacy Competence They Will

1. Demonstrate movement to being increasingly aware of and sensitive to their own multicultural identity and how their race, ethnicity, socioeconomic class, age, gender identity and expression, sexual orientation, religion, and spirituality, are impacted by their own experiences and histories.
2. Demonstrate movement towards being increasingly aware of and sensitive to the multiple dimensions of the multicultural and multilayered identities of group members.

3. Demonstrate an awareness of different connecting and communicating styles. Group workers recognize different communication styles related to the various nuances of one's cultural worldviews. They are aware of how myths, stereotypes, and assumptions learned by living in a society that bases one's cultural identity on excluding and devaluing others, impacts group dynamics.
4. Seek to understand the extent to which general group leadership skills and functions may be appropriate or inappropriate for group work facilitation with multicultural group members.
5. Recognize obstacles that group members encounter based on lack of opportunities and systems of oppression (e.g., sexism, classism, heterosexism) and gain awareness of how to integrate an advocacy focus into group learning to address these barriers.
6. Increase awareness and deeper level of understanding through educational, consultative, and training and cultural immersion experiences in order to become more fluent with culturally-based practices.

Initiating Courageous Conversations

One of the key roles you have in the counselor education classroom is to facilitate courageous conversations (Singh & Salazar, 2014). Courageous conversations are also commonly called "difficult dialogues" or "intergroup dialogues," and commonly explore diversity issues such as racism, ableism, classism, and other oppressions. Courageous conversations can be planned explorations of various diversity concerns, such as discussing the impact of anti-transgender bathroom laws on the mental health of transgender and gender nonconforming (TGNC) people or the mental health impact of police brutality on African American men. These conversations can also be spontaneous and address issues of privilege and oppression that arise in the classroom in the course of other content learning. For instance, a heterosexual counselor educator or student may unintentionally say something that is heterosexist in nature (e.g., "Counselors should be sure to talk to both the mother and father when working with families"), and the need arises for a courageous conversation about embedded heteronormativity in discussing course content.

Regardless of how courageous conversations arise or are planned, there are some key elements your should keep in mind in the counselor education classroom:

- Creating an environment of safety for exploration of diversity issues
- Developing an environment where exploring privilege and oppression are part of the courageous conversation
- Naming tensions and similarities in student sharing during class discussions
- Validating the risk and resilience it takes to engage in courageous conversations
- Cutting off students who monopolize discussion or divert emotionality and process of the class
- Drawing out students with privilege to share their perspectives
- Connecting courageous conversation content to larger systems in society

See Case Illustration 4.1 for an example of facilitation of a courageous conversation.

Case Illustration 4.1

Facilitating a Courageous Conversation

Delilah is an African-American, transgender counselor educator who is teaching an interpersonal helping skills course. In the news, there have been numerous stories of the murders of unarmed Black men and women by police. A Black, cisgender, heterosexual student—Brad—raises his hand and says that he "wants to talk about recent news events, and is tired of waiting for White people to bring up the topic." Delilah names and validates the emotions that Brad is feeling in terms of frustration, and reminds the class of the utility of a discussion about racism in a class exploring helping skills. In doing so, she connects course content and theory about building the counseling relationship to these current concerns and reminds the class about their initial group agreements as they have this discussion.

A White woman—Laurie—raises her hand and says her partner is a Black police officer. She shares that she is offended by "all of the Black Lives Matter activists who don't care about cops protecting them." Delilah draws out the similarities and tensions between Brad and Laurie, and invites them both to share reactions to one another's sharing. After doing so, Delilah opens to the class for reactions and sharing, paying close attention to ensuring that students of color do not feel positioned to educate the White students, and also to drawing out White students who are not sharing about their thoughts and feelings about the interaction between Brad and Laurie. Delilah also connects the frustration and tensions that the class experiences in discussing these issues, while also talking about the larger system of White privilege and over-criminalization of African American communities.

Considerations for Diversity Training With Resistant Students

When you engage in diversity explorations within your classrooms, you will naturally notice resistance from students who are exploring their own privilege and oppression experiences for the first time (Mildred & Zúñiga, 2004). It is important that you do not take these situations personally, but rather use their training in counselor education, multicultural and social justice competencies, CACREP standards, and the ACA Ethics Code (2014) to guide their interventions with these students. Resistance can be expected in many cases, as all students—and instructors—have various stages of identity development related to social identities of race/ethnicity, sexual orientation, gender, etc. For instance, a major part of White identity development is experiencing denial that White privilege is an issue, and denial is also an initial stage of many social identity development models (Bloom, Peters, Margolin, & Fragnoli, 2015). Here are some actions you may decide to take as a counselor educator within class when you notice student resistance to diversity training, or even distinct aspects of diversity training:

- Return to group agreements related to class discussions of diversity that can remind students of the importance of self-awareness, knowledge, and skill development related to diversity learning
- Use self-disclosure in class discussions related to model your own process of understanding your privilege related to a certain identity (e.g., African American heterosexual woman disclosing her awareness of heterosexual privilege, White trans man disclosing her awareness of White privilege)
- Challenge student sharing that is explicitly racist, sexist, ableist, etc. with research from within and outside of counselor education
- Review the specific ACA Ethics Code (2014) components, CACREP Standards (2016), and other counseling competencies that apply to student learning that related to diversity training to remind students of the expectations and best practices of counselor education, in addition to ethical concerns
- Share the feelings (e.g., concern) you have when you hear a student express a lack of awareness, knowledge, or skills and long-term implications of their thoughts

If none of the above strategies within class work—or if the resistant student is overtly displaying oppressive attitudes within class—then you may need to engage in one of the following actions:

- Explore further the student's openness to building diversity awareness, knowledge, and skills
- Ask to speak to the student outside of class and express concerns that are clearly linked to the ACA Ethics Code (2014), CACREP Standards (2016), and other counseling competencies
- Share that you will be consulting with other program faculty about follow-up training needs with the student
- Review the student within a program faculty meeting related to gatekeeping. Acquire assistance from your department chair and/ or Dean if necessary
- Consult with the Ethics Department at ACA if there are questions about gatekeeping that your program faculty need help understanding

As noted above, addressing student resistance to diversity explorations, you should assess whether the resistance is linked to an ethical issue in training (Davidson & Haseer, 2015). For instance, when a student says they do not want to work with immigrants, there are ethical considerations of the student's ability to work with a wide range of clients. If issues of resistance are not ethical in nature, typically class discussions or individual meetings further exploring diversity issues that the student is resistant to should be a priority. When the student resistance is linked to an ethical concern, then you should use consultation and supervision with their fellow faculty and peers to move through an ethical decision-making model to identify next steps. These are issues where gatekeeping and ethical/legal issues often can come into play within the program, department, and larger university levels. See Case Illustration 4.2 for an example of addressing a resistant student furthering oppression within the classroom.

Case Illustration 4.2

A Case Study Addressing Oppression in the Classroom

Mark is White, heterosexual, cisgender, male student who during a class discussion about heterosexism says to the instructor that he "thinks being gay is against the Christian faith." The counselor educator, Mansur, challenges Mark to share more about the sources of his beliefs in this regard. As Mark shares more deeply, he says "I truly think these people are going to hell." Mansur knows that there are several LGBTQ+ people within the classroom, and he stops the class and makes it clear that he as a counselor educator has an ethical and legal mandate to be able to work with a range of client identities. Mansur also reminds the entire class of how issues of privilege and oppression shape the lives of LGBTQ+ people in terms of their mental and physical health disparities. Mark crosses his arms and does not share any other thoughts in the class, despite Mansur attempting to engage him. After class, Mansur asks for an individual meeting with Mark and shares that he wants to have a follow-up discussion with Mark about his beliefs.

I believe that an additional important area for us to explore within the topic of resistance to diversity includes our own resistance we can feel in response to learning about diversity, as well as the resistance we may feel from colleagues within counselor education. Again, resistance to diversity training within counselor education is a natural part of the process as we talked about earlier. Many racial/ethnic and other identity development models each have a "stage" where there is either obliviousness to issues related to social identity or flat-out denial that oppression exists. The good news is, in my experience, that when you encounter resistance within students, colleagues, or even within yourself, you can validate that this resistance is *simply part of the process of learning*. For instance, a student or fellow faculty may have presented a family case study in class, but upon reflection realize that it was heteronormative in that it excluded LGBTQ families. It is important to explore this exclusion in a courageous conversation geared toward new learning and understanding.

It can be frustrating to stumble upon places within us that have this resistance, but it is more important to have regular accountability practices within our own diversity training and learning as counselor educators that help acknowledge that this is part of the process. We can engage in reflection, consultation, supervision, discussions with faculty and students, and ongoing professional development related to diversity to learn how to be more effective in identifying the places we still need to grow within our own diversity learning.

With regard to diversity-resistant colleagues, it can be tempting to be frustrated and not have conversations about the mutual learning that should be taking place amongst faculty related to diversity. However, it is more helpful to move to an action place, where you use theories and training models that help counselor educators assess the extent to which diversity is integrated in a program (Haskins et al., 2013). For instance, if you want to ensure attention to issues of race/ethnicity are integrated within your counselor education program, you can use a theory such as Critical Race Theory to assess how responsive your admission tools, curriculum content, and faculty-student interacts to these issues (Haskins & Singh, 2015). See Guiding Practice 4.3 for an example of how you as a counselor educator can identify programmatic ways to identify faculty resistance (including your own) to diversity.

Guided Practice 4.3

Identifying Our Diversity Resistance as Faculty

Use the following questions at the start of the academic year or at a program faculty retreat to begin to create a culture of shared accountability to diversity learning:

- What are the strengths and growing edges faculty have individually and as a program related to diversity knowledge?
- What are the ongoing diversity continuing education opportunities that faculty have engaged in recently?
- How can faculty integrate their new diversity learning into course content, as well as interactions with students and one another?
- What are the gaps that exist in diversity training across faculty? How can these gaps be addressed with future diversity learning opportunities?
- How is the program's commitment to diversity and ongoing learning communicated to students and applicants to the program?
- What are the diversity areas that are most difficult to access information about or challenging to discuss amongst students and program faculty?
- How do issues of privilege and oppression related to social identities influence comfort level among faculty in discussing diversity issues?

It is important to note that issues of power are embedded within any accountability work done within counselor education program faculty, as there are faculty who have lower rank (e.g., Assistant versus Associate or Full Professor or Clinical Faculty versus Tenure Track) and faculty who have historically marginalized identities (e.g., White versus people of color, heterosexual versus queer). Therefore, the roles of privilege and oppression are vitally important to discuss, as evidenced in Guided Practice 4.3.

Summary

In this chapter, the critical importance you have as a counselor educator of integrating diversity discussions and explorations into the classroom across content areas was discussed. From developing multicultural and social justice competence with counseling trainees to using a privilege and oppression framework both within and outside of the classroom when interacting with students and fellow faculty, you should embed diversity within all instructional activities. Pedagogical strategies exploring diversity can range widely, and issues of timing of these discussions during courses and how group dynamics influence these discussions are important considerations.

The following websites can provide you with additional information relating to the chapter topics.

Useful Websites

Association for Lesbian, Gay, Bisexual, and Transgender Issues in Counseling (ALGBTIC). www.algbtic.org

Association of Multicultural Counseling and Development (AMCD). www.multiculturalcounseling.org

Critical Multicultural Pavilion Awareness Activities. www.edchange.org/multicultural/activityarch.html

National Conference on Race and Ethnicity. www.ncore.ou.edu

National Intergroup Dialogue in Higher Education. https://igr.umich.edu/article/national-intergroup-dialogue-institute

White Privilege Conference. www.whiteprivilegeconference.com

Additional Resources

The following resources provide additional information relating to the chapter topics.

Adams, M. (2015). Pedagogical frameworks for social justice education. In Adams, Bell, & Griffin (Eds.) *Teaching for Social Justice and Diversity* (2nd ed) (pp. 15–34). New York, NY: Routledge.

Adams, M., Blumenfeld, W. J., Castaneda, C. R., Hackman, H. W., Peters, M. L., & Zuniga, X. (2015). *Readings for diversity and social justice*. New York, NY: Routledge.

Adams, M., Bell, L. A., & Griffin, P. (2015). *Teachings for diversity and social justice*. New York, NY: Routledge.

Goodman, D. J. (2000). *Promoting diversity and social justice: Educating people from privileged groups*. Thousand Oaks, CA: Sage.

Sue, D. W. (2010). *Microaggressions in everyday life: Race, gender, and sexual orientation*. New York, NY: Wiley.

References

Adams, M., Blumenfeld, W. J., Castaneda, C. R., Hackman, H. W., Peters, M. L., & Zuniga, X. (2015). *Readings for diversity and social justice*. New York, NY: Routledge.

American Counseling Association. (2014). ACA ethics code. Retrieved from www.counseling.org/resources/aca-code-of-ethics.pdf

American Counseling Association. (2010). American Counseling Association competencies for counseling with transgender clients. *Journal of LGBT Issues in Counseling, 4*, 135–159. doi:10.1080/15538605.2010.524839

Arredondo, P., Toporek, R. S., Brown, S., Jones, J., Locke, D. C., Sanchez, J., & Stadler, H. (1996). *Operationalization of the multicultural counseling competencies*. Alexandria, VA: American Counseling Association.

Bloom, D. S., Peters, T., Margolin, M., & Fragnoli, K. (2015). Are my students like me? The path to color-blindness and White racial identity development. *Education and Urban Society, 47*(5), 555–575. doi:10.1177/0013124513499929

Council for Accreditation of Counseling & Related Educational Programs. (2016). *2016 CACREP Standards*. Retrieved from www.cacrep.org/for-programs/2016-cacrep-standards/

Davidson, M. M., & Haseer, C. T. (2015). Multiculural counseling meets potentially harmful therapy: The complexity of bridging two discourses. *The Counseling Psychologist, 43*(3), 370–379. doi:10.1177/0011000014565714

Goodman, R. D., Williams, J. M., Chung, R. C. Y., Talleyrand, R. M., Douglass, A. M., McMahon, G. H., & Bemak, F. (2015). Decolonizing traditional pedagogies and practices in counseling and psychology education: A move towards social justice and action. In R. D. Hoodman & P. C. Gorski (Eds.), *Decolonizing "multicultural" counseling through social action*. New York, NY: Springer.

Harper, A., Finnerty, P., Martinez, M., Brace, A., Crethar, H. C., Loos, B., Harper, B., Graham, S., Singh, A. A., Kocet, M., Travis, L., & Lambert, S. (2013). Association for Lesbian, Gay, Bisexual, and Transgender Issues in Counseling (ALGBTIC) competencies for counseling lesbian, gay, bisexual, queer, questioning, intersex, and ally individuals. *Journal of LGBT Issues in Counseling, 7*(1), 2–43.

Haskins, N., Whitfield-Williams, M., Shillingford, M. A., Singh, A. A., Moxley, R., & Ofauni, C. (2013). The experiences of Black master's counseling students: A phenomenological inquiry. *Counselor Education and Supervision, 52*, 162–178.

Haskins, N., & Singh, A. A. (2015). Using critical race theory to enhance counselor education: Creating equitable training. *Counselor Education and Supervision, 54*(5), 288–301.

Lewis, J., Arnold, M. S., House, R., & Toporek, R. L. (2002). ACA Advocacy Competencies. Retrieved from http://www.counseling.org/Resources/Competencies/Advocacy_Competencies.pdf

McIntosh, P. (1988). White privilege and male privilege: A personal account of coming to see correspondences through work in Women's Studies, Working paper 189. Wellesley, MA: Wellesley Center for Research on Women.

Meyer, I. (2003). Prejudice, social stress, and mental health in lesbian, gay, and bisexual populations: Conceptual issues and research evidence. *Psychological Bulletin, 129*, 674–697. doi:10.1037/0033-2909.129.5.674

Mildred, J., & Zúñiga, X. (2004). Working with resistance to diversity issues in the classroom: Lessons from teacher training and multicultural education. *Smith College Studies in Social Work, 74*(2), 359–375. doi:10.1080/00377310409517721

Ober, A. M., Granello, D. H., & Henfield, M. S. (2009). A synergistic model to enhance multicultural competence in supervision. *Counselor Education and Supervision, 48*(3), 204–221. doi:10.1002/j.1556-6978.2009.tb00075.x

Pack-Brown, S., Coulter, S., & Fuller, L. (2012). Multicultural counseling: Training culturally intentional, competent, and ethical counselors for the 21st century. In D. M. Perera-Dilitz & K. M. MacCluskie (Eds.), *The counselor educator's survival guide: Designing and teaching outstanding courses in community mental health counseling and school counseling* (pp. 93–114). New York, NY: Taylor & Francis.

Parham, W. D., & Clauss-Ehlers, C. S. (2016). Celebrating our elders led us across the bridge: A call to action for the academy. *Journal of Multicultural Counseling and Development, 44*(1), 4–27. doi:10.1002/jmcd.12034

Ratts, M., D'Andrea, M., & Arredondo, P. (2004). Social justice counseling: 'Fifth force' in the field. *Counseling Today, 47*, 28–30.

Ratts, M., Singh, A. A., McMillan-Nasser, S., Butler, S. K., & McCullough, R. (2016). Multicultural and social justice competencies: Guidelines for the counseling profession. *Journal of Multicultural Counseling and Development, 44*(1), 28–48.

Roysircar, G. (2010). Introduction to a special issue on the association for multicultural counseling and development leadership history. *Journal of Multicultural Counseling and Development, 38*(4), 194–1995. doi:10.1002/j.2161-1912.2010.tb00128.x

Singh, A. & Salazar, C. (2010). The roots of social justice in group work. *The Journal for Specialists in Group Work, 35*(2): 97–104. doi 10.1080/01933921003706048

Singh, A. & Salazar, C. (2014). Using groups to facilitate social justice change: Addressing issues of privilege and oppression. In DeLucia-Waak, Gerrity, Kalodner, & Riva (Eds). *Handbook of Group Counseling and Psychotherapy*. Thousand Oaks, CA: Sage.

Singh, A. A., Merchant, N., Skuryzk, B., & Ingene, D. (2012). Group worker principles for seeking multicultural and social justice competence. *Journal of Specialists in Group Work, 37*(4), 312–325.

Smith, L. C., & Shin, R. Q. (2008). Social privilege, social justice, and group counseling: An inquiry. *Journal for Specialists in Group Work, 33*(4), 351–366. doi:10.1080/01933920802424415

Sue, D. W. (2010). *Microaggressions in everyday life: Race, gender, and sexual orientation*. New York, NY: Wiley.

Sue, D. W., Arredondo, P., & McDavis, R. (1992). Multicultural counseling competencies and standards: A call to the profession. *Journal of Counseling and Development, 70*(4), 477–486. doi:10.1002/j.1556-6676.1992.tb01642.x

Xie, D. (2014). Multicultural considerations: Within and byond traditional counseling theories. In R. D. Parsons & N. Zhang (Eds.), *Counseling theory: Guiding reflective practice*. Thousand Oaks, CA: Sage.

5 Classroom Engagement and Evidence-Based Teaching Strategies With Adult Learners

Melissa Ockerman and Breanna Adams

> Education is the kindling of a flame, not the filling of a vessel.
> —Socrates

Often *counselor education* programs spend ample amounts of time developing the *counselor* with little, if any, directed instruction aimed towards increasing competence in *education* (Watcher Morris, Barrio Minton, & Gibson, 2016). Thus, unlike graduates from teacher education programs, many advanced degree counselor education students exit programs with only a cursory understanding of both the art and science of teaching, largely predicated upon their own experiences as a student. Yet, all students have experienced the magic of a gifted teacher; one who understands their students and inspires them to not just achieve academically, but to also become better human beings. Conversely, most students at some point in their educational careers have endured classes with poor instruction and lackluster teaching. This chapter is designed to prepare counselor educators to teach adult learners in engaging and efficacious ways. We begin by reviewing learning styles and multiple intelligences. Next, we explore the unique needs of adult learners and the increasing use of online learning. Prevalent issues common in counselor identity and skill development, including the imposter syndrome, critical reflection, and group dynamics, are also discussed with corresponding evidence-based teaching strategies. Finally, case studies and guided practices are included to help burgeoning counselor educators begin to tackle the complex challenge of meeting students where they are while guiding them towards becoming competent professionals who possess a sounder knowledge of themselves and the world around them.

Learning Objectives

After reading this chapter, you will be able to:

1. Demonstrate an understanding of knowledge acquisition basics.
2. Differentiate learning styles from multiple intelligences.
3. Apply online instruction strategies for adult learners.
4. Describe imposter syndrome as it relates to counselor education students and its implications for learning.
5. Apply evidence-based and engaging teaching strategies to adult learners.

CACREP Standards

The following CACREP Standards regarding professional identity and teaching for counselor education doctoral students align with this chapter:

B. Doctoral Professional Identity

    3. Teaching

        a. roles and responsibilities related to educating counselors
        b. pedagogy and teaching methods relevant to counselor education
        c. models of adult development and learning
        d. instructional and curriculum design, delivery, and evaluation methods relevant to counselor education
        e. effective approaches for online instruction

Learning Basics

There is a rich, complex history of attempting to identify optimal conditions for development, teaching, and learning (Tokuhama-Espinosa, 2011). From early philosophers to prominent theorists in developmental psychology, researchers have made strides in seeking to understand relationships between emotion and psychology, between the environment and brain development, and between psychology and neuroscience (Olson & Hergenhahn, 2016). We now know how and where specific learning occurs in the brain and better understand best practices for this learning to occur. This chapter will discuss these concepts in detail with a focus on adult learners and the cognitive and affective conditions needed for learning to flourish. Later, we discuss effective teaching strategies to enhance these conditions for graduate students in counselor education.

Learning Styles and Intelligence

Experiential Learning

David Kolb was the first to develop specific learning styles based on his ideas of experiential learning in the 1970s. In his model, he described four stages of the learning cycle: concrete experience (feeling), reflective observation (watching), abstract conceptualization (thinking) and active experimentation (doing) (Kolb, 1976). This cycle of learning can start at any of these points of entry and functions as a continuous process. On this spectrum, Kolb posited four learning styles, each a blend of two stages (see Table 5.1).

Honey and Mumford

Kolb's model influenced many others in the field, including Honey and Mumford, who described four different learning styles or preferences (Table 5.2). Based on one's preference, Honey and Mumford (1986) believed that individuals should be aware of their own style and seek out learning activities that match. Further,

Table 5.1 Kolb's Learning Styles

Learning Style	Description	Activities/Preferences
Diverging (feeling + watching)	Prefer watching over doing; gather information from different perspectives; sensitive and emotional	Brainstorming Receiving feedback Group work
Assimilating (thinking + watching)	Concise and logical; prefer ideas and abstract concepts to people	Use of data or models Reading and lecture Time to process
Converging (thinking + doing)	Problem-solver; prefer technical tasks or problems over social issues; often unemotional; more specific interests	Experimentation Simulation (skits or role-play)
Accommodating (feeling + doing)	Follow intuition over logic; quick-thinking; tends to take risks	Group work Goal-setting Analysis of material

Table 5.2 Honey and Mumford Learning Preferences

Learning Style	Description	Activities/Preferences
Activist	Approaches learning with an open mind; learns by doing	Brainstorming Problem-solving
Theorist	Prefers analyzing and understanding theory behind the action	Data/research Models/examples
Pragmatist	Wants theory put into action	Case studies Problem-solving
Reflector	Learns by thinking and watching	Observations/interviews Group discussion

people should seek to build capacity in all areas in order to broaden their skills sets and increase their comfort level with different types of learning activities.

Multiple Intelligences

In light of the new attention to how individuals approach learning, Howard Gardner proposed his theory of multiple intelligences in the early 1980s. Easily confused with learning styles, Gardner stated that while learning styles describe how individuals approach the task of receiving information, his theory of multiple intelligences relies on individual differences in learning (Gardner, 1983). He proposed eight types of intelligences that all individuals possess and argued that people vary in their aptitudes, typically exhibiting strengths and weaknesses across the eight intelligences. Table 5.3 includes brief descriptions of these multiple intelligences and examples of learning activities best suited for someone with high

Table 5.3 Gardner's Multiple Intelligences

Type of Intelligence	Description	Activities/Preferences
Verbal/linguistic	Expresses oneself and solves problems best using words	Written responses Storytelling Debate
Logical/mathematical	Excels with patterns, relationships and numbers	Use of data Classifying/categorizing Problem-solving (logic)
Visual/spatial	Best at design and visualizing, respond well to visual stimuli	Use of charts, diagrams and timelines Concept mapping
Musical	Processes information best with sound, rhythmically talented	Play relaxing music during down time Find songs with thematic similarities to content
Naturalistic	Learns via connection with environmental interest and impact	Tie in biology (metacognition) Highlight relationships with science/nature
Bodily/kinesthetic	Benefits from learning through movement and touch	Role-play/skits Movement breaks
Interpersonal	Interacts and works exceptionally well with others	Group work Opportunities for leadership Interviewing
Intrapersonal	Extreme self-awareness and inward focus	Reflection Journals/logs

intelligence in each area. Placing multiple intelligences in the context of learning style research helps illuminate the intricacies in individual differences, not only in style and preference, but in aptitude as well. Gardner was among the first to argue against a singular measure for intelligence, and his writings highlight the diversity of strengths and predilections among learners.

Mind Styles

Around the same time Howard Gardner was studying multiple intelligences, Gregorc (1984) combined learning from decades of research into the *Mind Styles Model*. This model presents a quadrant-style theory: concrete vs. abstract, and sequential vs. random. Thus, individuals fall into one of four categories, as depicted in Table 5.4. The concrete and abstract components of this theory describe how we perceive information—either through the senses (concrete) or through intuition and reasoning (abstract). Once the information is taken in, Gregorc (1984) posited that individuals process this information in one of two ways: linear and logical (sequential) or impulsively, in chunks (random).

Table 5.4 Gregorc's Mind Styles

Mind Style	Description	Activities/Preferences
Concrete sequential	Prefers order, logic and data; methodical, structured learning	Charts/data Hands-on
Concrete random	Likes to find answers; practical and inquisitive, prefers independent learning	Experiments Trial and error
Abstract sequential	Analyzes and applies logic to find solutions	Theory and analysis Research projects
Abstract random	Focuses on building relationships with others; perceptive	Unstructured learning Discussions/group work

Table 5.5 VARK Learning Modes

Learning Mode	Description	Strategies/Preferences
Visual	Learns best by seeing information and relationships depicted in a variety of ways (not words)	Graphs and charts Making plans Video clips
Aural	Prefers hearing or speaking to learn information; likes to verbalize options	Group discussions Lectures/stories Guest speakers
Read/write	Opts for reading and writing information in all forms (articles, reports, essays, PowerPoints)	Reading a variety of texts/articles Note-taking Lists
Kinesthetic	Likes to use reality and practical experience to learn; prefers experiencing through all senses	Examples and case studies Role-play Practical examples

VAK/VARK

In the 1920s, psychologists and teachers developed the acronym VAK: Visual, Auditory, and Kinesthetic learning (Romanelli, Bird, & Ryan, 2009). Fleming (2006) split the V into Visual and Read/Write to develop the more popular VARK, displayed in Table 5.5. Fleming titled these *learning modes* and astutely noted, "We often have quite strong preferences for such things as cars, colours [sic], food and partners. So why not look into our preferences for the ways in which we learn?" (Fleming, 2006, p. 2). Comments one may hear in a classroom related to this theory include, "I'm a visual learner" or "I just can't sit still during a lecture!" VARK is one of the more common theories of learning preference and a helpful guide for educators when planning a lesson or course.

Limitations

Despite, or perhaps because of, the many different ways to measure and conceptualize learning strategies and styles, recent research suggests learning styles are over-emphasized. Pasher, McDaniel, Rohrer, and Bjork (2008) found that over the past 30 years, studies of various learning style models failed to validate any of the over 70 proposed theories. They argued that until we have scientific evidence supporting one of these theories, educators should not spend considerable time or resources with learning style tests or teaching tools. Willingham, Hughes, and Dobolyi (2015) added that perhaps true scientific support for learning styles is unavailable due to the difficulty of measuring these models and the lack of one cohesive theory around learning styles. While instructors need not barrage students with learning style inventories, the insights gained from meta-cognition and a better understanding of one's own styles or preferences can help inform future practice (Griffith & Frieden, 2000).

Adult Learners

As noted in the aforementioned section, societal definitions of not only *what* it means to learn but *how* one learns continue to evolve. Traditionally thought of as individual and cognitive-based phenomena, learning is now seen as multidimensional—encompassing brain, body, emotional well-being, and spirituality (Hill, 2014). For many years, scientists thought of the adult brain as fairly inelastic, similar to a computer with circuits. We know now the brain is capable of adjusting and retains much more flexibility than previously believed (Killen, 2007). As such, there has been a significant shift away from solely viewing learning as what happens in the brain, towards a focus on the conditions in which one learns. Specifically, contemporary theorists purport that learning happens in multiple contexts including culture, relationships, values, knowledge and skills—and through these constructs students create meaning (Olusegun, 2015). Researchers and practitioners alike are recognizing that this constructivist and holistic view is of particular importance to adult learners and therefore influences the way in which instructors can best teach them.

Constructivism

While different perspectives on constructivism exist, some common themes emerge that help educators create a framework for the *how* behind teaching. When operating from a constructivist perspective, "it is essential to place the learner at the centre [sic] of your teaching endeavours [sic], and structure learning environments and activities to help learners construct knowledge rather than just absorb it" (Killen, 2007, p. 8). Adult learners bring to the classroom a plethora of life experiences from which to draw, matching new information with existing knowledge and making connections. Students engage in a narrative process (that is, allowing one's story to educate and inform), by trying to make meaning from new experiences based on how they relate to what they already know (Olusegun, 2015). Adult students learn best when the instructor views them as self-directed, "shift[ing] the focus away from the teacher as the gatekeeper to knowledge" and instead "view[ing] the teacher as a facilitator and collaborator of knowledge" (Chen, 2014, p. 407). Indeed, instructors are wise to tap into adult students' previous experiences as a resource for their learning (Brady, 2014) and to share those experiences as an integral part of the teaching process. While providing both challenge and support through a constructivist lens is important (Larkin &

Richardson, 2012), we know "support is valuable to students only when it leads to development, and ultimately, to student autonomy" (Devereux & Wilson, 2014, p. 92).

For a concrete depiction of utilizing a constructivist framework with future counselor educators, consider the following example. Rather than creating a lecture on different stages of career development, a professor could ask students to reflect and document some developmental milestones throughout their own lives. After this reflection, students could work in pairs or groups (more on this below) to compare and contrast their experiences, each adding their own perspective and background knowledge to the conversation. Bringing the discussion back to the large group, the professor could facilitate a discussion helping the class make connections from their peers' career choices to the developmental process. Doing so not only increases student engagement but also successfully allows for the integration of students' past knowledge to serve as a basis for new and meaningful understanding. In the example provided, students had a chance to reflect individually and make connections within their existing knowledge base, construct their own meaning, and later share that meaning with classmates, comparing and contrasting their unique experiences. Students were situated at the center of this activity, and the primary role of the instructor was to facilitate discussion based on where students were, helping them to make connections between student experience and course content.

Perry's Stages

Constructivism can be enhanced by connecting student developmental models to students' learning overtly. Specifically, instructors can assist students in noticing patterns among their own developmental experiences and then applying that understanding to their future clients and students. Perhaps the most seminal student development model to the counseling field is *William Perry's Theory of Intellectual and Ethical Development* (1970). Perry, a counselor and educator at Harvard, recognized the need for a new cognitive development theory with adults given the changing demographics of the student populations in the late 1960s. Interviewing his students, Perry and his colleagues saw distinct stages of cognition through which the students journeyed (Hall, 2013). Briefly, the first stage, *dualistic thinking*, is characterized by absolutes (e.g., "There is a right way to respond to this client or a wrong way"). Students thus believe there is an authority (i.e., the professor), who holds the only correct answers and to whom they should be obedient. As students learn more, they move into *multiplistic thinking* (e.g., "There are many ways to respond to this client"); a period often marked by stress and fear. At this stage, students may express sadness that there is no absolute universal truth and therefore still rely on the professor to help them decipher which option is right, believing that uncertainty is only temporary. The stage ends when students demonstrate *relativistic thinking*, a phase marked by viewing answers as dependent on analysis, comparison, and evidence (Granello, 2011; Hall, 2013). Thus students' learning becomes more self-directed with the realization that *what* they think is less important than the *way* they think. Through critical reflection and self-examination, students come to realize that some responses are more legitimate than others. Often this line of thinking is applied not only to their studies, but to other spheres in their lives (i.e., a changed reliance on authority, a commitment to viewing issues relativistically) (Gibson, Dooley, Kelchner, Moss, & Vacchio, 2012). As students progress through a dualistic or simplistic way of thinking to a meaningful construction of knowledge, they experience incongruence between firmly held beliefs and new information. As discussed below, when this contradiction is processed in meaningful ways, it can become the catalyst for personal transformation.

Application to Counselor Education Students

The process of self-discovery noted above can be facilitated through analytical cogitation and introspection, a common phenomenon in counseling (Coll, Doumas, Trotter, & Freeman, 2013). While enrolled in introduction and basic skills courses, students may rely heavily on their professors for knowledge. Common questions include "What should I say if a client says this . . .?" or "How am I supposed to respond in this scenario?" Anxiety about what to say, when to say it, fears about "getting it wrong" and self-questioning (e.g., "Maybe I'm not cut out for this profession") may be prevalent within reflection assignments and class discussions (Chapman, 2015). This type of cognitive dissonance, often referred to as the *imposter syndrome*, occurs when individuals begin to experience "intense feelings that their achievements are undeserved and worry that they are likely to be exposed as a fraud" (Sakulku & Alexander, 2011, p. 72). Unchecked, imposter syndrome can lead to feelings of insecurity and the inability and/or the unwillingness to take credit for one's work. In extreme situations, individuals with impostor syndrome experience intense feelings of worry that cause severe stress, low self-esteem, and dysfunctional or impaired behavior (Gibson-Beverly & Schwartz, 2008; Sakulku & Alexander, 2011).

As students progress into more advanced coursework, students may signify a transition into multiplistic thinking, acknowledging the varied responses given by their peers, but still believing the instructor has the ultimate answer. Additionally, expressions of relativism may begin to occur with more frequency (Granello, 2011). During this phase, questions tend to be more grounded in context and in critical and reflective reasoning. Interestingly, it has been our experience that some cognitive regression takes place when students enter into their final year of practicum and internship. These new experientially based courses push students towards putting into practice their learning in new, unpredictable environments. Thus, a rigidity in thinking returns as do questions about what constitutes a right versus wrong way to respond to their clients. Self-doubt and criticism surface and the imposter syndrome seems particularly prevalent (e.g., "What if my client or supervisor finds out I have no idea what I am doing?"). As students experience more success with their clients, become more acclimated to their new surroundings, and spend time reflecting through on-site and in-class supervision, this type of dualistic thinking gives way towards multiplistic and relativistic reasoning (Granello, 2011). By the end of the program, an integration of past knowledge, practical experience and self-reflection are marked by confidence in voice, autonomy of decisions, and a commitment to continued learning (Mullen, Uwamahoro, Blout, & Lambie, 2015; Patterson & Levitt, 2012).

Interestingly, professors are not immune to imposter syndrome either, a phenomenon often prevalent in intelligent and high-achieving individuals (Chapman, 2015; Hutchins, 2015; Parkman & Beard, 2008). This feeling seems to be exacerbated by the 'publish or perish' academic culture (Hutchins, 2015) and especially when newly minted assistant professors are close in age to their graduate students (Kreuter, 2012). Imposter syndrome impacts the way in which faculty interact with students, how available they make themselves to students outside of class, and thus how students evaluate their effectiveness (Parkman, 2016). As observed by Bixby (2011), the cornerstone of teaching is to model vulnerability, because "whether you like it or not, some students will make it their aspiration to find out where [your] limits lie" (p. 33). Therefore, just as counseling students struggle to find self-efficacy in the beginning of their counselor education preparation programs (Mullen et al., 2015), new counselor educators teaching these courses may face fear of inadequacy as well. The key for an instructor then is to help students go beyond their own knowledge, while simultaneously challenging themselves to do the same.

Efficacious Teaching

While graduate students believe an instructor's ability to teach content is vital, they also report that an instructor's ability to connect with them emotionally and to form a relationship with them is equally as important (Hill, 2014). As reported by Hill (2014) in his study of 107 adult learners, students looked to instructors to stimulate discussion and employ various teaching techniques as a means to facilitate their learning. Graduate students tended to favor practical, relevant knowledge slightly over content and theory-based subject matter. Moreover, they emphasized their relationship with instructors, highlighting approachability and availability in both electronic and face-to-face formats. These needs dovetail adult learners' desire for instructors to demonstrate fairness, show flexibility, and give timely feedback via email and phone because of the multiple demands on their lives (Hill, 2014). As such, adult learners prefer instructors who are accommodating, passionate, warm, enthusiastic, and engaging, given their long work days and frequent evening classes (Pietrzak, Duncan, & Korcuska, 2008). Lastly and importantly, as noted by Hill (2014), trust and safety are key to students' perceptions of effective teaching (i.e., students' ability to trust in the design and implementation of the course and in creating a non-judgmental classroom environment). Furthermore, graduate students value instructors who are culturally competent and provide a safe place for risky yet important discussions about our increasingly global society (Hill, 2014). As our educational systems continue to evolve and include more advanced technology, it is critical that these skill sets can be transferred to online classroom learning communities as well.

Online Learning

Given that most adult learners are juggling multiple responsibilities (work, family demands, and school), online learning is an opportunity to advance their education while balancing multiple roles (Park & Choi, 2009). However, while online education may open up opportunities for prospective students to further their education, some adult students taking online courses may struggle with time management or motivation and may experience feelings of isolation or lack of support. In the following section we offer strategies to mitigate some of these struggles and suggestions for increasing student engagement online.

Autonomy

Adult students tend to be more autonomous and self-sufficient, and because of this, need both freedom to direct themselves and a framework in which they can learn and grow (Cercone, 2008). Conaway and Zorn-Arnold (2015) also discussed the importance of fostering a sense of autonomy and self-directedness in online environments. They asserted, "Taking every opportunity to relate learning material to past experience they [students] have disclosed or to future career aspirations will help students narrow the gap between what they already know and need to learn by helping them identify what is relevant" (p. 5). Instructors can help foster this process by getting to know students. In this vein, instructors should consider a brief introductory message and create a forum for students to do the same. One example for an online course could be a video introduction from the professor, including course expectations, instructions for the online platform, and current research or interests. Students can then make a video introduction or use the discussion boards to answer some basic questions about previous experiences and related career interests.

This personalization may prove especially important when instructors are unable to create their own content and must use pre-developed course material. Examples like the video introduction above could supplement other requisite course work and offer ways to form connections with and among students. Another way to enhance this connection is by creating context around course material. For example, posting current articles, video clips, or engaging and relevant resources with a brief explanation about why and how the material relates can also help with personalizing required content. You could also ask students to evaluate particular concepts or lessons by connecting the ideas to their own experiences, and to share this via a discussion board or similar tool. Although it may seem challenging to find ways to personalize something you yourself did not develop, attempts to do so will help engage and motivate students, as we discuss in more detail below.

Motivation

Yoo and Huang (2013) specifically studied adult learners' motivational needs, finding that online degree programs need to include ongoing opportunities for career development and material relevant to the workplace. By getting to know the career aspirations and background of students, instructors can find ways to increase connection with the new material and in doing so, increase engagement that fosters autonomy. Moreover, by having an understanding of students' background and interests, instructors can implement relevant online automatic polls to solicit real-time responses from students. These feedback loops allow instructors to know how students are feeling about course specifics (assignments, readings, discussion, etc.) and help clarify potential difficulties or misunderstandings more quickly and adeptly, thereby improving students' motivation to learn (Moran & Milsom, 2015).

Isolation

Sher (2009) discussed the isolation many online learners feel, and highlighted the importance of the instructor's role in not only positively interacting with students but in facilitating student-student interaction as well. Thus, we encourage you to diversify methods of communicating with your students (beyond email) and foster multimodal communication among students. Revere and Kovach (2011) highlighted this need and offered, "the capabilities of existing online course management systems can be supplemented by incorporating additional communication technologies, webbased [sic] applications and handheld/mobile devices within online courses" (p. 123). We recommend exploring some third-party collaborative spaces and instructor resources such as Google Docs, Group.me, YouCanBook.me, Doodle, and Padlet.

Finally, employing strategies we discuss throughout this chapter to predominately online courses will help increase engagement and combat resistance. For example, online instructors, just as brick and mortar instructors, should pay attention to students' self-awareness in terms of their learning styles and preferences and ensure they remain flexible, available, and responsive to students' needs. Chapter 10 provides a more in-depth discussion of different learning environments, including online formats.

Developing and Sustaining a Positive Learning Environment

Regardless of the class setting (face-to-face, online, or hybrid), instructors must help students process their own learning through making connections, thereby narrowing the gap between theory and practice. Below we highlight several teaching strategies designed to support a variety of types of learning and cultivate self-knowledge.

Group Work

Counseling is a multi-layered subject matter that can often lead to emotionally laden conversations, revealing deeply rooted beliefs. Honoring these differences while exposing students to divergent points of view can be facilitated by executing small group teaching strategies. Killen (2007) posited the most productive small groups are comprised of four or five students with clear goals and ongoing prompts and feedback from the instructor. He suggested posing the question, "What would happen if . . . ?" (p. 172) at multiple times throughout the group process to assist students in opening up new lines of thinking and encouraging varied perspectives to solve the issue at hand. Similarly, Moran and Milsom (2015) in their study of flipped classrooms techniques, found that counselor education students rated group work very favorably, noting students' comments such as, "Grouping up allows us to learn from one another and feed off each other's ideas . . . Hearing the questions my classmates had caused me to think differently and appreciate their ideas" (p. 39). Below are common strategies employed in counseling courses that highlight how small group work can be incorporated into teaching practices with fidelity.

Case Studies and Problem-Based Learning (PBL)

Case studies are often used to demonstrate the intersection of social, cultural, political, familial and educational backgrounds of future clients. They help bring to bear the multifaceted influences clients confront, pushing them to think beyond the client's initial presenting problem (Killen, 2007). Case studies can be open (i.e., there are many possible solutions) or closed (there is a specific response or diagnosis). Closed case studies are typically used to ascertain students' knowledge and application of specific data or theories while open case studies are employed to help students weigh various options, determining the merits of their recommended actions (Killen, 2007). Open cases encourage constructivist thinking, prompting students to "see they can develop their understanding of theory and their problem-solving skills simultaneously while struggling with realistic problems" (Killen, 2007, p. 277).

Tackling real-life issues prepares students for the often complicated realities they will confront in their professional practice. In fact, the American Counseling Association (ACA) specifically lists the use of case studies in its Ethical Codes (ACA, 2014) during supervision and field work as well as recommends infusing the application of ethical responsibilities throughout counseling curriculum. Thus, case studies delineating common ethical concerns counselors may face (e.g., negotiating boundaries between the client and counselor, distance counseling, or the use of social media) could easily be incorporated into ethics courses. Additionally, case studies can be effectively employed in psychopathology courses to introduce complex cases that prompt students to determine diagnostic features, associated risks and prognoses, and culturally related diagnostic issues. Similarly, students may be given case studies in a couples and family course to assess family dynamics and systems, addressing a wide range of presenting issues, including parenting, mental and behavioral issues, violence and substance abuse patterns, impact on career and finances, and support systems (See the American Counseling Association's *International Counseling Case Studies Handbook* (2015) and *Case Studies in School Counseling* (2007) for further discussion and examples.).

In a small group format, you can provide either the same case study or vary cases based on specialty area with attention to a particular skill (e.g., assessing for safety or identifying areas of support). Depending on time constraints and the objective of the case, instructors may then guide a whole class discussion, linking common themes and recognizing divergent ones. Killen (2007) recommended classroom discussion conclude with consolidation of learning by students, facilitated either through a follow-up assignment that builds upon the case or assigning personal reflection activities aimed at helping students summarize key learning outcomes they gained.

Similarly, problem-based learning (PBL) asks students to solve challenging real world problems and to work collectively to solve them (Karge, Phillips, Jessee, & McCabe, 2011). As such, you would encourage students to apply their own experiences, find supporting evidence, and to collaborate with their peers to create solutions. The objective is to help students acquire new knowledge through the problem-solving process itself. When utilizing this strategy, you should be careful to select problems that cannot be solved with prior knowledge alone and are relevant, comprehensive, and complex (Killen, 2007). Doing so motivates students to identify what they need to learn thus honing their research skills while simultaneously seeing the relevance to their own life experiences and those of their peers (Karge et al., 2011; Killen, 2007). PBL can be employed in a variety of counseling courses to address multidimensional systemic problems, such as violence in schools or managed health care reform. Problems should be linked to course objectives provided in the syllabus, and address both deep conceptual issues and the development of a particular skill set (Karge et al., 2011; Killen, 2007).

Chalk or Gallery Walk

Exposing students to multiple facts and/or statistics followed by time for personal reflection and then large group processing can also be an effective teaching tool (Killen, 2007). The chalk or gallery walk technique is one way to engender this experience. Students first move out of their chairs, circle the room, and quietly assess a gallery of information (e.g., a collection of quotes, pictures, statistics, etc.) about a specific topic, typically on big a sheet of paper or poster board taped or pinned to a wall. Students then offer written individual comments, feedback and/or questions on the paper, remaining silent. Once the allowed time is up for individual contributions, students again circulate the room to read the comments of their classmates prior to returning silently to their seats. Thereafter, the instructor facilitates large group processing, delving deeper into the topic, encouraging students to share their comments, questions, and observations with each other. This method is especially helpful for students who are less verbal or are visual/spatial or bodily/kinesthetic learners. See Sidebar 5.1 for an example of how a gallery walk can be put into action.

Guided Practice Example 5.1

Chalk Talk Using Root Cause Analysis

In order to help students understand the complex nature of the achievement and opportunity gap among White students and students of color in a large, urban city, Brea employs a Chalk Talk/Gallery Walk strategy. She uses a few pieces of chart paper with a blank tree drawn in the middle (see Figure 5.1). In the trunk, she writes a statistic that highlights this gap; for example, "In 2013, 52% of White males obtained a four-year agree, compared to 30% of Latino males and 34% of African American males" and "In 2013, 67% of Asian females, 59% of White females, 44% of African American females and 37% of Latino female CPS (Chicago Public Schools) graduates received a four-year college degree within six years" (University of Chicago College & Career Readiness Research Brief, 2014). When students arrive, this poster paper is already on the wall. Brea describes the idea of a root cause analysis, inviting students to brainstorm outcomes and reasons why this statistic exists. The outcomes become the branches;

these are the *effects* of the issue. The "why," or the *root causes*, become the roots—the potential reasons for the statistic in the first place. Students are asked to spend 10–15 minutes walking around the room silently, with their only method of communication a writing utensil, post-it notes and the chart paper. They should think about and try to fill in roots and branches for each tree (statistic). When their time is up, Brea gives them three questions to answer, in writing, at their seats. These questions may ask students to make connections between the issues, or to notice similarities and differences between the causes and effects (sometimes, an outcome can be a cause and an effect; for example, a potential cause of obesity could be depression, and a possible effect of obesity could be depression.) Once students have responded to the questions, Brea asks them to turn to a partner and discuss their answers. Each pair will then share with the class (think-pair-share strategy). The combination of these two strategies helps students to think critically on their own, making as many connections as possible. Students who may not feel comfortable sharing with the class may appreciate the chance to first bounce their ideas off a partner, and these strategies together should elicit a variety of responses in the group discussion to ensue thereafter.

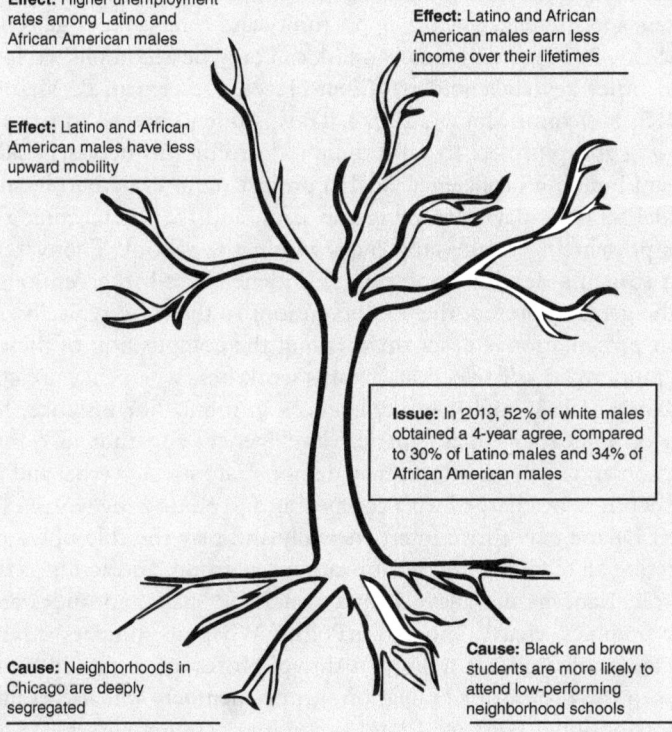

Figure 5.1 Root Cause Tree

Think-Pair-Share

As not all students have the need for high affiliation and small group work, instructors should vary class interaction to include one-on-one peer dialogue. One such strategy, first established by Lyman (1981, 1987), *think-pair-share* allows students time to first think about their responses to a learning prompt, write it down, and then pair up with someone sitting close by to share their responses with each other, discussing both common and divergent themes. During the "pair-share," students discuss not only their viewpoints but their reasoning behind them. According to Karge et al. (2011), this strategy encourages more introverted students to share their opinions and engage in dialogue during class. Once ample time is allowed for this process, you can ask for examples from groups, linking responses and noting differences. Hearing from multiple groups helps to gauge student learning and engage the entire class. You may also collect students' written responses for added assessment of understanding.

Group Assignments

As noted above, adult learners expect clear criteria and evaluation methods to guide their work (Hill, 2014; Yorks & Kasl, 2002). Creating a team-based assignment therefore necessitates clearly defined roles, grading expectations, and rubrics. For example, in the school counseling specialty area, students must learn how to assess and use data to close opportunity and achievement gaps present in schools (ASCA, 2012). This herculean task can only be accomplished in collaboration with other key stakeholders (Chen-Hayes, Ockerman, & Mason, 2014; Hatch, 2015; Holcomb-McCoy, 2007). Thus, students are asked to complete a *closing the gap* group project to assist them in learning this necessary skill and to develop team building proficiency. Such a project requires gathering and assessing an actual school's data, analyzing this data, and then determining achievement gaps present in certain subgroups within the school. Thereafter, school counseling students develop appropriate, evidence-based interventions to help eradicate the gap and present these interventions to the class, typically through a PowerPoint presentation. Rather than leaving the composition of these student groups to random or self-selection, groups work best when they are comprised with Gardner's (1983) multiple intelligences in mind. For instance, Sally may score high on logical and mathematical intelligences and thus take the lead in data collection and analysis. Yilmaz may demonstrate strong verbal and linguistic traits and therefore be charged with composing and editing the written section of the project. Duane may thrive interpersonally and play the role of team facilitator, connecting all team members, motivating the group, and acting as the group spokesperson. Kanesha may have strong visual and spatial aptitudes and therefore create graphics, charts, and PowerPoints. When all students' strengths are optimized and evaluated, team projects thrive. Moreover, it should be clear that in addition to the professor's evaluation, group members will also evaluate each other's contributions. We have found this joint accountability increases group participation and helps to distribute tasks more equally. Box 5.1 is an example of language from a syllabi indicative of this expectation.

> **Box 5.1 Syllabi Excerpt**
>
> *Each member of the team should contribute equally to this project.* Group presentations will be given during the weeks before the final class. *Students and school teams will assess themselves on this assignment at the end of the presentation, as will the instructor.* See the attached rubric for grading expectations. **On the date of the presentation**, you will also hand in an evaluation of both your own and your peers' contributions. TYPE responses to the following prompts:
>
> - Indicate percentage of work each member (including yourself) has completed as well as a list of tasks each member was responsible for/completed for needs assessment & community mapping
> - Indicate how well you believe you worked as a group member
> - List any additional information you believe is important in evaluation
> - **Please note, your individual score will be deducted should your teammates denote inadequate contribution on your part. Equal contribution is mandatory.**

Ongoing Evaluation and Feedback

As elucidated earlier, adult learners care about both the preparedness of instructors and their flexibility (Hill, 2014; Pietrzak, Duncan, & Korcuska, 2008). While end-of-the-quarter teaching evaluations are helpful, they do nothing to assist with teaching in real time. As such, we encourage you to take time to administer mid-quarter evaluations. Similar to Just-in-Time Teaching (JITT), which allows "instructors to provide minilectures, [sic] discussions, and activities to address questions that still exist and concepts that may be misunderstood" (Moran & Milsom, 2015, p. 33), mid-quarter evaluations can assist you in immediate feedback that helps you modify your teaching to specific student needs. Mid-quarter evaluations are administered through an anonymous survey. Students are prompted to assess specific teaching strategies employed in the first half of the course and how they have been helpful (or not) to their learning. Additionally, students are asked to reflect upon their own participation in the course to encourage them to think about how they may alter their behavior and/or participation in order to maximize their knowledge acquisition. Box 5.2 provides an example of an open-ended question mid-term evaluation. The week following the mid-term evaluation, you present common themes expressed by students, facilitate discussion around differing ideas and how to manage them, and clarify any questions or concerns. This helps to address any misunderstandings about course expectations before they escalate, encourages students to engage more fully in class and with the course material, and gives ample time for you to improve upon or modify your teaching methods and instruction. Discussions often lead to the parallel process of trying to accommodate multiple learning styles in one classroom, cultivating an appreciation for differences in their peers' learning, and recognizing the need to do so themselves as future counselors and collaborators. This shared process is beneficial for not only this particular class but also helps instructors, both new and experienced, hone their skills related to the course. As aptly noted by Brady (2014, p. 26), "When all of the students are engaged, not only do the students learn, but also the teacher," thus creating a recursive and generative relationship.

Box 5.2 Mid-Quarter Course Evaluation

Please do not write your name on this form. Use the back of the form if you need more space. As school counseling professionals, we must consistently strive to obtain evaluative DATA! DATA! DATA! in order to become better and more competent at our chosen occupations. The following questions were designed to gain valuable information from you, so that I can keep improving this course and my teaching practices. Please answer the questions thoughtfully and truthfully.

1) Generally, how is this course working for you?
2) Are you satisfied with your participation? Please explain your answer.
3) Of all the activities/readings (small group activities, video, group ice breakers, practice SFBC, reviewing report cards/data, guest speakers, Education Forum on Latino Issues, etc.) which ones have been most helpful in your development and understanding of this course? Please explain your answer.
4) Of all the activities/readings (see above), which have been the least helpful? Please explain your answer.
5) Suggestions for improvement:

Considerations for Resistant Students

Instructors at all levels will inevitably come across some measure of resistance from their students. We have discussed at length the importance of engagement and connection, particularly with adult learners. Despite our best intentions, students may not feel certain material is personally relevant to them, and as instructors we need to find ways to show students how particular topics will help them in their future endeavors. For example, we have both encountered students with an aversion to data and a misconception about about how they will use data in future practice. While students may not be running t-tests, they must still understand basic research concepts in order to assess needs and create interventions for their future clients. Discussing the need to be familiar with evidence-based techniques for efficacious treatment and developing their ability to collect and analyze future client/student evaluations can assist counselor education students in understanding how data is relevant to best practice and necessary for the success of their clinical clients or school-based programs.

In addition to helping students make personally relevant connections with course material, Dirkx (2006, 2008) discussed the idea of giving adults the opportunity to grow on the unconscious level by examining their own emotions and resistance more deeply. Once seen as an impediment to reason and learning, many researchers now see emotions as intrinsic and essential for knowledge acquisition (Dirkx, 2008). For example, a student in class may show consistent resistance to group work and express anger after another group task is assigned. Dirkx (2006) encouraged instructors to

> think of a learner's emotions in a transparent or literal manner, as windows that reveal experiences realities. For example, a student's anger at the instructor might be interpreted literally as being unhappy and dissatisfied with the instructional methods being used.
>
> (p. 2)

However, this anger may also reveal some unconscious issues, such as a history of being left out, feeling overwhelmed by a group, or having past experiences where the student felt out of control. Thus, issues around control are bound to evoke anger, not necessarily at group work per se, but rather triggered from past experiences. This aligns with what we have already learned about adult learners—a cache of experiences with attached emotions—and corresponds with the work of a counselor. As an instructor, you can help students process their feelings of resistance and help them explore unresolved conflicts that still cause difficulty. This Jungian perspective on transformative learning creates self-awareness and insight, as the learning environment itself is laden with emotion (Dirkx, 2008). Helping students shed light on the "why" behind their emotions will help instructors minimize resistance, assist students build self-awareness and break through unconscious barriers in order to fully engage with the material and their future clients.

Summary

The metamorphosis from a counselor to a counselor educator is achieved through understanding the building blocks of becoming an effective counselor and learning how to transmit this knowledge in engaging and meaningful ways. In order to accomplish this feat, you must have a basic understanding of how students acquire knowledge through various learning styles and intelligences. This information is particularly relevant with adult learners who draw extensively from their own life experiences and value practical knowledge, flexibility, and passion for the subject matter. Graduate students thrive when professors deliver information using varied evidence-based teaching techniques that are fairly and consistently evaluated in both face-to-face and online formats. When implemented properly and with fidelity, you can create optimal environments in which personal and professional transformation occur, kindling a flame for lifelong learning and self-discovery.

Useful Websites

The following websites provide additional information relating to the chapter topics.

Multiple Intelligences: What Does the Research Say?. www.edutopia.org/multiple-intelligences-research
  This website gives the research behind the theory of multiple intelligences.
Learning Style. https://teach.com/what/teachers-teach/learning-styles/
  This website offers sample assessments for VARK and SWOT learning styles.

Adult Education. http://adulted.about.com/od/teachers/a/teachingadults.htm
This website offers tips on teaching adult learners.

Faculty Focus. www.facultyfocus.com/articles/effective-teaching-strategies/tips-for-teaching-adult-students/
This website offers additional tips on teaching adult learners.

Facing History & Ourselves. www.facinghistory.org/resource-library/teaching-strategies
This website provides a database of varied teaching strategies.

ASCD. www.ascd.org/publications/books/107003/chapters/Diverse-Teaching-Strategies-for-Diverse-Learners.aspx
This website provides diverse teaching strategies for diverse learners.

Northwestern Searle Center for Advancing Learning and Teaching. www.northwestern.edu/searle/resources/teaching-strategies-materials.html
This website provides a wealth of resources around postsecondary teaching/learning.

The Imposter Syndrome. https://uwaterloo.ca/centre-for-teaching-excellence/teaching-resources/teaching-tips/planning-courses/tips-teaching-assistants/impostor-phenomenon-and
This website offers information about the imposter syndrome.

Case Examples

Case Example 5.1

Learning Styles

You are currently teaching a multicultural counseling course comprised primarily of first-year counselor education students. The majority of your students present as Caucasian, middle class, cisgender, heterosexual females, ages 22–32. Although students present as the "same," it is evident that some students are more vocal and others appear to be uncomfortable with the subject matter. Recently, topics about immigration, law enforcement, and mass shootings have permeated class conversation. Applying the VARK theory to this case, how would you create a classroom environment that emphasizes the learning styles of all students to increase participation, particularly around uncomfortable and potentially difficult in-class discussions? How would you apply this theory to online learning?

Case Example 5.2

Complaining About a Group Assignment

You worked diligently to create a small group assignment in a family therapy class where students design a manual for therapists based on a particular demographic comprised of relevant theories, current evidence-based strategies, and national and local resources. Students then are required to make a short presentation to the class highlighting key elements present in their manual before turning it in to be graded. Two of the three groups complete the project exceptionally well; however, one group appears to be disjointed, unorganized, and lacking cohesion, resulting in a subpar manual and presentation. After class, you receive an email from a group member who states all group members did not contribute equally and she should receive a higher grade than her peers. How might you configure groups in the future to minimize this type of problem? Should you give the student more credit? What types of evaluation tools will you need to create greater equality and accountability in the future?

References

American Counseling Association. (2014). *ACA code of ethics*. Alexandria, VA: Author.

American School Counselor Association. (2012). *The ASCA national model: A framework for school counseling programs* (3rd ed.). Alexandria, VA: Author.

Barrio Minton, C. A., Gibson, D. M., & Watcher Morris, C. A. (2016). *Evaluating student learning outcomes in counselor education*. Alexandria, VA: American Counseling Association.

Bixby, D. W. (2011). Shut up and teach. *Talent Development* (4), 32–34. Retrieved from www.td.org/Publications/Magazines/TD

Brady, L. (2014). Relationship, relationship and relationship in teaching/learning. *Educational Practice and Theory*, *36*(2), 27–34. doi:10.7459/ept/36.2.03

Cercone, K. (2008). Characteristics of adult learners with implications for online learning design. *AACE Journal*, *16*(2), 137–159.

Chapman, A. (2015). Using the assessment process to overcome imposter syndrome in mature students. *Journal of Further and Higher Education*, *41*(2), 112–119.

Chen, J. C. (2014). Teaching nontraditional adult students: Adult learning theories in practice. *Teaching In Higher Education*, *19*(4), 406–418. doi:10.1080/13562517.2013.860101

Chen-Hayes, S. F., Ockerman, M. S., & Mason, E. C. M. (2014). *101 solutions for school counselors and leaders in challenging times*. Thousand Oaks, CA: Corwin Press.

Coll, K. M., Doumas, D. M., Trotter, A., & Freeman, B. J. (2013). Developing the counselor as a person and as a professional: Attitudinal changes in core counseling classes. *Journal of Humanistic Counseling*, *52*, 54–66. doi:10.1002/Í.2161-1939.2013.00032.x

Conaway, W., & Zorn-Arnold, B. (2015). The keys to online learning for adults: The six principles of andragogy. *Distance Learning*, *13*(1), 1. Retrieved from http://web.b.ebscohost.com/ehost/pdfviewer/pdfviewer?vid=1&sid=2b389e0a-d8f2-43 b3-9741-0ea3f3e63f37%40sessionmgr102

Devereux, L., & Wilson, K. (2014). Scaffolding theory: High challenge, high support in academic language and learning (ALL) contexts. *Journal of Academic*

Language & Learning, 3(8), 91–100. Retrieved from http://journal.aall.org.au/index.php/jall/article/view/353/210

Dirkx, J. M. (2006). Engaging emotions in adult learning: A Jungian perspective on emotion and transformative learning. *New Directions for Adult and Continuing Education, 2006*(109), 15–26. doi:10.1002/ace.204

Dirkx, J. M. (2008). The meaning and role of emotions in adult learning. *New Directions for Adult and Continuing Education, 2008*(120). doi:10.1002/ace.311

Fleming, N. D. (2006). VARK visual, aural/auditory, read/write, kinesthetic. *Bonwell Green Mountain Falls, New Zealand.*

Gardner, H. (1983). *Frames of mind: The theory of multiple intelligences.* New York, NY: Basic books.

Gibson-Beverly, G. & Schwartz, J. P. (2008). Attachment, entitlement, and the imposter syndrome in female graduate students. *Journal of College Counseling, 11*(2), 119–132. DOI: 10.1002/j.2161-1882.2008.tb00029.x.

Gibson, D. M., Dooley, B. A., Kelchner, V. P., Moss, J. M., & Vacchio, C. M. (2012). From counselor-in-training to professional school counselor: Understanding professional identity development. *Journal of Professional Counseling, Practice, Theory, & Research, 39*(1), 17–25.

Golden, L. B., & Henderson, P. (2007). *Case studies in school counseling.* Upper Saddle River, NJ: Pearson/Merrill/Prentice Hall.

Granello, D. (2011). Cognitive complexity among practicing counselors: How thinking changes with experience. *Journal of Counseling & Development, 88*, 92–100.

Gregorc, A. F. (1984). *Gregorc style delineator: Development, technical and administration manual.* Columbia, CT: Gregorc Associates, Inc.

Griffith, B., & Friden, G. (2000). Facilitating reflective thinking in counselor education. I, *40*(2), 82–93.

Hatch, T. (2015). *Managing to change: How schools can survive (and sometimes thrive) in turbulent times.* New York, NY: Teachers College Press.

Hall, M. (2013). Perry's scheme-understanding the intellectual development of college-age students. *Innovative Instructor Blog* at Johns Hopkins University. Retrieved from http://ii.library.jhu.edu/tag/william-g-perry/

Hill, L. H. (2014). Graduate students' perspectives on effective teaching. *Adult Learning, 25*(2), 57–65. doi:10.1177/1045159514522433

Holcomb-McCoy, C. (2007). *School counseling to close the achievement gap: A social justice framework for success.* Thousand Oaks, CA: Corwin Press.

Honey, P., & Mumford, A. (1986). *The manual of learning styles.* Cooktown: Peter Honey Associates.

Hutchins, H. (2015). Outing the imposter: A study exploring imposter phenomenon among higher education faculty. *New Horizons in Adult Education and Human Resource Development, 27*(2), doi.org/10.1002/nha3.20098.

Karge, B. D., Phillips, K. M., Jessee, T., & McCabe, M. (2011). Effective strategies for engaging adult learners. *Journal of College Teaching & Learning, 12*(8), 53–56. doi:10.19030/tlc.v8i12.6621

Killen, R. (2007). *Effective teaching strategies: Lessons from research and practice* (4th ed.). South Melbourne, VIC: Thomson Social Science Press.

Kolb, D. A. (1976). Management and the learning process. *California Management Review, 18*(3), 21–31. doi:10.2307/41164649

Kreuter, N. (2012). Walk like a duck. *Inside Higher Education.* Retrieved from www.insidehighered.com/advice/2012/08/20/essay-how-new-faculty-members-can-deal-impostor-syndrome

Larkin, H., & Richardson, B. (2012). Creating high challenge/high support academic environments through constructive alignment: Student outcomes. *Teaching* in *Higher Education, 18*(2). Retrieved from www.tandfonline.com/doi/abs/10.1080/13562517.2012.696541

Lyman, F. (1981). The responsive classroom discussion. In A. S. Anderson (Ed.), *Mainstreaming Digest*. College Park, MD: University of Maryland.

Lyman, F. (1987). Think-pair-share: An expanding teaching technique. *Cooperative News*, 1(1), 1–2.

Moran, K., & Milsom, A. (2015). The flipped classroom in counselor education. *Counselor Education and Supervision, 54*(1), 32–43. doi:10.1002/j.1556-6978.2015.00068.x

Mullen, P. R., Uwamahoro, O., Blout, A. J., & Lambie, G. W. (2015). Development of counseling students' self-efficacy during preparation and training. *The Professional Counselor, 5*(1), 175–184. doi:10.15241/prm.5.1.175

Olusegun, S. (2015). Constructivism learning theory: A paradigm for teaching and learning. *Journal of Research & Method in Education, 5*(1), 66–70.

Olson, M. H., & Hergenhahn, B. R. (2016). *An introduction to theories of learning* (9th ed.). New York, NY: Routledge.

Park, J. H., & Choi, H. J. (2009). Factors influencing adult learners' decision to drop out or persist in online learning. *Educational Technology & Society, 12*(4), 207–217.

Parkman, A. (2016). The imposter phenomenon in higher education: Incidence and impact. *Journal of Higher Education Theory and Practice, 16*(1), 51–60.

Parkman, A., & Beard, R. (2008). Succession planning and the imposter phenomenon in higher education. *CUPA-HR Journal, 59*(2), 29–36.

Patterson, C. A., & Levitt, D. H. (2012). Student-counselor development during the first year: A qualitative exploration. *The Journal of Counselor Preparation and Supervision, 4*(1), 6–19.

Pasher, H., McDaniel, M., Rohrer, D., & Bjork, R. (2008). Learning styles: Concepts and evidence. *Psychological Science in the Public Interest, 9*(3), 1–17. doi:10.1111/j.1539-6053.2009.01038.x

Perry, W. G. (1970). *Forms of intellectual and ethical development in the college years: A scheme*. New York, NY: Holt, Rinehart and Winston.

Pietrzak, D., Duncan, K., & Korcuska, J. S. (2008). Counseling students' decision making regarding teaching effectiveness: A conjoint analysis. *Counselor Education and Supervision, 48*(2), 114–132. doi:10.1002/j.1556-6978.2008.tb00067.x

Revere, L., & Kovach, J. V. (2011). Online technologies for engaged learning: A meaningful synthesis for educators. *The Quarterly Review of Distance Education, 12*(2), 113–124. Retrieved from http://search.proquest.com/docview/920291723/fulltextPDF/B7FD2EAB58044B94PQ/1?accountid=10477

Romanelli, F., Bird, E., & Ryan, M. (2009). Learning styles: A review of theory, application and best practices. *American Journal of Pharmaceutical Education, 73*(1), 1–5. Retrieved from http://pubmedcentralcanada.ca/pmcc/articles/PMC2690881/pdf/ajpe9.pdf

Sakulku, J., & Alexander, J. (2011). The impostor phenomenon. *International Journal of Behavioral Science (IJBS), 6*(1). Retrieved from http://ejournals.swu.ac.th/index.php/jbse/article/view/1712

Sher, A. (2009). Assessing the relationship of student-instructor and student-student interaction to student learning and satisfaction in web-based online learning environment. *Journal of Interactive Online Learning, 8*(2), 102–120.

Tokuhama-Espinosa, T. (2011). A brief history of the science of learning. *New Horizons for Learning Online Journal, 9*(1). Retrieved from http://education.jhu.edu/PD/newhorizons/Journals/Winter2011/

Wang, H. (2010). The influence of the socratic tradition on Cambridge practice and its implication on Chinese higher education. *Journal of Cambridge Studies, 5*, 1–18.

Willingham, D. T., Hughes, E. M., & Dobolyi, D. G. (2015). The scientific status of learning styles theories. *Teaching of Psychology, 42*(3), 266–271. doi:10.1177/0098628315589505

Yoo, S. J., & Huang, W. D. (2013). Engaging online adult learners in higher education: Motivational factors impacted by gender, age, and prior experiences. *The Journal of Continuing Higher Education, 61*(3), 151–164. doi:10.1080/07377363.2013.836823

Yorks, L., & Kasl, E. (2002). Learning from the inquiries: Lessons for using collaborative inquiry as an adult learning strategy. *New Directions for Adult and Continuing Education, 2002*(94), 93–104.

6 Acquisition of Knowledge and Skills

Michael P. Chaney and Jennifer J. Matthews

One of the many goals of counselor education programs is to provide a comprehensive education according to the ACA *Code of Ethics* (2014) and Council for Accreditation of Counseling and Related Educational Programs (CACREP). To this end, programs seek to prepare future counselors who are culturally competent, ethical, and empathic practitioners and educators. Therefore, the role of counselor educators is to foster student learning and development along with facilitating an environment that challenges yet supports students. Thus, the aim of this chapter is to describe how counselor educators can create effective learning objectives that consider the needs of adult learners. Additionally, the authors describe how the integration of Bloom's Taxonomy of Educational Objectives is necessary within counseling curricula to encourage higher order critical thinking skills. Lastly, practice exercises and a case study is included to enhance self-awareness, engage the chapter material, and promote discussion with peers and the professor.

Learning Objectives

After reading this chapter, you will be able to:

1. Understand the educational needs of adult learners.
2. Apply pedagogical strategies for teaching adult learners.
3. Utilize Bloom's Taxonomy for developing learning objectives.
4. Create effective learning objectives for a variety of counseling courses.
5. Evaluate learning objectives.

CACREP Standards

The content in this chapter meets the following 2016 CACREP Standards:

1. Syllabi are available for review by all enrolled or prospective students, are distributed at the beginning of each curricular experience, and include (1) content areas, (2) knowledge and skill outcomes, (3) methods of instruction, (4) required text(s) and/or reading(s), (5) student performance evaluation criteria and procedures, and (6) a disability accommodation policy and procedure statement. (Section 2: D)

2. Theories of learning (Section 2: F.3.b)
3. Evaluation of counseling interventions and programs (Section 2: F.8.e)
4. Pedagogy and teaching methods relevant to counselor education (Section 6: B.3.b)
5. Models of adult development and learning (Section 6: B.3.c)
6. Instructional and curriculum design, delivery, and evaluation methods relevant to counselor education (Section 6: B.3.d)
7. Assessment of learning (Section 6: B.3.g)

Overview of Teaching Methods

As a new or seasoned counselor educator, our teaching philosophy informs the teaching methods we choose. Generally speaking, two main instructional methods are teacher-centered and student-centered teaching. Teacher-centered instruction is often related to passive learning, where professors provide direct instruction (e.g., lectures and teacher-led discussions) to convey knowledge (Carpenter, 2006). This method posits the instructor as an expert authority, while providing a model for students to emulate. Teacher-centered instruction can be beneficial when presenting new information or demonstrating a skill (Mascolo, 2009). For example, in a skills-based course such as basic counseling techniques, it is helpful for students to learn basic counseling micro-skills (e.g., reflection of feeling, paraphrasing, etc.) by understanding the concepts through mini-lectures and discussions, then to observe the skill demonstrated through an instructor-led role-play, and lastly to practice the skill themselves. However, if over-used, this approach could be limiting as it may stifle student participation and autonomy. Additionally, students may feel intimidated by the professor, inadequate in their own abilities, or perceive the classroom environment to be rigid and unwelcoming.

Conversely, student-centered learning is based on a constructivist approach where students construct knowledge, while the teacher is a facilitator helping students to accommodate new information (Mascolo, 2009). This teaching method promotes autonomy, critical thinking, and student ownership of learning. Therefore, inquiry-based learning is present through student-led group discussions, along with cooperative learning through group projects. Utilizing an example of teaching students how to reflect feelings, a student-centered approach involves students discussing the skill, considering their professional experience, and then practicing the skill in triads or dyads. Students often like the discussion; however, if over-utilized, students may become frustrated due to the lack of direction from the instructor and might desire more content instruction. Another effective method to teach students in counseling or counselor education is an andragogical approach.

Adult Learners

Andragogy, by definition, is the art and science of helping adults learn (Knowles, 1970, 1990). The term was first coined by a German high school teacher, Alexander Kapp, in 1833 as a way to explain Plato's theories regarding lifelong learning (Henschke, 2009a). Over time, Knowles (1970) developed four main assumptions of adult learners: a) self-concept becomes more self-directed as a result of maturity, b) experience is an invaluable resource that informs learning and accommodating new information, c) readiness to learn is based on performing social tasks more effectively (e.g., losing a job and now on the job market), and d) orientation to learning is based on present applications instead of future applications (e.g., problem-centered vs. subject-centered learning). Henschke (2009b) further stated that adults learn based on what makes sense to them and connects with a purpose. Additionally, adult learners tend to be more intrinsically motivated versus learning solely for external rewards (Henschke, 2009b).

These assumptions of adult learners are especially important for faculty of counselor education programs. Counseling graduate students come from various cultures, possess diverse skills, and have distinct life and work experiences. Therefore, faculty needs to be ethical, culturally competent, and "skilled as teachers and practitioners." (ACA, 2014, F.7.a, p. 14). It is essential for counselor educators to consider the diverse learning styles of adult learners, as well as pedagogical methods that reflect the needs of counseling graduate students.

Learning Styles of Adult Learners

Due to the copious theories of adult learning styles, there is a lack of consensus in the learning style research (Cercone, 2008; Coffield, Moseley, Hall, & Ecclestone, 2004). However, two of the most researched models are Kolb (1984) and Fleming and Mills (1992). David Kolb's theory of experiential learning posits that learning is based on transformational experiences and four learning styles, including the converger, diverger, assimilator, and accommodator (Kolb, 1984). A *converger* learns effectively with practical applications of concepts; *divergers* learn best when observing; *assimilators* gain knowledge through logical theories; and *accommodators* learn by doing (hands-on activities) (Kolb, 1984). The VARK model is an acronym describing four learning styles: visual, aural, read/write, and kinesthetic (Fleming & Mills, 1992). Visual learners thrive on seeing knowledge and content; therefore, videos, role-plays, PowerPoint presentations, and assigned readings help them to retain information. Aural or auditory learners learn best from listening to content in lectures and discussions. Students who learn best from reading and writing tend to be introspective. Kinesthetic learners, on the other hand, learn from doing; thus, retaining information is based on simulations, writing, experiential activities, and role-plays.

Although critics debate the reliability of learning style measurements, the models can be useful by opening lines of communication between instructors and students (Coffield et al., 2004). Having a discussion about learning styles at the beginning of a course allows students to reflect on how they learn and provides faculty with guidance on how to effectively convey information and construct learning objectives. Counselor educators can use learning style inventories or discussions at the beginning of the semester to inform their teaching methods.

Andragogical Methods for Counselor Education Students

Eriksen and McAuliffe (2001) recommended that counselor educators: (a) question categorical thinking, (b) encourage expression of conflict, (c) show commitment in the face doubt, (d) process interpersonal dynamics and metacognition awareness, (e) value approximation over precision (e.g. half-formed ideas), (f) personalize teaching, (g) vary the structure, (h) value and promote experience, and, lastly, (i) emphasize multiple perspectives. Considering the four assumptions of adult learners (adult learners are self-directed, work/life experience is a resource that informs learning, readiness to learn is linked to performing social tasks more effectively, and orientation to learning is based on present applications instead of future applications), a balance of teacher-centered and student-centered instruction seems beneficial for all students and their respective learning styles (Mascolo, 2009). Direction from the professor is integral to modeling appropriate behavior; however, it is equally as important to allow students to engage themselves in the content. Counselor educators maintain this balance within the structure of the course, through engaging activities throughout the curriculum, and by means of evaluation of student learning. One way to immediately engage students is through a learning contract. As defined by Lemieux (2001), learning contracts are a collaborative agreement between instructors and students regarding learning objectives, assignments, and evaluation of student learning. Halloran and Delaney (2011) surveyed 54 counseling graduate students on their perception of learning contracts and found that 89% of the students either preferred or strongly preferred the learning contract as opposed to instructor-assigned objectives and assignments. Learning contracts promote self-directed learning and autonomy; therefore, learning contracts are useful with adult learners in helping professions such as counseling and social work (Boitel & Fromm, 2014; Halloran & Delaney, 2011).

Experiential learning is another teaching method appropriate for adult learners as the experience is the catalyst for learning (see Kolb, 1984). Counseling literature supports the benefits of experiential learning to enhance cultural competence (Arthur & Achenbach, 2002; DeRicco & Sciarra, 2005; Kim & Lyons, 2003; Tomlinson-Clarke & Clarke, 2010), increase cognitive complexity, which informs ability to conceptualize client problems (Osborn & Dames, 2013), and enhance professional development (Furr & Carroll, 2011). McAuliffe (2002) even found that experiential learning was the preferred type of learning, along with social construction, for counseling students. Experiential learning can be utilized throughout counseling curricula, including group counseling (Young & Hundley, 2013), couples and family (Lim, 2008) multicultural courses (Arthur & Achenbach, 2002; Kim & Lyons, 2003), and career counseling courses (Fulton & Gonzalez, 2014). Experiential activities can include role-plays, case studies or vignettes, guided imagery, psychodrama, peer learning, and service learning projects within the community (Fulton & Gonzalez, 2014; Murray, Pope, & Rowell, 2010). Once the most appropriate teaching methods have been chosen, it is imperative that teaching methods complement educational learning objectives.

Defining Learning Objectives

Whether a new professional or a seasoned counselor educator, one of the most exciting, challenging, and time-consuming aspects of teaching is new course preparation. From deciding what textbook to adopt, to crafting a coherent syllabus, these initial steps often determine how successful your course and students will be. In addition to the course description, university and departmental policies, instructor contact information, course requirements and schedule, a comprehensive syllabus also must include a list of learning objectives. The creation of course learning objectives is often the first step to course preparation because they help guide the direction and activities within a course. In counseling, clients are more successful when counselors construct concrete, measurable goals and objectives at the onset of the therapeutic relationship. Similarly, students also are more successful when clear and observable learning objectives are integrated for your courses and syllabi. The learning objectives generated for a respective course should be based on the focus of the course, the individual values of the instructor, applicability to students, and university objectives (Svinicki & McKeachie, 2011). The educational standards of professional accrediting bodies (i.e., CACREP) also must be considered.

Broadly, a learning objective is a brief description of what an individual should be able to demonstrate at the conclusion of a particular experience (Van Melle & Pinchin, 2008). Specifically in the context of teaching, a learning objective is a concise statement that describes what knowledge, skills, and attitudes students should be able to demonstrate at the end of a course. In addition to acquisition of knowledge, development of skills, and adjustment in attitudes, Suskie (2009) added that learning objectives include cognitive habits that students adopt as a result of a particular learning experience. Now that an operational definition of learning objectives has been presented, a next logical step is to explore some of the purposes for learning objectives.

There are several important reasons for integrating clear and concise learning objectives into your courses. First, learning objectives help to underscore the central purpose of particular learning experiences. Second, learning objectives help instructors determine how and where course activities fit within the broader curriculum. Third, learning objectives allow educators to choose relevant learning experiences for a particular course. Fourth, learning objectives assist the instructor with developing pertinent assessments to measure students' acquisition of knowledge, skill competence, and attitude changes (Homa et al., 2013). Fifth, learning objectives link course content and assessment to what is supposed to be learned in a respective course. Finally, learning objectives provide students with an idea of course and instructor expectations. A real-life example may clarify the preceding reasons for crafting course learning objectives. In a doctoral-level, Advanced Group Counseling course, where students eventually lead their own groups, the first author of this chapter listed a course objective on his syllabus as follows: *To assist students in recognizing group process dynamics as a leader of group work.* This particular objective highlighted the purpose (to recognize group dynamics) for the students leading their own groups (Reason 1); informed the instructor to place the course requirement of a group leadership experience a few weeks to midway into the semester so students could gain background knowledge about group process and dynamics prior to leading their own groups (Reason 2); and directed the instructor to include a group leadership experience into the course (Reason 3). Because of the group leadership requirement, the instructor integrated the use of group process case notes and video recordings as a way to assess students' group leadership competence and knowledge (Reason

4). In addition, the example objective is in line with what is supposed to be taught in this course as determined by CACREP (Reason 5), and based on this sample objective, students expected to lead some type of group as part of this class (Reason 6). You are encouraged to review the chapter on assessment for additional contextual examples of learning objectives. To help you develop your ability to construct effective learning objectives, take a few moments to complete the proceeding guided practice exercise. Upon completion of the exercise, share your results with a fellow student and give each other constructive feedback.

> **Guided Practice Exercise 6.1**
>
> You have been asked to teach an Introduction to Counseling and Ethics course next semester. Construct one learning objective for this course and identify how it meets each of the six purposes of a learning objective as described above.

As previously discussed, there are a variety of reasons to include learning objectives in each of the courses you teach. Additionally, there are a few characteristics that should be described within each learning objective. Van Melle and Pinchin (2008) suggested that learning objectives should describe the following items. First, the individuals whom you expect to demonstrate the learned behavior need to be reflected in learning objectives. Second, clearly describe the desired outcome behaviors that your students will perform. Next, the context in which the objectives will be acquired needs to be clear. Lastly, delineate the level of competency that you expect of your students after the learning experience. Indeed, there are many factors to consider when constructing effective learning objectives, and although professional accrediting bodies may dictate the courses to which students are to be exposed in their training, the learning objectives for each of those courses may contain a great deal of variability because of the individual educators who developed the objectives. Interestingly, a recent study found that although most psychology instructors included learning objectives in their syllabi, the types and how they were utilized diverged greatly across instructors (Homa et al., 2013). Moreover, the study also revealed that although the American Psychological Association (APA) has recommended student-learning outcomes, educators were not always using APA's guidelines. This could lead to unbalanced education and training among students. Therefore, counseling instructors are strongly encouraged to utilize the Council for the Accreditation of Counseling and Related Educational Programs (CACREP) standards (2016) as a resource when crafting student learning objectives.

According to CACREP (2016), within the general counseling curriculum, there are eight core areas considered to be foundational knowledge standards for all students graduating from counselor education programs. The eight core areas include professional counseling orientation and ethical practice, social and cultural diversity, human growth and development, career development, counseling and helping relationships, group counseling and groupwork, assessment and testing, research and program evaluation. Listed under each core content area there are about 85 specific standards associated with the respective core areas. In addition to the standards affiliated with the general counseling curriculum, CACREP delineated distinct standards for the entry-level specialty areas of Clinical Mental Health Counseling (23 standards) and School Counseling (34 standards). The CACREP standards can and should be adapted into learning objectives for the courses you teach. Another way to structure educational learning objectives is by using Bloom's Taxonomy of Educational Objectives.

Bloom's Taxonomy of Educational Objectives

Bloom's Taxonomy of Educational Objectives was developed as a way to classify learning, establish educational goals, and evaluate learning outcomes (Bloom, Engelhart, Furst, Hill, & Krathwohl, 1956). Bloom's Taxonomy focuses on cognitive learning that is hierarchal, advancing from recalling basic information to higher order learning, such as creating knowledge (Bloom et al., 1956). Although other classifications were created, such as affective taxonomy or emotional knowledge (Krathwohl, Bloom, & Masia, 1964) and psychomotor or physical knowledge (e.g., Harrow, 1972), the cognitive taxonomy is most utilized for curriculum development (Tansey, Schopieray, Boland, Lane, & Pruett, 2009). Therefore, in this chapter we focus on the cognitive taxonomy in creating and evaluating course objectives and lesson planning.

The cognitive domain of Bloom's Taxonomy describes a sequential process of learning. In its original version, nouns and verbs were used to denote categories and subcategories that learners must master before moving to the next level (for a full description see Bloom et al., 1956; Krathwohl, 2002). The main categories in the cognitive domain were: Knowledge, Comprehension, Application, Analysis, Synthesis, and Evaluation. However, in 2001, Lorin Anderson, David Krathwohl, and colleagues revised Bloom's Taxonomy to: Remembering, Understanding, Applying, Analyzing, Evaluating, and Creating (Anderson et al., 2001).

Revised Bloom's Taxonomy

The revised version of Bloom's Taxonomy (Remembering, Understanding, Applying, Analyzing, Evaluating, and Creating) retains the essence of the original version with a few changes. *Remembering* consists of recalling or memorizing information (e.g., defining person-centered counseling). *Understanding* is when an individual comprehends a concept and can verbalize it in his or her own words (e.g., explaining and giving examples of empathy in person-centered counseling). *Applying* is the ability to use a concept in a new situation (e.g., using reflection of feeling to demonstrate empathy in a role-play). *Analyzing* involves a deeper understanding of a concept in order to identify patterns, themes, hidden meanings (e.g., explaining the efficacy of person-centered counseling with different populations). *Evaluating* is discriminating and comparing ideas (e.g., compare and contrast person-centered counseling and cognitive behavioral therapy). *Creating* builds on the previous developmental stages and encourages creativity of knowledge acquisition (e.g., developing your own personal theory of counseling). Historically conceptualized as a pyramid, more recently it has been

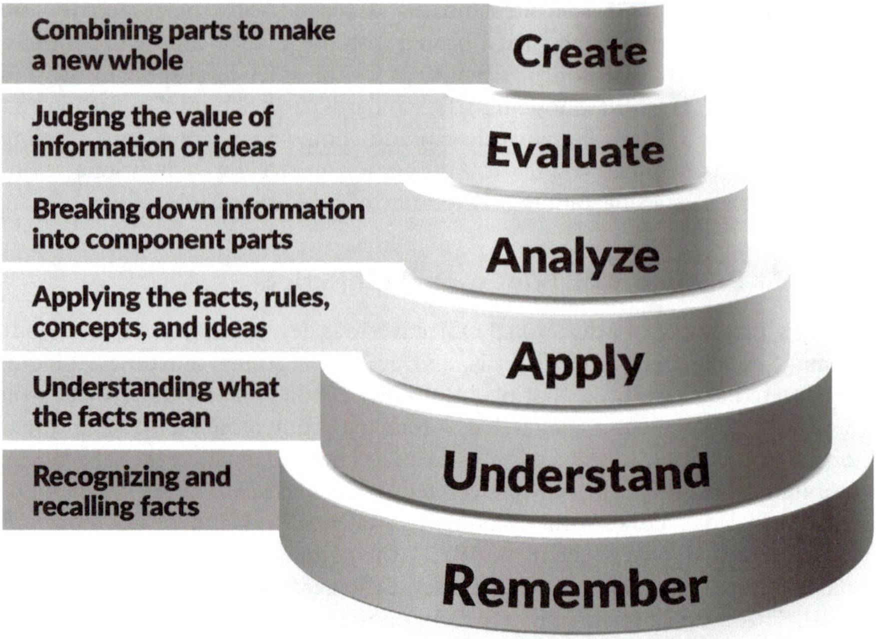

Figure 6.1 Bloom's Taxonomy

Copyright 2018: Jessica Shabatura, used with permission.

- Create: Combining parts to make a new whole
- Evaluate: Judging the value of information or ideas
- Analyze: Breaking down information into component parts
- Apply: Applying the facts, rules, concepts, and ideas
- Understand: Understanding what the facts mean
- Remember: Recognizing and recalling facts

presented as a layered-cake hierarchy (see Figure 6.1) because learning at higher levels can only take place when students have acquired understanding and skills at lower levels (Shabatura, 2013).

The most notable change between the original and revised Bloom's Taxonomy is the addition of metacognitive knowledge (awareness of one's own cognition) to the established subcategories (factual, conceptual, and procedural knowledge), which was included in the original taxonomy (Krathwohl, 2002). Therefore, as an individual moves from Remembering to Creating, they retain concrete and abstract information while exploring higher order thinking (evaluating their own learning and creating). Additionally, the revised taxonomy utilizes verbs (e.g., Remembering) instead of primarily nouns (e.g., Knowledge), which denotes active participation and engagement from the student (Krathwohl, 2002). Lastly, the revised taxonomy acknowledges that evaluating a concept is a necessary step prior to creating; therefore, Evaluating is placed before Creating in the revised version (Anderson et al., 2001). The revised Bloom's Taxonomy reminds us as educators to provide opportunities for metacognitive learning, emphasize learning in action, and integrate self-evaluating and peer evaluation into our courses. When as an educator you successfully incorporate the cognitive domain of Bloom's Taxonomy, students may be more engaged and motivated to learn.

Bloom's Taxonomy in Counselor Education: Creating Effective Lesson Plans

Literature has supported the use of Bloom's Taxonomy in counselor education, specifically in rehabilitation counseling curricula (Tansey et al., 2009), promoting cognitive complexity in graduate writing (Granello, 2001), in clinical supervision (Granello, 2000), and in multicultural counseling curricula (Dollarhide, 2013; Whitfield, 1994). Since the integration of Bloom's Taxonomy elicits high order thinking in counseling students, it is important to explore how to create an atmosphere of intellectual curiosity in graduate counseling courses. While course objectives set the tone and delineate information students are expected to learn (Krathwohl, 2002), creating effective lesson plans can help you promote higher order thinking for each class meeting.

Implementing teaching practices such as lesson planning can be challenging for faculty members who balance multiple tasks on a daily basis (e.g., publishing research, being a committee member) (Demir, Czerniak, & Hart, 2013). Typically, lesson planning is a task associated with K–12 teachers; however, it can be a productive and effective tool for instructors of graduate students. The benefits of lesson planning include clarifying and creating logical progressions in teaching, aiding instructors to match course objectives with daily class meetings, and integrating theory to practical applications (Solatini Arabshahi, Karimi, & Ghaderi, 2003). An online search of lesson plans for college professors yielded templates that included the following: learning objectives, content that will be taught, activities, assessment of learning objectives, materials needed, and Bloom's Taxonomy level(s), to name a few.

Developing Effective Learning Objectives

One of the first skills counselors-in-training learn as they begin to work with clients is effective goal-setting. The same characteristics of quality therapeutic goals apply to effective learning objectives. First, the learning objectives that you create for your courses should be *specific*. Objectives that are too broad or ambiguous are often times difficult to achieve due to lack of clarity. Second, effective learning objectives should be *measurable*. If course objectives are not measurable or observable, how will you or your students know whether or not they have been achieved? Third, learning objectives must be *attainable*. Students might feel discouraged and defeated if learning objectives are too far out of reach. Fourth, your course learning objectives must be *relevant*. Not only should learning objectives be related to the expected outcomes for respective courses, but they should be relevant to your students. Students will be more invested to meet course objectives if they find personal and professional relevance within the objectives. Fifth, learning objectives should *match the level of the students*. For example, if using Bloom's Taxonomy as a framework, it is recommended to focus objectives on Bloom's lower order skills (e.g., remembering and understanding) for beginning students in introductory courses because at this level they are developing a foundational knowledge base (Shabatura, 2013). For advanced graduate students, it may be more effective to construct objectives that exercise higher order skills such as analyzing and evaluation. Advanced graduate students may become disinterested or indifferent in class if course objectives and activities are based on lower order skills, whereas students with less experience may become frustrated and resentful if objectives are focused on higher order skills (Shabatura, 2013). In class, students are more likely to remain engaged, feel excited, and be successful when the course learning objectives match their developmental level of learning and, at the same time, gently challenge students to move to the next level.

Learning Objectives for Adult Learners

Increasingly, adult learners, also called non-traditional students, are filling up classrooms. Ross-Gordon (2011) described characteristics of many adult learners that contribute to their "non-traditional" label, including having children, being a single parent, holding a full time job, being financially independent, attending school part time, or not having a high school diploma. Based on these characteristics and because of these additional responsibilities, responsive educators should take these factors into consideration when crafting learning objectives for adult learners. Dean and Fornaciari (2014) suggested that efficacious learning objectives for adult learners should be andragogical. As discussed earlier in this chapter, andragogy pertains to helping adult learners. Therefore, an andragogical approach to learning objectives means that you are able to differentiate between what you as the instructor believe is pertinent compared to what your adult students think is necessary. To illustrate a real-life example, I (M.C.) used to hand out hard copies of an 11-page syllabus in my Introduction to Counseling and Ethics Class. Although I thought *everything* contained within the syllabus was crucial for students' (many of whom were adult learners) ability to be successful in class, they informed me that the syllabus was overwhelming and that they were unable to filter what was relevant and what was not, and frankly, did not have time to decipher the important aspects of the syllabus. Based on their feedback, I adopted a more andragogical approach by posting online only pertinent information that they needed to know such as course learning objectives, assignments and readings, and due dates. When constructing your course objectives, you should take into consideration the six characteristics pertaining to andragogy.

There are six tenets associated with andragogy (Knowles, Holton, & Swanson, 2005). First, adult learners are most interested in the "why" of learning. In other words, why is this information necessary for the student to know? Second, adult learners acquire knowledge via trial and error experiences. Third, decisions about learning should involve the adult learner; what is learned should be a collaborative decision. Fourth, adult students are more successful when they are able to discover how what is being learned is relevant to their lives presently. Fifth, adult students learn best from solving open-ended problems compared to being immersed in content-heavy classrooms. Finally, adult students learn best when they are motivated intrinsically rather than extrinsically. Note that a common theme among the aforementioned principles is that influence, onus, and motivation are student-centered and move further from the educator as a more andragogical approach to teaching is exercised. This is the core of andragogy (Fornaciari & Dean, 2014).

Although over a decade old, Weimer's (2002) summarization of the shifts toward student-centered instructional practices is still relevant today and has direct implications for developing effective student learning objectives, particularly for adult learners. Consider the following educational transformations when constructing learning objectives for the courses you teach:

1. Functions of power move toward the student from the educator.
2. Instruction should focus on course process versus content. In other words, how learning takes place rather than what is learned is underscored.
3. Educators serve as mentors who empower rather than directors who assert.
4. Onus of learning moves from educator to student.
5. Evaluation and assessment of learning is a collaborative process involving both student and educator, which in itself is a learning experience.

To summarize, the demography of graduate students is rapidly changing. As a result of adult learners having to manage and prioritize numerous personal and professional responsibilities, including work, family, and coursework, responsive educators should take these factors into consideration when constructing student learning objectives.

Constructing Learning Objectives

The key to constructing effective learning objectives is to first have a clear understanding of the general goals for each course. You should ask yourself, *what do I want students to know and demonstrate at the end of the course?* Van Melle and Pinchin (2008) recommended a first step to developing course objectives is to list the topics you want to cover in a course and the overall goals for the respective course. Additionally, course objectives may also come from an instructor's areas of scholarship (Homa et al., 2013). For instance, if an instructor's research is in the area of grief and loss within the African American community, a course objective for a grief and loss counseling course could be: Students will understand cultural factors that may influence the grieving process for clients of color. Other sources from where learning objectives may emerge are from CACREP standards and various professional competencies, such as the Multicultural and Social Justice Counseling Competencies (Ratts, Singh, Nassar-McMillan, Butler, & McCullough, 2015) and the Competencies for Counseling Lesbian, Gay, Bisexual, Queer, Questioning, Intersex and Ally Individuals (ALGBTIC LGBQQIA Competencies Task Force, 2013). Next, educators must realize how and where a particular learning experience belongs within the overall curriculum. Finally, before learning objectives can be created, delineate relevant concepts and learning experiences for students to have the most beneficial classroom experience possible.

The next step is to define the course learning objectives. In a practical sense, learning objectives are comprised of specific elements of grammar. For example, remember that verbs are used to represent aspects of the cognitive domain of Bloom's Taxonomy, while nouns represent the knowledge domains (Cannon & Feinstein, 2005). Shabatura (2013) recommended that effective learning objectives should contain the following characteristics. There should be one observable verb associated with each learning objective. Additionally, if using Bloom's Taxonomy, make sure that verbs for individual lesson level objectives are at a high enough taxonomy level so they can support overall course objectives. For

Table 6.1 Learning Objective Outcome Terms for Bloom's Taxonomy

Remember	Understand	Apply	Analyze	Evaluate	Create
Define	Exemplify	Utilize	Organize	Critique	Plan
Recall	Summarize	Use	Discriminate	Monitor	Generate
List	Predict	Apply	Select	Examine	Hypothesize
State	Demonstrate	Demonstrate	Integrate	Appraise	Solve
Identify	Describe	Construct	Structure	Compare	Collaborate
Locate	Illustrate	Report	Analyze	Assess	Formulate
Read	Observe	Develop	Classify	Consider	Design
Record	Conclude	List	Prioritize	Summarize	Infer
Recognize	Rewrite	Explain	Correlate	Distinguish	Propose
Memorize	Describe	Practice	Conceptualize	Choose	Manage

example, if an overall objective for a Social Justice and Diversity Counseling course is for students to be able to *Evaluate* (higher domain) disparities between diagnosis among diverse cultural groups, it would not make sense to construct a lesson objective that has students only memorize or *Remember* (lower domain) terms and definitions related to diagnosis. Note that the last four categories (Apply, Analyze, Evaluate, Create) of Bloom's Taxonomy require higher order, critical thinking skills (Bissell & Lemons, 2006). When creating learning objectives, it can be helpful to utilize a verb table such as the sample table included in this chapter.

Once you have crafted the learning objectives for your course, make sure each one is measurable, descriptive, and brief. To write effective learning objectives, the following steps may be helpful:

1. Choose the topic or the content and skills students need to learn.
2. Using Bloom's Taxonomy, identify students' level of learning. Decide in which domain of learning (see Bloom's Taxonomy: cognitive, psychomotor, affective) students will be engaged throughout the course or lesson.
3. Write a tentative learning objective. Assess whether or not the objective contains what Van Melle and Pinchin (2008) referred to as the A-B-C-D of learning objectives. Where A is the audience expected to demonstrate a learning outcome, B is the new learned behavior, C are conditions in which objectives should be acquired, and D is the degree of competency expected at the conclusion of the learning experience.
4. Evaluate and revise if appropriate.

Now, take time to review the case study presented in Guided Practice Exercise 6.2 and work through the questions following the case vignette.

Guided Practice Exercise 6.2

Amir is a recent doctoral graduate of a counselor education program. He accepted a faculty position as a counselor educator at a medium-sized institution. The counseling department is CACREP-accredited and offers a master's degree in Clinical Mental Health. Amir's faculty appointment begins in the fall so he is using the summer to move and prepare for his two courses (Diversity & Social Justice in Counseling and Addictions Counseling). His future colleagues have graciously emailed examples of syllabi for both courses. As he reviews the syllabi, he reflects on the course learning objectives and begins to brainstorm experiential activities that reflect diverse student learning styles, along with the multiple domains of Bloom's Taxonomy.

1. After reviewing CACREP guidelines for the multicultural and addictions courses, what would be important learning objectives to include on the syllabus?
2. During the lesson planning process, Amir wants to include activities for diverse student learners. Review the learning styles from the chapter (Kolb's Theory of Experiential Learning the VARK model). In small groups, discuss activities that could engage each learning style for either the multicultural course or the addictions course.
3. Counselor educators strive to promote higher order thinking in graduate counseling students. Using Bloom's Taxonomy as a guide, create a sample lesson plan for either the multicultural or addictions course. The lesson plan should be for a three-hour graduate level course. How can you engage students in remembering, understanding, applying, analyzing, evaluating, and creating?
4. What are other factors that Amir should consider as a new faculty member teaching a multicultural and addictions counseling course?

Recommendations for Incorporating Learning Objectives in Courses

Now that you have a general sense of what makes learning objectives effective and how to construct measurable and concise learning objectives, there are a couple of other considerations. Thus far, this chapter has focused primarily on developing learning objectives grounded in the cognitive domain of Bloom's Taxonomy. However, in counseling and counselor education coursework, it may be beneficial to integrate learning objectives that address the affective domain of the taxonomy. Components of the affective domain include class attendance, participation, interest and value in particular subjects, and student motivation. It is recommended that affective domain characteristics be integrated into course syllabi and a student's final grade (Lei, 2010). Affective traits in the class could translate into future positive or negative counseling behaviors. For example, a student who demonstrates a great deal of motivation to educate herself on a particular topic beyond what is being taught in class may later develop into a counselor who goes out of her way to educate herself about issues of multiculturalism and diversity. A student who is consistently tardy or misses multiple classes may continue this pattern of behavior as a counselor who struggles with managing session time boundaries with clients. Therefore, it could be beneficial for counselor educators to include learning objectives on syllabi that not only target the cognitive domain but the affective domain of Bloom's Taxonomy as well.

Integrating Learning Objectives Into Clinical Courses

Because expected student learning outcomes are often different for content courses (knowledge-based) versus clinical courses (skill-based), this section highlights particular aspects of learning objectives for courses and experiences in counselor education under which students may receive supervised training. These courses include counseling skills, practicum, and internship.

Cabaniss, Arbuckle, and Moga (2014) purported that supervisory learning objectives serve several purposes. Learning objectives have the capacity to connect what is being taught in the classroom to what is occurring in clinical work. Next, learning objectives transparently inform students and supervisees how they will be evaluated. Objectives may offer instructors and supervisors an opportunity to collaborate and consult on the development of assessments and evaluations. Finally, learning objectives in supervisory practice have the potential to standardize supervision.

Learning objectives for clinical courses have been classified into six areas: assessment, diagnosis, and treatment; the therapeutic relationship; empathy and reflective listening; technique; formulation and writing; and supervision (Cabaniss, 2008). Therefore, competent instructors will formulate concrete, cogent objectives that fall under one or more of the aforementioned categories. Research has shown that when learning objectives were not understandable, supervisees reported feeling confused and unclear about the goals of supervision and anxious about being evaluated (Cabaniss et al., 2014). Students in clinical courses are likely to feel similarly when learning objectives are ambiguous. As a result, it is strongly encouraged to develop learning objectives that are appropriate for the developmental phase in which helping professionals-in-training or supervisees are currently functioning (Rojas, Arbuckle, & Cabaniss, 2010). To illustrate, for students in a counseling micro-skills course, objectives might focus on the ability to demonstrate invitational or attending skills, reflective listening, and exploration skills, whereas for students in practicum, learning objectives might focus on assessment and diagnosis, case conceptualization, and ability to select effective theoretical interventions to treat clients. Taking into consideration counseling students' stages of clinical development when creating learning objectives is consistent with other helping professions. A recent study found that internship directors identified the three most crucial learning objectives for psychology interns during internship training to be more advanced learning outcomes such as assessment and diagnosis, therapeutic interventions, and cultural diversity issues (Stedman, Schoenfeld, & O'Donnell, 2013).

Constructing Learning Objectives for Clinical Courses

Adapted from the work of Cabaniss et al. (2014) who conceptualized steps to create learning objectives for supervision specifically, this section suggests steps you might take to draft learning objectives for clinical coursework, including basic counseling skills, practicum, and internship.

1. Brainstorm an inclusive list of general learning objectives for effective counseling. The objectives may be related to CACREP standards, other professional competencies, and ethical standards. Remember that the most effective learning objectives are measurable and concrete and take into consideration a counselor-in-training's stage of development. Within this broad list, include common therapeutic factors such as the helping relationship, empathy, goal-setting, and cultural competence. Additionally, learning outcomes related to intervention knowledge, awareness, and skills and case conceptualization should be included.
2. Select learning objectives that are appropriate for clinically based courses in which there is a supervisory component and whch are able to be evaluated within a supervisory context. For example, learning objectives related to individual or group supervision, utilization of professional resources, case formulation, self-evaluation skills, use of technology (e.g., diagnostic software, electronic record keeping, etc.), and ethical practice are required facets of effective counseling skills and supervision.
3. For each learning objective, develop instructional activities, exercises, and evaluation methods appropriate for each respective objective. Effective activities include collaborative reviews of recorded simulated or actual counseling sessions, role-plays, and shared case formulation and conceptualization.

Summary

An exciting and anxiety-provoking aspect of counselor education is teaching counselors-in-training. There are broadly two primary types of teaching methods. Teacher-centered teaching places responsibility for instruction on the educator, who directly presents students with information and content. Student-centered teaching allows learners to contribute to and generate knowledge in the classroom. When adopting teaching methods, competent educators take into consideration the characteristics of their students. Because counseling graduate students tend to be adult learners who have diverse learning styles, counselor educators should develop lesson plans, course exercises and activities, and learning objectives that are equally variant. Learning objectives delineate expected student outcomes at the conclusion of a course. Effective learning objectives are clear, concise, and measurable. This chapter explored how to apply Bloom's Taxonomy of Educational Objectives to construct quality student learning objectives in counseling and counselor education curricula. Lastly, step-by-step instructions were presented to assist new and seasoned counselor educators to generate their own learning objectives for core and clinical counseling courses.

Additional Resources

The following resources provide additional information relating to the chapter topics.

Anderson, L. W. (2013). *A taxonomy for learning, teaching, and assessing: A revision of Bloom's taxonomy for educational objectives, abridged edition*. New York, NY: Pearson.

The Association for LGBT Issues in Counseling. www.algbtic.org
This website hosts competencies for counseling LGBTQ+ individuals, which can serve as potential learning objectives.

Council for the Accreditation of Counseling and Related Educational Programs. www.cacrep.org
This website presents the 2016 CACREP Standards, which can and should be adapted into course learning objectives.

Gershon, M. (2015). *How to use Bloom's Taxonomy in the classroom: The complete guide*. Charleston, SC: CreateSpace Independent Publishing Platform.

Vanderbilt University, Center for Teaching. https://cft.vanderbilt.edu/guides-sub-pages/blooms-taxonomy/
This website includes more information about Bloom's Taxonomy for Educational Objectives. It also includes a list of potential action verbs.

References

ALGBTIC LGBQQIA Competencies Task Force. (2013). Association for lesbian, gay, bisexual, and transgender issues in counseling competencies for counseling with lesbian, gay, bisexual, queer, questioning, intersex, and ally individuals. *Journal of LGBT Issues in Counseling*, 7, 2–43. doi:10.1080/15538605.2013.755444

American Counseling Association. (2014). *ACA code of ethics*. Alexandria, VA: Author.

Anderson, L. W., Krathwohl, D. R., Airasian, P. W., Cruikshank, K. A., Mayer, R. E., Pintrich, P. R., . . . Wittrock, M. C. (2001). *A taxonomy for learning, teaching, and assessing: A revision of Bloom's taxonomy of educational objectives*. New York, NY: Pearson, Allyn & Bacon.

Arthur, N., & Achenbach, K. (2002). Developing multicultural counseling competencies through experiential learning. *Counselor Education and Supervision*, 42(1), 2–14.

Bissell, A. N., & Lemons, P. P. (2006). A new method for assessing critical thinking in the classroom. *BioScience*, 56(1), 66–72.

Bloom, B. S., Engelhart, M. D., Furst, E. J., Hill, W. H., & Krathwohl, D. R. (1956). Taxonomy of educational objectives: The classification of educational goals. Handbook I. *Cognitive Domain*. New York, NY: David McKay.

Boitel, C. R., & Fromm, L. R. (2014). Defining signature pedagogy in social work education: Learning theory and the learning contract. *Journal of Social Work Education*, 50(4), 608–622.

Cabaniss, D. L. (2008). Becoming a school: Developing learning objectives for psychoanalytic education. *Psychoanalytic Inquiry*, 28, 262–277. doi:10.1080/07351690801960814

Cabaniss, D. L., Arbuckle, M. R., & Moga, D. E. (2014). Using learning objectives for psychotherapy supervision. *Psychotherapy*, 68(2), 163–176.

Cannon, H. M., & Feinstein, A. H. (2005). Bloom beyond Bloom: Using the revised taxonomy to develop experiential learning strategies. *Developments in Business Simulations and Experiential Learning*, 32, 348–356.

Carpenter, J. M. (2006). Effective teaching methods for large classes. *Journal of Family & Consumer Sciences Education*, 24(2), 13–23.

Cercone, K. (2008). Characteristics of adult learners with implications for online learning design. *Association for the Advancement of Computing in Education Journal*, 16(2), 137–159.

Coffield, F. J., Moseley, D. V., Hall, E., & Ecclestone, K. (2004). *Learning styles and pedagogy in post-16 learning: A systematic and critical review.* London: Learning and Skills Research Centre.

Council for the Accreditation of Counseling and Related Educational Programs. (2016). *2016 CACREP standards.* Retrieved from www.cacrep.org

Dean, K. L., & Fornaciari, C. J. (2014). The 21st-century syllabus: Tips for putting andragogy into practice. *Journal of Management Education, 38*(5), 724–732. doi:10.1177/1052562913504764

Demir, K., Czerniak, C. M., & Hart, L. C. (2013). Implementing Japanese lesson study in a higher education context. *Journal of College Science Teaching, 42*(4), 22–27.

DeRicco, J. N., & Sciarra, D. T. (2005). The immersion experience in multicultural counselor training: Confronting covert racism. *Journal of Multicultural Counseling and Development, 33*(1), 2–17.

Dollarhide, C. T. (2013). Using a values-based taxonomy in counselor education. *Counseling and Values, 58*(2), 221–236.

Eriksen, K., & McAuliffe, G. (2001). *Teaching counselors and therapists: Constructivist and developmental course design.* Westport, CT: Greenwood Publishing Group, Inc.

Fleming, N. D., & Mills, C. (1992). Not another inventory, rather a catalyst for reflection. *To Improve the Academy, 11,* 137–149.

Fornaciari, C. J., & Dean, K. L. (2014). The 21st-cenrtury syllabus: From pedagogy to andragogy. *Journal of Management Education, 38*(5), 701–723. doi:10.1177/1052562913504763

Fulton, C., & Gonzalez, L. (2014). Making career counseling relevant: Enhancing experiential learning using a "flipped" course design. *Journal of Counselor Preparation and Supervision, 7*(2), 38–67.

Furr, S. R., & Carroll, J. J. (2011). Critical incidents in student counselor development. *Journal of Counseling & Development, 81*(4), 483–489.

Granello, D. H. (2000). Encouraging the cognitive development of supervisees: Using Bloom's taxonomy in supervision. *Counselor Education and Supervision, 40*(1), 31–46.

Granello, D. H. (2001). Promoting cognitive complexity in graduate written work: Using Bloom's taxonomy as a pedagogical tool to improve literature reviews. *Counselor Education and Supervision, 40*(4), 292.

Halloran, K. C., & Delaney, M. E. (2011). Using learning contracts in the counselor education classroom. *The Journal of Counselor Preparation and Supervision, 3*(2), 69–81.

Harrow, A. (1972). *A taxonomy of psychomotor domain: A guide for developing behavioral objectives.* New York, NY: David McKay.

Henschke, J. A. (2009a). Beginnings of the history and philosophy of andragogy 1833–2000. In C. V. Wang (Ed.), *Integrating adult learning and technology for effective education: Strategic approaches* (pp. 1–30). Hershey, PA: IGI Global.

Henschke, J. A. (2009b). Movement toward staying ahead of the curve in developing and managing human capital. In V. C. X. Wang & K. P. King (Eds.), *Human performance models in the global context* (pp. 1–27). Charlotte, NC: Information Age Publishing.

Henschke, J. A. (2012). Counseling in an andragogical approach. In C. V. Wang (Ed.), *Technology and its impact on educational leadership: Innovation and change* (pp. 272–286). Hershey, PA: IGI Global.

Homa, N., Hackathorn, J., Brown, C. M., Garczynski, A., Solomon, E. D., Tennial, R., . . . Gurung, R. A. R. (2013). An analysis of learning objectives and content coverage in introductory psychology syllabi. *Teaching of Psychology, 40*(3), 169–174. doi:10.1177/0098628313487456

Kim, B. S. K., & Lyon, H. Z. (2003). Experiential activities and multicultural competence training. *Journal of Counseling and Development, 81*(4), 400–408. doi: https://doi.org/10.1002/j.1556-6678.2003.tb00266.x.

Knowles, M. S. (1970). *The modern practice of adult education*. New York, NY: Associate Press.

Knowles, M. S. (1990). *The adult learner: A neglected species* (4th ed.). Houston, TX: Golf Publishing Company.

Knowles, M. S., Holton, E. F., & Swanson, R. A. (2005). *The adult learner: The definitive classic in adult education and human resource development* (6th ed.). Burlington, MA: Elsevier.

Kolb, D. A. (1984). *Experiential learning: Experience as the source of learning and development*. Englewood Cliffs, NJ: Prentice Hall.

Krathwohl, D. R. (2002). A revision of Bloom's taxonomy: An overview. *Theory into Practice, 41*(4), 212–264.

Krathwohl, D. R., Bloom, B. S., & Masia, B. B. (1964). *Taxonomy of educational objectives, the classification of educational goals. Handbook II: Affective domain*. New York, NY: David McKay Co., Inc.

Lei, S. A. (2010). College research methodology courses: Revisiting general instructional goals and objectives. *Journal of Instructional Psychology, 37*(3), 236–240.

Lemieux, C. M. (2001). Learning contracts in the classroom: Tools for empowerment and accountability. *Social Work Education, 20*(2), 263–276.

Lim, S. (2008). Transformative aspects of genogram work: Perceptions and experiences of graduate students in a counseling training program. *Family Journal: Counseling and Therapy for Couples and Families, 16*, 35–42.

Mascolo, M. F. (2009). Beyond student-centered and teacher-centered pedagogy: Teaching and learning as guided participation. *Pedagogy and the Human Sciences, 1*(1), 3–27.

McAuliffe, G. J. (2002). Student changes, program influences, and adult development in one program of counselor training: An exploratory inductive inquiry. *Journal of Adult Development, 9*, 205–216.

Murray, C. E., Pope, A. L., & Rowell, P. C. (2010). Promoting counseling students' advocacy competencies through service-learning. *Journal for Social Action in Counseling and Psychology, 2*(2), 29–47.

Osborn, D. S., & Dames, L. S. (2013). Teaching graduate career classes: A national survey of career instructors. *Counselor Education & Supervision, 52*, 297–310.

Ratts, M. J., Singh, A. A., Nassar-McMillan, S., Butler, S. K., & McCullough, J. R. (2015). *Multicultural and social justice counseling competencies*. Retrieved from www.counseling.org/docs/default-source/competencies/multicultural-and-social-justice-counseling-competencies.pdf?sfvrsn=20

Rojas, A., Arbuckle, M., & Cabaniss, D. (2010). Don't leave teaching to chance: Learning objectives for psychodynamic psychotherapy supervision. *Academic Psychiatry, 34*(1), 46–49.

Ross-Gordon, J. M. (2011). Research on adult learners: Supporting the needs of a student population that is no longer nontraditional. *Peer Review, 13*(1), 26–29. Retrieved from www.aacu.org/publications-research/periodicals/research-adult-learners-supporting-needs-student-population-no

Shabatura, J. (2013). *Using Bloom's taxonomy to write effective learning objectives*. Retrieved from https://tips.uark.edu/using-blooms-taxonomy/

Solatini Arabshahi, S. K., Karimi, H., & Ghaderi, A. (2003). The effect of educational workshops on appropriate design of lesson plan & application of different levels of cognitive domain in faculty staff of (Shaheed Sadooghi's) Yazd University of medical sciences. In 2000–2001: An Iranian experience. *Journal of Medical Education*, *4*(1), 11–15.

Stedman, J. M., Schoenfeld, L. S., & O'Donnell, L. (2013). An investigation of internship directors' perspectives on the learning objectives required by the commission on accreditation. *Training and Education in Professional Psychology*, 134–138. doi:10.1037/a0031660

Suskie, L. (2009). *Assessing student learning: A common sense guide* (2nd ed.). San Francisco, CA: Jossey-Bass/Wiley.

Svinicki, M., & McKeachie, W. J. (2011). *Teaching tips: Strategies, research, an theory for college and university teachers* (13th ed.). Belmont, CA: Wadsworth.

Tansey, T. N., Schopieray, S., Boland, E., Lane, F., & Pruett, S. R. (2009). Examining technology-enhanced coursework in rehabilitation counselor education using Bloom's taxonomy of learning. *Rehabilitation Education*, *23*(2), 107–117.

Tomlinson-Clarke, S. M., & Clarke, D. (2010). Culturally focused community-centered service learning: An international cultural immersion experience. *Journal of Multicultural Counseling and Development*, *38*(3), 166–175.

Van Melle, E., & Pinchin, S. (2008). *Writing effective learning objectives*. Retrieved from www.entcanada.org/Word_Files/CreatingLearningObjectives.pdf

Weimer, M. (2002). *Learner-centered teaching: Five key changes to practice*. San Francisco, CA: Jossey-Bass.

Whitfield, D. (1994). Toward an integrated approach to improving multicultural counselor education. *Journal of Multicultural Counseling and Development*, *22*(4), 239–252.

Young, M. E., & Hundley, G. (2013). Connecting experiential education and reflection in the counselor education classroom. In J. D. West, D. L. Bubenzer, J. A. Cox, & J. M. McGlothlin (Eds.), *Teaching in counselor education: Engaging students in learning* (pp. 51–66). Alexandria, VA: Association for Counselor Education and Supervision.

7 Curriculum Development

J. Kelly Coker and Savitri Dixon-Saxon

The best thing about being a counselor educator is the responsibility you have to ensure that students are given access to an engaging course experience that allows them the opportunity to develop the knowledge, skills, and abilities based on your program learning outcomes aligned with your university's mission and CACREP standards. Does that sound daunting? For those of you who do feel a little intimidated by that process, we can assure you that you can and will be successful if you are committed to a process of learning and growing yourself. In this chapter, we want to encourage you to engage in an iterative process of identifying what students need to know, how they need to develop, and what they need to be able to do as a result of completing a course; selecting the right course materials and artifacts to accomplish those objectives; and creating a course syllabus that serves as a guide or roadmap throughout the curricular experience for you and your students.

Learning Objectives

After reading this chapter, you will be able to:

1) Select appropriate course assignment and evaluations based on 2016 Council for Accreditation of Counseling and Related Education Programs (CACREP) standards.
2) Select appropriate textbooks, supplemental readings, and other materials and media to support learning objectives.
3) Identify the appropriate modality of delivery (i.e., face to face, hybrid, online) for your development curriculum.
4) Create a course syllabus that serves as an institutional contract with students and incorporates required 2016 CACREP standards.

CACREP Standards

The 2016 CACREP standards provide a framework for developing curriculum, activities, and assessments for counseling courses. Relevant standards related to doctoral professional identity in the teaching domain that inform the development of courses and curriculum include:

1) 6.B.3.d. instructional and curriculum design, delivery, and evaluation methods relevant to counselor education.
2) 6.B.3.e. effective approaches for online instruction (CACREP, 2015).

In addition, standards under Section 2 of the 2016 CACREP standards related to the elements required in program syllabi and curriculum are relevant to the discussions in this chapter:

1) 2.D. Syllabi are available for review by all enrolled or prospective students, are distributed at the beginning of each curricular experience, and include (1) content areas, (2) knowledge and skill outcomes, (3) methods of instruction, (4) required text(s) and/or reading(s), (5) student performance evaluation criteria and procedures, and (6) a disability accommodation policy and procedure statement.
2) 2.E. Current counseling related research is infused in the curriculum (CACREP, 2015).

Depending on the course being developed, 2016 CACREP standards related to the eight common core areas for entry level programs (CACREP standards 2.F.1–8), the specialty areas (CACREP standards 5. A–G), or the doctoral core areas (CACREP standards 6.B.1–5), will need to be taken into account in curriculum development. It is crucial that the development of an individual course aligns with the overall requirements of adhering to CACREP curriculum standards across the program, and that requirements for assessing program effectiveness and individual student progress and student learning outcomes (CACREP standards in Section 4) are also considered.

Curriculum Development—Getting Started!

You are a new assistant professor at XYZ University, and your department chair tells you that you now will be the primary instructor for the Research and Assessment course. She comes into your office with an armful of books and a folder of papers and happily drops them on your desk. "This course has been taught by the same person for years. Dr. West retired at the end of last year, so here is everything we can find about how he taught the course. It is yours now, so use of this what you want but it is now up to you to develop it. Remember, the semester starts in two weeks, so good luck!"

This is an all-too-familiar situation for faculty in many institutions, whether the delivery method be face to face, hybrid, or online. According to Felder and Brent (2007), many faculty members who are faced with developing a new course will make the mistake of feeling like it is up to them and them alone to develop everything, teach everything under the sun, know everything about the topic, and basically try to work things out as you go and hold on tight. Developing a course that is engaging, includes relevant and current research, is guided by identified learning objectives, contains key performance indicators that align with accreditation standards, and includes varied learning activities and opportunities may seem daunting, but it is definitely doable! Felder and Brent (2007) offer a few initial suggestions when tasked with developing a new course. First, start as early as you can. Sometimes externally imposed timeframes can make this one difficult, but the more you can fully develop before the semester or quarter begins the better. Second, do not reinvent the wheel. You may find that Dr. West has some outdated and antiquated information that needs to be brought up to date, but you may also find he has developed over the years some great activities or lectures on various topics that you can incorporate into your own development. Consulting with colleagues about materials, topics, assessments, and evaluations helps to keep you from having to develop everything from scratch. Another key suggestion and one that is doubly important for those working in CACREP accredited programs is to ensure that there are detailed learning objectives that guide the construction of lesson plans, assignments, and tests (Felder & Brent, 2007). These should also serve as a framework for creating an alignment table between learning objectives, CACREP standards met in the course, and student activities and assignments that demonstrate these objectives have been met.

Learning Objectives: Begin With the End in Mind

According to the 2016 CACREP standards, counseling programs must develop program objectives that reflect current knowledge and needs concerning counseling practice in a multicultural and pluralistic society that address student learning. In addition, syllabi for courses and course curricula must contain knowledge and skills outcomes and performance evaluation criteria and procedures (CACREP, 2015). In developing curriculum, it is important to first think about what your students will know, understand, and/or be able to do after completing the course. Working backwards from outcomes, to assessments and evaluations, to activities, to curriculum can help ensure all paths lead to enhanced student knowledge, skills, and/or dispositions.

Learning objectives, also known as student learning outcomes (SLOs) or key performance indicators (KPIs), should be developed thoughtfully and represent the level of learning expected. Bloom's Taxonomy is often utilized to help frame learning outcomes to reflect the developmental level of the learner and subsequently the learning level achieved. Bloom's Taxonomy moves from lower level learning (i.e. knowledge-based, remembering information, understanding concepts) to higher order learning (i.e., applying, analyzing, evaluating, and creating; Granello, 2000). For graduate-level counseling programs, learning outcomes are often written to reflect what the student will be able to do at the end of the course and/or program. Using words such as "analyze, apply, evaluate" helps to frame the expectations that students will need to do more than simply demonstrate that they have understanding of concepts. According to Granello (2000), the use of progressively higher levels of Bloom's Taxonomy across learning experiences can reflect the ability to capture developmental learning around a concept. In writing about applying Bloom's to the practice of supervision in a counselor training program, Granello (2000) suggested that in an introductory experience such as a first skills course, students might be expected to demonstrate their ability to learn, conceptualize, and understand different methods of client intake and assessment. In a practicum course, students might be asked to analyze and explain patterns of client behaviors that might impact a particular clinical approach. Finally, in an internship experience, students could be called upon to assess and evaluate client progress based on identified goals and interventions. The previous chapter provides specific information about developing student learning outcomes, so for the purposes of this discussion, keep in mind that they are a key anchor for the rest of your curriculum development.

Course Materials—NOT Everything and the Kitchen Sink!

After wading through all of Dr. West's materials from the previously taught Research and Assessment class, you realize that while there is some strong foundational information, the articles and resources are largely out of date. According to the 2016 CACREP standard 2.E, current counseling-related research must be infused in the curriculum (CACREP, 2015). This has implications for both the choice of resources and materials as well as lectures, discussions, and assignments. It is not uncommon for counseling programs to identify one specific course to primarily cover all learning objectives around a particular topic, so the challenge can be to balance creation of a curriculum that is both comprehensive and focused. This process often starts with finding course materials that can support the content that needs to be delivered.

Textbook Selection

One might assume that the first place to start in determining which course materials to use would be to start with the selection of a textbook. Historically, textbooks were what provided the primary information for a course and were what drove the delivery of information through lectures and discussions. Zaghab and Beckenholdt (2014) indicated in their discussion of a textbook-free approach to course development that a combination of high costs of textbooks and the slow pace at which they are published and updated make them a less-relevant option when selecting materials. Nonetheless, many counseling courses are anchored by textbooks because they can provide a solid framework to establish curriculum, activities, and assessments. Zaghab and Beckenholdt (2014) contend that there are some considerations when determining to go "textbook-free" or not. First, is the field of study the course is being developed around in a state of dynamism and change, or is the information pertaining to the topic in a state of enduring equilibrium? For example, if you are developing a History of the Counseling Profession course, and the curriculum you are developing pertains to the history and development of the field, a well-established and positively reviewed textbook is probably a good choice as it will likely provided the pertinent early theorists, development, legislation, and key dates driving the advances in the field. If the course under consideration, however, represents a newer and dynamic field of study, or even a field of study that has recently gone through a major transformation or new way of thinking, then ensuring course materials are cutting edge, up to date, research based, and representing emerging trends and theories will be important (Zaghab & Beckenholdt, 2014). The field of multicultural counseling, for example, has gone through much iteration, from learning about different cultural groups, to focusing on advocacy and social justice, to ensuring inclusion of people with disabilities and the LGBT communities in our consideration of multicultural constructs. For these reasons, adoption of the 2nd edition of the *Handbook of Multicultural Counseling* published in 2001 for a newly developed course in the subject would be missing newer and more relevant information found in the 3rd edition of the same text published in 2010. This represents another challenge with textbook adoption—namely, that if you are developing a course that needs to retain the same materials for a given period of time, such as in some online courses, even a current edition of a textbook could end up being out of date before the course is revised again.

This is not to say that textbooks should not be considered. More and more, textbooks are now available electronically, significantly reducing the cost for students and allowing for easier access. Many publishers, recognizing the changing landscape of course materials, are focusing increasingly on digital product management and creating dynamic resources better fit for adaptive learning environments (Opidee, 2014). Course developers searching for a new edition of a textbook are likely to find more interactive platforms, including accompanying media, online or digital versions, and partner websites or other online resources with relevant and current information. One final consideration for textbook adoption as we move into a discussion of other learning materials; a textbook does not have to be viewed as a linear document. As you develop weekly objectives, readings, and activities, you are encouraged to not feel bound by the linear outline of chapters in textbooks. You might have students read chapter three in week one of the course along with viewing a video, and you might have them read chapter eight in week two along with two supplemental articles. Sometimes the textbook itself becomes the supplement to other materials. Also consider this: the time it can take for a student to read, analyze, interpret, and discuss assigned readings may be slower than it takes you as the instructor. When planning weekly readings, take into account the amount of time you expect students to spend on the consumption of information to best prepare them for the week's work. It might be preferable to assign less in the way of textbook or article readings to ensure students have a maximum understanding of the information they do read. Guided Practice Exercise 7.1 will encourage consideration of whether adding a textbook or not to your course is warranted.

Guided Practice Exercise 7.1

In considering the use of a textbook or not, what is your preference? Do you feel a course is stronger if it is anchored by a comprehensive textbook, or would you rather use different learning resources to provide the learning for your course? Consider your own experiences as a graduate student. Have you found that textbooks, other materials, or a combination provide the best information to facilitate learning?

Other Learning Materials

Finding supplemental articles, assessments, media, and websites is one way to augment or even replace the textbook-only model of course design. Whether offering an online, face-to-face, or hybrid class, we know that the majority of college students learn in different ways, so having a blend of resources and deliveries can help foster engagement throughout the class. The difference between having a class that is structured as a "read/lecture/test" format from one that is a "read/debate/view/practice/demonstrate" format can potentially have very different results as the first format focuses on instructor delivery, while the second focuses on student learning (Opidee, 2014). According to the Association for Supervision and Curriculum Development (ASCD), using materials that promote differential learning is key to bridging the gap between research and practice (ASCD, 2015). Selecting materials that help focus on "doing" rather than "knowing" can help students achieve a higher order learning outcome.

It is also important that learning materials are able to be used by all students, including those with documented disabilities. According to Rao, Edelen-Smith, and Wailehua (2015), often faculty developing a course, particularly one where technology will be integral to the delivery of content, do not know what needs future students will have. Applying Universal Design (UD) principles can assist course developers with building in flexible options that take into account learner variability (Rao et al., 2015). UD frameworks actually originated in the field of architecture, with a focus on designing functional, physical environments. Expanded to course design and development, the concept has the goal of creating accessible learning environments (Rao et al., 2015). For course development, a UD design framework would include having varied learning materials and experiences that consider diverse learning styles and learning needs. In both online and face-to-face course development, develop teaching methods and learning resources that allow for multiple ways for students to take in information and demonstrate knowledge (Rao et al., 2015). UD principles can be applied to face-to-face, online, and hybrid learning environments. An important component of online learning, in particular, is ensuring that resources built into the course can be accessed by all students. Providing a video resource, for example, would require the addition of a written transcript that can be read in lieu of viewing if needed.

The Internet and its potential to provide immediate, up-to-date, and interactive resources has opened up a new world of learning materials options for the course developer. The use of online articles, assessments, videos, podcasts, and other websites offers ways to significantly augment the traditional read/lecture/test format of yesterday. Many textbook publishers are now providing digital products, technology, and services as well as curriculum design and online tutoring resources to support the creation of dynamic, interactive, and engaging curriculum (Opidee, 2014).

A word of caution about the use of digital materials and media: the Internet is not always a stable place, and that wonderful YouTube video you wanted students to view and respond to in week eight of the course, which is there today, could be gone tomorrow. Similarly, the use of live webpages, assessments, online articles, and other Internet-based resources would need to be checked and checked again to ensure the content is still available, links are still working, and the information presented is clear and accurate. One reason we consistently rely on peer-reviewed journal articles instead of just web-based articles is that we can ensure that there has been a deliberate review and editing process to ensure information is research based, representing agreed-upon best practices, and standing the test of time.

Finally, remember that potentially the best learning material and resource is YOU. As the teacher of the content, you are the one who breathes life into your topic and makes it come alive for your students. Whether you are teaching an online, hybrid, or face-to-face course, think about how you will present your materials. Try to think outside the box of PowerPoint/lecture. Tell stories about your own experiences, rely on the expertise of students in your class, look for ways to deliver information in fun, engaging, and yes, even entertaining ways. Even if you are teaching online, the technology of today provides ever-increasing opportunities to actively engage with your students and create new ways to differentiate learning.

Considerations for Different Delivery Platforms: What IS the Difference?

One of the authors of this chapter had an experience several years ago in which she was teaching a face-to-face practicum course at one institution while also teaching an online practicum course at another institution. This was during a time that online counselor training was relatively new and viewed with skepticism. This experience, however, demonstrated to this author how similar counselor training can be despite platform. For both courses, the author held "real time" group supervision, reviewed tapes of counseling sessions, and engaged in instruction around specific counseling skills appropriate for practicum-level learning. Students in both experiences grew in their skill development, had meaningful experiences at their sites and with peers in supervision, and received positive reports from their respective counseling sites. Since this time, online counselor training has grown significantly. At the time of this writing, there are currently 39 CACREP accredited counselor and counselor educator training programs that operate online (CACREP, 2016). While CACREP programs, regardless of delivery platform, are held to the same standards and therefore must demonstrate that student learning has occurred across the curriculum, the role a faculty member plays in development courses and curriculum for online versus face-to-face programs can look quite different.

According to Delaney-Klinger, Vanevenhoven, Wagner, and Chenoweth (2014), there are three primary options when faced with developing a new online course: develop a brand new course, modify an existing course from another delivery method, or adopt an existing online course "as is." Going back to our previous example at XYZ University, Dr. West has left many materials and information from a previously taught course. Imagine that in addition to creating a section of this course to be taught face to face, you are also being asked to develop a version that will be taught online. While you might develop the same learning outcomes and even have the same learning materials, you will need to give some thought to your delivery of information and how you plan to foster engagement and interaction and evaluate learning. According to Cicco (2012a), if online classes, particularly those that focus on skill acquisition, are to be comparable to on-ground counterparts, they need to include opportunities for supervisory and practice experiences. In a study to evaluate perceptions of online versus face-to-face counselor training, Cicco (2012a) found that there is a general lack of confidence in the efficacy of skills training among faculty and counseling students for online classes. She also found, however, that students indicated if online classes included video clips, the use of synchronous interactions via SKYPE or other video conferencing tool, and other tools such as podcasts, the perceived efficacy of online skills training would increase (Cicco, 2012a).

For those course developers looking at online delivery, selecting tools and materials that create an engaging and interactive atmosphere with opportunities for both synchronous and asynchronous exchanges may serve to enhance the overall delivery of the course. Hrastinski (2008) conducted a study of the benefits of both asynchronous and synchronous learning opportunities in online learning built on the basis that there are three types of communication important for building and sustaining effective e-learning communities. These are "content-related communication, planning of tasks, and social support" (Hrastinski, 2008, p. 52).

In the development of your online and face-to-face versions of the Research and Assessment course, you can consider how each of the three communication types above will be managed in your online version. For the face-to-face class, you will probably rely on class lectures and guided discussions to deliver content-related communications. For your online version, you may craft discussion post prompts to support readings for the week. This method allows for an asynchronous experience where students ask or answer content-related questions, share information, and express ideas or thoughts (Hrastinski, 2008). To plan for tasks in the face-to-face class, you might develop a case study and group students to collectively determine the best assessments to use to evaluate the client concern. You could also employ a case study activity in your online version, and even provide opportunities for students to "meet" with their fellow group members to work through their assessments using tools such as SKYPE or Blackboard Collaborate. In both online and face-to-face versions of the class, this activity could allow students to plan their work, allocate tasks, and coordinate efforts (Hrastinski, 2008). Of course, you might need to consider how developed activities would work in a hybrid format. In this case, students might spend one week on ground in a face-to-face class, and the next week completing activities in an asynchronous online classroom. Developing activities that span the two deliveries and provides a seamless experience is important.

A question at this point might be how to address the social support desired to express companionship, emotional support, and talk about things other than class work. In your face-to-face course, this may not require much planning on the course developer's part; this tends to happen more organically when students are gathering for class, on breaks together, or grabbing a bite to eat after class. But even creating group activities in class, creating group projects to occur outside of regular class time, having class debates, and encouraging sharing of different thoughts and ideas can foster this type of engagement. In the online environment, however, this aspect of communication needs more thoughtful consideration. Synchronous opportunities for interaction can be an experience built into the online learning platform where students can come together with one another and even with their professor and talk through issues they are facing as online learners, questions about the class or assignments, or opportunities to discuss concepts and even practice skills.

Hrastinski (2008) found in his assessment of synchronous versus asynchronous learning opportunities in classes that both have benefits and drawbacks. Asynchronous interactions provide the online student with more flexibility in how and when they engage and participate in class, but these interactions can also lead to feelings of isolation and a more singular focus on content-related interactions. Synchronous interactions provide more support for other types of communication (i.e., planning for tasks, allocating work, stronger social support), but may diminish students' ability to take more time to consider a concept and thoughtfully respond. Hrastinski (2008) also noted that previous research supports that synchronous communication in online platforms can increase psychological arousal and can increase motivation. The key message for considering curriculum development in online platforms is that what happens in the face-to-face classroom is not likely to automatically translate to the online world without some careful planning around materials, communication types, and the use of technologies to support both asynchronous and synchronous interactions.

The Course Syllabus: The Roadmap for an Engaging Learner Experience

In a counselor education program, every aspect of the educational experience should contribute to learners' professional development, especially those aspects that we often consider mundane, necessary aspects of education like the course syllabus. The syllabus allows everyone to be clear about expectations throughout the course and sets the tenor of the course. A syllabus is one of the most important tools in the course, because it communicates to students the tools they will need to be successful in the course and it also guides them in the policies that will impact that success. (Cornell University Center for Teaching Excellence, 2016).

Traditionally, the course syllabus has been thought of as the contract between the professor, as an agent of the institution, and the student. In reality, the syllabus is a contract between the student, the instructor, the university, and, in the case of accredited counseling programs, CACREP. The syllabus provides a roadmap or blueprint for the course experience. It also clearly communicates to all stakeholders what students should learn as a result of completing the course experience. The syllabus is one of the most important pieces of evidence for the overall learning experience.

The syllabus is the primary aid in guiding the students through the course and making sure that each student has a clear understanding of the learning expectations throughout the course and the learning outcomes as a result of the educational experience. The Center for Teaching and Learning at Brigham Young University (n.d.) suggests that the syllabus establishes the first connection for the instructor and the learner, and it allows the learner to decide if he or she is adequately prepared to be successful in the course.

Building Relationships Through the Course Syllabus

Imagine that you, the new instructor for the Research and Assessment course, distributed a partially completed syllabus. While some points of the syllabus were complete, like the academic integrity policies, course learning outcomes, resources for students with disabilities, and the instructor's teaching philosophy, the section on expectations regarding student behavior and the course schedule was incomplete. Taking a page from your counseling training, you, the counselor educator, have decided to collaborate with your students in determining the ground rules for behavior in the course and the order of learning in the course. While implementing such an idea is not easy, it would certainly have the potential to change the traditional power dynamic in the course, create the opportunity for a more egalitarian relationship between the instructor and student, and foster the sense that both are responsible for the outcome of the course. Using the syllabus as an avenue to relationship building is particularly important for counselor education because every aspect of the course experience should be used to model and practice those skills that are required for training counselors and counselor educators. This is one strategy for relationship building. It could be as beneficial to the instructor-learner relationship to have clearly articulated expectations (Cicco, 2012b), especially in courses that involve the acquisition of extremely challenging concepts and skill development expectations.

Traditionally, the syllabus has been one-way communication and a mandate to the student instead of a contract between two people (Ludwig, Bentz, & Fynewever, 2011). However, the syllabus can be an opportunity to not only guide students in the educational process with clear expectations, learning objectives, and evaluation and assessment measures, but it can also be used to motivate students and help them understand the particular course experience as one part of the student's professional preparation.

Fornaciari and Lund Dean (2014) argue that educators should rethink how they use the syllabus to build culture in the classroom and to collaborate with students. Their recommendations are based on the idea the principles of andragogy, the science of teaching adults.

Andragogy and Students' Influence on Courses

The science of andragogy recognizes that adults have a wide variety of experiences that can serve as learning resources (Akin, 2014). Additionally, there is the recognition that the best education results from the practical application of learning and relating new information to each student's lived experiences. The principles of andragogy also suggest that authority and responsibility should be shared by the learner and the instructor and the actual classroom should be arranged by the learner and the instructor.

It may be challenging to involve students in the syllabus design process, especially in an online environment, but if we regard the syllabus as an iterative process, it is very possible for a faculty member to incorporate feedback from students in each successive iteration of a syllabus and make it known to future students how past students' feedback has been incorporated. Cicco (2012a) also recommends giving students the opportunity to choose assignments reflective of their learning styles and preferences. For example, students could be given options to do a 100% written assignment or do a narrated PowerPoint. Cicco (2012a) also offers that for counseling courses, it is important to include assignments that allow students to practice their counseling skills throughout the program and for the syllabus to include objective assessments in order to prepare students for credentialing examinations and to get an objective measure of students' learning. In keeping with the tenets of andragogy that allow for faculty and students to collaborate, students can also be invited to work together to establish the ground rules for in-class behavior and communication.

An additional consideration in course development, as well as syllabus design, is both online and in-person diverse learning styles of students. Activities like reflective writing, role-playing, mock counseling sessions, group projects, and group discussions can all be used to be inclusive and allow for diversity in learning. Another important consideration when designing the course syllabus is the diversity of the students in the course and of the populations they will serve (Cicco, 2012a). Throughout the course, students should be given the opportunity to increase their self-awareness as cultural beings, but to also develop skills and knowledge appropriate to serve a diverse client population.

Student Disposition Evaluations

A very important feature of each course experience in a counseling program is the group of activities designed to evaluate each student's dispositions. Section 4 of the 2016 CACREP standards specifically identifies the assessment of professional dispositions as an essential part of the counselor training experience and mandates that training programs include an ongoing evaluation process (CACREP, 2015). Redekop and Wlazelak (2010) define dispositions as those characteristics that make an individual an effective counseling professional. For the last two decades, a host of ideas have been generated to concretely define those behaviors or characteristics that are indicative of the appropriate dispositions for counselors (Meara, Schmidt, & Day, 1996; Pope & Kline, 1999; Spurgeon, Gibbons, & Cochran, 2012). Using the example of Redekop and Wlazelak (2010), we can generally characterize the very long lists of attitudes by healthy perceptions of self, others, and purpose and an appropriate frame of reference. As you develop your syllabus, be sure to include course assignments, activities, and discussions that allow you to evaluate these dispositions throughout the course. In the spirit of relationship building, a good practice is to generally remind your students that the course includes evaluations of knowledge, skills, and dispositions.

Resistant Students

In almost every course you teach, there will be a student who is difficult to work with for one reason or another. You will have to learn to manage these situations, not take it personally, and respond to the student in a way that effectively manages expectations around the student-instructor relationship for the future. Your syllabus coupled with your behavior can be a great tool for working through issues with difficult or resistant students.

Consistency and Congruence

Every year, as summer comes to a close and a world of academics prepare for fall, social media pages are filled with lamentations about preparing syllabi that students never read, and the end of terms see the same kind of social media traffic about academics who are preparing to go on the defensive against students who want faculty to make exceptions for their inattention to details in the final days and hours of the course. However, there are many students who pore over every word—some who are trying to absorb the essence of the course and retrieve important details and others who are looking for loopholes of which they can take advantage. Your role as the instructor is to be as clear and detailed as possible, provide an experience that is congruent with what you have described, and be consistent with holding everyone, including yourself, accountable to what is described in the syllabus. Students are less engaged and committed to the classroom experience when an instructor communicates that a high value will be placed on student participation and then lectures the students for the majority of the in-class time. It is equally frustrating for students when they are unsure of their responsibilities for a course when, for example, a professor fails to make the distinctions between required and suggested assignments and rarely attends to or assesses the knowledge from the learning resources assigned.

Instructors have to consistently uphold the information in the syllabus and enforce the course requirements and expectations. We have found that the students who are often the most challenging are the students for whom you have made unjustified exceptions to your policies without extending them to all students. As the old adage appropriately states, "No good deed goes unpunished." Not holding students accountable to what has been described in the syllabus can essentially make the syllabus null and void in a student's mind. Instructors create challenges for themselves when they inconsistently hold students accountable to the expectations laid out in the syllabus, and it sets a tone for students that they will take to other courses. As administrators, we frequently have students protest one instructor's evaluation of scholarly writing because a previous instructor did not have the same level of accountability.

Clarity

In addition to being consistent and congruent, instructors need to provide as much clarity as possible about the expectations in a course. Later we will speak to the differences in this regard for the syllabi for online courses, but for all courses, it is important that all aspects are clear and easy to understand with the appropriate attention given to the details to the components of the syllabus like due dates, applicable time zones, and assignment and project requirements.

Here is an important caution though. No matter how much you have prepared, your syllabus will not be perfect and sometimes a student will find a loophole you did not intend. While you will encounter students who would rather take advantage of your human error in order to avoid following the path you have designed in order for them to meet the learning outcomes, your best approach is to give the student the benefit of the doubt and correct the problem in the future (Comer, 2016). Comer (2016) also recommends that faculty consider the dynamic nature of the syllabus and work with colleagues to uncover ambiguous areas in syllabi that might create problems later.

Preparing to Craft the Syllabus

In creating a syllabus, you must consider what you want to accomplish in each week of a course, the students' professional and academic development (Small, 2014), and students' prior learning. For master's courses, it is important that course activities foster critical thinking, while providing students with the foundational knowledge about the profession. Prior to creating the syllabus, you need to reflect on any institutional and department policies that will need to be included and be sure that you have the most up-to-date information for your institution. You will need to review any guidelines around the amount of work for the number of credit hours assigned to the course. You will need to determine if there are differences in expectations for credit hours for content courses, skill development courses, and field experience courses. In addition, you will need to review both the program assessment plan and the applicable CACREP standards. It is also advisable to create a checklist or template to ensure that you have all of the necessary components accounted for in your syllabus. Finally, you need to review logistics that will impact your course and how you will be accounted for in your syllabus. For instance, you should clearly state how and when you will be available to your students outside of the regularly scheduled class time and how quickly students can expect you to respond. In order to be sure that you will be available when you say you will, you will need to review other institutional activities and responsibilities that may impact your availability prior to creating your syllabus. Another logistical consideration is the course platform. The activities included in the syllabus should be reflective of thought about those instructional activities that work best in a particular platform. For example, we have found that managing group work in an asynchronous, online environment is very difficult for students, primarily because students find it difficult to convene for assignment planning and preparation. These are things you will have to consider before designing your syllabus.

The course should include activities that allow the adult learner to practice and experience what he or she is learning; to relate new learning to prior learning and experience; and to relay his or her expertise and knowledge (Small, 2014). The preparatory work allows you to create a vision of what you want the course to be for you and your students as both experts and learners.

Components of a Syllabus

Once you have done the pre-work for your syllabus, it is then time to start creating a draft syllabus that sets the tone for the class and models for the students the professionalism with which you expect them to present their work. Many institutions have a course template that includes all of the required elements of a course syllabus. In their template for a course syllabus, the Cornell University Center for Teaching Excellence (2016) includes the following elements for each course syllabus:

- course title
- term and year
- class location and meeting time

- instructor name and contact information
- the course grading scale
- schedule of course activities

In addition, they offer that each syllabus should include a rationale for the course that describes how the course fits with the rest of the curriculum (Cornell University Center for Teaching Excellence, 2016). They recommend that each course syllabus include the format and procedures, describing how the class will be implemented and what the expectations will be for each member of the course with regard to behavior like participation, attendance, open-mindedness, and respect. The syllabus should also clearly describe the platform for each aspect of the course (Cornell University Center for Teaching Excellence, 2016.) For courses in counselor education, it is advisable to include an expanded course description of the course, followed by a visual demonstration of the CACREP standards and program learning outcomes the course is designed to meet. The course requirements should be aligned with the learning outcomes, and it is important that the alignment is clear and valid for CACREP programs or programs intending to adhere to the CACREP requirements. In the previously referenced Section 2.D of the 2016 CACREP standards (CACREP, 2015), the accrediting body lists all of the required components of the syllabus that should be available to students and prospective students.

You can use your institution's template to start building your syllabus, being sure to customize it so that it is reflective of your teaching style. If your university does not have a template, we will review those components of a syllabus that we believe are critical to engaging learners and setting expectations for the course.

We suggest that every syllabus meets the requirements prescribed in the CACREP standards and includes an expanded course description, faculty expectations of the student, the faculty member's commitment to the student, university and course policies, course activities, and due dates. However, there are other things that will be discussed in these next sections that we believe increase student engagement and commitment.

Philosophy of Teaching

Your teaching philosophy is composed of your thoughts and theories on how students learn and your approach to facilitating the learning process (Caughlin, 2014). A clearly articulated teaching philosophy allows you to organize your comprehensive approach to teaching and allows you to select resources and instructional activities reflective of that philosophy. The teaching philosophy should describe your expectations of your students and your goals for their learning. It should also describe how you will facilitate learning. Your teaching philosophy should not be a static document, but should be dynamic and reflective your growth and development. Your stated teaching philosophy also allows you to consider student behaviors that detract from the learning process and prepare to respond to those. One of the most important aspects of a teaching philosophy is that it gives you an orientation and purpose to your teaching that guides your behavior in the learning process. By providing a teaching philosophy in the syllabus, a counselor educator is modeling the need for professional self-awareness and values to inform professional behavior much in the same way a professional attestation demonstrates that for a practicing counselor or supervisor. (Please see Chapter 2 of this textbook for more about the teaching philosophy.)

While it might be tempting for you to only rely on Dr. West's blueprint for the Research and Assessment course, you must determine how you want the course to be reflective of your teaching philosophy. Many times individuals include learning artifacts on a course syllabus to provoke thought around issues and topics they find engaging, but that may be very difficult for another faculty member to facilitate discussion.

Expanded Course Description

While the catalog course description allows students to decide if they want to take a course, the expanded course description should extend that description to give students an overview of the learning process they can expect in a particular course and how the specific course fits with the larger program of study designed to prepare them as professionals in their specific area of counseling. The expanded course description should also address prerequisite knowledge required for the course.

Attendance and Participation Policy

The course requirements sections should include the specifics about attendance and participation. It is advisable to specifically describe the quality of participation, as well. For example, most instructors want the students' comments and feedback to reflect preparation and critical analysis of the instructional materials. Instructors should be clear to note how students should prepare for each class session.

Instructional Materials

The syllabus should specifically describe any text, media, equipment, software, and electronic capabilities required for courses. It is also necessary to describe what materials will be required during class times. For example, will students need laptops, tablets, or mobile devices to access the Internet during class sessions? If electronic resources are reserved in the library for a course, it should be clear to students how to access those and any limits to access. Today, it is common for faculty to require students to review streamed video and audio and be available for synchronous telecommunication. It is important to specify any software, hardware, video, Internet, and telephone requirements in the course syllabus.

Grading

We would love it if all students enjoyed learning for learning's sake and grades did not matter. But because grades have traditionally been evidence of student learning, they remain necessary to the assessment and evaluation process. Your goal with the syllabus is to make sure that you have accurately described the grading criteria and rubric for each assignment and that you have described how each assignment will be weighted. Being clear about this allows students to understand how to manage their time and effort in the course.

Academic Integrity and Student Conduct

All students in a course are expected to adhere to institution's academic integrity and student conduct codes. It is crucial that you highlight the most important elements of these in the course syllabus and refer students directly to where both codes are located. We have found that there may be institutional differences in policies around academic integrity and there may be times when collaboration is allowed (Cornell University Center for Teaching Excellence, 2016), therefore the policies around academic integrity should be stated clearly and exceptions should be listed.

Accommodations for Persons With Disabilities

The Rehabilitation Act of 1973, the Section 504 Amendments to the act, and the American with Disabilities Act of 1990 (ADA) resulted in barriers being removed that limited access to higher education for students with disabilities. However, only 53% of students with disabilities complete their higher education degree or certificate in comparison to 64% of students with no disability. One of the challenges is that students with disabilities often do not avail themselves of the services designed to support them and impact their success. Both ADA and Section 504 make it illegal for faculty to refuse accommodations or question the necessity of accommodations (Tincani, 2004).

As educators, we should create an educational environment with reasonable accommodations aimed at helping students be successful in the course. Instructors can make accommodations in the course that have universal benefit. With regard to the syllabus, the instructor should make the syllabus accessible to all students and the syllabus should inform the students that the instructor will be available for private conversations to discuss the accommodations with each student with a disability (Tincani, 2004). However, the syllabus should advise students of their right to only disclose the nature of their disabilities to the office or agent responsible for supporting students with disabilities (Legal Roundup, 2015). This is usually a disabilities services office.

Other Academic and Student Support Resources

Graduate programs are designed to stretch students as scholars and practitioners. At the master's level, we want our students to critically evaluate evidence and research about best practices and determine when and how to apply it to support and individual, couple, or family. At the doctoral level, we want our students to be able to critically evaluate existing research and be able to fill the gaps in existing research by providing us with new information and evidence. At different points in a graduate program, when the challenges get high, students may experience the imposter syndrome—the general belief that they do not really deserve to be in a graduate program and they will eventually be found out as an imposter (Pishva, 2010). You can help students overcome the imposter syndrome by informing them of the academic resources at your institution designed to support them through their struggles. Providing them with a connection to these services allows them to see the use of services like the writing center, counseling services, and statistics support as an expected part of the graduate student experience.

Inclusiveness Statement

Important to the classroom experience is creating an environment where all students feel safe and respected. The inclusiveness statement should be an acknowledgement of students' diverse backgrounds and should promote respect and authenticity among and between peers. It should also encourage an intellectual exchange of ideas and experiences that allows students to gain a cognitive, professional, and interpersonal advantage from that diversity. The statement of inclusiveness should also set the expectations for behavior (University of Washington Center for Teaching and Learning, 2016) and contribute to students' self-awareness.

Class Schedule, Assignments Schedule, and Requirements

Many students head straight to the course assignments section when they receive the syllabus. It is crucial that this section is laid out with great care and detail. It should be written with students' perspectives and development in mind. The schedule should include the topic, learning resources, and assignments due for each class session (University of Washington Center for Teaching and Learning, 2016). Included in this large section should be the due dates of assignments and projects and examination days along with explicit criteria and rubrics for assignments and projects. Instructors should include details like due dates and times for a specific time zone and page lengths and formatting requirements for written assignments. It is important that you also communicate to students what your policies are for late submissions and make sure that your policies are aligned with your institution or graduate program's policies. As mentioned before, it is important that you consistently enforce the policies you have outlined in your course.

Additionally, it is important to communicate other logistics to your students as well. Clearly state when you will have office hours and describe the process for making an appointment. Also, inform students the timeframe within which they should expect a response to email or phone messages. Finally, be sure that students know when they should expect feedback on assignments. This is a very important feature of the syllabus and it will be important for you to describe a feedback timeline that is reasonable and accounts for both the course content and your other responsibilities. The concepts and competencies in assignments often build on one another; therefore, you want to be sure that your feedback can be incorporated in the next assignment. As you consider the key components of an effective syllabus, it is also important to think about how your students use this document to guide their work in your course. The next guided practice will ask you to reflect on your own experiences with course syllabi as a student.

Guided Practice Exercise 7.2

At this point, readers have seen their fair share of course syllabi. In reflecting on your academic history, what was it about a course syllabus that engaged you in a course? What could have been added to a course syllabus to increase your likelihood of success? How have previous course syllabi allowed you to collaborate and build relationships with your classmates and your instructor? The answers to these questions will allow you to create a syllabus that guides your counseling students through an engaging learning process.

Syllabi for Online Courses

Philosophically, there are very few differences in how the online course syllabus serves as a tool for student learning in comparison to the syllabus for the face-to-face, in-person course syllabus. There are, however, some considerations specifically for the online learning platform. Unlike the face-to-face environment, instructors in online classes rely very heavily on students' ability to understand course requirements through the reading material available to them. For that reason, online instructors have syllabi that are very information heavy. An emerging best practice in online learning is for instructors to employ videos or narrated presentation software like PowerPoint to guide students through difficult course content and the same strategy could be used for in-person courses. Whenever possible, synchronous teleconferenced course orientations could achieve even better results, allowing students the opportunity to ask clarifying questions.

Online courses, especially, require faculty to define technological resources like video and streaming capabilities and Internet speed on the syllabus. A very useful activity to outline on the syllabus is a requirement for students to test their technology at the beginning of the course so that they can make the appropriate adjustments if there are problems.

Technology continues to advance, and some of the activities that were challenges to online learning a decade ago are much less so today. For example, video streaming and teleconferencing are no longer the challenges they once were, and faculty are able to incorporate more engaging activities that employ new technology.

While you will be creating your own syllabi based on the guidelines of your institution, it can be helpful to review course syllabi and syllabi templates already created. Case Illustration 7.1 provides one such syllabi template for consideration.

Case Illustration 7.1

Example Syllabus Template

This section of the chapter looks at syllabus construction and important components. You will likely find, however, that different institutions, colleges, or even departments have some specific expectations for syllabus construction. For example, in this chapter we discussed the importance of including a teaching philosophy in your syllabus. Other factors impacting the structure of the syllabus and specific components can also include whether you are teaching in a CACREP accredited program or not and whether you are adhering to other accreditation guidelines (i.e., Council for the Accreditation of Education Professionals [CAEP], Higher Learning Commission [HLC]). Finally, whether the course is to be delivered online, hybrid, or face to face may also impact the specific components of the syllabus. There are several available resources that can offer guidance in the construction of your syllabus. The American Counseling Association (ACA) hosts on their website a joint syllabus clearinghouse with the Association for Counselor Education and Supervision (ACES). The syllabi available are organized by CACREP content area, and offer examples from several different faculty in several different counseling programs. This resource can be found at: www.counseling.org/knowledge-center/clearinghouses/syllabus-clearinghouse. Another resource is to use a syllabus template to organize the structure of your syllabus. Often, faculty, teaching, and learning centers at different universities provide supporting resources in developing syllabi. The template below is provided by North Dakota State University and includes links to relevant academic policies and considerations for distance education courses:

SYLLABUS TEMPLATE—MINIMUM REQUIRED INFORMATION

This template reflects NDSU Policy 331.1 Course Syllabus (www.ndsu.edu/fileadmin/policy/331_1.pdf). Please check your College policy for any additional elements required by your College. Syllabi requirements for **Distance & Continuing Education** courses can be found at www.ndsu.edu/dce/faculty_resources/forms_and_templates.

Basic Information

Course prefix, catalog number, and title:
Number of credits: (Note for faculty calculating credit hours: Using the Carnegie Unit system, one semester credit is equivalent to one lecture period [50 minutes] in class per week for one regular semester [15 weeks, not including final examination week]. A minimum of two 50-minute laboratory periods per week for one semester is equivalent to one credit [see bulletin.ndsu.edu/undergraduate/academic-policies/academic-credit].)

Term and year:
Instructor's name:

Office location:
Office hours:
Phone number:
Email address:

Bulletin Description

Description on syllabus must be consistent with the description listed in the current NDSU Bulletin (bulletin.ndsu.edu/course-catalog). Additional information may be included after the bulletin description.

Course Objectives

List the objectives, goals, aims, and/or outcomes for the course.

All General Education course syllabi and course websites must identify the course as having been approved for General Education and include the General Education category and outcomes. See General Education Syllabi Requirement (www.ndsu.edu/facultysenate/gened/syllabi).

For courses offered for both undergraduate and graduate credit, course objectives should be written to clearly define the increased expectations for graduate students in these courses.

Required Student Resources

List books, lab manuals, technology, supplies, calculators, and any other materials required or recommended for the student to complete the course requirements.

Course Schedule/Outline/Calendar of Events

Provide students with a tentative projected outline of significant events that occur throughout the semester, including assignments, projects, examinations, field trips, guest speakers, etc. *For example:*

Week	Topic	Reading /Assignment
1	Introductions; Role of Cultural Competence	Chapter 1
2	Cultural Self-Assessment	Chapter 2; Articles 1–4
3	Cultural Identity	Chapter 3; "White Like Me" due
4	EXAM #1	
5	Cross Cultural Communication	Chapter 4–5
etc.	Working with Interpreters	Article 4–6; Reflection Paper due

Note the NDSU Dead Week policy, which limits the amount and type of exams/quizzes that may be given during the last two weeks of the semester and identifies exceptions. See NDSU Policy 336: Examinations and Grading (www.ndsu.edu/fileadmin/policy/336.pdf).

Evaluation Procedures and Grading Criteria

Indicate how students are evaluated, including tests, quizzes, papers, assignments, weight of the assignments, etc. Clearly identify how the course grades are determined.

If a course is offered for both **undergraduate and graduate credit**, the additional requirements for graduate students must be clearly described on the syllabus. These courses require a significant, identifiable higher level of expectations for the performance of the graduate students.

Criteria for grading includes the grading scale used for the course. If points are earned, be sure the total number of points is correct and all points are accounted for in the grading scale. *See examples below:*

Ex.			Ex.		
Assignment "A"	50 points		A =	> 360 points
Assignment "B"	50 points		B =	320 to < 360 points
Mid-Term Exam	100 points		C =	280 to < 320 points
Final Exam	100 points		D =	240 to < 280 points
Total Points	400 points		F =	< 240 points

Ex.			Ex.		
Assignment "A"	20% of final grade		A =	> 90%
Assignment "B"	20% of final grade		B =	80 to < 90%
Mid-Term Exam	20% of final grade		C =	70 to < 80%
Final Exam	40% of final grade		D =	60 to < 70%
	100%		F =	< 60%

Attendance Statement

"According to NDSU Policy 333 (www.ndsu.edu/fileadmin/policy/333.pdf), attendance in classes is expected." The course instructor must clearly inform students on the first day of class and in writing in the syllabus of their (1) policy regarding class absence and (2) policy, if any, for making up missed assignments. If class attendance is a component of the course grade, the course instructor must clearly communicate this to the class in writing in the syllabus. See NDSU Policy 333 for faculty and student responsibilities related to attendance, including for university-sponsored activities.

Faculty are encouraged to provide the following statement on syllabi: "Veterans and student service members with special circumstances or who are activated are encouraged to notify the instructor as soon as possible and are encouraged to provide Activation Orders."

Americans with Disabilities Act for Students with Special Needs Statement

The following statement must appear on all syllabi: "Any students with disabilities or other special needs, who need special accommodations in this course, are invited to share these concerns or requests with the instructor and contact the Disability Services Office (www.ndsu.edu/disabilityservices) as soon as possible."

Approved Academic Honesty Statement

The following statement must appear on all syllabi: "The academic community is operated on the basis of honesty, integrity, and fair play. NDSU Policy 335: Code of Academic Responsibility and Conduct applies to cases in which cheating, plagiarism, or other academic misconduct have occurred in an instructional context. Students found guilty of academic misconduct are subject to penalties, up to and possibly including suspension and/or expulsion. Student academic misconduct records are maintained by the Office of Registration and Records. Informational resources about academic honesty for students and instructional staff members can be found at www.ndsu.edu/academichonesty."

In addition to the above, a statement of a college honor code, if applicable, should be included.

Syllabi on Web Pages

Syllabi presented on web pages shall contain the date of last update.

(Copied from: www.ndsu.edu/fileadmin/facultysenate/docs/syllabus-template.docx).

Summary

In many ways, curriculum development represents the starting point for effective course delivery. From identifying learning outcomes, to selecting materials and activities, to developing learning activities and assessments, to developing the course syllabus—all of these activities represent what you hope will create the optimal learning experience for your students. As with any exercise in course development, however, it is important to be prepared to learn from the "real world" experiences of you and your students as you actually deliver the course. Sometimes what looks and sounds good on paper does not always translate in the delivery. Paying attention to student and faculty workload, effectiveness of materials and activities, and the attainment of student learning as measured by designed assessments will be vital in your efforts to continue to improve your course. As discussed at the beginning of this chapter, there might be times that you do not have to reinvent the wheel. Using syllabi and course material from previously designed courses can provide a foundation for building your own course. Balancing using pre-existing materials with current and empirically based information is a key consideration, as outlined in Case Illustration 7.2.

Case Illustration 7.2

As the new faculty member for XYZ University, you have taken Dr. West's curriculum and syllabus as a framework for your Research and Assessment course and have taken it to your department chair for approval. The department chair, a former colleague of Dr. West, asks you to defend the choices you made that are different than what he has done. How do you defend your choices for changing and updating the course given that Dr. West's original course was viewed as "exemplary"? Consider the building blocks of your course and syllabus: CACREP standards, learning objectives, learning materials, and syllabus components, in your answer. Remember that one challenge of taking an existing course and modifying/updating it is that there can sometimes be resistance to change. What evidence and research can you provide that supports the need for the updates you've made?

Useful Websites and Other Resources

The following websites and other resources provide additional information relating to the chapter topics.

Association for Supervision and Curriculum Development (ASCD) Website. www.ascd.org/research-a-topic/differentiated-instruction-resources.aspx
  This association provides information and resources about developing and delivering innovative curriculum. While more focused on teaching in K–12 settings, it does have valuable information about differentiated learning in the construction of curriculum and learning materials.
American Counseling Association Syllabus Clearinghouse. www.counseling.org/knowledge-center/clearinghouses/syllabus-clearinghouse
  The ACA in partnership with ACES provides actual syllabi for counseling courses based on the eight core areas of CACREP.
Brigham Young University Center for Teaching and Learning. http://ctl.byu.edu/creating-syllabus

The Brigham Young University Center for Teaching and Learning has several resources that are helpful in the "Planning a Course" section of their website. This specific link provides you with tips and resources to assist you in developing a syllabus.

Chronicle of Higher Education ProfHacker: Teaching, Tech, and Productivity. www.chronicle.com/blogs/profhacker/tag/syllabus-design
This site is a collection of blogs from professors and instructors about various topics relating to syllabus development.

Cornell University Center for Teaching Excellence Website. www.cte.cornell.edu/teaching-ideas/designing-your-course/writing-a-syllabus.html#what
Resources for creating elements of an effective syllabus are provided.

Council for the Accreditation of Counseling and Related Educational Programs (CACREP) website. www.cacrep.org
2016 CACREP standards, policy documents, and accreditation information and procedures are provided on this website.

University of Washington Center for Teaching and Learning Website. www.washington.edu/teaching/teaching-resources/preparing-to-teach/designing-your-course-and syllabus/
The learning resource center at the University of Washington provides resources for developing and enhancing college-level curriculum and syllabi.

Yale Center for Teaching and Learning Website. http://ctl.yale.edu/teaching/ideas-teaching/diversity-classroom
This site provides several links to help instructors create an inclusive learning experience and includes links to other useful resources around diversity and inclusion in the classroom.

References

Akin, G. A. (2014). The term of andragogy and the difference between andragogy and pedagogy. *Journal of Faculty of Educational Sciences, 47*(1), 279–300.

Association for Supervision and Curriculum Development. (2015). *Differentiated instruction*. Retrieved from www.ascd.org/research-a-topic/differentiated-instruction-resources.aspx

Brigham Young University Center for Teaching and Learning. (n.d.). *If your syllabus were graded, would you pass?* Retrieved August 17, 2016, from Designing a Course Syllabus: A Learning-Centered Approach, http://ctl.byu.edu/sites/default/files/designing-a-course-syllabus_0.pdf

Caughlin, D. E. (2014). Enhancing your teaching experience: Developing your teaching philosophy, course syllabus, and teaching portfolio. *TIP: The Industrial-Organizational Psychologist, 52*(2), 94–99.

Cicco, G. (2012a). Counseling instruction in the online classroom: A survey of faculty and student perceptions. *i-manager's Journal on School Educational Technology, 8*(2), 1–10.

Cicco, G. (2012b). Strategic lesson planning in online courses: Suggestions for counselor educators. *Journal for School Educational Technology, 8*(3), 1–8.

Comer, A. R. (2016, July 27). The syllabus as a contract: How do you deal with clever students who find loopholes you didn't intend? *Chronicle of Higher Education*. Retrieved from http://chronicle.com

Cornell University Center for Teaching Excellence, 2012. (2016, April 14). *Writing a syllabus*. Retrieved August 13, 2016, from Writing a Syllabus, www.cte.cornell.edu/teaching-ideas/designing-your-course/writing-a-syllabus.html#what

Council for Accreditation of Counseling and Related Education Programs (CACREP, 2016). *Directory of programs*. Retrieved from www.cacrep.org/directory

Council for Accreditation of Counseling and Related Education Programs (CACREP, 2015). *2016 CACREP standards*. Retrieved from www.cacrep.org

Delaney-Klinger, K., Vanevenhoven, J., Wagner, R., & Chenoweth, J. (2014). Faculty transitions in online delivery: Make or buy? Tips for developing a "new to you" online course. *Journal of College Teaching & Learning, 11*(1), 45–52.

Felder, R. M., & Brent, R. (2007). How to prepare new courses while keeping your sanity. *Chemical Engineering Education, 41*(2), 121–122.

Fornaciari, C. J., & Lund Dean, K. (2014). The 21st-century syllabus: From pedagogy to andragogy. *Journal of Management Education, 38*(5), 701–723.

Granello, D. H. (2000). Encouraging the cognitive development of supervisees: Using Bloom's taxonomy in supervision. *Counselor Education and Supervision, 40*(1), 31–46.

Hrastinski, S. (2008). Asynchronous and synchronous e-learning. *Educause Quarterly, 4,* 51–55.

Legal Roundup. (2015). Policies and procedures: Revised policies, faculty training resolve noncompliance concerns. *Disability Compliance for Higher Education, 20*(10), 11–12. doi:10.1002/dhe

Ludwig, M. A., Bentz, A. E., & Fynewever, H. (2011). Your syllabus should set the stage for assessment for learning. *Journal of College Science Teaching, 40*(4), 20–23.

Meara, N. M., Schmidt, L. D., & Day, J. D. (1996). Principles and virtues: A foundation for ethical decisions, policies, and character. *The Counseling Psychologist, 24*(1), 4–77. http://dx.doi.org/10.1177/0011000096241002.

Opidee, J. (2014). College textbook forecast: Radical change ahead. *University Business.* Retrieved from www.universitybusiness.com/article/college-textbook-forecast-radical-change-ahead

Pishva, R. (2010, Summer). "Phew, I fooled 'em this time . . . but I may not be so lucky next time": The imposter syndrome among graduate students. *Psynopsis: Canada's Psychology Newspaper,* 35.

Pope, V. T., & Kline, W. B. (1999). The personal characteristics of effective counselors: What 10 experts think. *Psychological Reports, 84,* 1339–1344.

Rao, K., Edelen-Smith, P., & Wailehua, C. U. (2015). Universal design for online courses: Applying principles to pedagogy. *Open Learning, 30*(1), 35–52.

Redekop, F., & Wlazelak, B. (2010). Counselor dispositions: An added dimension for admissions decisions. Retrieved November 20, 2016 from www.counseling.org/docs/vistas/vistas_2012_article_17.pdf?sfvrsn=5

Small, D. (2014). Essay: Teaching adult students: Creating a syllabus. *International Forum of Teaching & Studies, 10*(2), 60–65.

Spurgeon, S. L., Gibbons, M. M., & Cochran, J. L. (2012). Creating personal dispositions for a professional counseling program. *Counseling & Values, 57*(1), 96–108. doi:10.1002/j.2161–007X.2012.00011.x

Tincani, M. (2004). Improving outcomes for college students with disabilities: Ten strategies for instructors. *College Teaching, 52*(4), 128.

University of Washington Center for Teaching and Learning. (2016). *Course and syllabus design*. Retrieved August 17, 2016, from Course and Syllabus Design, www.washington.edu/teaching/teaching-resources/preparing-to-teach/designing-your-course-and-syllabus/

Zaghab, R. W., & Beckenholdt, P. (2014). *Textbook-free learning: A framework for critical analysis*. Paper presented at the International Conference on eLearning, 190–199. Retrieved from http://search.proquest.com.ezp.waldenulibrary.org/docview/1545530948?accountid=14872

8 Evaluation of Student Learning
Instructor Feedback and Developmental Assessment

Kristi Cannon

Assessment is a two-fold process. The first element of appropriate assessment is the development of learning objectives based on a program's mission and goals (Bailie, Marion, & Whitfield, 2010). This is the driver of curriculum development and ensures assignments are created to appropriately meet the goals of the program, course, and weekly objectives. Chapters 6 and 7 provide a detailed overview of this side of the assessment process. The second part of assessment is the evaluation of performance relative to the established objectives or outcomes. Specifically, if an assignment is designed to meet a learning objective, the corresponding assessment should reflect an evaluation of the extent to which a student actually met the learning objective (Bailie et al., 2010). Further, aggregate performance of a student across the span of a course and program should be assessed to the extent that it reflects the goals of the course and overall program (Minton & Gibson, 2012). In this way we can effectively measure learning. To reach these goals faculty must first determine the appropriate evaluation methods for each assignment, develop the corresponding assessment instrument (where necessary), analyze the resulting data, and use that data to improve student and program performance (Bailie et al., 2010). The current chapter will orient you to this assessment process and your role in supporting assessment practices as a faculty member. Below you will find the specific learning objectives and CACREP standards that will be covered in the chapter material.

Learning Objectives

After reading this chapter, you will be able to:

1. Differentiate between formative and summative assessment.
2. Evaluate the impact of outcomes-based assessment practices on counselor education programs.
3. Synthesize the ACA ethical codes specific to assessment.
4. Analyze assessment methods specific to counselor education.
5. Develop analytic rubrics for use in the classroom.
6. Create assessment practices that support gatekeeping in counselor education.

CACREP Standards

6.B.3.a. roles and responsibilities related to educating counselors
6.B.3.b. pedagogy and teaching methods relevant to counselor education
6.B.3.d. instructional and curriculum design, delivery, and evaluation methods relevant to counselor education
6.B.3.f. screening, remediation, and gatekeeping functions relevant to teaching
6.B.3.g. assessment of learning
6.B.3.h. ethical and culturally relevant strategies used in counselor preparation

The Evolution of Assessment

Assessing student work and progress through a counseling program is paramount to the learning process. The combination of ongoing feedback and point-specific evaluation provides students the ability to self-assess, engage and re-engage with program material, and develop mastery of the specific knowledge, skills, and dispositions required of the program. Likewise, the assessment process affords faculty the ability to monitor their own teaching effectiveness and evaluate ways in which curriculum and overall program goals are appropriately aligned to student work and performance. In this way, assessment provides an excellent vehicle to evaluate both student and program level performance across time. When assessment processes are used effectively, a feedback loop is created, providing necessary information on individual student performance and support needs as well as ways in which faculty and programs can and should change to support those needs.

In order to best understand the current state of assessment in counselor education, it is important to understand some key concepts and their evolution across time. Let's start with the terms *assessment* and *evaluation*. It is not uncommon for these words to be used interchangeably in both practice and the larger research literature. In the context of student performance, the goal of both is the same: a process whereby the submitted work, skills, or disposition of the student is reviewed against expected performance goals. The differentiator is in how that information is ultimately used. More specifically, the term *assessment* frequently refers to a developmental process whereby student performance is evaluated as part of ongoing growth and advancement across time—student performance is evaluated and feedback from the evaluator is provided to help guide the student in modifying future performance (Andrade, 2007). The term *evaluation* is frequently used as to refer to a point of final review. That is, it reflects a summative appraisal of student performance at key points in time in order to reflect mastery of the necessary benchmark (Andrade, 2007). To this end, the term *assessment* is often used to reflect student formative assessment, while *evaluation* is used to reflect summative assessment experiences. And, while it is common to associate these terms with student-level performance, it is important to note that they can be, and increasingly are, used for program-level performance as well (Ewell, 2005).

The terms *formative* and *summative* assessment, much like *assessment* and *evaluation*, are complex and intertwined. These terms were first introduced by

Scriven (1967) in a paper on educational programs and curriculum development. For Scriven (1967), the term *summative evaluation* reflected the final evaluation of curriculum or a program, whereas *formative evaluation* was used to reflect the process of curriculum construction—the process of practicing and refining curriculum before the final summative evaluation. Bloom, Hastings, and Madaus (1971) took these concepts further and applied them to student learning. The term "evaluation" was swapped out for "assessment," but the key idea remained the same: *summative assessment* reflected the final evaluation of student performance at the end of a course or program, while *formative assessment* reflected the ongoing process of receiving and integrating feedback in order to remediate or improve (Bloom et al., 1971).

There have been significant differences in how to interpret formative and summative evaluation since these terms first came about, with much of the concern tied to which type of assessment is more important and which comes before the other in the overall assessment process (Lau, 2016; Taras, 2010; Taras & Davies, 2012). The general consensus among the newer lines of thought is that both assessment approaches hold value for student learning if the following conditions are met: (a) formative and summative assessment are connected to one another and to the overall learning process, (b) students are actively involved in their own learning process with a desire to improve, and (c) faculty and students work together in an active and involved relationship (Lau, 2016). By and large, the end goal is the same—whether it is assessment *for* learning (formative assessment) or assessment *of* learning (summative assessment) (Bennett, 2011; Taras & Davies, 2013), learning is the common denominator.

Finally, and perhaps equally important to the discussion of terminology in assessment, is an understanding of the evolution of assessment practices in higher education. When taken at face value, the assessment process and its outcomes-based benefits seem quite clear: students, faculty, and programs increase knowledge and understanding of performance and are able to make modifications that improve learning and overall output. However, this shift to data-driven results, particularly with regard to using student learning outcomes as a guide to overall student and program performance, has only evolved and been prioritized in the past few decades (Ewell, 2005; Urofsky & Bobby, 2012).

Within the United States, the movement toward evidence-based practices and learning outcomes driven assessment has most notably reflected in the evidence-based requirements for institutional accrediting bodies as well as those that support individual programmatic accreditation (Urofsky, 2013). The movement toward more stringent and outcomes-based assessment practices for accreditors is the trickle-down effect of increased pressure from the U.S. Department of Education (USDE) and the Council for Higher Education Accreditation (CHEA). CHEA, a non-profit and private membership organization of institutions of higher education, and the USDE, a department of the federal government, provide *recognition* to accrediting bodies, which is "the equivalent process to accreditation for accreditors" (Urofsky, 2013, p. 7). Both CHEA and the USDE have shifted their expectations of the accreditors they provide recognition to, due in large part to the evolving needs of higher education, a need for increased accountability by institutions and programs, a push for educational outcomes, and an overall attempt to prevent fraud (Urofsky, 2013). The final effect is that institutions of higher education and individual programs within those institutions are heeding the call for a systematic, data-driven, and comprehensive approach to student learning (Dwyer, Millett, & Payne, 2006). As you might imagine, this has had, and continues to have, a profound effect on how institutions and programs support students and evaluate the learning process—an impact that you will clearly see as you move through this chapter.

Assessment of Learning in Counselor Education

Now that you have some exposure to the history of assessment, it is important to look at the value of the assessment process, specific to the field of counselor education and supervision. Namely, how is assessment tied to ethical requirements and larger accreditation standards and what does this mean for the work you do as an instructor? Answering these questions will ultimately help prepare you to better understand your role as a counselor educator and help to facilitate the necessary "buy in" to the process of student and program level assessment practices that support overall student learning.

Requirements of American Counseling Association (ACA) Ethical Codes

When you think about the ACA Ethical Codes (2014), your first thought is likely not student-level assessment. That being said, hopefully your review of Chapter 3 has begun to shift your thinking about the ethical obligations you will soon hold as a counselor educator and supervisor. To that end, one of your key responsibilities as a professor will be that of student evaluator. The introduction to Section F of the ACA Code of Ethics (2014) speaks to the requirement for counselor educators and supervisors to "be fair, accurate, and honest in in their assessment of counselors, students, and supervisees" (p. 12). This early emphasis on evaluation highlights the important role you serve in supporting appropriate assessment practices and sets the stage for what is to come in Sections F.8, Student Welfare, and F.9, Evaluation and Remediation.

Primary to your responsibility as an ethical evaluator is the need to clearly communicate the assessment process during orientation (ACA, 2014, F.8.a; Foster & McAdams, 2009) as well as throughout the student's program of study (ACA, 2014, F.9.a). Doing so will foster the necessary transparency needed for students to understand on what elements they will be evaluated, when those evaluations will occur, and how those processes will take place. These ethical mandates help to support students in their preparedness for receiving feedback across the life of their program. They also highlight the fact that student assessment is not a solitary event. Truly evaluating student performance means assessing students across a variety of skills, dispositional requirements, and knowledge from the beginning through the end of their programs. Arming students with this information helps them to become active agents in their own learning and growth processes.

Another important assessment related code pertains to student limitations (ACA, 2014, F.9.b). Within this ethical code you will find your responsibility deepens, requiring you to not only observe and evaluate student performance, but to also provide the necessary remediation efforts and dismissal of the student, when deemed appropriate. There will be a larger discussion on gatekeeping responsibilities related to assessment later in the chapter. However, it is important to note the initial emphasis the ACA Ethical Codes put on this responsibility and the connection it has to the ongoing assessment practices you will engage in as a counselor educator and supervisor.

Requirements of Accrediting Bodies

While not all counselor education and supervision programs are accredited, it is important to reflect on the impact accrediting bodies have on the assessment process. The reason for this is that accreditation, both institutionally and programmatically, serves as a mechanism for providing quality assurance to the public (Eaton, 2015; Urofsky, 2013), which can have indirect effects on accredited and non-accredited programs, alike. Accreditation occurs through a vigorous self-study and peer review process whereby institutions seeking institutional accreditation and programs seeking programmatic accreditation, demonstrate adherence to a set of standards and policies established by the accrediting body (Eaton, 2015; Urofsky, 2013). This high level of internal and external scrutiny serves to ensure that a minimum set of standards are met and ultimately provide access to state and federal student loan funding (Eaton, 2015; Urofsky, 2013).

Beyond funding, accreditation at the program level, and with specific reference to field of counseling, is indirectly tied to licensure and portability. The Council for Accreditation of Counseling and Related Educational Programs (CACREP) serves as the specialized programmatic accreditor for entry- and doctoral-level counselor preparation programs. In large part, due to the public perception of quality associated with accredited programs, many states are now looking to CACREP as the guide for licensure requirements (Urofsky, 2013). Some states are actively seeking to mandate graduation from a CACREP-accredited program as a requirement for licensure, while many require graduation from a CACREP-equivalent program (Urofsky, 2013). In addition to licensure, this has an impact on the potential for portability of licenses. Currently, state license portability does not exist within the counseling profession—each state has its own licensing requirements and rules. However, there is a growing demand for licensure portability in order to facilitate moves and professional opportunities for licensed counselors (Mascari & Webber, 2013). To this end, CACREP accreditation is valuable because it provides a standardized set of requirements for programs and thereby offers some level of assurance as to having met curriculum requirements necessary for licensure in most states (Mascari & Webber, 2013; Urofsky, 2013).

So what does all of this have to do with assessment? Given the increased climate for outcomes-based performance data in higher education, accrediting bodies have taken note and modified their standards accordingly. Specific to counseling and CACREP, this evolution began in the 1988 version of the standards, which moved from a singular focus on individual student learning to learning within the broader context of the overall program (Urofsky & Bobby, 2012). With each new version of the published CACREP standards, there has been an increased emphasis on assessment and outcomes-based data reporting that has gotten us where we are today. The 2016 version of the CACREP standards now has a dedicated section to student and program-level assessment (Section 4), emphasizing the systematic assessment of students' skills, knowledge, and dispositions across time and using "multiple measures" (p. 17). This is coupled with a requirement for review of the data collected at both the program and student level and an emphasis on making data-driven decisions for remediation and program change (CACREP, 2015). This level of heightened requirement demonstrates a significant shift and evolution of assessment practices in counselor education, where we are now responsible for not only effectively teaching counselors and future counselor educators specific material, but we are also fully demonstrating that learning has actually occurred. Where it has not, the onus is now on us to make the necessary changes to do so.

Creating a Culture of Assessment as a Counselor Educator

Hopefully, what has become clear to you is the fact that assessment and accountability in higher education has increased over the past 30 years and resulted in potential gains for students and institutions (Ewell, 2005; Urofsky & Bobby, 2012). Even more important is the fact that this accountability requirement is now impacting the counseling profession and counselor education programs directly (Levitt & Janks, 2012; Minton & Gibson, 2012). Unfortunately, one of the significant challenges of developing a culture of assessment within a program can be getting the program faculty to "buy in" and actively support it. This is not because faculty do not value assessment practices or want to be involved in the assessment process, but often that they do not fully understand them (Ewell, 2005; Reddy & Andrade, 2010) or are not involved in the process of developing learning outcomes and therefore are not appropriately trained in their purpose and need (Ewell, 2005). As a result, it is important that counselor education programs not only work to develop strong and consistent assessment practices, but that they also engage faculty in that process and communicate with faculty on new developments and assessment needs in an ongoing capacity.

Evaluation Methods Relevant to Counselor Education

Counselor and counselor educator preparation is built on the development of learning outcomes specific to key skills, knowledge, and dispositions, and there are now a wide variety of programs and program types that support this learning. Regardless of the orientation of the program, assessment practices are important to effectively teaching and preparing the next batch of well-prepared counseling professionals. This is best achieved by providing students with a variety of learning experiences, offering opportunities for direct practice of learned concepts, and utilizing a mixture of assessments for student evaluation (Cicco, 2011; Tate, Bloom, Tassara, & Caperton, 2014). Within a student's program of study there are likely to be a variety of assessment tools used to meet this need. This next section focuses on some of the most commonly used evaluation methods in counselor education today.

A Developmental Approach to Assessment

It is important begin the discussion of counselor assessment with an understanding of the developmental process of counselor preparation. Due to the nature of the work we do in counselor training programs, there is a significant need to ensure appropriate development and preparation for the students we are graduating (ACA, 2014, F.9.b; CACREP, 2015, 4.F and 4.G). However, that ultimate preparation does not occur overnight or in a vacuum. The counseling profession is ever-evolving and the learning curve students face in a counselor preparation program can be quite steep. As a result, the assessments and assessment practices that are created to support student work should be developmental in nature (Hamlet & Burnes, 2013), allowing for the necessary balance of formative and summative assessment. This translates into a few fundamental requirements. First, students need to be provided ample opportunity to engage with the necessary concepts prior to assessment points (Cicco, 2011). Second, student performance should be assessed based on what the student has learned up to that point (Reicherzer et al., 2012). Finally, in courses such as skills and techniques courses, where the emphasis is on applied skill demonstration, there should be multiple opportunities for practice and feedback prior to any final summative evaluation (Cicco, 2011). When we provide the necessary exposure and supportive feedback to students along the continuum of their program of study, they have the best chance to succeed at graduating with the requisite skills and knowledge needed for the profession.

Knowledge-Based Assessment

Students are exposed to a wealth of material in the process of their training programs that they are expected to comprehend, synthesize, and retain as future counselors. Knowledge-based assessments afford us the opportunity to directly test understanding and retention of course-based curriculum at a variety of points and through various means. It can be formatively assessed through assignments such as written papers, reflection or journal assignments, and participation in classroom discussions. Here, the focus is on allowing students to synthesize course content and receive feedback for future evaluation. Content knowledge can also be assessed summatively. In cases where an instructor wants to evaluate the final comprehension of course material, quizzes, mid-term evaluations, final exams, and final projects can be used. The goal with summative evaluation of student course comprehension is to determine a baseline mastery of the course content prior to moving the student forward. To this end, final course grades also serve as a summative evaluation of content knowledge.

Many counseling programs also require comprehensive exams as the culminating summative evaluation process for content knowledge. The Counselor Preparation Comprehensive Exam (CPCE) is a standardized exit exam that is frequently used by counselor training programs for this purpose (Minton & Gibson, 2012). The National Counselor Exam (NCE) is another standardized exam frequently used in the counseling profession. Although it is national certification exam and therefore not used within programs for summative evaluation of students, it can be taken by students in CACREP-accredited programs while they are internship.

Additionally, many states use the NCE as the licensure exam. Counselor training programs, particularly those that are CACREP-accredited, frequently use NCE pass rate and testing data from their graduates to assist with program-level assessment (Minton & Gibson, 2012). This aggregate performance data can provide programs with key insights into the areas of curriculum strength and weakness and allow for necessary program changes.

Skills-Based Assessment

Some of the most significant assessments you will do of your future counseling students are of their skill performance. Skills assessments can take many forms and occur at a variety of points within a student's program of study (Hamlet & Burnes, 2013). Beginning with course-based assessments, you will find that counseling students are frequently assessed in skill and practice courses or techniques-oriented courses. These courses traditionally utilize live role-play demonstrations, video submissions of mock sessions, or a combination of both (Minton & Gibson, 2012). The assessment of these performance-based skills demonstrations is typically done through a rubric (Cicco, 2011; Tate et al., 2014). The rubric may be summative in that it evaluates specific skills that should be mastered at that given point in time, or formative, in that it provides initial feedback to students on skills criteria that will be evaluated again at a later point. Additionally, skills rubrics may standardized and used at multiple points in the program or they may be independent rubrics of specific skill sets required at various benchmarks.

Beyond skills-based courses, skills assessments are also commonly completed in the field experience courses. This is a natural place for student skill assessment and often reflects a more summative evaluation of overall skill development. Skills assessments completed in field experience often come from site supervisors who evaluate student performance on criteria established by the program. In addition to feedback from the site supervisor, many counselor education programs also include skills assessments by the field experience faculty member as well. Regardless of the evaluator, field experience skills assessments most often include the review of video or live client sessions and are evaluated on a corresponding rubric. These are frequently accompanied by an end-of-term evaluation that is completed by the site supervisor, faculty member, or both.

Dispositional Assessment

Formally evaluating student disposition is of great importance to counselor educators due to the ethical responsibility we hold as gatekeepers to the profession (ACA, 2014, F.6.b). Perhaps more so than knowledge or skills, this area of assessment is significant to determining a student's preparedness and fitness to enter the counseling profession. The challenge with dispositional assessment is that it is a bit more nebulous than skills or content-based knowledge. To truly and effectively assess disposition, a variety of assessments should be used and the assessment process should be carried out from the start to the end of a student's program (ACA, 2014, F.6.b; CACREP, 2015, 4.G; Kelly, 2011). Course-based assignments provide a good opportunity to begin evaluating student disposition. Here, you can use real-life scenarios that require students to face situations they are likely to find challenging, such as ethical or multicultural case dilemmas. Although course assignments are largely intended to assess content learning, these types of assignments have the potential to provide some indirect assessment of student makeup as well.

More formally, counselor education programs can use standardized assessments for evaluating student disposition (Tate et al., 2014). These come in a variety of forms, including checklists, inventories, and rubrics, and can reflect evaluation by faculty members, site supervisors, and the individual student. Regardless of the assessment format, it is important that student development assessments reflect behaviorally based criteria so that if an issue is noted, it can be effectively remediated.

Now that you have some exposure to the basic evaluation methods used in counselor education, it is important to start thinking about how you might use them when you are in your faculty role. Take a moment to look at Case Illustration 8.1 and ponder what your action steps would be in the example provided.

Case Illustration 8.1

Your counseling program has decided to seek CACREP accreditation; something it does not currently have. As a result, you and two of your fellow faculty members have been asked to help develop the comprehensive assessment plan for your program. At present, the program evaluates skill development at six key places: the techniques course, the group course, the prevention course, and in all three field experience courses. Additionally, content knowledge is assessed through a variety of course projects, final papers, and exams. However, there is no formal assessment of student disposition beyond basic oversight by faculty in the classroom. Given the need to address this CACREP requirement and in an attempt to strengthen your program's gatekeeping process, what assessment practices would you put in place to address student dispositional development?

Rubrics

One of the primary tools you will use to assess student progress, both formatively and summatively, is a rubric. Rubrics serve as scoring guides, comprised of required content and categories of achievement, which assist in evaluating performance on designated constructs. Rubrics can be either holistic or analytic (Popham, 1997). *Holistic* rubrics evaluate the performance or submitted work product as a whole rather than breaking it down into various categories (Reddy, 2011). They may include a variety of assessed areas, but the emphasis is in the overall performance score rather than any one contributing part. These types of rubrics are often used in a summative capacity or when large groups of students are evaluated at a single point in time, such as a benchmark performance assessment. In contrast, *analytic* rubrics allow for the scoring of individual components or categories of performance within the same rubric (Reddy, 2011). They provide for an aggregated final score, as do holistic rubrics; however, each evaluated component is scored separately so that students are allowed more detailed feedback on specific areas of strength and weakness that contributed to the overall score. To this end, analytic rubrics are often beneficial and frequently used in providing formative feedback to students (Reddy, 2011).

Regardless of type, rubrics provide substantial value to both students and faculty alike. For students, rubrics serve two key goals: (a) clarifying the purpose and requirements of an intended assignment or performance outcome (Andrade, 2005; Reddy & Andrade, 2010; Tractenberg, Umans, & McCarter, 2010; Taub, Servaty-Seib, Wachter Morris, Prietro-Welch, & Werden, 2011; Wyss, Freedman, & Siebert, 2014) and (b) providing students with detailed and specific feedback about areas of strength and weakness (Wyss et al., 2014). The first goal is an important one—students come into a counselor training program knowing they will be evaluated on specific criteria. However, what may not be clear is *how* that will occur. Rubrics afford students the necessary clarity for understanding initial expectations of their work as well as the opportunity to be active participants in their own achievement (Andrade, 2005; Minton & Gibson, 2012). To this end, students who utilize rubrics for this purpose can make determinations on what score they want to achieve through their submitted work or demonstrated performance and respond accordingly. Thus, as faculty, you will less likely encounter that all-too-common question of "How do I earn an A"? Additionally, when rubrics are used, students have been found to substantially increase assignment or course grades (Andrade, 2007; Reddy & Andrade, 2010; Wyss et al., 2014). The increase is directly related to students having the ability to determine the requirements at the outset and direct their own achievement in the process.

In the case of formative assessment, feedback provided by rubrics can assist students in self-assessing their own work and modifying performance on future tasks (Reddy & Andrade, 2010). Rubrics are designed as inherent vehicles of information on achievement of learning objectives. By reviewing scores within a rubric students are able to determine what areas they mastered and what areas show needed improvement. What cannot be guaranteed is that students will look at their rubric feedback in great detail or use that information to modify future performance. However, when students are informed of the assessment process and encouraged to use rubrics as a tool for self-assessment and growth, there is great potential for that improvement to take place (Andrade, 2005).

Much like students, faculty members stand to gain from the incorporation of rubrics in their curriculum design and assessment practices. When appropriately constructed, rubrics allow for a much more objective (Reddy & Andrade, 2010) and consistent (Taub et al., 2011) evaluation of student performance. The reason for this is that well-defined and descriptive rubrics provide clear guidelines as to what criteria should be evaluated and the extent to which performance at any given level meets those criteria. As a result, rubrics remove much of the "guesswork" from the grading process—grades are determined based on the extent to which performance met criteria within the designated performance level. This limits the opportunity for subjective bias on the part of the instructor and the potential to evaluate students against one another (*norm referencing*) rather than based on the criteria required (*criterion referencing*) (Reddy, 2011). This level of increased consistency and objectivity is true for the use of a rubric by the same instructor across time or students, as well as when multiple faculty or raters are using the rubric (Taub et al., 2011). One important caveat to mention is the importance of providing clarity and detail in the development of rubrics, along with training in the use of rubrics once they have been developed. These added steps help to ensure that faculty using the rubric will have a consistent understanding of how to interpret the categories and descriptors within the rubric itself.

While rubrics require some time investment on the front end (Andrade, 2005), they have the potential of providing an extensive amount of feedback to students in a condensed time frame when it comes to the grading process itself (Andrade, 2005; Reddy & Andrade, 2010). The reason for this is that the categories and descriptors have already been created through the rubric development process. When students review feedback from a rubric there is built-in clarity as to where points were gained and lost as well how their overall performance measured up against required criteria. This is certainly a benefit when it comes to initial feedback to students on performance, but it also has the added benefit of serving the instructor when it comes to the need to clarify or justify grades. Specifically, faculty can require the student to utilize the rubric prior to and in the process of contesting a grade or when questions of evaluation come into play (Wyss et al., 2014). By directing students to the rubric as the objective measuring tool, faculty can engage students in an enhanced self-assessment process whereby justification for a grade change is not only driven by the student but also reflects the objective criteria pre-established in the rubric. This does not mean that a faculty member will never make errors with the use of rubrics; however, it does offer another opportunity for students to serve as active participants in their own learning process. It also emphasizes the need to remain consistent in the interpretation of the rubric categories and descriptors for all students being evaluated.

One final benefit rubrics provide to faculty is the potential for more detailed feedback about areas of curriculum that are effectively covered or may need to be enhanced (Reddy, 2011). Just as students can use rubric evaluations to determine the strength of their performance on the evaluated content, so can faculty determine the extent to which their developed curriculum and teaching helped students to achieve mastery of that content. For example, if multiple students demonstrate poor overall performance relative to the application of the ACA Code of Ethics on a required case study assignment, it may mean that this material was not sufficiently covered in the course resources or by the instructor. By assessing the aggregate performance of students with rubrics, faculty are provided with a heightened level of visibility into their own instruction processes. To this end, they are then able to make necessary adjustments to curriculum or teaching practices to better meet the learning needs of their students.

Rubric Development

There are many ways to construct rubrics, depending on the purpose and level of specificity desired by the creator. Rubric development begins with a strong understanding of learning objectives to be measured and how those can be effectively measured through the rubric itself (Bailie et al., 2010). This is a key point, because without a clear end-goal, rubrics hold no real value. Once the purpose of the rubric has been established, the process of developing the actual rubric can begin. Most rubrics contain three key elements: (a) evaluation criteria, (b) performance categories and (c) a corresponding scoring metric (Reddy & Andrade, 2010; Popham, 1997). The detail associated with each element is fluid, but the basic structure is the same.

Pulling from the learning objectives, the first step in rubric design is to develop the evaluation criteria so that they align with the intended goal of the rubric (Popham, 1997; Suskie, 2009). Within this step you will determine what criteria are necessary for inclusion in the rubric in order to meet the predetermined learning objectives. As noted earlier, this step is important to providing clarity and specificity for the student who is being evaluated and for the faculty member who will be completing the evaluation (Reddy, 2011). As you work through identifying these criteria, it is important to hone in on the most critical and salient elements of the learning objectives. This will ensure that criteria speak directly to the performance requirements but are not overly cumbersome for grading or confusing for students (Suskie, 2009). One other important consideration is to include criteria that can be taught (Popham, 1997). If the goal of the rubric is to demonstrate mastery of learning, it is important that the rubric reflect material that is teachable and that students have been exposed to. Doing so ensures accurate evaluation of the learning and provides opportunities for material that has been missed to be re-learned.

The next step involves the development of the performance categories (Popham, 1997; Suskie, 2009). These categories serve as the varied levels of performance students can achieve on each of the evaluation criteria. There is no set number of categories required within a rubric, relative to performance criteria. However, it is typically recommended that rubrics include between three and five performance categories (Popham, 1997; Suskie, 2009). This will ensure that there is enough variability between categories to assess meaningful differences in performance levels, while not so much that it becomes overly prescriptive or difficult to parse out more nuanced differences (Bailie et al., 2010; Suskie, 2009). In addition to selecting an appropriate number of performance categories, it is important to develop categories based on behaviors that can be observed (Popham, 1997). This helps to maintain an increased level of objectivity, while keeping the focus on demonstration of content, skill, or dispositional mastery. Finally, when developing performance categories, it is also helpful to begin with the highest level a student might achieve (Bailie et al., 2010), followed by the lowest (Tractenberg et al., 2010). Doing so clarifies the upper and lower limits of expected performance and can then aid in fleshing out the categories that fall in between.

Once the actual categories have been established, the next step involves developing the descriptors associated with those categories (Bailie et al., 2010). This is the detailed narrative information that reflects what must be included in the performance of the student in order for that category to be achieved (Reddy, 2011). When developing this material, it is important to be detailed and meaningful—effectively spelling out what is required of students will help them understand initial expectations as well as where they may have fallen short once an evaluation has been completed. To this end, the language should be clear and understandable for students (Reddy, 2011). It should not be too complex or too long, which can result in rubrics that are unwieldy, or so specific that performance variability cannot be effectively captured. On the flip side, performance descriptors should not be too broad or ambiguous such that the category descriptions hold no real meaning (Reddy, 2011). When completed, the category descriptors should make it clear for both students and faculty what performance is aligned with the designated performance category.

The final step of the rubric development process involves assigning a scoring metric to the categories (Popham, 1997). Scoring metrics can be relatively straightforward or quite complex to determine, depending on the goal of the rubric. This process begins by determining if performance is to be evaluated holistically, meaning all performance criteria are aggregated into a total score (less complicated), or analytically, meaning each criteria will be evaluated and scored individually (more complicated) (Popham, 1997). Assuming an analytic approach is chosen, the next step in development would be to consider weights between evaluation categories. For example, if an analytic rubric was designed to assess a student's written assignment, there might be four evaluation criteria. Depending on the emphasis of each criterion, you could make it so that they were of equal weight, accounting for 25% of the overall grade, each. Or, you could determine that categories one and two required were more significant learning objectives and should each be weighted at 30% apiece, leaving the final two categories at 20% each. The second step of this process is to then determine the associated value of each of the performance categories. Again, these categories can be of equal value or different and can be point-based (e.g. 1, 2, 3, 4), range-based (e.g. 0–1, 2–3, 4–5, 6–7), or even percentage-based (e.g. 25%, 50%, 75%, 100%). The final scoring metric is the resulting marriage between the evaluation categories and the performance categories, and should ultimately reflect the overall point values you want associated with an assignment.

Table 8.1 provides an example analytic rubric I developed to evaluate performance on a written assignment for a diagnosis and assessment case vignette. The evaluation criteria are listed down the left-hand column, while the performance categories are listed horizontally across the top. The detailed descriptors of the performance categories are included within each column. This particular example illustrates a scoring metric reflective of different weights for the evaluation criteria. You will note that the first and second categories were considered more significant to the assignment, and therefore the point values for those rows are of higher value than the two following. Another consideration made to the development of this rubric was the translation of performance category point totals to the final grade. Specifically, because my second performance category was determined to be "satisfactory" and the criteria within that column were written to reflect students having met the minimum requirement or baseline mastery of the learning objective, I wanted to ensure that the points they received would correspond to what I believed to be an appropriate grade for a satisfactory response. In this case, it was 80%. You will note that, regardless of the weight of the evaluation category, the satisfactory column minimum point allocation always reflects 80% (i.e. 8/10 = 80% and 4/5 = 80%). In order to achieve my goal of weighted evaluation criteria and the 80% threshold, I did have to use point ranges. This is not always optimal, as it can pose challenges in cleanly determining a score. However, it is sometimes necessary, depending on the needs of the rubric developer.

Table 8.1 Example Rubric for a Diagnosis and Assessment Case Vignette

Criteria	Exemplary	Satisfactory	Progressing	Emerging	Score
Assessment Explain the family and social issues that might be significant to the diagnosis of the client	Student provided a detailed and accurate outline of all of the family and social issues impacting the case. 8–10 points	Student provided a detailed and accurate outline of the primary social issues impacting the case. 6–7 points	Student provided an outline of some of the family and social issues impacting the case; however, many were missed, lacking in detail, and/or were inaccurate. 2–5 points	Student did not provide an outline of the family and social issues impacting the case OR was fully inaccurate in what was submitted. 0–1 points	/10
Diagnosis Construct and explain your diagnosis. Provide specific supporting information from the DSM and include necessary specifiers.	Student provided an accurate DSM diagnosis for the case, reflecting necessary specifiers and a detailed explanation of the chosen diagnosis. 8–10 points	Student provided an accurate DSM diagnosis, but did not include necessary specifiers and/or the explanation of the chosen diagnosis lacked detail. 6–7 points	Student did not provide an accurate DSM diagnosis for the case but did include necessary specifiers and an explanation of the chosen diagnosis. 2–5 points	Student did not provide an accurate DSM diagnosis for the case and did not provide a detailed explanation of the chosen diagnosis. 0–1 points	/10
Intervention Describe the interventions you would recommend and explain why you would make these recommendations.	Student provided detailed and accurate interventions for the client supported by a strong rationale for doing so. 5 points	Student provided detailed and accurate interventions for the client but the rationale for doing so was somewhat lacking. 4 points	Student provided interventions for the client; however, they were inaccurate or the rationale for the interventions was limited. 2–3 points	Student did not provide interventions for the client OR what was submitted was both inaccurate and lacking in rationale. 0–1 point	/5

| Cultural Biases
Describe any difficulties you might have in assessing or diagnosing this individual, and any cultural factors or biases you might have that would contribute to making this a challenging case for you to assess, diagnosis, and provide counseling. | Student provided thoughtful and detailed response to potential biases, reflecting on personal cultural background and the direct implications for the assessment, diagnosis, and counseling of the client.
5 points | Student provided thoughtful and detailed responses to potential biases, reflecting on personal cultural background and the direct implications for assessment, diagnosis, or counseling of the client, but not all three.
4 points | Student provided a response to potential biases; however, the response lacked in detail or personal cultural reflection OR did not address the direct implications for the assessment, diagnosis, and counseling of the client.
2–3 points | Student did not provide a response to potential biases OR what was submitted lacked in personal cultural reflection and detail and did not address the direct implications for the assessment, diagnosis, and counseling of the client.
0–1 point | /5 |
|---|---|---|---|---|---|
| Total Score | | | | | /30 |

Reliability and Validity of Rubrics

A noted challenge of rubric development is in creating ones that are both reliable and valid (Reddy, 2011). Rubrics that are reliable demonstrate consistency in rating across time by the same evaluator (*intra-rater reliability*) and between evaluators (*inter-rater reliability*) (Reddy, 2011; Reddy & Andrade, 2010). Intra-rater reliability is important when a single faculty member is assessing students on performance within the same term or even from term to term. More specifically, is the faculty member consistently evaluating student performance of the same caliber on the same level within the same cohort group and across cohort groups? Inter-rater reliability is also significantly important to the assessment process, particularly in counselor education. The reason for this is that often students are assessed on skill and dispositional dimensions across time and by various faculty members. Having a rubric that has high inter-rater reliability will result in consistent scores, regardless of who is doing the evaluating.

Valid rubrics are those that are well founded and meaningful (Reddy, 2011). Validity encapsulates reliability—you cannot have a valid rubric that is not also consistent. However, it goes beyond a level of consistency to ensure that the fundamental goal of the rubric is being achieved. There three types of validity that are important to rubric development: content, criterion, and construct. *Content validity* refers to the extent to which the evaluation criteria fully address the learning objective or objectives (constructs) of the assignment (Reddy, 2011). *Criterion validity* refers to the extent to which the criteria effectively measure an outcome (Reddy, 2011). In many cases, criterion validity is used for predictive purposes—can the scores on a given rubric predict future performance? Finally, there is *construct validity*, which refers to the extent to which a rubric actually measures what it is intending to measure (Reddy, 2011).

One way to ensure reliability and validity or rubrics as assessment tools is to gather initial feedback during and following the development process (Chow, Ko, Li, & Zhou, 2012; Reddy, 2011). How effectively are the criteria defined? Do the rubrics demonstrate the potential to measure what is intended to be measured? Gathering this initial feedback from fellow faculty as well as students provides an increased potential for achieving rubric intra-rater reliability and validity (Andrade, 2005; Reddy, 2011). For rubrics that will be used by multiple reviewers, the next step to ensuring inter-reliability is to sufficiently train faculty in the interpretation of the rubric categories and criteria (Minton & Gibson, 2012). This requires that faculty have preliminary discussions about how the descriptors are to be interpreted and is often best achieved through the practice of scoring sample work across faculty (Reddy, 2011). In this process, you should look for inter-rater reliability of 70% or higher (Reddy & Andrade, 2010).

Beyond standard reliability and validity, it is also important to account for accuracy across applications of diverse students. More specifically, rubrics must be evaluated to ensure they are equally and appropriately applied across students of all races, ethnicities, socioeconomic statuses, ability levels, and the gender continuum (Andrade, 2005). This is yet another reason to seek consultation from colleagues and students prior to using a rubric in practice. In addition to this, it is a good idea to consult published standards on any topic you plan to incorporate into a rubric (Andrade, 2005). While not fail-safe, consulting the literature has the potential of not only enhancing your rubric content, but also helping to ensure your constructs are consistent and equitably applied. A good rubric should provide a strong, consistent, and objective measure of observable criteria, regardless of whose performance is being evaluated.

Using Rubrics in Practice

One thing to keep in mind is that even well-developed rubrics hold little real value if they are not implemented correctly. This means faculty need to use them in accordance with the intention of the assessment process. However, this also means faculty need to ensure they are communicating the role and purpose rubrics serve (Chow et al., 2012). Students benefit not only from being exposed to rubrics ahead of the assessment point, but also taught how to actively use the rubric to guide and assess their own work (Reddy & Andrade, 2010). When this occurs, students are allowed the opportunity to be active agents in their own learning process and the benefits noted above can be achieved.

Now that you have been exposed the finer points of rubrics and rubric development, it is time to practice! Using the information provided in Guided Practice Exercise 8.1, develop an analytic rubric that can be used to assess student performance on the example assignment.

Guided Practice Exercise 8.1

Imagine that you have been asked to teach a Child and Adolescent Development course. The learning objectives for the week are to:

- Evaluate how culture, gender, or social factors might influence the development and persistence of an adjustment issue in children and adolescents.
- Evaluate how the adjustment issue might manifest in children and adolescents.
- Develop an evidence-based intervention for the adjustment issue of an example case vignette.

Using the steps outlined in the section above, develop an analytic rubric for the case vignette assignment that includes four evaluation criteria and three performance criteria. Consider that this is a written assignment and an additional evaluation category is writing quality. For practices purposes, assume that all four evaluation criteria hold equal weight, and develop a corresponding scoring metric for your rubric.

Once you have had the opportunity to construct your rubric, reflect on the development process. What steps did you find most challenging to complete? What value do you think having a rubric like this might provide to you and your students? And finally, what next steps might you take after this one to ensure reliability and validity of your rubric?

Assessment for the Purposes of Screening, Remediating, and Gatekeeping

Gatekeeping is not only good practice in counselor training, but an ethical requirement as well (ACA, 2014). Counselors and counselor educators work with people, not widgets, and the potential impact of this working relationship is significant. As faculty, we have to understand this significance and we have to be prepared to execute our gatekeeping responsibility. Assessment is a key part of this. As the section in the earlier part of this chapter alluded to, counselor educators and supervisors have to be up front about the assessment process and communicate this to students at orientation and throughout the program (ACA, 2014, F.8.a, F.9.a). This is the relatively easy part. The harder part of the ethical codes tied to assessment is the part requiring necessary remediation and, at times, student dismissal (ACA, 2014, F.9.b). This ethical mandate requires us to be ready and willing to have the tough conversations and take the necessary steps with students when performance in skills, knowledge, or disposition is lacking.

Assessment practices assist in this effort by serving as screening tools for the work we do with students. Whether in classroom assignments, on skill demonstrations, or in the overall dispositional assessment we do of students, these measures of student performance give us objective information about the abilities of students that allow us to make data driven decisions to support the student and the profession. When it comes to identifying student deficiencies and supporting remediation efforts, this is vital (Swank & Lambie, 2012). By setting benchmarks, facilitating student support through feedback and remediation, and regularly communicating about student progress, counselor preparation programs can establish a framework to assist with the gatekeeping process (Kelly, 2011; Lumadue & Duffey, 1999) This not only assists us to ensure student preparedness for the profession, but also serves to model the importance of assessment practices and the ethical and professional requirements of counselors and counselor educators to students (Foster & McAdams, 2009). This is an important message and part of overall professional development.

While it can certainly be the case that students struggle with coursework or demonstrate performance concerns in skills or dispositions in a typical classroom setting, gatekeeping issues tend to present themselves most often and be of most concern when students are in active practice, such as field experience courses where the potential for skills and interpersonal issues are at their height. To this end, faculty teaching clinically based or applied skills-based courses need to be particularly aware of their gatekeeping responsibility and efforts to ensure student fitness for the profession when completing student assessments (Foster & McAdams, 2009).

Considerations for Resistant Students

While there is inherent value in the assessment process for students, it is not uncommon for students to resist the idea of being evaluated or otherwise find it to be an anxiety-provoking experience. One of the most important ways faculty can avoid this type of resistance or anxiety is to promote a high level of transparency in the assessment process itself. Early and regular communication with students on assessment practices and consistently applying those practices across all students is important (Foster & McAdams, 2009). This includes sharing with students the rubrics and other assessment measures that will be used to evaluate them in advance (Chow et al., 2012; Cicco, 2011) as well as providing a dialogue about assessment practices at regular intervals in a student's program of study (Foster & McAdams, 2009). Doing so fosters necessary trust between students and faculty and helps students to develop an understanding of the necessary gatekeeping role required of counselors and counselor educators (Foster & McAdams, 2009). To this end, students can begin to see assessment practices as not only a way to gauge individual performance, but also as a larger part of the counselor development process and good ethical practice.

Another valuable way to both minimize student resistance is to work directly with students on the co-creation of rubrics (Reddy & Andrade, 2010) or other assessment practices. This not only fosters transparency in the assessment process, but provides an enhanced opportunity for "buy in" by students who now have a voice in their own assessment process (Andrade, 2007; Reddy & Andrade, 2010). When co-creation is not an option, you may want to allow for an ungraded peer review process on early drafts of projects, assignments, or skill demonstrations (Andrade, 2005; Cicco, 2011; Swank & Lambie, 2012). This allows for direct feedback that is both meaningful and objective, without the consequence of a final grade. Either approach provides opportunities for students to communicate with you about their experiences, needs, and opinions of the assessment process. This type of "bottom-up" communication helps faculty to see the assessment process through the eyes of the students and provides opportunities for increased trust between students and faculty (Foster & McAdams, 2009, p. 276).

Finally, when remediation efforts are needed, it is important to frame them from a positive perspective—as one of support and an opportunity for student improvement rather than an independent student critique (Foster & McAdams, 2009). Students are often self-conscious about their performance in counselor training programs and can personalize assessment results and feedback as an attack. As a result, it is our job as faculty members to help them understand the assessment results and normalize the process of receiving feedback. During these times that is helpful to have an established framework for gatekeeping and remediation it allows you to support students in a proactive and positive way (Kelly, 2011).

It is, once again, time to give you some practice putting your new knowledge to the test. Utilizing the information above, determine how you might best approach the student situation provided in Case Illustration 8.2.

Case Illustration 8.2

Lala is in your group counseling course. She is a very strong student, academically, but is, admittedly reserved and introverted and struggles with performance anxiety when she is working on skills demonstrations. As part of the group course, she is required to role-play a group member

> as well as help facilitate the group in her designated week. She has come to you noting that she fears she will never be able to complete the course knowing that she will be evaluated in this way. After first normalizing the anxiety she is feeling, what types of formative assessment might you put into place to assist Lala (and her peers) in developing the requisite skills for her final evaluation as the group facilitator?

Summary

The landscape in higher education has changed substantially over the last three decades, with an increasing demand for outcomes-based assessment and data-driven results taking center stage. The emphasis on assessment has significant meaning for counselor preparation programs, both programmatically as well as for the students they serve. In particular, counselor educators are now being charged with developing a culture of assessment to support best practices in teaching, overall student learning, and program performance. At the heart of this process is an effort to use formative and summative feedback measures to facilitate the developmental process of counseling students in the key areas of knowledge, skills, and student disposition.

There are a variety of assessment tools and measures available to counselor educators to support this effort, regardless of the program in which they teach. Among the most popular are course-based assignments, exams, skill demonstrations, and standardized assessments. Rubrics are frequently used as a part of the evaluation processes for course-based assignments as well as skills and dispositional assessments, and hold significant value for faculty and students alike. The development of rubrics involves a multi-step process of creating evaluation criteria, determining performance criteria, and establishing a scoring metric. The end-result is an assessment instrument that can be used to provide both formative and summative feedback, depending on the design and need.

It is important that counselor education programs have an assessment plan that is clearly communicated to students in the orientation process and throughout the student's program of study. Doing so facilitates students' awareness of the assessment process and allows them to be actively involved in their own growth and development. Additionally, counselor educators have an ethical obligation to serve as gatekeepers in the profession. Assessments and assessment plans support faculty and programs in screening for student issues as well as supporting remediation efforts. Ultimately, faculty can best support students in understanding the assessment process by regularly engaging them in assessment practices and maintaining transparency along the way.

Useful Websites

The following websites provide additional information relating to the chapter topics.

The Association for Assessment of Learning in Higher Education. www.aalhe.org/

National Institute for Learning Outcomes Assessment. www.learningoutcomesassessment.org/

University of West Florida Rubric Development. http://uwf.edu/offices/cutla/supporting-pages/rubric-development/

Additional Resources

The following resources provide additional information relating to the chapter topics.

Black, P., & William, D. (1998). Assessment and classroom learning. *Assessment in Education, 5*(1), 7–74. doi:10.1080/0969595980050102

Dixson, D. D., & Worrell, F. C. (2016). Formative and summative assessment in the classroom. *Theory into Practice, 55*(2), 153–159. doi:10.1080/00405841.2016.1148989

Haberstroh, S., Duffey, T., Marble, E., & Ivers, N. N. (2014). Assessing student-learning outcomes within a counselor education program: Philosophy, policy, and praxis. *Counseling Outcome Research and Evaluation, 5*(1), 28–38. doi:10.1177/2150137814527756

Perera-Diltz, D., & Moe, J. (2014). Formative and summative assessment in online education. *Journal of Research in Innovative Teaching, 7*(1), 130–142.

Suskie, L. (2009). *Assessing student learning: A common sense guide* (2nd ed.). San Francisco, CA: Wiley.

Taras, M. (2010). Assessment—summative and formative—some theoretical reflections. *British Journal of Educational Studies, 53*(4), 466–478. doi:10.1111/j.1467-8527.2005.00307.x

References

American Counseling Association. (2014). *ACA code of ethics*. Alexandria, VA: Author.

Andrade, H. G. (2005). Teaching with rubrics: The good, the bad, and the ugly. *College Teaching, 53*(1), 27–30. doi:10.3200/CTCH.53.1.27-31

Andrade, H. (2007). Self-assessment through rubrics. *Educational Leadership, 65*(4), 60–63.

Bailie, F., Marion, B., & Whitfield, D. (2010). How rubrics that measure outcomes can complete the assessment loop. *Journal of Computing Sciences in Colleges, 25*(6), 15–25.

Bennett, R. E. (2011). Formative assessment: A critical review. *Assessment in Education: Principles, Policy & Practice, 18*(1), 5–25. doi:10.1080/0969594X.2010.513678

Bloom, B. S., Hastings, J. T., & Madaus, G. F. (1971). *Handbook on formative and summative evaluation of student learning*. New York, NY: McGraw-Hill.

Chow, T., Ko, E., Li, C., & Zhou, C. (2012, August). *The systematic development of rubrics in assessing engineering learning outcomes*. Paper presented at the IEEE International Conference on Teaching, Assessment, and Learning for Engineering (TALE), Hong Kong.

Cicco, G. (2011). Assessment in online courses: How are counseling skills evaluated? *i-manager's Journal of Educational Technology, 8*(2), 9–15.

Council for Accreditation of Counseling and Related Educational Programs [CACREP]. (2015). *2016 standards for accreditation*. Alexandria, VA: Author.

Dwyer, C. A., Millett, C. M., & Payne, D. G. (2006). *A culture of evidence: Postsecondary assessment and learning outcomes. Recommendations to policymakers and the higher education community*. Princeton, NJ: Educational Testing Service.

Eaton, J. S. (2015). *An overview of U.S. accreditation*. Washington, DC: Council for Higher Education Accreditation.

Ewell, P. (2005). *Applying learning outcomes concepts to higher education: An overview prepared for the Hong Kong University Grants Committee*. Retrieved from www.ied.edu.hk/obl/files/OBA_2nd_report.pdf

Foster, V. A., & McAdams III, C. R. (2009). A framework for creating a climate of transparency for professional performance assessment: Fostering student investment in gatekeeping. *Counselor Education & Supervision, 48*(4), 271–284. doi:10.1002/j.1556- 6978.2009.tb00080.x

Hamlet, H. S., & Burnes, T. (2013). Professional school counseling internship: Developmental assessment of counseling skills (CIDACS). *Counseling Outcome Research, 4*(1), 55–71. doi:10.1177/2150137812472196

Kelly, V. A. (2011). Assessing individual student progress: Meeting multiple accreditation standards and professional gatekeeping responsibilities. *Journal of Counselor Preparation and Supervision, 3*(2), 110–122.

Lau, A. M. S. (2016). Formative good, summative bad?—A review of the dichotomy in assessment literature. *Journal of Further and Higher Education, 40*(4), 509–525. doi:10.1080/0309877X.2014.984600

Levitt, D. H., & Janks, F. A. (2012). Outcome-based assessment in counselor education: A proposed model for new standards. *Counseling Outcome Research and Evaluation, 3*(2). 92–103.

Lumadue, C. A., & Duffey, T. H. (1999). The role of graduate programs as gatekeepers: A model for evaluating student counselor competence. *Counselor Education & Supervision, 39*(2), 101–109. doi:10.1002/j.1556–6978.1999.tb01221.x

Mascari, J. B., & Webber, J. (2013). CACREP accreditation: A solution to license portability and counselor identity problems. *Journal of Counseling & Development, 91*(1), 15–25. doi:10.1002/j.1556–6676.2013.00066.x

Minton, C. A., & Gibson, D. M. (2012). Evaluating student learning outcomes in counselor education: Recommendations and process considerations. *Counseling Outcome Research and Evaluation, 3*(2), 73–91. doi:10.1177/2150137812452561

Popham, W. J. (1997). What's wrong—and what's right—with rubrics. *Educational Leadership, 55*(2), 72–75.

Reddy, M. Y. (2011). Design and development of rubrics to improve assessment outcomes: A pilot study in a master's level business program in India. *Quality Assurance in Education, 19*(1), 84–104. doi:10.1108/09684881111107771

Reddy, M. Y., & Andrade, H. (2010). A review of rubric use in higher education. *Assessment & Evaluation in Higher Education, 35*(4), 435–448. doi:10.1080/02602930902862859

Reicherzer, S., Coker, K., Rush-Wilson, T., Buckley, M., Cannon, K., Harris, S., & Jorissen, S. (2012). Assessing clinical mental health counseling skills and practice standards in distance education. *Counseling Outcome Research and Evaluation, 3*(2), 104–115. doi:10.1177/2150137812452558

Scriven, M. (1967). The methodology of evaluation. *AERA Monograph Series on Curriculum Evaluation, 1*, 39–83.

Suskie, L. (2009). *Assessing student learning: A common sense guide* (2nd ed). San Francisco, CA: Jossey-Bass.

Swank, J. M., & Lambie, G. W. (2012). The assessment of CACREP core curricular areas and student learning outcomes using the counseling competencies scale. *Counseling Outcome Research and Evaluation, 3*(2), 116–127. doi:10.1177/2150137812452560

Taras, M. (2010). Back to basics: Definitions and processes of assessments. *Práxis Educativa, 5*(2), 123–130.

Taras, M., & Davies, M. S. (2012). Perceptions and realities in the functions and processes of assessment. *Active Learning in Higher Education, 14*(1), 51–61. doi:10.1177/1469787412467128

Tate, K. A., Bloom, M. L., Tassara, M. H., & Caperton, W. (2014). Counselor competence, performance assessment, and program evaluation: Using psychometric instruments. *Measurement and Evaluation in Counseling and Development, 47*(4), 291–306. doi:10.1177/0748175614538063

Taub, D. J., Servaty-Seib, H. L., Wachter Morris, C. A., Prieto-Welch, S. L., & Werden, D. (2011). Developing skills in providing outreach programs: Construction and use of the POSE (Performance of Outreach Skills Evaluation) rubric. *Counseling Outcome Research and Evaluation, 2*(1), 59–72. doi:10.1177/2150137811401019

Tractenberg, R. E., Umans, J. G., & McCarter, R. J. (2010). A mastery rubric: Guiding curriculum design, admissions and development of course objectives. *Assessment & Evaluation in Higher Education, 35*(1), 17–35. doi:10.1080/02602930802474169

Urofsky, R. (2013). The council for accreditation of counseling and related educational programs: Promoting quality in counselor education. *Journal of Counseling & Development, 91*, 6–14.

Urofsky, R., & Bobby, C. L. (2012). The evolution of a student learning outcomes focus in the CACREP standards in relation to accountability in higher education. *Counseling Outcome Research and Evaluation, 3*(2), 63–72. doi:10.1177/2150137812452562

Wyss, V. L., Freedman, D., & Siebert, C. J. (2014). The development of a discussion rubric for online courses: Standardizing expectations of graduate students in online scholarly discussions. *TechTrends, 58*(2), 99–10

9 The Role of Gatekeeping in Counselor Education

Janet L. Muse-Burke, Amanda S. Hanko, and Jennifer S. Barna

Gatekeeping within counselor education has been established as a means of preventing unsuitable students from entering the counseling profession. This may be accomplished through remediation processes where interventions are put into place to help correct deficits or through steering unfit students toward professions to which they are better suited (Ziomek-Daigle & Christensen, 2010). A standard approach to remediation and gatekeeping has not been established within the field of counseling (Brear & Dorrian, 2010b; Crawford & Gilroy, 2013), although many recommendations for addressing problem students have been presented (e.g., Forrest et al., 2013; Johnson & Campbell, 2002). Further, despite its importance to the field, there are numerous factors that deter counselor educators from effectively carrying out the role of gatekeeper in counselor training (e.g., Hoffman, Hill, Holmes, & Freitas, 2005; Robiner, Fuhrman, & Ristvedt, 1993; Strom-Gottfried, 2000). As such, the purpose of this chapter is to enable you to develop skills in remediation and gatekeeping, which are essential to safeguard clients, students, and the counseling profession.

Learning Objectives

After reading this chapter, you will be able to:

1. Identify which CACREP (2015a) standards address gatekeeping and remediation.
2. Understand the importance of gatekeeping for clients, students, and the profession.
3. Discuss what knowledge, skills, and dispositions characterize competent counselors.
4. Describe the opportunities for gatekeeping through admissions, clinical supervision, curriculum, and due process.
5. List various strategies for remediation and gatekeeping, including objective measures that might be used for evaluation.
6. Analyze the obstacles to effective gatekeeping that counselor educators might encounter.
7. Consider how diversity factors might impact the gatekeeping process.

CACREP Statement and Standards

According to the Council for Accreditation of Counseling and Related Educational Programs (CACREP; 2015b), it is "the ethical responsibility of counselor educators and supervisors to monitor and evaluate an individual's knowledge, skills, and professional dispositions required by competent professional counselors and to remediate or prevent those that are lacking in professional competence from becoming counselors." Moreover, the following 2016 CACREP Standards (2015a; Section 6, Doctoral Standards for Counselor Education and Supervision: B. Doctoral Professional Identity) relate to the gatekeeping function:

1. Counseling
   - e. Methods for evaluating counseling effectiveness
2. Supervision
   - f. Assessment of supervisees' developmental level and other relevant characteristics
   - i. Evaluation, remediation, and gatekeeping in clinical supervision
3. Teaching
   - a. Roles and responsibilities related to educating counselors
   - f. Screening, remediation, and gatekeeping functions relevant to teaching

Importance of Gatekeeping

The role as gatekeeper serves the important purpose of ensuring the training of effective clinicians and protection of the community from individuals unsuitable to practice (Bernard & Goodyear, 2014; Brear, Dorrian, & Luscri, 2008). There is a responsibility to prevent trainees who lack competence or ethical adherence from graduating and practicing due to the risk of harm to the public (Kitchener, 1992). A fundamental ethical principle of the American Counseling Association's Code of Ethics (ACA, 2014) attests that counselors must demonstrate nonmaleficence (i.e., do no harm to clients). In addition, the Code (ACA, 2014) asserts that counselors have a primary responsibility to promote the welfare of clients. Counselor educators serve in the key role to ensure that trainees lacking in competence do not enter the counseling profession and do not harm future clients (ACA, 2014; Bernard & Goodyear, 2014).

Not only is it important to address incompetent students to uphold the tenets of the profession and protect public safety, but it is also necessary for the well-being of other trainees. Rosenberg and colleagues (2005) found that problematic students influenced their surroundings, impacting other students and the learning environment. In fact, 95% of students reported that problematic peers impacted them negatively. Similarly, Veilleux et al. (2012) determined that problematic students influenced their peers' training experience by reducing their confidence in faculty and the doctoral degree and negatively affecting their learning process. Furthermore, Shen-Miller and colleagues (2015) found that peers of trainees with problems of professional competence noted several negative consequences, including decreased contact and increased conflict with peers as well as emotional withdrawal from and increased conflict with faculty. These negative outcomes for peers highlight the need to rehabilitate deficient students and, if necessary, steer them to another profession.

Counselor Competence

For counselor educators to facilitate the professional growth of trainees, first you must know what characterizes an effective counselor. Overholser and Fine (1990) indicated five areas of competence regarding clinical practice: (a) factual knowledge, (b) generic clinical skills, (c) orientation-specific technical skills, (d) clinical judgment, and (e) interpersonal attributes. Factual knowledge refers to information such as models of treatment. Clinical skills include the ability to develop a working alliance, manage self-disclosure, and guide the client with little to no advice giving. Orientation-specific technical skills involve the ability to utilize appropriate techniques within a theoretical framework. Clinical judgment encompasses a high degree of professional insight and judgment into client care. Lastly, interpersonal attributes consist of positive characteristics that aid in developing a working alliance (Overholser & Fine, 1990).

While knowledge, skills, and experience are important to the outcome of treatment, common factors (e.g., personal characteristics, working alliance) have been found to be more predictive of treatment outcomes (Herman, 1993). Wampold and Budge (2012) suggested that effective counseling is a product of the interaction of both common factors (i.e., empathy, working alliance, and expectations) and specific factors (i.e., theoretical orientation and techniques). As such, all of these domains of clinical competence are typically considered in the formal and informal evaluation of students to determine readiness for the profession (Bernard & Goodyear, 2014). For the purpose of this chapter, each of these areas will be addressed, using CACREP's (2015b) classifications: knowledge, skills, and dispositions.

Knowledge

The knowledge required to become an effective professional counselor has been clearly delineated in the 2016 CACREP Standards (CACREP, 2015a). These standards assert there are eight core competency areas that are foundational to professional counseling: (a) professional counseling orientation and ethical practice, (b) social and cultural diversity, (c) human growth and development, (d) career development, (e) counseling and helping relationships, (f) group counseling and group work, (g) assessment and testing, and (h) research and program evaluation. The eight domains are further broken down into specific knowledge criteria, all of which are required to demonstrate competence. In addition, several specialty areas exist in counseling (i.e., addiction counseling; career counseling; clinical mental health counseling; clinical rehabilitation counseling; college counseling and student affairs; marriage, couples, and family counseling; school counseling). Each of these specialty areas contains its own set of knowledge requirements (CACREP, 2015a).

Skills

The practice requirements of each specialty identified by CACREP (2015a) provide an overview of the basic skills required by counselors. For example, clinical mental health counselors are expected to implement prevention and intervention techniques to address various mental health difficulties (CACREP, 2015a). However, the skills described by CACREP (2015a) are general, and counseling programs typically seek greater depth and breadth when evaluating students' counseling skills. Additional information regarding some specific skills necessary to be a competent counselor are ascertained from ACA's Competencies for various specialties (e.g., ALGBTIC, spiritual and religious issues, multicultural career counseling). For example, the Association for Spiritual, Ethical, and Religious Values in Counseling (ASERVIC, 2009) stated that a spiritually competent counselor is able to utilize religious or spiritual techniques that are consistent with the client's perspective. While these guidelines are useful for evaluating skills in specialty areas, many broad-based counseling skills are not addressed.

Notably, there are no general counseling skills competencies for counseling, and no core foundational skills have been promoted by ACA. However, Larson and colleagues (1992) developed a list of competencies based on five empirical studies in which counseling students were evaluated. Five skill areas were derived from that research: (a) microskills, such as comfort with use of confrontation and interpretation; (b) process, as related to the therapeutic relationship; (c) difficult client behaviors, including ability to manage resistance; (d) cultural competence, encompassing appropriate awareness of diversity and effectiveness in the treatment of diverse clients; and (e) awareness of values, so as not to impose values on clients (Larson et al., 1992). These foundational skills suggested by Larson et al. (1992) provide a research-based, objective option for assessing general counseling skills.

Dispositions

In their meta-analytic review of the literature, Fluckiger, Del Re, Wampold, Symonds, and Horvath (2012) explored the factors that influence the outcome of treatment and found the working alliance was the most important. Certain personality characteristics are associated with the ability to develop a strong working alliance. For example, Sperry (2010) indicated effective counselors present themselves as warm, friendly, confident, experienced, honest, open, flexible, supportive, empathic, able to facilitate affective expression, able to accurately interpret, and able to explore deeply. Rogers (1992) also identified empathy, genuineness, and unconditional positive regard as essential components to facilitate clients' psychological change. Moreover, Rieck and Callahan (2013) found that emotional intelligence significantly affected counseling outcomes. These personality qualities speak to the interpersonal functioning and personal character of competent counselors.

In addition, counselor educators need to understand the personal qualities that are characteristic of ineffective counselors to provide a framework for gatekeeping (Brear & Dorrian, 2010a). Brear and Dorrian (2010a) presented negative characteristics of an unsuitable trainee, which include (a) limited self-awareness, (b) inadequate sensitivity and relationship development, (c) a judgmental attitude, (d) inability to demonstrate empathy, and (e) failure to demonstrate ethical and legal practice (Brear & Dorrian, 2010a). Additionally, Ganske, Gnilka, Ashby, and Rice (2015) found that perfectionism and rigidity negatively influenced the supervisory relationship and inhibited training.

Peers have reported additional qualities of trainees with deficiencies in professional competence (Veilleux, January, VanderVeen, Reddy, & Klonoff, 2012), including lack of professionalism (Shen-Miller et al., 2011), interpersonal deficits (Mearns & Allen, 1991), insufficient insight and awareness of emotional state (Rosenberg, Getzelman, Arcinue, & Oren, 2005), and psychopathology (Oliver, Bernstein, Anderson, Blashfield, & Roberts, 2004). Early identification of these characteristics through admissions screening is most beneficial. However, if students with these concerns enter a counseling program, identifying these characteristics early would help facilitate gatekeeping procedures (Grant, Schofield, & Crawford, 2012). In addition to understanding the current research on dispositional factors, it is meaningful to reflect on your interpersonal interactions with various faculty and peers. Please see Guided Practice Exercise 9.1 and further explore your thoughts, feelings, and experiences with effective and ineffective counselor educators or trainees.

Guided Practice Exercise 9.1

Think about peers or counselor educators who were effective at their positions. What personal and professional traits did they exhibit? How did you feel interacting with them? What impact have they had on your growth and development?

Now, consider peers or counselor educators who were lacking in competence. How would you describe their personal qualities and professional demeanor? How have they influenced your thoughts, feelings, and behaviors as you are training to become a counselor educator?

Opportunities for Gatekeeping

When the need for gatekeeping arises, counselor educators are charged with two tasks. First, gatekeepers must establish and maintain a set of professional standards by which prospective students are accepted into a program. After admission, gatekeepers must evaluate and monitor students according to those professional standards, attending to students who demonstrate shortcomings (Crawford & Gilroy, 2013). The Association for Counselor Education and Supervision (ACES, 1995) proposed ethical guidelines for remediation (i.e., the process by which problematic students are addressed). The guidelines assert that you must be aware of any personal or professional limitations of trainees that might negatively influence future professional behavior. Likewise, you are responsible for suggesting remedial assistance to these challenging students.

Admissions Gatekeeping

According to a recent survey of counseling master's programs, coordinators and department chairs reported typically employing the following screening tools during admissions: (a) undergraduate GPA, (b) reference letters, (c) a personal statement, (d) relevant experience, (e) GRE scores, (f) individual interview, and (g) group interview (Crawford & Gilroy, 2013). Lyons and Calicchia (2008) ascertained similar findings, adding to the list of admissions standards: (a) prerequisite course work, (b) writing samples, (c) projective tests, and (d) role-plays. While academic admissions factors (i.e., undergraduate GPA and GRE) have some correlation with counseling knowledge and skills, research has shown that they appear to have no relationship with the dispositional factors necessary to become a competent counselor (Smaby, Maddux, Richmond, Lepkowski, & Packman, 2005). As such, screening prospective students for character fitness prior to admittance would add a layer of protection to prevent unfit students from entering the field (Johnson & Campbell, 2002; McCaughan & Hill, 2015). This would benefit both counselor educators and the prospective students; counselor educators would be spared the challenging issues that arise during remediation and gatekeeping, and prospective students would be more efficiently steered toward suitable careers (McCaughan & Hill, 2015).

Johnson and Campbell (2002) proposed a template for screening the character and fitness of mental health clinicians after reviewing the strict character screenings done by the legal profession (Baude, 1993; National Conference of Bar Examiners, 1998). These researchers provided a preliminary list of characteristics that are essential to being an effective counselor, which should be assessed before admission into graduate training. These characteristics include: (a) personality adjustment, (b) psychological health, (c) use of substances, (d) integrity, (e) prudence, and (f) caring (Johnson & Campbell, 2002). Additionally, Muse-Burke and Surace (2014) provided a list of 39 personality traits of effective counselors, which was based on a review of the literature as well as interviews and ratings of 14 clinical supervisors and faculty. These traits, such as being warm, open, trustworthy, genuine, and affirming, provide counseling programs with additional descriptors of what dispositional factors might be assessed pre-admission. Without adequate assessment of dispositional qualities, counselor education programs will have the added burden of implementing remediation and gatekeeping strategies with problem students later.

Program Gatekeeping

Clinical Supervision

The practice of clinical supervision is widely utilized and viewed as a primary component of counselor education. Bernard and Goodyear (2014) presented the goals of supervision to be (a) providing support and education to supervisees to facilitate professional development, (b) gatekeeping to ensure the integrity of the field, (c) ensuring the welfare of supervisees regarding competence and client care, and (d) providing the skills for supervisees to have the ability to self-supervise. As such, Bernard and Goodyear (2014) identified gatekeeping as a critical requirement of clinical supervision.

Relatedly, an important component of supervision is evaluation and monitoring a supervisee's performance relative to required standards (Brear & Dorrian, 2010b). Wood (2005) indicated the necessity of giving trainees feedback in clinical supervision. The evaluative aspect of clinical supervision distinguishes it from other forms of practice, such as counseling or consultation, and this evaluation serves as a source of motivation for supervisees to utilize feedback and initiate professional growth (Bernard & Goodyear, 2014). Without evaluation, supervisees have little to no guidance as to their strengths or deficits.

Further, Bernard and Goodyear (2014) specified that there are two types of evaluation in supervision: formative and summative. Formative evaluation refers to utilization of direct feedback in the examination of skills and the facilitation of professional growth (Robiner et al., 1993). This type of evaluation causes little discomfort in the supervisory process. Conversely, summative evaluation encompasses all work the supervisee has done to determine whether he or she is effective overall. This type of evaluation has been found to elicit more discomfort (Bernard & Goodyear, 2014). The difficult nature of evaluation can lead to avoidance and overshadowing of deficits (Bernard & Goodyear, 2014); however, both forms of evaluation are central supervisory responsibilities. By sharing feedback of progress, strengths, and growth edges, supervisors facilitate the development of the supervisee and oversee client care, which are the main functions of clinical supervision (Wood, 2005). In your role as supervisor, you will be required to provide positive and critical feedback as well as address interpersonal issues. Please see Case Illustration 9.1 and consider what interventions you might implement if you were in the role of clinical supervisor.

Case Illustration 9.1

Fatima is a 25-year-old counseling student who is experiencing considerable distress due to ongoing conflict with a fellow supervision group member, Amber. Fatima believes Amber is passive aggressive and creates an unsafe atmosphere in group. Fatima has attempted to settle this conflict with Amber one on one; however, Amber was not receptive to Fatima's feedback and became defensive. Fatima met with the group supervisor individually, and he listened to and validated Fatima's concerns. As weeks passed, Fatima became increasingly frustrated because the group supervisor did not address ongoing issues with Amber during group. Again, Fatima met with the group supervisor, seeking to clarify her needs. The group supervisor said, "Try to act like adults and deal directly with Amber." How might Fatima respond in this situation? What might the group supervisor have done differently? What remediation or gatekeeping strategies (if any) might be used with Amber? What remediation or gatekeeping strategies (if any) might be implemented with Fatima?

Curriculum and Due Process

Counseling program faculty and administrators have an added responsibility of addressing deficient trainees through program curriculum and proper due process. According to Crawford and Gilroy (2013), the counseling program curriculum can focus on issues related to the prevention of deficits through (a) ethics training, (b) self-care endorsement, and (c) personal growth. The ACA Code of Ethics (2014) succinctly addresses the ethical mandates of the counseling profession. Moreover, it requires counselors to self-monitor and address any physical, mental, or emotional challenges that might impede professional performance. Likewise, CACREP (2015a) requires competence in professional behavior, ethics, self-care, and personal self-evaluation and improvement. Thus, programs adhering to the 2016 CACREP Standards (2015a) will be mandated to address each of these curricular components relevant to gatekeeping.

In addition to these prevention measures, you are advised to conduct student evaluations at regular and predetermined intervals throughout the training program to assess for difficulties (Crawford & Gilroy, 2013). In the event that a remediation plan is required, several steps have been described in the literature for due process (Crawford & Gilroy, 2013). These include (a) meeting with the advisor, (b) meeting with the program coordinator or department chair, (c) providing verbal and written lists of concerns, (d) writing a remediation plan, (e) providing notification of the appeals process, (f) providing notification of the dismissal process, (g) meeting with a faculty committee, and (h) conducting an informal hearing.

Additionally, when implementing remediation due process procedures, several important recommendations have been provided by Gilfoyle (2008). First, you should provide prospective and current students with written documentation of performance standards and due process procedures related to competency issues. Second, faculty should apply the competencies and assessments consistently across all students in the program. Third, programs should develop remediation plans that are concrete, well-defined, and linked to program standards. Fourth, student confidentiality should be maintained; information should only be shared on a need-to-know basis (Family Educational Rights and Privacy Act, 1974). Finally, all correspondence, meetings, assessments, remediation plans, and outcomes should be documented (Gilfoyle, 2008).

Box 9.1 Sample Remediation Plan

Corrective Action Plan

Counseling Program

University
Student Name:
Date of Corrective Action Plan:
Date of Evaluation of Outcome of Corrective Action Plan:

Overview of a Corrective Action Plan (CAP): *Describe the nature and purpose of a CAP. Address all possible outcomes of the CAP and how outcomes will be determined. This section should include information and* citations from program and university student handbooks, ethics codes, and/or professional competencies standards. This section should remain consistent for all students.

Rationale for Corrective Action Plan: *Specify the particular reasons why the CAP is being written for the student with problems of professional competence. Be concrete, and describe behavioral indicators. State any informal methods of resolution that were attempted but unsuccessful.*

Corrective Action Plan Criteria: *List and describe the specific requirements of the remediation plan. Be as clear and concise as possible. Indicate how achievement of each criterion will be determined; specify who will make each determination and by what date.*

Consent Statement: *Include a consent statement, such as "I have read the above and understand the identified expectations. I am aware of the administrative actions possible following the evaluation of the outcome of this Corrective Action Plan."*

Signatures: *Signatures should be ascertained from the student, program coordinator/department chair, and other faculty or administrators as determined by the university.*

Documentation: *Copies of the signed plan should be forwarded to the student, the student's academic file, and other faculty or administrators as determined by the university.*

(Adapted from the *Counseling Student Handbook* for the Clinical Mental Health and School Counseling programs at Marywood University, Scranton, PA.)

Strategies for Gatekeeping

It is important for you to utilize the professions' standard language when describing and documenting student difficulties. There has been some debate within the mental health field regarding the terminology used to describe trainees experiencing difficulties; both *impairment* and *problems of professional competence* have been employed (Bernard & Goodyear, 2014). Because the term *problems of professional competence* specifies the assessment of proficiency, rather than the diagnosis of an impairment or disability, that construct is recommended (Bernard & Goodyear, 2014). Additionally, Ladany, Friedlander, and Nelson (2016) provided descriptions of other terms related to remediation and gatekeeping. They asserted that students demonstrating problems with acquiring skills might be experiencing a *skill difficulty* (i.e., when a student is experiencing the normal, expected challenges of learning a new counseling skill) or a *skill deficit* (i.e., when a student appears incapable of developing a new counseling skill). With skill difficulties, students demonstrate that practice and feedback improve the counseling skill; however, with a skill deficit, students appear resistant to working on enhancing their skills (Ladany et al., 2016). Further, Ladany and colleagues (2016) specify that problematic trainees once demonstrated a skill but has experienced a situation that impedes their ability to effectively exhibit counseling efficacy. On the other hand, an *incompetent trainee* has never demonstrated certain counseling proficiencies. Understanding the type and longevity of the problem of professional competence will inform you about how to proceed with gatekeeping strategies.

Program Level Strategies

Fortunately, researchers have provided meaningful suggestions to assist counselor educators and counseling programs in the gatekeeping process. Johnson et al. (2008) provided a list of nine recommendations to help practice ethical gatekeeping: (a) prepare faculty for the role of both advocating for and evaluating students and the tension associated with this conflict; (b) ensure familiarity with all ethical guidelines, especially those regarding gatekeeping responsibilities; (c) ensure competence in supervisors concerning the ability to identify deficits and provide corrective feedback; (d) acknowledge competence to be neither dichotomous nor static in nature, and evaluate trainees on current performance; (e) attempt to separate dual roles, such as mentoring and evaluation roles, when possible; (f) attempt to prevent inflation of evaluation and recommendations based on likability and alliance with the student; (g) regularly provide timely and accurate feedback in the form of summative and formative evaluations of trainees, including documentation from multiple sources; (h) develop standard methods of assessment that are valid and reliable for measuring competence based on accrediting regulations; and (i) utilize formal and informal methods to establish cooperation among training programs, internship sites, and licensing boards, and create a comprehensive system to address problems of competence.

Kaslow et al. (2007) also proposed a series of recommendations when identifying, evaluating, and remediating trainees with problems of professional competence. Suggestions unique from Johnson et al. (2008) include: (a) define terms utilized in evaluations and provide a categorization of deficits; (b) establish policies that allow for appropriate plans, which are thoroughly communicated with the trainee; (c) when evaluating deficits, encourage self-assessment to facilitate improvement and prevent future competency issues; (d) be aware of the influence of culture on actions in evaluation, remediation, and gatekeeping; (e) clearly explain the limitations of the trainee's confidentiality before any actions are put in place; and (f) take ethical, regulatory, and legal implications into consideration (Kaslow et al., 2007). Overall, Forrest and colleagues (2013) found that effective strategies for dealing with problematic students included positive actions that were deliberate rather than reactive. They recommended identifying and documenting problems early, responding at a program level, engaging in difficult conversations, attending to diversity issues, and participating in ongoing education about working with problem students (Forrest et al., 2013).

Student Level Strategies

Furthermore, the literature provides strategies for how training programs might intervene with a student who is lacking competency. The remediation and gatekeeping suggestions provided by Russell, DuPree, Beggs, Peterson, and Anderson (2007) include: (a) conversing with the identified student about the perceived problem, (b) consulting with other faculty, (c) providing a referral for a psychological or psychiatric assessment, (d) providing a referral for personal counseling, (e) recommending a leave of absence, (f) increasing supervision, (g) repeating coursework, (h) increasing informal interactions and communications with the student, (i) assigning peer shadowing, (j) assigning a co-therapist, (k) observing the student more in session with clients, (l) constructing a letter of concern, (m) providing a written remediation plan, (n) counseling the student out of the program, (o) putting the student on probation, (p) dismissing the student, and (q) filing a complaint with an ethics committee. Veilleux et al. (2012) provided some additional remediation strategies: (a) counseling the trainee out of the field, (b) requiring the trainee to repeat practicum, and (c) recommending tutoring. Other suggestions include shifting a student's client caseload (Lamb et al., 1987) and reducing a student's course load (Crawford & Gilroy, 2013).

Some additional strategies have been implemented by the authors of this chapter in our experiences as counselor educators. Remediation plans with previous students have included: (a) reviewing professionalism DVDs or Webinars (e.g., ACA's On-demand Webinars), (b) observing master counselors (e.g., American Psychological Association [APA] Psychotherapy Training Videos), (c) writing a paper, (d) writing a personal conduct statement, (e) assigning readings from counseling skills texts (e.g., Hill, 2014), (f) transcribing portions of counseling sessions and writing alternative responses to say to clients, (g) completing a plagiarism tutorial and test (e.g., Indiana University Bloomington, School of Education, *How to Recognize Plagiarism*), and (h) submitting papers for a plagiarism check (e.g., Turnitin).

Box 9.2 Gatekeeping Strategies in Order of Intrusiveness

Consult about trainee with other faculty
Talk with trainee about perceived problem
Increase informal communication and interactions with trainee
Assign readings related to counseling, supervision, or teaching skills
Complete a plagiarism tutorial and test
Submit papers for plagiarism checking
Review professionalism DVDs or Webinars
Observe master counselor, supervisor, or teacher DVDs
Write a personal conduct statement
Write a paper
Transcribe a portion of counseling or supervision sessions and provide alternative responses
Increase supervision of trainee's counseling, supervision, or teaching
Increase direct observation of trainee's counseling, supervision, or teaching

> Obtain tutoring
> Provide a referral for personal counseling
> Provide a referral for psychological or psychiatric assessment
> Reduce course load
> Assign a peer mentor for trainee to shadow
> Shift client caseload
> Assign a co-counselor, co-supervisor, or co-teacher
> Require to repeat coursework
> Require to complete extra coursework
> Require to repeat practicum in counseling, supervision, or teaching
> Write a letter of concern
> Develop a written remediation plan
> Put on probation
> Require a leave of absence
> Counsel out of the program or field
> Dismiss from the program
> File a complaint with an ethics committee

A particularly sensitive remediation task is personal counseling, and you might struggle with making a referral and assessing outcomes. Both the ACA Code of Ethics (2014) and empirical research (e.g., Byrne & Shufelt, 2014) affirm the value of personal counseling for counselor trainees, and you are encouraged to support students' involvement in personal counseling. In the current authors' experience, documentation has been required from the student's counselor, specifying the dates of service and providing an evaluative statement regarding the student's readiness to return to clinical work. For our purposes, this level of documentation was sufficient to determine the student's successful completion of the remediation task while also honoring the integrity of the client/counselor relationship.

When applying these approaches, it is recommended that you consider the type and severity of the student deficit; in standard cases, faculty typically begin with less intrusive strategies and advance to more invasive approaches when less formal methods are not successful. However, serious ethical or professional breaches might require more intense action earlier in the gatekeeping process. During implementation of a remediation plan, you are advised to be concrete and specific regarding the behavioral changes expected and how successful completion will be determined (Gilfoyle, 2008). For example, if a corrective plan requires a student to transcribe counseling session recordings and provide alternative interventions, the plan should indicate how many recordings are required as well as how many minutes of each recording should be transcribed. Further, the plan should delineate who will review the transcripts, and how the transcripts will be evaluated. Rubrics are often useful to assess these types of tasks (Smith & Hanna, 1998). In all cases, due process procedures should be followed, and the student should be kept informed through each step.

Objective Measures for Gatekeeping

Peers have indicated that faculty identify only slightly more than half of problematic students (Veilleux et al., 2012). This finding shows a need for better methods of assessment so that trainees with competence problems can be detected. Bethune and Johnson (2013) compared subjective and objective methods of assessment as predictors of graduate GPA and internship evaluation scores. These researchers found that an objective measure of personality (i.e., Minnesota Multiphasic Personality Inventory-2) was a significant predictor of graduate GPA and internship evaluations, whereas the subjective method (i.e., program-developed rating scale created to assess interview performance) did not predict success (Bethune & Johnson, 2013). As such, you are urged to consider using objective measures to assess the suitability of prospective and current students. To assist you with the selection of measures, several instruments that assess knowledge, skills, and dispositions are recommended.

Measure of Knowledge

Counselor Preparation Comprehensive Examination (CPCE)

The CPCE is offered by the Center for Credentialing and Education (CCE) and was created to assess the core eight areas of counseling (i.e., professional counseling orientation and ethical practice, social and cultural diversity, human growth and development, career development, counseling and helping relationships, group counseling and group work, assessment and testing, and research and program evaluation; Erford, Hays, & Crockett, 2015). It is employed by more than 400 counseling programs (CCE, n.d.) as an exit exam (Erford et al., 2015). It contains 160 items; 17 items per content area are included for a maximum score of 136. There is no overall score to pass; counseling programs determine the cutoff score for their students (Erford et al., 2015).

Measures of Skills

Counseling Competencies Scale (CCS)

The CCS (Swank, Lambie, & Witta, 2012) is a 32-item, rubric-style measure completed by the supervisor or counselor educator, which was created to assess counseling skills, professional dispositions, and behaviors. The CCS includes five subscales: (a) professional behaviors, (b) counseling relationship, (c) counseling skills, (d) assessment and application, and (e) professional dispositions. Reliability and validity are supported by research (Swank et al., 2012), and the CCS is recommended for evaluating student learning outcomes in CACREP programs (Swank & Lambie, 2012).

Counseling Self-Estimate Inventory (COSE)

The COSE (Larson et al., 1992) is a 37-item self-report assessment intended to measure counseling self-efficacy. The COSE contains five subscales: (a) execution of microskills, (b) attending to process-related work, (c) dealing with difficult client behaviors, (d) cultural competence, and (e) self-awareness of personal values. Larson and colleagues (1992) demonstrated reliability and validity for the COSE's overall score and subscales. With the authors' permission, programs might easily adapt phrasing of the items to be supervisor-rated rather than trainee-rated.

Cross-cultural Counseling Competence Inventory-Revised (CCCI-R)

The CCCI-R (LaFromboise, Coleman, & Hernandez, 1991) is a 20-item, observer-report scale that assesses effectiveness of treatment with culturally diverse clients. This measure reflects the multicultural competencies developed by the Society of Counseling Psychology of the APA (Owen, Leach, Wampold, & Rodolpha, 2011), and it includes three subscales: (a) cross cultural counseling skill, (b) sociopolitical awareness, and (c) cultural sensitivity (LaFromboise et al., 1991). Recent research utilizing this measure has reported strong reliability and validity (Owen et al., 2011).

Measures of Dispositions

Characteristics of an Effective Psychotherapist Index (CEPI)

The CEPI (Muse-Burke & Surace, 2014) was created to measure character traits of mental health trainees for the purpose of gatekeeping. The instrument was generated from the character deficits and common factors literature (e.g., Rogers, 1992; Sperry, 2010; Wampold & Budge, 2012). The 39-item bipolar adjective measure has undergone two expert reviews and a validation study, which obtained strong reliability (Surace, 2015). While early evidence of the CEPI is promising, additional reliability, validity, and norming data is needed. During the admissions process, this measure could be completed by references to evaluate prospective candidates. While in training, faculty could assess students, and students could self-assess.

Working Alliance Inventory-Short Form (WAI-SF)

The WAI (Horvath & Greenberg, 1986) was created to measure the three components of Bordin's (1979) therapeutic working alliance: (a) mutual agreement on goals, (b) mutual agreement on tasks, and (c) emotional bond. Using confirmatory factor analysis of the original measure, Tracey and Kokotovic (1989) maintained the three factor structure along with a primary alliance factor. Further, they reduced the number of items, creating a 12-item short form. Reliability and validity of the original WAI were good (Horvath & Greenberg, 1986). Importantly, having clients evaluate counselor trainees on the strength of the working alliance would provide valued input from another constituent invested in the gatekeeping process.

Obstacles to Gatekeeping

Many difficulties can arise when gatekeeping, such as establishing and evaluating the necessary competencies, utilizing a proactive method as opposed to reactive methods, and legal implications (Falender & Shafranske, 2004). While competencies of knowledge, applied skills, and dispositions have been established, a clear method for measuring all components has not been widely adopted, making it difficult to obtain clear evidence of deficiencies (Brear & Dorrian, 2010b). Specific examples of problems are needed to provide feedback to students and develop concise plans for trainee growth (Falender & Shafranske, 2004). In trainees who fail to improve, explicit data is needed to support the decision to dismiss (Brear & Dorrian, 2010b).

University factors also might deter counselor educators from gatekeeping. It has been shown that the pressure to maintain enrollment (Strom-Gottfried, 2000) and institution reputation (Robiner et al., 1993) influence whether counselor educators intervene with problem students. Students being dismissed from an institution reflect negatively on that institution's screening process (Robiner et al., 1993). Also, the number of students enrolled in a program is important for funding or accreditation, making it difficult to deny students admission (Robiner et al., 1993). Hoffman et al. (2005) found another significant influence is perceived support from colleagues; without support from faculty and administration, educators are less likely to remediate or gatekeep when necessary. Additionally, Forrest et al. (2013) discovered that faculty struggle in their work with problematic students when there is a culture of avoidance, individualistic attitudes, and concerns about multicultural competence.

The social psychological phenomena of "social loafing" also presents as a deterrent to gatekeeping, as faculty might believe that another counselor educator or clinical supervisor will follow through with remediation (Elman, Forrest, Vacha-Haase, & Gizara, 1999). This has been called "the Hot Potato Game" (Johnson et al., 2008) or *gate slippage* (Gaubatz & Vera, 2002). With the expectation that others will take responsibility, unsuitable students fall through the cracks and enter the field. Another barrier that might come from within the counselor educator is valuing unconditional positive regard and autonomy. While these principles are paramount in counseling, they might feel contradictory to the tasks of gatekeeping (Bernard & Goodyear, 2014). Many supervisors view evaluation as a "necessary evil" or an essential but unpleasant part of successful clinical supervision (Cohen, 1987). Notably, Russell and colleagues (2007) found that few supervisors indicated the need for formal intervention or gatekeeping procedures despite severe hypothetical violations, including sexual relationships and blatant ethical breaches. Because remediation and gatekeeping might feel uncomfortable, some counselor educators appear inclined to avoid it. Please see Guided Practice Exercise 9.2 and consider how gatekeeping and remediation might affect your thoughts, feelings, and actions.

Guided Practice Exercise 9.2

Imagine yourself as a counselor educator in the not-so-distant future. You are sitting in your office with a student who requires remediation, and you are responsible for addressing the concerns. What feelings arise within you? What thoughts come to mind about the trainee, yourself, and the gatekeeping process? Describe how these reactions might influence your conversation with the trainee as well as the remediation plan you implement. What strategies might you employ to effectively manage your countertransference?

Multicultural Considerations in Gatekeeping

While gatekeeping has been identified as a main function of counselor educators and supervisors (Bernard & Goodyear, 2014), little research has been conducted examining the effects of multicultural competence on gatekeeping practices. Forrest et al. (2013) asked training directors about how faculty interact with trainees who have problems related to overall competence and multicultural competence. These researchers found an ineffective strategy is avoiding discussing the problem as well as circumventing cultural issues, especially difficult discussions differentiating between culture and competence (Forrest et al., 2013). Openness to cultural discussions is necessary during gatekeeping and includes self-exploration and introspection into how the supervisor might be contributing to the problem. These researchers suggested that cultural and diversity issues should be addressed early, and faculty should acknowledge how diversity might impact competency assessment (Forrest et al., 2013).

In the realm of clinical supervision, Burkard, Knox, Clarke, Phelps, and Inman (2014) examined cross-ethnic/racial supervisory relationships before and after providing difficult cultural competence feedback. These researchers indicated that providing difficult feedback regarding cultural competence helped establish a stronger working alliance between supervisors and supervisees. Further, supervisees became more engaged in the supervision process following the feedback (Burkard et al., 2014). These findings highlight the importance of addressing cultural issues as a part of feedback, evaluation, remediation, and gatekeeping. Please see Case Illustration 9.2 and reflect on how issues of diversity and power might affect gatekeeping and remediation practices in a graduate counseling program.

Case Illustration 9.2

Dr. Nina Mejia is a 34-year-old, untenured counselor educator. In her role as individual supervisor, she has experienced a master's level student, Andre, as defensive, disrespectful, and rude. He often questions Dr. Mejia's competency and refuses to accept feedback in supervision. Although Andre is quite intelligent and excels academically, Dr. Mejia is concerned about his disposition and ability to function as an effective counselor. She brings her concerns to her colleagues at their monthly

> faculty meeting. During the conversation, most faculty continue to highlight Andre's academic achievements. When Dr. Mejia attempts to redirect the conversation back to personality concerns, the Department Chair states, "to let such a bright young man go would be a detriment to the program, and I suspect we might even have legal problems, if we act." How do you think Dr. Mejia feels during this meeting? What diversity and power dynamics might be affecting this situation? How do you think Dr. Mejia should proceed?

Considerations for Resistant Students

Deficient trainees might have a variety of responses to your attempts to initiate remediation or gatekeeping procedures. In these authors' experiences, while some students express relief at having problems identified and addressed, others become defensive and resist attempts to ameliorate issues. Regardless, it is important that remediation and gatekeeping initiatives be provided in a supportive atmosphere; you should acknowledge students' strengths and successes, even in the face of shortcomings (Ladany et al., 2016). Likewise, you are advised to spend more time than might be typical building trust with sanctioned trainees (Kress, O'Neill, Protivnak, Stargell, & Herman, 2015). Similarly, you are urged to use relational and reflective strategies initially and move towards more challenging approaches as time progresses (Grant et al., 2012). Bernard and Goodyear (2014) also recommended that you collaborate with students in developing the remediation plan, empowering the trainee to actively participate in resolving shortcomings. Essentially, you are encouraged to focus on the relationship with the problematic student; you should integrate your counseling skills with the skills required for student evaluation, remediation, and gatekeeping. In so doing, it is more likely that challenging students will experience growth and improvement through the remediation process.

Summary

Counselor educators have a critical responsibility to serve as gatekeeper with the purpose of ensuring the training of effective clinicians and protecting the community from individuals unsuitable to practice. This function begins at pre-admission and continues until termination, which might come through degree completion or early dismissal. Although you are likely to experience barriers when implementing gatekeeping procedures, the literature provides meaningful suggestions to help with the implementation of effective strategies for student improvement. To ensure best practice, you are encouraged to remain up-to-date on gatekeeping practices, consider the impact of power and diversity, reflect on your personal reactions, and utilize core counseling skills that build relationships with trainees experiencing problems of professional competence.

Author Note

Thank you to Melissa M. Gericke for her assistance with searching the literature and checking the references and Micalena I. Sallavanti for her assistance with editing the manuscript.

Additional Resources

The following resources provide additional information relating to the chapter topics.

American Counseling Association Competencies. www.counseling.org/knowledge-center/competencies
This link provides access to counseling competency guidelines endorsed by ACA.

American Counseling Association Webinars. www.counseling.org/continuing-education/webinars
This link provides access to purchase ACA's on-demand webinars for counselors.

American Psychological Association Psychotherapy Supervision Video Series. www.apa.org/pubs/videos/browse.aspx?query=series:Psychotherapy+Supervision
This link provides access to purchase APA's DVDs for psychotherapy supervision training.

American Psychological Association Psychotherapy Training Videos. www.apa.org/pubs/videos/index.aspx
This link provides access to purchase APA's DVDs for psychotherapy training.

Cross-Cultural Counseling Inventory—Revised (CCCI-R). www.researchgate.net/file.PostFileLoader.html?id=514a3783d2fd648e0400002b&assetKey=AS%3A271834333810690%401441821763650
This link provides free access to the CCCI-R with permission to reproduce by the author.

Indiana University Bloomington, School of Education, How to Recognize Plagiarism. www.indiana.edu/~academy/firstPrinciples/
This link provides access to a free tutorial and test on plagiarism.

Turnitin. http://turnitin.com
This link provides access to purchase online plagiarism checking services.

Working Alliance Inventory-Short Form (WAI-SF). http://wai.profhorvath.com/downloads
This link provides free access to the WAI with permission to reproduce by the author.

References

American Counseling Association. (2014). *ACA code of ethics.* Washington DC: Author.

Association for Counselor Education and Supervision. (1995). Ethical guidelines for counseling supervisors. *Counselor Education and Supervision, 34,* 270–276. doi:10.1002/j.1556-6978.1995.tb00248.x

Association for Spiritual, Ethical, and Religious Values in Counseling. (2009). *Competencies for addressing spiritual and religious issues in counseling.* Retrieved from www.aservic.org/resources/spiritual-competencies/

Baude, P. L. (1993). An essay on the regulation of the legal profession and the future of lawyer's characters. *Indiana Law Journal, 68*, 647–658.

Bernard, J. M., & Goodyear, R. K. (2014). *Fundamentals of clinical supervision* (5th ed.). Upper Saddle River, NJ: Merrill.

Bethune, M., & Johnson, B. D. (2013). Predicting counselors' academic and internship outcomes: Evidence for the incremental validity of the MMPI-2. *Training and Education in Professional Psychology, 7*, 257–266. doi:10.1037/a0033025

Bordin, E. (1979). The generalizability of the psychoanalytic concept of the working alliance. *Psychotherapy: Theory, Research and Practice, 16*, 252–260. doi:10.1037/h0085885

Brear, P. D., & Dorrian, J. (2010a). Does professional suitability matter? A national survey of Australian counseling educators in undergraduate and post-graduate training programs. *International Journal for the Advancement of Counselling, 32*, 1–13. doi:10.1007/s10447-009-9084-2

Brear P. D., & Dorrian, J. (2010b). Gatekeeping or gate slippage? A national survey of counseling educators in Australian undergraduate and postgraduate academic training programs. *Training and Education in Professional Psychology, 4*, 264–273. doi:10.1037/a0020714

Brear, P., Dorrian, J., & Luscri, G. (2008). Preparing our future counseling professionals: Gatekeeping and the implications for research. *Counselling and Psychotherapy Research, 8*, 93–101. doi:10.1080/14733140802007855

Burkard, A. W., Knox, S., Clarke, R. D., Phelps, D. L., & Inman, A. G. (2014). Supervisors' experiences of providing difficult feedback in cross-ethnic/racial supervision. *The Counseling Psychologist, 42*, 314–344. doi:10.1177/0011000012461157

Byrne, J. S., & Shufelt, B. (2014). Factors for personal counseling among counseling trainees. *Counselor Education and Supervision, 53*, 178–189. doi:10.1002/j.1556-6978.2014.00056.x

Center for Credentialing and Education. (n.d.). *Counselor Preparation and Comprehensive Examination (CPCE)*. Retrieved from www.cce-global.org/AssessmentsAndExaminations/CPCE

Cohen, B. Z. (1987). The ethics of social work supervision revisited. *Social Work, 32*, 194–196.

Council for Accreditation of Counseling and Related Programs. (2015a). *2016 CACREP standards*. Retrieved from www.cacrep.org/wp-content/uploads/2012/10/2016-CACREP-Standards.pdf

Council for Accreditation of Counseling and Related Programs. (2015b). *Gatekeeping*. Retrieved from www.cacrep.org/glossary/gatekeeping/

Crawford, M., & Gilroy, P. (2013). Professional impairment and gatekeeping: A survey of master's level training programs. *The Journal of Counselor Preparation and Supervision, 5*, 28–37. doi:10.7729/51.0030

Elman, N., Forrest, L., Vacha-Haase, T., & Gizara, S. (1999). A systems perspective on trainee impairment: Continuing the dialogue. *The Counseling Psychologist, 27*, 712–721. doi:10.1177/0011000099275005

Erford, B. T., Hays, D. G., & Crockett, S. (2015). *Mastering the national counselor examination and the counselor preparation comprehensive examination* (2nd ed.). Boston, MA: Pearson.

Falender, C. A., & Shafranske, E. P. (2004). *Clinical supervision: A competency-based approach*. Washington, DC: American Psychological Association. doi:10.1037/10806-000

Family Educational Rights and Privacy Act of 1974, 20 U.S.C. § 1232g. (1974).

Fluckiger, C., Del Re, A. C., Wampold, B. E., Symonds, D., & Horvath, A. O. (2012). How central is the alliance in psychotherapy? A multilevel longitudinal meta-analysis. *Journal of Counseling Psychology, 59*, 10–17. doi:10.1037/a0025749

Forrest, L., Elman, N. S., Huprich, S. K., Veilleux, J. C., Jacobs, S. C., & Kaslow, N. K. (2013). Training directors' perceptions of faculty behaviors when dealing with trainee competence problems: A mixed method pilot study. *Training and Education in Professional Psychology, 7*, 23–32. doi:10.1037/a0032068

Ganske, K. H., Gnilka, P. B., Ashby, J. S., & Rice, K. G. (2015). The relationship between counseling trainee perfectionism and the working alliance with supervisor and client. *Journal of Counseling and Development, 93*, 14–24. doi:10/1002/j.1556-6676.2015.00177.x

Gaubatz, M. D., & Vera, E. M. (2002). Do formalized gatekeeping procedures increase programs' follow up with deficient trainees? *Counselor Education and Supervision, 41*, 294–305. doi:10.1002/j.1556-6978.2002.tb01292.x

Gilfoyle, N. (2008). The legal ecosystem: Risk management in addressing student competence problems in professional psychology training. *Training and Education in Professional Psychology, 2*, 202–209. doi:10.1037/1931-3918.2.4.202

Grant, J., Schofield, M. J., & Crawford, S. (2012). Managing difficulties in supervision: Supervisors' perspectives. *Journal of Counseling Psychology, 59*, 528–541. doi:10.1037/a0030000

Herman, K. C. (1993). Reassessing predictors of therapist competence. *Journal of Counseling & Development, 72*, 29–32. doi:10.1002/j.1556-6676.1993.tb02272.x

Hill, C. E. (2014). *Helping skills: Facilitating exploration, insight, and action* (4th ed.). Washington, DC: American Psychological Association.

Hoffman, M. A., Hill, C. E., Holmes, S. E., & Freitas, G. F. (2005). Supervision perspective on the process and outcome of giving easy, difficult, or no feedback to supervisees. *Journal of Counseling Psychology, 52*, 3–13. doi:10.1037/0022-0167.52.1.3

Horvath, A., & Greenberg, L. (1986). The development of the Working Alliance Inventory. In L. Greenberg & W. Pinsoff (Eds.), *The psychotherapeutic process: A research handbook* (pp. 529–556). New York, NY: Guilford Press.

Johnson, W. B., & Campbell, C. D. (2002). Character and fitness requirements for professional psychologists: Are there any? *Professional Psychology: Research and Practice, 33*, 46–53. doi:10.1037//0735-7028.33.1.46

Johnson, W. B., Elman, N. S., Forrest, L., Robiner, W. N., Rodolfa, E., & Schaffer, J. B. (2008). Addressing professional competence problems in trainees: Some ethical considerations. *Professional Psychology: Research and Practice, 39*, 589–599. doi:10.1037/a0014264

Kaslow, N. J., Rubin, N. J., Forrest, L., Elman, N. S., Van Horne, B. A., Jacobs, S. C., . . . Thorn, B. E. (2007). Recognizing, assessing, and intervening with problems of professional competence. *Professional Psychology: Research and Practice, 38*, 479–492. doi:10.1037/0735-7028.38_5.479

Kitchener, K. S. (1992). Psychologist as teacher and mentor: Affirming ethical values throughout the curriculum. *Professional Psychology: Research and Practice, 23*, 190–195. doi:10.1037/0735-7028.23.3.190

Kress, V. E., O'Neill, R. M., Protivnak, J. J., Stargell, N. A., & Herman, E. R. (2015). A qualitative study of supervisors' reflections on providing sanctioned supervision. *The Clinical Supervisor, 34*, 38–56. doi:10.1080/07325223.2014.1003740

Ladany, N., Friedlander, M. L., & Nelson, M. L. (2016). Addressing skill difficulties, deficits, and competency concerns. In *Supervision essentials for the critical events in psychotherapy supervision model* (pp. 57–84). Washington, DC: American Psychological Association.

LaFromboise, T. D., Coleman, H. L. K., & Hernandez, A. (1991). Development and factor structure of the Cross-cultural Counseling Inventory-Revised. *Professional Psychology: Research and Practice, 22,* 380–388. doi:10.1037/0735-7028.22.5.380

Lamb, D. H., Presser, N., Pfost, K., Baum, M., Jackson, R., & Jarvis, P. (1987). Confronting professional impairment during the internship: Identification, due process, and remediation. *Professional Psychology: Research and Practice, 18,* 597–603. doi:10.1037/0735-7028.18.6.597

Larson, L. M., Suzuki, L. A., Gillespie, K. N., Potenza, M. T., Bechtel, M. A., & Toulouse, A. L. (1992). Development and validation of the Counseling Self-estimate Inventory. *Journal of Counseling Psychology, 39,* 105–120. doi:10.1037/0022-0167.39.1.105

Lyons, C., & Calicchia, J. (2008). Admissions criteria in counselor education: Traditions and trends. *Counselor Education and Supervision Spectrum, 69,* 24–27.

McCaughan, A. M., & Hill, N. R. (2015). The gatekeeping imperative in counselor education admission protocols: The criticality of personal qualities. *International Journal for the Advancement of Counselling, 37,* 28–40. doi:10.1007/s10447-014-9223-2

Mearns, J., & Allen, G. J. (1991). Graduate students' experiences in dealing with impaired peers, compared with faculty predictions: An exploratory study. *Ethics & Behavior, 1,* 191–202. doi:10.1207/s15327019eb0103_3

Muse-Burke, J., & Surace. A. (2014). *Characteristics of effective psychotherapists index.* Unpublished instrument.

National Conference of Bar Examiners. (1998). The Bar Examiner Subject Index: 1989–1997. *The Bar Examiner, 67,* 1–24.

Oliver, M. N. I., Bernstein, J. H., Anderson, K. G., Blashfield, R. K., & Roberts, M. C. (2004). An exploratory examination of student attitudes toward "impaired" peers in clinical psychology training programs. *Professional Psychology: Research and Practice, 35,* 141–147. doi:10.1037/0735-7028.35.2.141

Overholser, J. C., & Fine, M. A. (1990). Defining the boundaries of professional competence: Managing subtle cases of clinical incompetence. *Professional Psychology: Research and Practice, 21,* 462–469. doi:10.1037/0735-7028.21.6.462

Owen, J., Leach, M. M., Wampold, B., & Rodolpha, E. (2011). Client and therapist variability in clients' perception of their therapists' multicultural competencies. *Journal of Counseling Psychology, 55,* 1–9. doi:10.1037/a0021496

Rieck, T., & Callahan, J. L. (2013). Emotional intelligence and psychological outcomes in the training clinic. *Training and Education in Professional Psychology, 7,* 42–52. doi:10.1037/a0031659

Robiner, W. N., Fuhrman, M., & Ristvedt, S. (1993). Evaluation difficulties in supervising psychology interns. *The Clinical Psychologist, 46,* 3–13.

Rogers, C. R. (1992). The necessary and sufficient conditions of therapeutic personality change. *Journal of Consulting and Clinical Psychology, 60,* 827–832. doi:10.1037/0022-006X.60.6.827

Rosenberg, J. I., Getzelman, M. A., Arcinue, F., & Oren, C. Z. (2005). An exploratory look at students' experiences of problematic peers in academic professional psychology programs. *Professional Psychology: Research and Practice, 36,* 665–673. doi:10.1037/0735-7028.36.6.665

Russell, C. S., DuPree, W. J., Beggs, M. A., Peterson, C. M., & Anderson, M. P. (2007). Responding to remediation and gatekeeping challenges in supervision.

Journal of Marital and Family Therapy, 33, 227–244. doi:10.1111/j.1752-0606.2007.00018.x

Shen-Miller, D. S., Grus, C. L., Van Sickle, K. S., Schwartz-Mette, R., Cage, E., & Kaslow, N. J. (2011). Trainees experiences with peers having competence problems: A national survey. *Training and Education in Professional Psychology, 5,* 112–121. doi:10.1037/a0023824

Shen-Miller, D. S., Schwartz-Mette, R., Van Sickle, K. S., Jacobs, S. C., Grus, C. L., Hunter, E. A., & Forrest, L. (2015). Professional competence problems in training: A qualitative investigation of trainee perspectives. *Training and Education in Professional Psychology, 9,* 161–169. doi:10.1037/tep0000072

Smaby, M. H., Maddux, C. D., Richmond, A. S., Lepkowski, W. J., & Packman, J. (2005). Academic admission requirements as predictors of counseling knowledge, personal development, and counseling skills. *Counselor Education and Supervision, 45,* 43–57. doi:10.1002/j.1556-6978.2005.tb00129.x

Smith, J., & Hanna, M. A. (1998). Using rubrics for documentation of clinical work supervision. *Counselor Education and Supervision, 37,* 269–278. doi:10.1002/j.1556-6978.1998.tb00550.x

Sperry, L. (2010). *Highly effective therapy: Developing essential clinical competence in counseling and psychotherapy.* New York, NY: Routledge; Taylor & Francis Gr.

Strom-Gottfried, K. (2000). Ethical vulnerability in social work education: An analysis of NASW complaints. *Journal of Social Work Education, 36,* 241–252.

Surace, A. L. (2015). *Factors influencing the gatekeeping practices of clinical supervisors working with trainees with deficiencies in character* (Unpublished doctoral project). Marywood University, Scranton, PA.

Swank, J. M., & Lambie, G. W. (2012). The assessment of CACREP core curricular areas and student learning outcomes using the Counseling Competencies Scale. *Counseling Outcome Research and Evaluation, 3,* 116–127. doi:10.1177/2150137812452560

Swank, J. M., Lambie, G. W., & Witta, E. L. (2012). An exploratory investigation of the Counseling Competencies Scale: A measure of counseling skills, dispositions, and behaviors. *Counselor Education and Supervision, 51,* 189–206. doi:10.1002/j.1556-6978.2012.00014.x

Tracey, T. J., & Kokotovic, A. M. (1989). Factor structure of the Working Alliance Inventory. *Psychological Assessment: A Journal of Consulting and Clinical Psychology, 1,* 207–210. doi:10.1037/1040-3590.1.3.207

Veilleux, J. C., January, A. M., VanderVeen, J. W., Reddy, L. F., & Klonoff, E. A. (2012). Differentiating amongst characteristics associated with problems of professional competence: Perceptions of graduate student peers. *Training and Education in Professional Psychology, 6,* 113–121. doi:10.1037/a0028337

Wampold, B. E., & Budge, S. L. (2012). The 2011 Leona Tyler Award Address: The relationship and its relationship to the common and specific factors of psychotherapy. *The Counseling Psychologist, 40,* 601–623. doi:10.1177/0011000011432709

Wood, C. (2005). Supervisory working alliance: A model providing direction for college counseling supervision. *Journal of College Counseling, 8,* 127–137. doi:10.1002/j.2161-1882.2005.tb00079.x

Ziomek-Daigle, J., & Christensen, T. M. (2010). An emergent theory of gatekeeping practices in counselor education. *Journal of Counseling & Development, 88,* 407–415. doi:10.1002/j.1556-6678.2010.tb00040.x

10 Teaching Across Settings

Corinne Bridges and Walter L. Frazier

Effective counselor educators engage students and create meaningful learning experiences regardless of the educational environment. This includes building positive faculty-student relationships as well as facilitating growth fostering peer-to-peer relationships across platforms. Attention to how we effectively communicate to students both in traditional and online environments is imperative to building meaningful relationships, messages, and student success. Face-to-face classrooms, virtual classrooms, and hybrid class constellations are all common options for students. In order to be an effective teacher across settings, you must consider your personal philosophy of teaching in concordance with evidence-based teaching strategies and how to adjust your approach to best fit the environment in which you work. Additionally, you must account for students' varying learning styles and access to the educational setting to maximize the potential for the learning process, particularly the students' professional development as counselor educators. Finally, the counselor educator must incorporate safeguards and standards established by the American Counseling Association (ACA) Code of Ethics, regional accrediting bodies, and professional accreditation standards such as Council for Accreditation of Counseling & Related Education Programs (CACREP).

Learning Objectives

After reading this chapter, you will be able to:

1. Apply strategies for effective teaching across educational platforms.
2. Evaluate current technologies in teaching across face-to-face, online, and hybrid platforms.
3. Analyze ethical guidelines, laws, and regulations related to the use of technology tools in multiple settings.
4. Apply strategies for incorporating technology tools in online, hybrid, and face-to-face platforms.
5. Analyze the implications of culture and diversity in teaching and learning.

CACREP Standards

The following CACREP standards represent those related to teaching, specific to this chapter, and are derived from Section 6, Doctoral Standards for Counselor Education and Supervision:

a. roles and responsibilities related to educating counselors
b. pedagogy and teaching methods relevant to counselor education
e. effective approaches for online instruction
h. ethical and culturally relevant strategies used in counselor preparation
i. the role of mentoring in counselor education

Platforms of Higher Learning

We recognize that the ACA Code of Ethics charges counselor educators to engage students in complex, critical, and reflective practices that encompass ethical standards with attention to multicultural issues across educational platforms (ACA, 2014; Remley & Herlihy, 2015. This higher level of learning includes the use of creative technological advancements to enhance scholar learning. Similarly, each platform, face-to-face, hybrid, and online, requires careful consideration of course planning, teaching strategies, tools, effective delivery of course content, and student participation (McKeachie & Svinicki, 2014; Smith et al., 2015; Albrecht & Jones, 2013). Moreover, all three environments can utilize technology and multimedia instruction (Hayes, 2008) to increase effective communication, be it faculty to student or peer-to-peer (McKeachie & Svinicki, 2014; Smith et al., 2015; Trepal, Haberstroh, Duffey, & Evans, 2007). The scope of this chapter introduces issues relating to faculty-student and peer-to-peer communication as well as the technological tools that facilitate that communication. However, it is important to understand that philosophical, pedagogical, ethical, and multicultural lenses as well as curriculum development and assessment strategies discussed in previous chapters interweave together with technology tools to strengthen content delivery across settings.

Face-to-Face Instruction

The traditional face-to-face classroom has much to offer counseling students. This forum allows for subjective evaluation (Smith, Ferguson, & Caris, 2002), in-person engagement and group activities, and the implementation of humor into the classroom. While many of these can be accomplished in other formats, when engaged in face-to-face environments, students are likely to feel a connection to faculty and fellow students on a seemingly more personal level (Summers, Waigandt, & Whittaker, 2005). Further, instructors are able to integrate technology creatively within their classes to enhance and deepen the overall learning experience (ACES, 2016). This can include utilizing technology to further experiential learning within lecture, discussion, and group work as well as individual and group communication. For example, a counselor educator can assign students to small group Discussion Boards online in which each group must assess individual aspects of the weekly topic. Students can participate in small group discussions, discourse throughout the week, and then bring the final critical analysis from the small online group to the large group in the traditional classroom.

However, there are still challenges to teaching in traditional face-to-face classrooms. For example, students are more likely to take a passive role in learning and participation when physically present (Benshoff & Gibbons, 2011). The learning environment is more structured; the weekly set schedule is not conducive to nontraditional students with families and careers (Robertson, Grant, & Jackson, 2005). In a face-to-face environment, students may become over dependent on their instructor (Robertson et al., 2005) rather than taking an active role in their learning. For example, in face-to face classrooms students may feel inhibited from participating in group discourse; however, in an online setting the perceived anonymity can allow more students to be engaged in active discourse (AbuSeileek, 2012) and application of course concepts.

Online Instruction

Technological advancements have paved the way for an increase in online education among institutions of higher education (ACES, 2016). This has become more common in part due to the cost effective nature for both students and institutions, ease of access, and improved student performance outcomes (ACES, 2016). Critical to the success of students in online forums is interaction between the scholar and course content, faculty, and peers (Smith et al., 2002). Connections between students and course information and materials can be met in a variety of ways online, allowing instructors to reach a diverse student body across multiple learning styles (McKeachie & Svinicki, 2014; ACES, 2016). Online education is more accessible and retains flexibility in scheduling and pace (Fedynich, 2014) which provides an educational opportunity for non-traditional students. Further, students experience enhanced levels of autonomy (Smith et al., 2002; ACES, 2016) which allows for an increase in self-driven participation in discussion and a decrease in student faculty power differential (Svinicki & McKeachie, 2014). Finally, online learning could help prepare students for distance counseling practices in which counselors are expected to understand and implement technological resources legally and ethically (ACA, 2014).

Online environments are not without challenges. Many instructors transition from traditional face-to-face classrooms and lack experience teaching in the online environment. While many students today might be comfortable utilizing multiple technological resources, educators may not transition as easily to an online forum (ACES, 2016); a lack of appropriate training and adequate technical skills can be barriers to faculty success online (McKeachie & Svinicki, 2014; ACES, 2016). Further, time constraints can be a deterrent for faculty. It takes more time to create and build an online classroom (ACES, 2016; Smith et al., 2002). The course preparation for online classrooms is significantly greater than in face-to-face forums (Fedynich, 2014) and educators can spend a substantial amount of time in email communication with students. According to Dougherty, Haddock, and Coker (2015) due to the increased level of "perceived sense of autonomy" (p. 4), students can become argumentative and hostile. This can be true in several aspects of online communication (e.g., email and group discussion forums), which could require additional mitigation and attention to ensure continued respect and consideration for all students (Dougherty et al., 2015). While these time constraints can have a negative impact on faculty, the increase in faculty time spent on communication allows students to feel faculty presence and build relationships, and without consistent interaction, students may be less likely to succeed (Smith et al., 2002; Worley & Tesdell, 2009). A perceived lack of faculty presence, guidance, and support can lead to feelings of isolation and decrease retention (Fedynich, 2014; Wang, Han, & Yang, 2015).

Just as important as training online educators to use technology is student preparedness (ACES, 2016). As adult learners, counselors-in-training represent a wide array of ages, which can result in varied experiences with technology. What may seem common sense for some students may be challenging for a student with less exposure to technology as part of their everyday life. A lack of proper technological understanding can act as a deterrent to learning as well as positive student-faculty relationships (ACES, 2016).

Hybrid Instruction

Hybrid or blended classrooms combine traditional face-to-face settings with online forums and or technological tools to enhance student learning. Hybrid classrooms may represent the best of both worlds in terms of learning outcomes for graduate counseling students. Renfro-Michel, O'Halloran, and Delaney (2010) found adult learners may benefit more from hybrid than traditional face-to-face classes due to the use of technological tools covering more diverse learning styles. This enhances the student experience by providing in-person access to faculty and simultaneously allowing for greater flexibility in pace and scheduling while offering technological tools for self-directed, experiential, and active learning practices.

However, there still remains a paucity of literature on hybrid and online classes in counselor education. While some studies indicate that adult learners seem to navigate technological additions with ease (Renfro-Michel et al., 2010), others found students frustrated by a perceived lack of support from faculty on incorporation of technology (Magil et al., 2015). Research is inconclusive as to whether adult learners are more or less likely to understand technology tools. Consideration must be given to technology use in terms of multicultural awareness and students with disabilities (ACES, 2016). This suggests the need for more research focused on evidence-based practices and student assessment specific to counselor education in hybrid and online settings.

Roles and Responsibilities

Relationships

Relationships remain an important aspect within counselor education. Similar to clinical relationships, counselor educators are ethically obligated to maintain relationships with students that will do no harm (ACA, 2014). In particular, standard 10.a of the ACA *Code of Ethics* (2014) stipulates educators must remain aware of the power differential across all educational platforms and refrain from engaging in clinical or sexual relationships with current students. As faculty, we aim to create a trusting, safe environment (ACES, 2016) in which our students feel comfortable interacting with both professor and peers. Positive faculty-student relationships have been shown to increase learning and reduce dropout (Lee, Pate, & Cozart, 2015) and are particularly important to counseling students (ACES, 2016). Students are more likely to respond positively to programs and in classrooms, when instructors actively participate in positive and consistent interaction (Dixson, 2010). These student-faculty relationships are multi-dimensional and extend to teaching, mentoring, research, and supervisory be it clinical or in teaching assistantships. Therefore, much like in clinical counseling, counselor educators must set appropriate boundaries and engage in self-reflection while simultaneously navigating and nurturing relationships throughout the duration of student's masters or doctoral counseling program (Bernard & Luke, 2013).

Professional Ethics and Boundaries

Due to the nature of serving in multiple roles with students, counselor educators must consider carefully the possible ethical issues that could arise as well as their continued ability to remain objective (Corey, Corey, & Callanan, 2011). In their efforts to provide unique growth fostering relationships with individual students, multicultural awareness and attention to the power differential are imperative (ACA, 2014; Remley & Herlihy, 2015). While the potential risk of boundary crossing and multiple roles with students could act as a deterrent for some faculty (Remley & Herlihy, 2015), these interactions remain highly beneficial to student self-concept, purpose, and intellectual and academic performance (Komarraju, Musulkin, & Gargi, 2010) across educational platforms.

At the same time, faculty must understand and anticipate that one day these students will serve as colleagues in their roles as counselor educators. Maintaining the balance can be difficult; it requires open communication, informed consent, transparent assessment strategies, and consistent and reasonable expectations to achieve success (ACA, 2014). Standard F.10.f of the ACA *Code of Ethics* (2014) supports the notion that effectively communicating and managing established professional boundaries to students from the beginning of the relationship would support ethical responsibilities to students and help decrease relationships outside the educational setting that may be beneficial only to the educator. Much like counselor-client boundaries, student-faculty professional boundary setting is informed by ACA (2014) ethical codes, which require awareness and reflection of the benefits of these relationships and make certain that counselor educators engage only in those that do no harm to their students.

Settings can facilitate and exacerbate efforts to maintain these appropriate boundaries. Digital environments lend to a high level of documented communication (Yates, Adams, & Brunner, 2009). For example, time-stamped email, time-stamped submission of documents, perpetual access to course information and syllabi—to name a few. However, the hybrid and online environments can create physical distance between parties thereby disrupting familiar means of communication, especially for faculty and students that bring less technological knowledge to the table (ACES, 2016; Summers et al., 2005). This emphasizes the need for gatekeeping and attention to individual student experience to help ensure those who are less tech-savvy are not at a disadvantage. Dougherty et al. (2015) recommend using a gatekeeping model in online or hybrid forums, which includes:

> (a) Proactive communication with students about expectations for professional development for the counseling profession, but also for interacting in a virtual environment; (b) Clear guidelines and process for assessing development of "professionalism" within a virtual environment, (c) Clear process

and guidelines for addressing identified issues in development within a virtual classroom, and (d) Clear process for intervention, remediation, and program dismissal for a virtual environment, as needed.

(p. 3)

Recall the multitude of relationships in which you will participate with your students. It is important that you explore how you can ensure best practices for maintaining ethical boundaries and building positive student faculty relationships across platforms. Review the following and allow for time to think about how you will effectively navigate the scenario, utilize gatekeeping strategies, and engage in self-reflection.

Guided Practice Exercise 10.1

You are a professor in an online Counselor Education and Supervision Doctoral Program. In this position, you serve in various roles. For example, you teach, mentor teaching assistants and student researchers, chair dissertation committees, and provide triadic supervision. Currently, you have been assigned a teaching assistant (TA) you have taught in several courses and who has asked you to serve as dissertation chair. You have an established relationship and have built good rapport; however, due to the online nature of the program you have yet to meet. One day your TA sends an abrupt email requesting a phone consult. In this discussion, the TA expresses frustration regarding another faculty member's opinion of the proposed dissertation research. While your TA is not belligerent, the TA becomes very upset and unprofessional in the language used to describe your colleague and questions your colleague's qualifications. However, you happen to agree with the TA's assessment of your colleague's opinion regarding the research.

1. How can you respond in a way that reflects professional expectations and guidelines without alienating your TA?
2. What role does culture play in your response?
3. Should consideration be given to gender identity and the power differential?
4. How can you ensure that you are maintaining appropriate ethical boundaries as well as your positive student-faculty relationship?
5. How would your response change if your TA had disclosed being upset via email rather than in a phone consult?

Faculty-Student Communication

When interacting with students, faculty must demonstrate a willingness to nurture student ideas and investment in student learning and knowledge. In doing so, faculty can model how to appropriately build collaborative professional relationships (ACES, 2016) which allows students to think critically about course concepts and materials and synthesize theory with real world situations. This growth begins with clear, concise, and respectful communication between faculty and students. Faculty who effectively communicate expectations from the beginning of class can build an interactive, experiential, and collaborative space for in-depth learning. For example, the course syllabus can be used as a contract between the student and faculty member that clearly delineates expectations and accountability of students and faculty, as well as procedures regarding grades and contacting the instructor (ACES, 2016). This is an effective communication tool across all settings and the tenets can apply to various aspects of group and individual faculty-student communication, including email interaction, conferencing in person or via telephone or video, and discussion.

In hybrid and online classrooms, the perceived autonomy can help create a more egalitarian relationship between faculty and students, which lends to an increase in communication and discussion (ACES, 2016; McKeachie & Svinicki, 2014). However, this emphasizes the need to further evaluate and decrease emotional reactions as well as increase awareness of our student audience, the purpose of what we are trying to do (e.g., evaluate whether our interaction is getting us what we or the student need), as well as professional and civil tone. When you effectively model positive communication (written and verbal), students can gain firsthand experience of your expectations and learn appropriate behavior that could have benefit in class and as future educators. For example, when engaging in email communication with students, you should avoid sending reactive, emotional responses. It is natural to experience emotional responses to emails; some might even incite anger, especially when there is a perceived lack of cyber civility. Further, while autonomy in online and hybrid classes can be positive, it can also have negative outcomes. You may experience students as unprofessional or disrespectful when students rely on the use of slang and a more conversational style via email (Lewin-Jones & Mason, 2014). Students may be more willing to say things in email that they would otherwise not articulate in person (Boshrabadi & Sarabi, 2016). Emotionally charged responses to students can adversely influence faculty-student relationships. Email communication is better received when it is concise, but not curt; positive; personal; and professional (Lewin-Jones & Mason, 2014).

Consider Case Illustration 10.1, in which, as a professor in an online counseling program, you receive an email from your student.

Case Illustration 10.1

Student Email

As a professor in an online Counseling program, you receive the following email from your student.

Hey,
I read the announcement about weekly discussion post clarification and I had a question! I understand that peer responses are a part of the

workload! I am confused because the syllabus states that we are required to respond to one other student by day 5! But in the clarification it states that we are required to respond to a minimum of two students! My other teachers in past courses have all supported my interpretation and NOT your clarification. idk with the first weeks grades if i will pass this class. Do I have to challenge this or are u going to allow my work? Please don't be the reason I am not allowed to follow my lifelong dream of becoming a counselor educator.

Student

1. What would your next steps be in addressing this student?
2. How could you address cyber civility and professionalism?
3. What role does culture play in your response?

Feedback

Feedback is another important element in communication with students. Effective feedback is consistent, timely, and detailed (Nicol, 2014). This is true across platforms, but even more so in asynchronous settings or online environments. Faculty should provide students with feedback that goes beyond quantitative evaluation that incorporates a personalized qualitative aspect; this can be as simple as addressing a student by name (Leibold & Schwarz, 2015). Leibold and Schwarz (2015) contend the most effective and well received feedback is that which is frequent, immediate, balanced, and specific; incorporates a positive tone; and poses questions that encourage creative and critical thinking. Feedback can be delivered in various ways, across platforms, and be synchronous and/or asynchronous; there are a variety of tools available that allow for verbal recorded feedback as well as live feedback via the web. For example, screen captures, rubrics, online grading, email, phone and video conferencing, or wikis, to name a few. However, you will find a more in-depth discussion on technological tools and options further on in this chapter.

Discussion with and among students is possible within all platforms and can allow various classroom objectives to be met. Online and hybrid synchronous components can increase communication (Benshoff, & Gibbons, 2011) and allow for the exploration of course content and materials on a deeper more meaningful level through written discussion (Leibold & Schwarz, 2015). The enhanced student autonomy (Smith et al., 2002) and decreased power differential between student and instructor allows self-driven students to engage in more critical and creative written discussion (Leibold & Schwarz, 2015; McKeachie & Svinicki, 2014). Online discussions provide students with more time to think and process responses to discussions as well as reach a wider array of resources through the Internet. The latter emphasizes the need for faculty to teach students how to differentiate between scholarly materials and non-scholarly resources (Smith et al., 2002). However, written communication is not the only avenue with which students and faculty can engage. For example, in an online or hybrid classroom faculty and students alike can utilize video discussions as a means to effective communication in a more personal manner. Active engagement in discussion will strengthen the relationships and communication between faculty and students as well as peer to peer.

Facilitating effective communication between students can be an essential element to student success and could help create a sense of community as well as more opportunities for social interaction (Hung, Flom, Manu, & Mahmoud, 2015). Peer-to-peer discussion increases student autonomy, encourages professionalism and critical and creative thinking, and helps create social and community presence. Further, building a safe, trusting, and collaborative environment could lend to more diverse student interactions online (Hung et al., 2015). In both asynchronous and synchronous settings faculty can encourage students to engage in discourse, ask questions, and further learning in a meaningful way that supports peer-to-peer interaction and communication. Across educational settings faculty can use technology tools such as IM, Skype, and Adobe Connect in and outside of the classroom to expand communication and strengthen peer-to-peer and student-faculty relationships. A more in-depth discussion of the various tools, utilization by students and faculty, and pros and cons follows.

Technology Options for the Classroom

Advances in educational technology have grown exponentially since the days Plato and other students dialogued at the feet of Socrates. Let us remember that significant educational technology advances occurred well before the development of the personal computer and the Internet. The invention of the chalkboard and pencils at the turn of the 19th century, nearly 100 years before the Internet, revolutionized education. Distance learning first occurred with on-air classes over the radio in the 1920s. A truly exceptional development for the future in counselor education, particularly skills-training courses, was the introduction of videotaping in the 1950s. We did not see the development of handheld calculators until 1972. So, by the time the Internet became more accessible to educators in the early 1990s, many developments in technology for educational use had occurred (Purdue University, n.d.). Today, the term *educational technology* relates mostly to computer and Internet applications, but we recognize that educational technology refers to any device that facilitates educational communication, from the chalkboard to the online discussion forum.

In the early 1990s, the Internet functioned mostly in a relatively inert, text-based environment (Rockinson-Szapkiw & Walker, 2009; Bory, Benecchi, & Balbi, 2016). Mostly, the experienced HTML code writers submitted content and updates to pages on the Internet; the Internet represented great potential for sharing information much like a highly accessible digital encyclopedia at best (Bory et al., 2016; Dumitrescu, 2015). But creative programming innovations and rapid hardware developments opened the door in the late 1990s for anyone surfing the Internet to add content to pages with relative ease, and the Internet transformed into what is called Web 2.0 (Rockinson-Szapkiw & Walker, 2009; Bory et al., 2016). The Web 2.0 version of the Internet facilitated opportunities for social interaction where persons could contribute and edit content in wikis, post viewpoints and ideas on blogs, and design interactive web pages that share and collect information from others surfing the Internet (Rockinson-Szapkiw & Walker, 2009). Social networking and peer-to-peer environments allowed persons to readily engage one another by sharing digital files and rapidly sending messages, tweets, and posts to private and public groups (Jencius & Wade, 2011).

Regardless of the setting (traditional, hybrid, or online), counselor educators enjoy an ever-growing number of technology options from which to choose. Whether the course developer wishes to create an integrated environment combining various technologies or simply to supplement course activities using very limited, static technologies, the options continue to grow. In fact, by the time the publishers distribute this text, many more options will become available (Main & Dziekan, 2012), so we do not anticipate we will provide an exhaustive list of known technologies. Instead, we wish to spur awareness and interest in technology use strategies so that newly developing tools will be more accessible and appreciated by the readers of this text.

Counselor educators need to consider many factors when choosing to incorporate technological resources, especially online tools. For instance, the instructor's skills and knowledge will significantly influence the quality and effectiveness of these tools, but the students' learning style will need to be considered as well (Cicco, 2012). Also, student accessibility to the classroom should be considered when determining the use of technology resources for course delivery (Main & Dziekan, 2012). Hybrid and online teaching pedagogy offers a plethora of opportunities for research studies as effective strategies for incorporating technologies in counseling education settings needs to be further assessed beyond theoretical applications. Doctoral students and counselor educators may find little evidence in the current literature that clearly identifies the pros and cons of various approaches to technology uses combined with instructors' skills and student learning styles (Carr, Zube, Dickens, Hayter, & Barterian, 2013).

As an instructor in an online counseling course, consider the scenario in Case Illustration 10.2, involving accessibility to a course.

Case Illustration 10.2

Student Accessibility to an Online Course

As part of the weekly activities of your course, you meet with your students through a video conferencing platform. Each student is required to attend and to engage in the process. You have a student that contacts you directly at the beginning of the course.

> Teacher,
> This will be my first experience with a course requiring a live video meeting, and I don't know if I can do it. I don't know if I can keep up with the conversation. I'm pretty sure I can listen to the conversation, but in crowds I don't do a good job of saying what I mean to say. That's why I'm in this

online degree program. I can type my thoughts better than I can speak, at least when I'm in a hurry. My words get jumbled. Did you get my disability letter from the disability office? I have an auditory processing disorder. You have to give me extra time to complete assignments.

1. What accommodations would make this component of the course accessible to this student?
2. What technology tools may be helpful to students with communication disabilities?
3. What are the barriers that your use of technology in the classroom creates for persons with various disabilities?

Table 10.1 Technology Toolbox

Category	Tools	URLs
Video Sharing Websites	Youtube Vimeo	www.youtube.com www.vimeo.com
Telephone and Video Conference	Adobe Connect Cysco Webex Ring Central for Business Skype for Business Turbobridge Zoom	www.adobe.com/products/adobeconnect.html www.webex.com/ www.ringcentral.com/ https://products.office.com/en-us/skype-for-business/online-meetings www.turbobridge.com/index.html https://zoom.us/
Telephone Conferencing	Turbobridge	www.turbobridge.com/index.html
Virtual Worlds	Second Life Kitely Active Worlds Quest Atlantis	http://secondlife.com/ www.kitely.com/ www.activeworlds.com http://atlantisremixed.org
Learning Management Systems	Blackboard Canvas Moodle	www.blackboard.com www.canvaslms.com www.moodle.com
Social Media	Twitter Facebook Pinterest Instagram Snapchat Tumblr	www.twitter.com www.facebook.com www.pinterest.com www.instagram.com www.snapchat.com www.tumblr.com

Ethical considerations should be considered when incorporating technology in the classroom. The American Counseling Association (2014) Code of Ethics includes guidelines for counselor educators utilizing technology as part of delivering course content through various forms of technology, particularly online applications. Specifically, the Code of Ethics (ACA, 2014) reminds supervisors and educators they must have competence in using any technology ranging from online classroom management systems to social media. In fact, Section H.6 explicitly addresses social media. Having knowledge and competence in utilizing online applications for supervision and education of counseling students involves knowing the limits and risks of using the technology. Wilkinson and Reinhardt (2015) recommend that counselor educators employ strategies consistent with the Health Insurance Portability and Accountability Act (HIPAA) and the Health Information Technology for Economic and Clinical Health (HITECH) Act. These regulations emphasize protection of confidentiality and the rights of those receiving the services provided by the professional in electronic mediums. We chose to organize this discussion as if these tools distinctly fall into one of two simple categories, synchronous and asynchronous delivery, and as if these technologies function separately from one another. This organization only serves to simplify the discussion, but we wish to emphasize that these distinctions are not so simple. We will present examples of combined and overlapping technologies to conclude this section because we recognize that any combination of technologies may be used across all course delivery settings.

Utilization of Technology in Counselor Education

Course Management Platforms

Many course management platforms exist, including Moodle, Blackboard, and WebCT, to name just a few. Many textbook publishers establish pre-developed content for course management platforms and even provide access to versions of these platforms for counselor education courses. Through the use of course management platforms, faculty may develop a course to cover weekly activities such as discussion forums, blogs, group projects, tests, and assignments. Instructors can provide course content, communicate via email and announcements, and post grades. In many cases universities integrate a classroom management platform with the campus-wide registration and enrollment systems, so the course platform may appear seamless with campus operations. For counselor educators teaching in programs that do not routinely or collectively utilize a specific course management platform, getting started may seem daunting. But the benefits of the coordinated resources available through these platforms gives reason for programs to consider adopting such a system. All types of classroom delivery can utilize some level of this technology to facilitate the learning experience for counseling students.

Combinations of Resources

Counselor educators have the opportunity to incorporate both synchronous and asynchronous technologies in the course delivery regardless of the setting. For instance, Moran and Milsom (2015) introduced a strategy of using the flipped classroom in counselor education by providing students on-demand videos, learning resources, and just-in-time teaching course content prior to class meetings; thereby, the students engage the material prior to class. Subsequently, the class meeting becomes an opportunity for the instructor to provide individualized hands-on skill development and experiential strategies where the students apply their knowledge (Moran & Milsom, 2015; Young, Bailey, Guptill, Thorp, & Thomas, 2014). With the growing use of the Internet and computer technologies, the idea of combining multiple technologies for classroom use has already started. Faculty and students routinely use conference calling, email, and online classroom management platforms to interact and deliver course materials. Familiarity with all this technology will enhance the counselor education experience for both faculty and students.

With this growing availability of technology for the classroom setting, a word of caution should be noted. Acceptance of technology by both faculty and students, and conversely resistance to technology, can impact the viability of the introduction of technology in the classroom. Researchers have sought to continually increase their understanding of the factors that contribute to technology acceptance. Davis (1989) developed the Technology Acceptance Model focusing upon the user's perception of the usefulness and ease of using the technology. But later, Venkatesh, Morris, Davis, and Davis (2003) and then Venkatesh, Thong, and Xu (2016) proposed the Unified Theory of Acceptance and Use of Technology which includes social and intrinsic values that influence a person's willingness to adopt technology use for different applications. While these theories appear to apply across cultures (Jung & Lee, 2015; Ortaçtepe, 2016; Simeonova, Bogolyubov, & Blagov, 2014), opportunities for research evaluating the characteristics of acceptance and resistance to technology use in the classroom by graduate students abound.

Asynchronous and Synchronous Technologies

Generally, technology falls under two categories representing the type of communication between users. Asynchronous technologies involve differentiated or separated communications. For instance, email communication between users occurs in distinct messages. While messages may be delivered in a back-and-forth interaction, the technology delivers the communication one packet at a time. This differs from synchronous communication such as a video conference between users. In a video conference, communication between parties occurs simultaneously with a fluid interaction. Other forms of asynchronous communication include texting, messaging, and discussion forums. Besides video conferencing, synchronous communication occurs via telephone and chat discussions (Chapman, Baker, Nassar-McMillan, & Gerler, 2011; Carlisle, Carlisle, Hill, Kirk-Jenkins, & Polychronopoulos, 2013). Counselor educators may utilize any combination of synchronous and asynchronous technology for the delivery of course material and peer-to-peer and faculty-and-scholar interaction.

Asynchronous Technologies

EMAIL

Counselor educators have used email long enough that we take for granted its many uses. In fact, counselor educators began using email as a mode of teaching and supervision communication about the same time the American public began widespread use of the electronic medium (Clingerman & Bernard, 2004;

Graf & Stebnick, 2002; Luke & Gordon, 2011; Romano & Cikanek, 2003). Email offers an asynchronous mode of communication that gives the author of the email time to formulate thoughts, construct the flow of the content, and edit the text before sending the message to a select individual or group of recipients (Watts, 2016). Whether the message is a single word or graphic or a long, complicated presentation of text with files of content, the author can send the email as a time-stamped communication. Students needing timely feedback and ready access to faculty may use email to ask questions, send course assignments for review and grading, and provide private information without engaging the rest of the class members (Clingerman & Bernard, 2004). Faculty may send email to individual or groups of students to record time sensitive notifications of gate-keeping steps, notes of a non-recorded audio and video communication, and instructions and announcements pertinent to course or program requirements and communication (Carlisle et al., 2013). Both faculty and students routinely utilize email as a strategy for sending an easy-to-access collection of important resources such as web links; tailored messages to individuals and groups; and of course documents, including assignments, paper submissions, syllabi, course instructions, course content (Zhao, Meyers, Timmerman, & Fonner, 2012). These features translate to the peer-to-peer relationships between students and between faculty members, also. Students may readily share documents and information with one another.

Because emails may be stored on an off-site computer server, the author and recipient may indefinitely store, organize, and access these emails for later reference without the danger of losing the content to technology failure or loss of a computer device. At the time of this publication, 47 states, Washington, DC, and the U.S. Virgin Islands have codified electronic transaction acts that establish that electronic records and signatures transmitted through emails may be recognized as legal documents no different than hard-copy records with hand-written signatures (Uniform Law Commission, 2016). Counselor education programs may transmit signature required agreements and commitments between students and faculty.

ON-DEMAND VIDEOS

Counselor educators have used demonstration videos to teach counseling students theory specific techniques since tape recording has been available (Jerry & Collins, 2005; Walz & Johnston, 1963). Many counseling degree programs stocked a library full of VHS tapes until college libraries began accessing online collections of these videos. With the easy use of smartphone and laptop computers with built-in cameras and video recording software, recording instructional videos and classroom activities for on-demand access can be a valuable tool for course content delivery (Renfro-Michel et al., 2010). Classrooms equipped with audio-video equipment may record class meetings that course instructors can provide in an online environment for students to download for later use. Educators may provide instructions and explain important components of a subject in brief videos to address different learning styles of online students. With the availability of social media (next section), these videos may be made available for student access through the Internet.

Roodt and Peier (2013) demonstrated that students from the Net Generation (those born in the 1980s or later) enjoyed and preferred YouTube videos as supplemental resources that increased student engagement. Using a camera equipped hand-held device or other digital video recorder, instructors can record videos that demonstrate techniques for skills-training classes or provide individualized in-person videos of instructor feedback (Carlisle et al., 2013; Jerry & Collins, 2005; Moran & Milsom, 2015). Also, instructors may record presentations of course content or instructions for completing specific course tasks (Renfro-Michel et al., 2010). Using online video management platforms such as YouTube or Vimeo, the instructor can upload those videos for classroom presentations or when students wish to view them on-demand. This author (Frazier) has used YouTube to make available to class members videos that explain his expectations for assignments. These videos are uploaded on a private YouTube channel registered through the YouTube website for free. The YouTube platform assigns a web address for each video, and the author shares the links to those addresses in emails and course announcements. The YouTube channel stores the videos, and the instructor can save them for subsequent sections of the course to be reused and distributed as needed.

YouSeeU is an online resource that provides a platform for video assignments, peer-to-peer and instructor video feedback, face-to-face interaction, and virtual skill practice both in synchronous and asynchronous formats (Bao, Moore, Tinianow, & Nideffer, 2017). A course instructor teaching counseling skills could create a video assignment for a specific skill demonstration. Students may demonstrate the use of a particular skill, potentially in collaboration with another student through a video, by recording the video interaction. Then the instructor and classmates may be able to access the video and record their own feedback to the student.

SOCIAL MEDIA (TEXTING/MESSAGING, TWITTER/FACEBOOK, DISCUSSION FORUMS, BLOGS, AND WIKIS)

When we talk about social media and the Internet, we are referring to Web 2.0 (Rockinson-Szapkiw & Walker, 2009). When Internet technologies opened the door for users to add and edit content placed on the Internet, the conversations became two-way streets (Jencius & Wade, 2011). Despite the common assumption that social media refers to sites like Facebook, Twitter, Pinterest, and Instagram, numerous applications fall under the very large umbrella of social media (Rockinson-Szapkiw & Walker, 2009). Social media involves any aspect where Internet users may engage with others by contributing and viewing and sometimes editing content on the Internet. Educators utilize various forms of social media to harness the potential for class members to collaborate, network, and engage beyond the typical classroom setting (Watts, 2016). Additionally, students utilize social media with or without the directives of the course, so counselor educators should become aware of the workings of social media at least for keeping abreast of their students' realities.

Discussion Forums/Blogs

Counselor educators may use discussion forums or interactive blogs to engage class members in discussions of specific topics (Watts, 2016). Class members may introduce topics and respond to peer and faculty contributions. We call an ongoing conversation about a specific topic a thread; in many cases the formatting of the forum links responses together so that the reader can follow the conversation. Specific topics may be initiated by the instructor or students. Many classroom management systems such as Blackboard or WebCT facilitate discussion forums for formal or informal discussions (Rockinson-Szapkiw & Walker, 2009). A special quality of classroom discussion forums is their relative privacy for members of the class. These platforms limit access to the discussion and other aspects of the classroom to those enrolled in the course as students, instructors, and support staff. In addition to class-wide communication between the instructor and students, this medium offers the instructor a confidential mechanism to evaluate student posts and offer constructive feedback. To encourage student development in the subject area, the discussion forums may serve as a mechanism for students to reflect their knowledge of topics, evaluate one another's posts, and practice sharing new ideas. Potentially with purposeful facilitation by the instructor, these forums serve as environments for students to post preliminary ideas for later course projects, and the feedback provided by the forum members offers a collegial and scholarly dialogue supporting further progress (Luhrs & McAnally-Salas, 2016).

Wikis

Educators use wiki platforms to encourage collaborative learning projects for groups of students (Zheng, Niiya, & Warschauer, 2015). Familiar with Wikipedia? Wikis allow groups to contribute and edit content on the same online document creating opportunities for student collaboration. While an abundance of platforms exists, some wikis require users to utilize basic codes to post content while other platforms allow contributions with little or no skills beyond basic Internet browsing experience (Griffith, 2012).

Twitter/Facebook/Pinterest/Instagram

Finally, we discuss those highly developed websites that provide specialized platforms for communication, better known as Twitter and Facebook. These two sites, along with numerous others, offer users unique mechanisms for engaging and interacting with one another. Unlike the closed discussion forums provided within the classroom management systems (Blackboard, WebCT, Moodle, etc.), these social media sites provide limited opportunities for private interaction. Public social media sites thrive on public exposure of content; therefore, classroom applications of these sites may be limited (at this point in time), at least as it relates to facilitating within-class activities. If the instructor posts videos on YouTube or Vimeo and neglects to select the check boxes indicating the video content is hidden from public searches, the videos may be publicly viewed. Posting these videos within classroom management platforms may be more private, thereby giving the instructor more control for managing privacy and compliance with the Family Educational Rights and Privacy Act. These platforms may be excellent environments for counselor educators to demonstrate the multiple opportunities for student counselors to engage in leadership roles, advocate for social change, solicit research volunteers, collect social data, and observe sociopolitical trends. As in other forms of social media, counseling students utilize these resources for out-of-class purposes, so counselor educators may learn more about the worldview of students by becoming more familiar with these media. At the same time, counselor educators' familiarity with this medium in the classroom can facilitate discussions about ethical use of these resources in the counseling arena.

Synchronous Technologies

Beyond the face-to-face experience of the classroom, various technologies offer opportunities for faculty and students to interact in real time. From old school communication by telephone to sophisticated landscapes such as online virtual worlds, many options should be considered for creating synchronous interactions. Supervisors with experience utilizing synchronous technologies have found that communicating with supervisees through both face-to-face and synchronous technology methods to be equally beneficial (Chapman et al., 2011). The following forms of synchronous technology offer counselor educators important resources for expanding their reach to student access that is both humanizing and responsive for student development.

Telephone Calls/Conference Calls

Much of the technology discussed in this chapter has evolved in the past 10 years, so even with cellular equipment, the telephone seems to be an old-school technology. The idea of talking over a telephone connection simply still works, and the longevity of telephone communication for the general public as well as education seems dependable and comforting in this world of dramatic technological change (Aborisade, 2012; Van Volkom, Stapley, & Malter, 2013). In some cases, a telephone call may serve as a substitute for a face-to-face conversation, but it is an effective communication link. For online courses, the telephone serves as a lifeline for students and faculty to communicate with one another in cases where confusion, frustration, or isolation overcome the educational experience. For distance education, long-distance toll charges may be less of a factor with cellular communication. Also, availability of conferencing multiple callers in one call allows faculty and students to gather by phone for presentations, tutoring, and collaboration. Recordings of phone conversations, whether a dyad or a whole group, can provide callers a record of the communication for later reference. So, an old-school technology has only become better with age. In cases where other forms of technology simply fail due to limited resources, limited technology, or technology failure, the phone conversations may serve as a steady and comfortable resource (Aborisade, 2012; Ladyshewsky & Pettapiece, 2015)

Video Conferencing

As an adjunct to phone communication, video conferencing adds the face-to-face component to a conversation or group connection that may be missed in the phone call. To whatever extent we rely upon non-verbal cues to communicate with one another, video conferencing brings to the telephone conversation the real-time presence of the caller. Additionally, with video conferencing many platforms offer data sharing capabilities that allow transmission of files and presentation of desktop display in the video layout. A common feature allows audio or audio-visual recordings of the video conference for future viewing, too. Many of these tools are available at no cost or free for limited uses with costs for longer recordings or time periods or for greater numbers of meeting attendees (Martinez & McLaughlin, 2017). For instance, Skype, GoToMeeting, and Webex offer free trials and free versions. Services that require fees may include operator assistance, toll-free call-in numbers, and cloud storage of recordings. See Table 10.1 for a list of several video conferencing resources and web addresses.

Virtual Worlds

Persons familiar with games such as Mindcraft and World of Warcraft have an idea of a virtual world. These two video games give insight to the potential for educational use of virtual worlds. Virtual worlds involve players (or students) who take on roles as avatars and interact with other players within a landscape. Players can control the actions, expressions, and movements of their avatars, communicate with other avatars, and complete tasks of the game. The aspects of the platforms that may be applicable to counselor education is the communication and interaction between students through avatars. A virtual world available is Second Life (McGhee, Brown, & Pressley, 2012). With this platform, it may be possible to create an environment where students play roles (counselor and client) to demonstrate and practice specific counseling skills. This interaction supports a constructivist approach to creating online learning environments for students (Reicherzer, Dixon-Saxon & Trippany, 2009). Counseling programs may use virtual worlds to conduct initial interviews with prospective students allowing for transmission of information between both parties but not requiring travel or face-to-face interaction (McGhee et al., 2012). Like other technologies, virtual worlds like Second Life offer many advantages to counselor educators, but faculty skill and understanding of the technology must be mastered in order to fully appreciate and utilize the resource for educational purposes. Additionally, as with other forms of social media, participants can engage in abusive or inappropriate behavior, so counselor educators need to understand the medium to protect participants from harassment and misuse of the technology (Behm-Morawitz & Schipper, 2016; Reed, 2010).

Virtual Classrooms

Of all the technologies discussed in this chapter, virtual classrooms may be the most cumbersome and expensive to establish, but it may be a very strong contender for some brick-and-mortar programs with satellite campuses. Virtual classrooms bring together multiple classrooms by audio-visual connection with cameras and video screens, particularly in situations that make it impossible to assemble the class, such as an astronaut demonstrating outer space science experiments to a classroom (An et al., 2016). In this arrangement, an instructor works from one classroom location with or without students while one or more groups of students in classrooms in other locations watch through audio-video technology. Students may communicate to the instructor from any of the locations, and the instructor can see students in all the classrooms. This would look much like a video conference call but with student-filled classrooms as participants. Much like a brick-and-mortar classroom, the virtual classroom adds to the benefits of real-time interaction between the instructor and students (Martin, Parker, & Deale, 2012), but classroom instruction must be tailored to account for the context of the technology-assisted interaction (Aydemir, Kursun, & Karaman, 2016).

Summary

In this chapter, we addressed the various settings—face-to-face, online, and hybrid classrooms—where counselors meet the task of facilitating learning opportunities for students. These environments involve numerous responsibilities, as the counselor educator must manage professional ethics and appropriate boundaries to establish the best conditions for communication and interaction with students and between students. The vast array of technologies available to the counselor educator can be daunting to negotiate as both synchronous and asynchronous options continue to multiply. Phone conversations have expanded to video conferencing, and assignment feedback has multiplied into numerous forums. Classrooms have become virtual environments through discussion forums, virtual classrooms, and virtual worlds. While the opportunities to incorporate various forms of technology in the learning environment, the basic relationship and need for clear communication between the teacher and the student remains the core of education.

Additional Resources

The following resources provide additional information relating to the chapter topics.

PC Magazine Reviews of Video Conferencing Resources includes a review of 10 different applications. www.pcmag.com/article2/0,2817,2388678,00.asp

Center for Credentialing and Education provides information and resources for training and credentialing for distance counseling. www.cce-global.org/Credentialing/DCC

Edutopia—12 Awesome Edtech Apps—an example of the plethora of applications adapted for educational purposes. www.edutopia.org/blog/12-awesome-edtech-apps-vicki-davis

Teachthought.com—50 Of The Best Teaching & Learning Apps For 2016—another example of the plethora of applications adapted for educational purposes at various developmental levels. www.teachthought.com/technology/best-teaching-and-learning-apps-for-2016/

G2Crowd.com—Best Learning Management System (LMS) Software—a comparison of numerous online learning management systems. www.g2crowd.com/categories/learning-management-system-lms

References

Aborisade, O. P. (2012). Telephone: The old technology that is never old. *International Journal of Emerging Technologies in Learning*, 7(3), 54–58.

AbuSeileek, A. F. (2012). The effect of computer-assisted cooperative learning methods and group size on the EFL learners' achievement in communication skills. *Computers & Education, 58*(1), 231–239.

Albrecht, A. C., & Jones, D. G. (2013). Using distance learning in teaching. In J. D. West, D. L. Bubenzer, J. A. Cox, & J. M. McGlothlin (Eds.), *Teaching in counselor education: Engaging students in learning* (pp. 97–113). Alexandria, VA: Associaton for Counselor Education and Supervision.

American Counseling Association. (2014). *ACA code of ethics.* Alexandria, VA: Author.

An, S. A., Zhang, M. Tillman, D. A., Robertson, W., Siemssen, A., & Paez, C. R. (2016). Astronauts in outer space teaching students science: Comparing Chinese and American implementations of space-to-earth virtual classrooms. *European Journal of Science and Mathematics Education, 4*(3), 397–412.

Association for Counselor Education and Supervision. (2016). Best practices in teaching in counselor education. Retrieved from www.acesonline.net/resources/aces-teaching-initiative-taskforce-report-october-2016

Aydemir, M., Kursun, E., & Karaman, S. (2016). Question-answer activities in synchronous virtual classrooms in terms of interest and usefulness. *Open Praxis, 8*(1), 9–19.

Bao, M., Moore, T. T., Tinianow, D., & Nideffer, J. (2017). Enhancing teaching and learning through technology: A comparative study of YouSeeU integration. *International Journal of Technologies in Learning, 24*(1), 15–23.

Benshoff, J. M., & Gibbons, M. M. (2011). Bring life to e-learning: Incorporating a synchronous approach to online teaching in counselor education. *Professional Counselor, 1*(1), 21–28.

Behm-Morawitz, E., & Schipper, S. (2016). Sexing the avatar: Gender, sexualization, and cyber-harassment in a virtual world. *Journal of Media Psychology: Theories, Methods, and Applications, 28*(4), 161–174.

Bernard, J. M., & Luke, M. (2015). A content analysis of 10-years of the clinical supervision literature in counselor education. *Counselor Education & Supervision, 54*(4), 242–257.

Bory, P, Benecchi, E., & Balbi, G. (2016) How the web was told: Continuity and change in the founding fathers' narratives on the origins of the World Wide Web. *New Media & Society, 18*(7). doi:10.1177/1461444816643788

Boshrabadi, A. M., & Sarabi, A. B. (2016). Cyber communic@tion etiquette: The interplay between social distance, gender and discursive features of student-faculty email interactions. *Interactive Technology and Smart Education, 13*(2), 86–106.

Carlisle, R. M., Carlisle, K. L., Hill, T., Kirk-Jenkins, A. J., & Polychronopoulos, G. B. (2013). Distance supervision in human services. *Journal of Human Services, 33*(1), 17–28.

Carr, C. T., Zube, P., Dickens, E., Hayter, C. A., & Barterian, J. A. (2013). Toward a model of sources of influence in online education: Cognitive learning and the effects of web 2.0. *Communication Education, 62*(1), pp. 61–85.

Chapman, R. A., Baker, S. B., Nassar-McMillan, S. C., & Gerler, Jr., E. R. (2011). Cybersupervision: Further examination of synchronous and asynchronous modalities in counseling practicum supervision. *Counselor Education & Supervision, 50*(5), 298–313.

Cicco, G. (2012). Strategic lesson planning in online courses: Suggestions for counselor educators. *i-manager's Journal on School Educational Technology, 8*(3), 1–7.

Clingerman, T. L., & Bernard, J. M. (2004). An investigation of the use of e-mail as a supplemental modality for clinical supervision. *Counselor Education and Supervision, 44,* 82–95.

Corey, G., Corey, M., & Callanan, P. (2011). *Issues and Ethics in the Helping Professions* (8th ed). Belmont, CA: Brooks/Cole.

Davis, F. D. (1989). Perceived usefulness, perceived ease of use, and user acceptance of information technology. *MIS Quarterly, 13*(3), 319.

Dixson, M. (2010). Creating effective student engagement in online courses: What do students find engaging? *Journal of the Studentship of Teaching and Learning, 10*(2), 1–13.

Dougherty, A. E., Haddock, L. S., & Coker, J. K. (2015). *Student development and remediation processes for counselors in training in a virtual environment.* Retrieved from //www.counseling.org/knowledge-center/vistas

Dumitrescu, V. M. (2015). *One step ahead: From web 1.0 to web 2.0 technologies in higher education.* The 11th International Science Conference eLearning and Software for Education, Bucharest, April 23–24. doi:10.12753/2066-026X-15-111

Fedynich, L. V. (2014). Teaching beyond the classroom walls: The pros and cons of cyber learning. *Journal of Instructional Pedagogies, 13*(1). Retrieved from http://files.eric.ed.gov/fulltext/EJ1060090.pdf

Graf, N. M., & Stebnicki, M. A. (2002). Using e-mail for clinical supervision in practicum: A qualitative analysis. *Journal of Rehabilitation, 68*(3), 41–49.

Griffith, E. (2012). *How to create your own wiki.* PC Magazine. Retrieved January 31, 2012, from www.pcmag.com/article2/0,2817,2399582,00.asp on 11/16/2016

Hayes, B. G. (2008). The use of multimedia instruction in counselor education: A creative teaching strategy. *Journal of Creativity in Mental Health, 3*(3), 243–253.

Hung, W., Flom, E., Manu, J., & Mahmoud, E. (2015). A review of the instructional practices for promoting online learning communities. *Journal of Interactive Learning Research, 26*(3), 229–252.

Jencius, M., & Wade, M. E. (2011). The digital psyway. *Counseling Today,* Oct., 24–25.

Jerry, P., & Collins, S. (2005). Web-based education in the human services: Use of web-based video clips in counselling skills training. *Journal of Technology in Human Services 23*(3/4), 183–199.

Jung, I., & Lee, Y. (2015). YouTube acceptance by university educators and students: A cross-cultural perspective. *Innovations in Education and Teaching International, 52*(3), 243–253. doi:10.1080/14703297.2013.805986

Komarraju, M. & Musulkin, S., & Bhattacharya, G. (2010). Role of student–faculty interactions in developing college students' academic self-concept, motivation, and achievement. *Journal of College Student Development, 51*(3), 332–342.

Ladyshewsky, R., & Pettapiece, R. G. (2015). Exploring adult learners usage of information communication technology during a virtual peer coaching experience. *Online Learning, 19*(2), 107.

Lee, E., Pate, J., & Cozart, D. (2015). Autonomy support for online students. *Techtrends: Linking Research & Practice to Improve Learning, 59*(4), 54–61. doi:10.1007/s11528-015-0871-9

Leibold, N. N., & Schwarz, L. M. (2015). The art of giving online feedback. *Journal of Effective Teaching, 15*(1), 34–46.

Lewin-Jonesa, J., & Mason, V. (2014). Understanding style, language, and etiquette in email Communication in higher education: A survey. *Research in Post Compulsory Education, 19*(1), 75–90.

Luke, M., & Gordon, C. (2011). A discourse analysis of school counseling supervisory email. *Counselor Education & Supervision, 50,* 274–291.

Luhrs, C., & McAnally-Salas, L. (2016). Collaboration levels in asynchronous discussion forums: A social network analysis approach. *Journal of Interactive Online Learning, 14*(1), 29–44.

Martinez, J., & McLaughlin, M. K. (March 14, 2017). *The Best Video Conferencing Software of 2017.* PC Magazine. Retrieved August 3, 2017, from www.pcmag.com/article2/0,2817,2388678,00.asp

Main, D., & Dziekan, K. (2012). Distance education: Linking traditional classroom rehabilitation counseling students with their colleagues using hybrid learning models. *Rehabilitation Research, Policy, and Education, 26*(4), 315–320.

Martin, F., Parker, M. A., & Deale, D. F. (2012). Examining interactivity in synchronous virtual classrooms. *International Review of Research in Open and Distance Learning, 13*(3), 227–261.

Martinez, M., & McLaughlin, M. K. (2017). *The best video conferencing software of 2017.* PC Magazine. Retrieved March 14, 2017, from www.pcmag.com/article2/0,2817,2388678,00.asp

McGhee, T. W., Brown M., & Pressley, F. (2012). Second life: Implications for counselor education. *Michigan Journal of Counseling: Research, Theory, and Practice, 39*(1), pp. 19–30.

McKeachie, W. J. & Svinicki, M. D. (2014). *McKeachie's teaching tips: Strategies, research, and theory for college and university teacher* (14th ed.). Independence, KY: Cengage Learning.

Moran, K., & Milsom, A. (2015). The flipped classroom in counselor education. *Counselor Education & Supervision, 54,* 32–43.

Nicol, D. (2014). Good designs for written feedback for students. In M. Svinicki & W. J. McKeachie (Eds.), Teaching tips: Strategies, research, and theory for college and University teachers (pp. 109–124). Belmont, CA: Wadsworth.

Ortaçtepe, D. (2016). Using webcasts for student presntations: A case study. *The International Journal of Information and Learning Technology, 33*(1), 57–74.

Purdue University. (n.d.). The evolution of technology in the classroom. Retrieved from http://online.purdue.edu/ldt/learning-design-technology/resources/evolution-technology-classroom

Reed, C. (2010). Why must you be mean to me? Crime and the online persona. *New Criminal Law Review, 13*(3), 485–514.

Reicherzer, S., Dixon-Saxon, S., & Trippany, R. (2009). Quality counselor training in a distance environment. *Counseling Today,* 46–47.

Renfro-Michel, E. L., O'Halloran, K. C., & Delaney, M. E. (2010). Using technology to enhance adult learning in the counselor education classroom. *Adultspan Journal, 9*(1), 14–25.

Remley, T., & Herlihy, B. (2015). *Ethical, Legal, and Professional Issues in Counseling* (5th ed.). Pearson

Robertson, J. S., Grant, M. M., & Jackson, L. (2005). Is online instruction perceived as effective as campus instruction by graduate students in education? *Internet and Higher Education, 8,* 73–86.

Rockinson-Szapkiw, A. J., & Walker, V. L. (2009). Web 2.0 technologies: Facilitating interaction in an online human services counseling skills course. *Journal of Technology in Human Services, 27.* doi:10.1080/15228830903093031

Roodt, S., & Peier, D. (2013). Using youtube© in the classroom for the net generation of students. *Issues in Informing Science & Information Technology, 10,* 473–488.

Romano, J. L., & Cikanek, K. L. (2003). Group work and computer applications: Instructional components for graduate students. *Journal for Specialists in Group Work, 28*(1), 23–34.

Simeonova, B., Bogolyubov, P., & Blagov, E. (2014). Use and acceptance of learning platforms within universities. *The Electronic Journal of Knowledge Management, 12*(1), 26–37.

Smith, G. G., Ferguson, D., & Caris, M. (2002). Teaching over the web versus in the classroom: Differences in the instructor experience. *International Journal of Instructional Media, 29*(1), 61–67.

Smith, R. L., Flamez, B., Vela, J. C., Schomaker, S. A., Fernandez, M. A., & Armstrong, S. N. (2015). An exploratory investigation of levels of learning and learning efficiency between online and face-to-face instruction. *Counseling Outcome Research and Evaluation*, 6(1), 47–57.

Summers, J., Waigandt, A., & Whittaker, T. A. (2005). A comparison of student achievement and satisfaction in an online versus a traditional face-to-face statistics class. *Innovative Higher Education*, 29(3), 233–250.

Trepal, H., Haberstroh, S., Duffey, T., & Evans, M. (2007). Considerations and strategies for teaching online counseling skills: Establishing relationships in cyberspace. *Counselor Education & Supervision*, 46(4), 266–279.

Uniform Law Commission. (2016). Retrieved November 14, 2016, from www.uniformlaws.org/LegislativeFactSheet.aspx?title=Electronic%20Transactions%20Act

Van Volkom, M., Stapley, J. C., & Malter, J. (2013). Use and perception of technology: Sex and generational differences in a community sample. *Educational Gerontology*, 39(10), 729.

Venkatesh, V., Morris, M. G., Davis, G. B., & Davis, F. D. (2003). User acceptance of information technology: Toward a unified view." *MIS Quarterly*, 27, 425–478.

Venkatesh, V., Thong, J. Y. L., & Xu, X. (2016). Unified theory of acceptance and use of technology: A synthesis and the road ahead. *Journal of the Association for Information Systems*, 17(5), 328–376.

Walz, G. R., & Johnston, J. A. (1963). Counselors look at themselves on video tape. *Journal of Counseling Psychology*, 10(3).

Wang, Y., Han, X., & Yang, J. (2015). Revisiting blended learning literature: Using a complex adaptive systems framework. *Educational Technology & Society*, 18(2), 380–393.

Watts, L. (2016). Synchronous and asynchronous communication in distance learning: A review of the literature. *The Quarterly Review of Distance Education*, 17(1).

Wilkinson, T., & Reinhardt, R. (2015). Technology in counselor Education: hippa and hitech as best practice. *Professional Counselor*, 5(3), 407–418.

Worley, W., & Tesdell, L. (2009). Instructor time and effort in online and face-to-face teaching: Lessons learned. *IEEE Transactions on Professional Communication*, 52(2), 138–151.

Yates, B. L., Adams, J. W., & Brunner, B. R. (2009). Mass communication and journalism faculty's perceptions of the effectiveness of email communication with college students a nationwide study. *Learning, Media and Technology*, 34(4), 307–321.

Young, T. P., Bailey, C. J., Guptill, M., Thorp, A. W., & Thomas, T. L. (2014). The flipped classroom: A modality for mixed asynchronous and synchronous learning in a residency program. *Western Journal of Emergency Medicine: Integrating Emergency Care with Population Health*, 15(7), 938–944.

Zhao, Q., Ahn, S., Meyers, R. A., Timmerman, C. E., & Fonner, K. L. (2012). Exploring students' use of e-mail for out-of-class communication: Frequency, satisfaction, and learning self-efficacy. *Journal on Excellence in College Teaching*, 23(4).

Zheng, B., Niiya, M., & Warschauer, M. (2015). Wikis and collaborative learning in higher education. *Technology, Pedagogy and Education*, 24(3), 357–374, doi:10.1080/1475939X.2014.948041

11 The Role of Mentoring in Counselor Education

Cirecie A. West-Olatunji, Kathryn Williams, and Christian D. Chan

A traditional definition of mentoring characterizes this concept as a close working relationship between an experienced person and one who is typically less knowledgeable and new to a profession or environment (Harvey, McIntyre, Heames, & Moeller, 2009). Beginning professionals are cited as particularly needing mentoring in order to increase skill, become socialized into the network, and learn to navigate the career journey. Other individuals, such as faculty of color and women, are often subject to poor or no mentoring experiences, contributing to negative work environments and encounters with glass ceiling career trajectories that limit their advancement (West-Olatunji, 2013). Ineffective mentoring may be due to mismatched goals between the mentor and mentee (Eby & Allen, 2002) or nonvoluntary participation in a mentoring experience (Allen, Eby, & Lentz, 2006). Additionally, demands for accountability at work can leave little time to provide mentoring (Clayton, Sanzo, & Myran, 2013). Scholars have also suggested that a pervasive attitude of elitism favors some individuals over others, with a talented few being chosen to prepare for career advancement (Sherman, 2005). Scholars who explore the concept of mentoring suggest that effective mentors can significantly impact the organization as a whole and have an effect on productivity, sustainability, and worker/member job satisfaction (Eby & Allen, 2002). This chapter provides an overview of the extant literature on mentoring with a focus on mentoring in counselor education and offers strategies for effective mentoring in the various roles in counseling practice.

Learning Objectives

After reading this chapter, you will be able to:

1. Apply concepts, theories, strategies, and skills related to mentoring for all areas of counseling specialties, including counselor education and supervision.
2. Develop a personal philosophy of mentoring.
3. Analyze: (a) ethical guidelines and (b) laws, regulations, and statutes, and reflect on your own moral and philosophical beliefs regarding mentoring.
4. Assess the implications of mentoring within a socially and culturally diverse society to broaden participation within the profession at all levels of practice.
5. Apply strategies for mentoring counselors-in-training and early career professionals.

Relevant CACREP 2016 Standards Included in This Chapter

Section 2: PROFESSIONAL COUNSELING IDENTITY; COUNSELING CURRICULUM;

- F.1.b. the multiple professional roles and functions of counselors across specialty areas, and their relationships with human service and integrated behavioral health care systems, including interagency and interorganizational collaboration and consultation.
- F.4.b. approaches for conceptualizing the interrelationships among and between work, mental well-being, relationships, and other life roles and factors

Section 6: DOCTORAL STANDARDS COUNSELOR EDUCATION AND SUPERVISION B. DOCTORAL PROFESSIONAL IDENTITY;

3. TEACHING

- B.3.h. ethical and culturally relevant strategies used in counselor preparation
- B.3.i. the role of mentoring in counselor education

5. LEADERSHIP AND ADVOCACY

- B.5.a. theories and skills of leadership
- B.5.b. leadership and leadership development in professional organizations
- B.5.c. leadership in counselor education programs
- B.5.k. strategies of leadership in relation to current multicultural and social justice issues
- B.5.l. ethical and culturally relevant leadership and advocacy practices

Why Is Mentoring Necessary in Counselor Education?

One of the key characteristics of the mentoring experience is *improved learning* for the mentee and enhancing professional competence and self-confidence (Harvey et al., 2009). Although mentoring is important in the professional development of all early career faculty, scholars have suggested that it is especially important for women and faculty of color (Butner, Burley, & Marbley, 2000; Casto et al., 2005; Tillman, 2001). Mentoring allows the opportunity for individuals receiving mentoring to connect with individuals who have traveled a similar road and survived. It also enables a relationship that provides moral support, guidance, feedback, and encouragement throughout the journey. As an informal teacher, mentors can assist early career professionals in mastering skills in order to advance in their careers (Borders et al., 2011). Second, mentors provide *clear guidance* to promote developmental progress in a mentee's career. According to the Principles and Practices of Leadership Excellence of Chi Sigma Iota, the international counseling honor society, mentors encourage and empower their mentees with the intent of helping them to advance (Lonn, Tello, Duffey, & Haberstroh, 2014). Finally, mentors assist mentees in the *socialization process* within their professional community (Borders et al., 2011; Casto, Caldwell, & Salazar, 2005; Harvey et al., 2009). Ultimately, mentors promote a sense of community, collaboration, and collegiality within the organization by fostering relationship and a sense of belonging. After reading Guided Practice Exercise 11.1, take a moment to reflect on your mentoring philosophy; what are your values and beliefs?

> **Guided Practice Exercise 11.1**
>
> In considering the characteristics of effective mentors, take a moment and reflect on your personal values, personality, and lived experiences that inform your career choices and decision-making. Who were your best mentors and what qualities did they have? Now, create a two-column table of your mentoring skills and characteristics. On the left column, list those mentoring elements that you currently possess and on the right column, list those skills and characteristics that you wish to acquire. Once you have completed your table, contemplate how these items reflect your mentoring philosophy.

Mentoring as an Aspect of Leadership

Perhaps the most prolific writings on mentoring and leadership have been authored by Kathy Kram, who focused primarily on women's experiences. Kram (1985) asserted that effective mentoring experiences significantly contributed to leadership engagement and influenced both career advancement and psychosocial outcomes. The relationship between mentoring and leadership has focused on two essential elements. First, mentoring is seen as a catalyst in the development of future leaders and helps to enhance their leadership skills (Olson & Jackson, 2009). Second, mentoring is a way to prepare individuals for leadership roles and leadership succession (McCloughen, O'Brien, & Jackson, 2009). In nursing, for example, scholars have asserted that mentoring necessitates: (a) engaging the mentee's own values and (b) facilitating awareness for opportunities that encourage self-discovery and growth (Metcalfe, 2010).

Although research in other disciplines has suggested that there is a relationship between leadership and mentoring, little is known about the role of mentoring in effective leadership in counselor education. In one such study, emerging leaders reported how influential their mentors were in deciding to serve in leadership roles (Meany-Walen, Carnes-Holt, Barrio Minton, Purswell, & Pronchenko-Jain, 2013). Future research exploring mentoring in counselor education might focus on mutuality and how the developmental nature of the mentoring relationship influences the outcomes of the mentoring experience.

Five Effective Mentoring Strategies

The use of planned mentoring events to link early career faculty to the surrounding community and other scholars of color can foster mentoring opportunities and relationships (Quezada & Louque, 2004). As outlined in the following section, we offer five strategies that have been shown to be effective for developing high quality mentoring experiences in: (a) advancing career development, (b) socialization into the counseling community, and (c) improving learning for mentees (Harvey et al., 2009).

Strategy #1

Sponsor advancement with counselors-in-training, doctoral students, and early career professionals (Harvey et al., 2009). For example, you can recommend counselors-in-training at the master's level, in particular, for fellowships, awards, research opportunities, professional development training, research assistantships, and doctoral studies. By recommending counselors-in-training for fellowships and awards, they are likely to be introduced to a new network of experienced counselors and educators who can enlighten them and expand their horizons. For those students who are interested in entering into the practice of counseling, professional development training will position them as future leaders in the counseling community. Often, counselors-in-training, particularly those from working class backgrounds, may not be aware of the nuances of doctoral studies (i.e., preparation, developmental milestones, and benefits/challenges; Warnock & Appel, 2012). Additionally, female counselors-in-training may be less inclined to pursue a doctoral program to become a counselor educator due to the lack of sufficient role models (Casto et al., 2005). It is imperative that mentors are proactive by not only introducing their mentees to these possibilities, but also actively sponsoring their advancement by writing letters of nomination and providing verbal recommendations.

As a mentor, you can sponsor the advancement of doctoral students by inviting them to collaborate on manuscripts, conference presentations, grant development, and teaching. The use of collaborative writing has been shown to be transformative in affecting the career trajectory of mentees (Jones, Jones, & Murk, 2012; Lamar & Helm, 2017). Additionally, doctoral students can be members of research teams to engage in the research process from design, such as grant proposal development, through dissemination (e.g., professional presentations and reports; Borders, Wester, Fickling, & Adamson, 2014b; Lambie & Vaccaro, 2011; Lambie, Hayes, Griffith, Limberg, & Mullen, 2014; Letourneau, 2015; Okech, Astramovich, Johnson, Hoskins, & Rubel, 2006). Mentors can also select doctoral students to serve as teaching assistants and co-facilitators of groups in addition to engaging in consulting opportunities (Baltrinic, Jencius, & McGlothlin, 2016). These examples and activities will enhance students' skills and prepare them for a career trajectory as a counselor educator.

For early career professionals, mentors can sponsor their advancement by asking them to collaborate on writing projects (Jones et al., 2012; Letourneau, 2015), participate in research groups (Lamar & Helm, 2017; Peterson, Hall, & Buser, 2016), pair them with other scholars (Borders et al., 2012, 2014b; Lambie et al., 2014), and engage in grant development activity (Borders et al., 2011; Briggs & Pehrsson, 2008). Thus, by inviting them to co-author manuscripts that can be submitted to refereed journals, mentors can model how to successfully publish the quality and quantity necessary for advancement (Borders et al., 2014b; Kuo, Woo, & Bang, 2017; Lambie & Vaccaro, 2011). Finally, assisting new faculty members in securing grants and fellowships, mentors can position them as having the intellectual capacity to consistently produce scholarly works and provide them with a sustainable research agenda that will ensure their success at their institution (Borders et al., 2011; Briggs & Pehrsson, 2008; West-Olatunji, 2013).

Strategy #2

Serve as a coach to socialize the mentee to the institutional norms with an emphasis on community, collaboration, and collegiality. You can socialize master's students as counselors-in-training to have a sense of *community* during their field experiences (Fulton & Shannonhouse, 2014). Regardless of the setting, counselors-in-training often require: (a) careful monitoring and feedback on their interactions, (b) re-positioning of their counselor identity when placed in environments that do not reflect our core assumptions, and (c) support when experiencing doubts about their career choice, abilities, or talents (Goldberg, Dixon, & Wolf, 2012). Additionally, you, as a mentor, can assist counselors-in-training to become oriented to the policies and procedures at their institution and counseling program. While handbooks are helpful in providing institutional information, the subtle, unwritten guidelines for behaviors and expectations are often provided within mentoring relationships (Boswell, Wilson, Stark, & Onwuegbuzie, 2015). Thus, your mentoring can serve as a key factor in ensuring whether a student graduates on time, registers for the correct courses in sequence, or is aware of options for areas of specialization within and outside of the department (Baltrinic, Waugh, & Brown, 2013).

Opportunities to *collaborate* can include membership in the local chapter of Chi Sigma Iota, participation in peer networks, and involvement in social justice initiatives. As mentors, you can also serve as coaches to counselors-in-training, particularly at the master's level, to facilitate development of their *collegiality* competencies by encouraging (a) involvement within the local counseling community, such as helping out with a National Alliance on Mental Illness (NAMI) walk or participating in National Depression Screening Day, (b) engagement with other mental health professionals to raise awareness about salient mental health issues, and (c) engage in disaster mental health initiatives that allow for interdisciplinary advocacy and interventions. With your assistance, mentees can inquire, discuss, and prepare for interactions within multiple, and sometimes complex, counseling networks.

Doctoral students can benefit from you to mentor as coaches when seeking *community* within the counseling department as instructors (or teaching assistants), supervisors, and as student representatives on committees at the local, state, or national level. In the role of supervisor of supervisors, the mentor who serves as coach to the doctoral students expends much of the time interpreting the counseling department's cultural norms to assist the doctoral student with supervision skills and supervisory development (Borders et al., 2014a; CACREP, 2015; Glosoff, Durham, & Whittaker, 2012). Within the context of higher education and counselor education, faculty mentors generate a contextual understanding of norms within the department. For example, you might serve as a teaching assistant, co-instructor, or instructor of record in which you build on your pedagogical practices, curriculum development, and professional identity as a counselor educator. The intention in departments of counselor education are for faculty to serve as mentors as you move forward in your professional journey, capitalizing on the breadth of your skills as a counselor educator (Baltrinic et al., 2016). Finally, when doctoral students are engaged in leadership activities at the state, branch, or national level as a student representative on a committee or task force, mentors can introduce doctoral students to the cultural norms within various professional organizations to aid them in their interpersonal skills (Meany-Walen et al., 2013). All of these activities frequently involve work with professionals, paraprofessionals, and lay people while requiring strong group work, interpersonal, and negotiation skills to jointly reach consensus about how to advocate for the target cause.

While working on research teams, doctoral students can learn how to successfully *collaborate* with other scholars and negotiate roles and responsibilities. A mentor can aid doctoral students in avoiding the pitfalls of collaborative scholarship and successfully advance their research agenda. This perspective is also true for other scholarly activities, such as preparing for presentations at conferences and other professional venues where similar planning processes exist. Finally, mentors can serve as coaches to facilitate *collegiality* when doctoral students engage in advocacy efforts to advance the profession, support marginalized clients, and engage in social justice projects. All of these activities frequently involve work with professionals, paraprofessionals, and lay people while requiring strong group work, interpersonal, and negotiation skills to jointly reach consensus about how to advocate for the target cause.

As emerging scholars, early career professionals have similar needs for community, collaboration, and collegiality. As a mentor, you can coach them in the politics of *community* within professional organizations (Cashwell & Barrio Minton, 2012). Also, mentors can help new scholars in learning how to *collaborate* on research projects, writing initiatives, and administrative tasks, such as accreditation and assessment reports (Borders, Wester, Fickling, & Adamson, 2014; Hays, Wood, & Smith, 2012; Lambie & Vaccaro, 2011). Lastly, mentors can facilitate the development of *collegial* skills for early career professionals by serving as coaches when new scholars are serving on university committees to help them navigate and avoid the pitfalls of intercollegiate discussions and joint decision-making (Borders et al., 2011).

Strategy #3

Protect from adversity. This strategy is arguably the most important because it incorporates the concepts of *prevention, intervention*, and *reflection*, particularly under stressful circumstances. In this role, the mentor who focuses on prevention can anticipate obstacles and advise mentees, at all levels, about situations that might place them at risk and provide coping strategies (Hill, Leinbaugh, Bradley, & Hazler, 2005; West-Olatunji, 2013). Useful techniques in this role might include the use of personal stories or metaphors that illuminate the possible dangers of certain situations or choices that the mentee is considering. As a buffer against adverse circumstances, the mentor can also intervene once the mentee is in the midst of a difficult situation. In this manner, the mentor can engage in damage control to remove obstacles to successful career advancement. It is imperative that the mentor maintains unconditional positive regard toward the mentee throughout this experience to allow for a teachable moment in the training and development of the mentee (Boswell et al., 2015; Butler, Evans, Brooks, Williams, & Bailey, 2013; Solomon & Barden, 2016). Post-crisis, the mentor can facilitate a process meeting to deconstruct the situation and debrief about the incident to determine how it can be prevented in the future. Debriefing techniques can include personal disclosure, role-plays, and cognitive exercises (e.g., journaling, creative writing, and list making) that facilitate increased self-awareness (Black, Suarez, & Medina, 2004; Solomon & Barden, 2016). In some situations, it might be useful to refer the mentee to personal counseling if it is discovered that the decision-making was flawed due to emotional or psychological dispositions that cannot be addressed within the mentoring relationship (Black et al., 2004; Dang & Sangganjanavanich, 2015; Myers, Trepal, Ivers, & Wester, 2016; Solomon & Barden, 2016). The final element of this strategy ends with inquiry about the lessons learned and contextualized within an encouraging framework (Solomon & Barden, 2016). This strategy in which the mentor serves as protector is applicable for counselors-in-training, doctoral students, and early career professionals. Counselors-in-training at the master's level would best benefit from this mentoring strategy when placed at their field sites, active in local counseling/civic organizations, or serving as leaders on campus (Fulton & Shannonhouse, 2014).

Doctoral students are often vulnerable in their "middle of the road" roles (i.e., not quite a faculty member and not quite a student either). Given that the ACA Code of Ethics (American Counseling Association, 2014) states that doctoral students "have the same ethical obligations as counselor educators, trainers, and supervisors" (F.7.g), it is ultimately the responsibility of experienced counselor educators to train, support, and encourage them (Boswell et al., 2015). Thus, it is important that the mentor is mindful of their vulnerability and, when critical incidents arise, serve as an advocate to protect the doctoral students' reputation and positioning as a worthy future counselor educator (Casto et al., 2005). Moreover, since many doctoral students serve as supervisors to master's level counselors-in-training, their assessment of master's students' clinical skills can place them at risk and challenge their existing clinical, interpersonal, and mediation skills. Finally, doctoral students who are involved in leadership activity within professional associations and interacting with seasoned practitioners and experienced counselor educators may need a buffer between the harsh realities of organizational politics and their idealized view of professional advocacy (Luke & Goodrich, 2010). Mentors can assist at every stage of adverse situations, from prevention to intervention to reflection (McKibben, 2016; McKibben, Webber, & Wahesh, 2017).

For early career scholars, the need for a senior scholar to serve as protector is paramount to their survival (Borders et al., 2011). Untenured faculty are highly vulnerable within higher education and can benefit from sage advice from a mentor to help them navigate through the murky landscape of the counselor education community. This issue is particularly evident for women and faculty of color (Casto et al., 2005). Thus, mentors must have as a primary goal to prevent obstacles that can have the potential to make or break an early career scholar. Often, there are no second chances and critical incidents that occur early on in a new faculty member's career can leave lasting impressions on their peers, who are often the individuals who will later make the initial nomination for their tenure and promotion. Once an incident has occurred, it is the mentor who is able to serve as the bridge between other colleagues and the early career scholar and can aid in repositioning the mentee or reinterpreting the events as a means of damage control. Finally, mentors can assist early career scholars in debriefing about the adverse incident by focusing on the idea that all is not lost, their career has not been destroyed and that it is possible to recover. Most importantly, mentors can outline the recovery steps while focusing on lessons learned.

Strategy #4

Challenge their performance to elevate their skills. Four elements of this mentoring strategy are worthy of attention: introduce them to new ideas, expose them to new experiences, expand their self-awareness, and identify strengths (Casto et al., 2005; Solomon & Barden, 2016). For counselors-in-training at the master's level, it is important that mentors aid them in developing a professional identity that is informed by both conventional concepts that undergird the profession and *new ideas* that are currently being investigated (Luke & Goodrich, 2010; McKibben, 2016). It is the task of the mentor to stay current with trends in counselor education in order to avoid the pitfall of relying on outdated perspectives on counseling practices and scholarship (Sweeney, 2012). By staying informed, mentors can help to position counselors-in-training as future leaders who are creative in their thinking, informative in their discussions and oral presentations, and cutting edge in their effective service delivery (Dollarhide, Gibson, & Saginak, 2008; Dollarhide, Gibson, Moss, & Leach, 2015; Gibson, Dollarhide, & McCallum, 2010; McKibben et al., 2017; Sweeney, 2012). All of these outcomes translate into successful career advancement for future practitioners.

Mentors are also responsible for exposing counselors-in-training to *new experiences* through the use of service learning activities embedded in the coursework; outreach experiences available during term breaks, including guest speakers in course development (either face-to-face or electronically using video conferencing software); and partnering with faculty teaching other counseling specialties to exchange dialogue during class time. Service learning activities have been shown to increase students' cultural awareness and enhance empathy for diverse individuals and communities (West-Olatunji, Watson, Nelson, Frazier, & St. Juste, 2008). Thus, service learning promotes expedient learning about bias and systemic oppression and social marginalization (Fulton & Shannonhouse, 2014). Rather than teaching about service learning, mentors can expose counselors-in-training to service learning activities and community experiences to promote curiosity, engagement, and responsiveness (Storlie, Shannonhouse, Brubaker, Zavadil, & King, 2016).

You, as a mentor, can design outreach experiences for all levels of mentees. Counselors-in-training, doctoral students, and early career scholars can benefit from live supervision, coaching, and instruction out in the real world, away from the home institution and city. Scholarship on outreach in counseling has suggested that these experiences aid in increasing participants' understanding of sociopolitical context (Goodrich, Hrovat, & Luke, 2014; Ratts, 2011) in clinical service delivery, awareness of their own biases toward diverse populations, and appreciation for a wider array of clinical interventions beyond the mainstay of Eurocentric strategies found in counseling textbooks (Chung, Bemak, & Talleyrand, 2007). Given the dominance of certain privileged perspectives, such as Eurocentrism, heterosexism, classism, and male gender bias, in our training (West-Olatunji, 2013), when mentors use guest speakers to give voice to alternate realities and lived experiences, they can aid in enhancing clinical efficacy for future clinicians. Another way that mentors can offer new experiences is to partner with a colleague to exchange classes. For example, a counselor educator who teaches rehabilitation counseling at a predominately White institution (PWI) partnered with a colleague who teaches clinical mental health counseling at a Historically Black College/University (HBCU) for several years to schedule two class periods in which their students visit each other's classrooms. The outcomes of this exchange served to aid in the unification of counselor identity and to simultaneously raise awareness about specific focus areas and dynamics that are not covered in their respective programs.

Doctoral students and early career scholars can be introduced to new experiences when recommended for professional development trainings, retreats, think tanks, research projects, and fellowships that bring together diverse scholars to focus on a particular instructional technique or program area. Faculty serving as mentors to doctoral students can effectively motivate mentees to be mindful of their skill development by giving them choices. Consider the situation provided in the sidebar and reflect on how you might respond.

Case Illustration 11.2

A first-year doctoral student asked to speak with a faculty member who could serve as a teaching mentor. As they discussed the level of responsibilities the student could assume, the counselor educator presented a three-tiered system of assisting in the class. In the first tier, the counselor educator leads the class and the student is an active observer. In the second tier, the counselor educator and doctoral student equally co-lead the class. The third tier allows for the doctoral student to lead the class with the counselor educator in the observing and supporting role. Since this doctoral student had some previous teaching experience with undergraduate courses, the student opted for the second tier. After the tier had been chosen, the counselor educator and doctoral student proceeded to discuss the student's strengths and areas for growth and subsequently identify ways to support the student's continued development as an instructor. The student agreed to be the primary instructor for at least three weeks of the term, with two of the weeks focusing on areas of strength with the remaining week reserved for an area that would challenge the student. *Which tier would you choose and why? In assessing the mentor's skills, what strategies were implemented? Would you characterize this mentor's behaviors as effective or ineffective?*

Without the assistance of a mentor, many doctoral students and early career professionals are unaware of opportunities for skill development.

Given that the developmental nature of the mentoring relationship suggests that mentees are often unaware of how important self-reflection and contemplation are to efficacy (Hicks, 2011), it is necessary that mentors encourage mentees to expand their self-awareness. Often, mentees are so busy trying to be successful that they are focusing on the *doing* rather than the *thinking*. Mentors can aid mentees, at all levels, to expand self-awareness by reflecting. Mindfulness has been shown to facilitate clear thinking, effective decision-making, and improve self-knowledge (Hicks, 2011). In his book, *The Seven Habits of Highly Effective People* (1989), Stephen Covey related a story of preparing for a lecture while in Hawaii in which he had his presentation papers stacked on several chairs. Suddenly, a gust of wind blew through the open windows and scattered his papers throughout the room. First the first few minutes, he tried to gather the papers (unsuccessfully) until he realized that the task would be easier if he first closed the windows and then picked up the papers. Reflection is often counter-intuitive because we often want to keep working—but, by thinking things through, we work more efficiently. Mentors can be critical allies in encouraging mentees to think before acting, schedule time to reflect, and see the value of taking time to increase self-awareness and self-knowledge.

Finally, mentors can challenge mentees to step up their game and elevate their skills by helping them to identify their strengths. Counselors-in-training, particularly at the master's level, often find it difficult to focus on their strengths given the degree of feedback they receive throughout their training (Goldberg et al., 2012). Thus, mentors who serve as advisors or supervisors, in particular, can emphasize what strengths they bring to their counselor training. This is also relevant for doctoral students, who often experience anxiety about moving from the student role to one of researcher, supervisor, and co-facilitator (Borders et al., 2014b; Lamar & Helm, 2017; Lambie et al., 2014; Lambie & Vaccaro, 2011; Milsom & Moran, 2015). Similarly, early career professionals may question their ability to perform at the level necessary to earn tenure at their institution (Barrett & Brown, 2014; Borders et al., 2011; Briggs & Pehrsson, 2008; Hill, 2004, 2009; Magnuson, Norem, & Lonneman-Doroff, 2009; Pente & Adams, 2010; Sangganjanavanich & Balkin, 2013). Mentors can use encouragement to scaffold mentees from where they are to where they could be. In this manner, mentors serve to facilitate career imagination and can aid mentees in crafting a career plan that incorporates personal challenges to build new skill sets along the career journey (Harvey et al., 2009). This empathic and encouraging challenge of mentees' performance also allows for the necessary critical feedback of their actions, thoughts, and productivity to allow for an authentic discussion about their scholarship, teaching, and activities within the counseling community to fuel self-awareness and self-knowledge for continuous improvement.

Strategy #5

Increase credibility of the mentee's worth by nominating them for tasks and positions requiring complex skills, appointing them to high profile roles, and situating them as knowledgeable and capable (Luke & Goodrich, 2010; Wahesh & Myers, 2014). For counselors-in-training, mentors serving as advisors (formal or informal) can recommend students for awards, appoint them as student representatives to various committees, and encourage them to participate in student organizations, such as Chi Sigma Iota and other similar student-led associations on campus and locally (Luke & Goodrich, 2010; Meany-Walen et al., 2013; McKibben, 2016; McKibben et al., 2017; Sweeney, 2012; Wahesh & Myers, 2014). For doctoral students, you can promote involvement in state branch and national associations by recommending them to colleagues. More importantly, you can invite doctoral students to accompany them to conferences so that they can be introduced to their peers as an emerging leader and scholar in counselor education. For early career professionals, you can nominate them for opportunities to publish or engage in consulting and professional development trainings. I [first author] remember a time when I was an untenured assistant professor and my department chair rarely recommended me to other scholars as a capable researcher. In one instance, I was the only faculty member in the college who had a restricted user license to work with a national data set. When one of the methodology faculty inquired about who in our department could partner with him to engage in collaborative research using that specific data set, my department chair recommended someone else. Eventually, this scholar located me, but it was not because my mentor had thought to increase my credibility as a scholar. This, in fact, was an example of ineffective mentoring in which I was being positioned as having little or no credibility, and it could have been disastrous for my career if it had not been for other informal mentors who were actively placing me in more high-profile roles and nominating me for opportunities that challenged my existing skills to enhance my competence as a scholar.

All of these strategies are tools that can be used by the mentee or the mentor. As a mentee, you can view the strategies as a checklist to evaluate your current mentoring experience. If you are not able to identify any (or few) of these strategies as part of your mentoring relationship, you probably need to find another mentor. Additionally, you can use this list of strategies to initiate a conversation with your existing mentor to discuss ways that you can enhance your mentoring relationship to potentially improve the outcomes. Consider Case Illustration 11.3 and imagine what steps you might take to advocate for yourself.

Case Illustration 11.3

A second-year doctoral student in Counselor Education and Supervision had focused extensively on clinical practice, supervision, and teaching experience during his first academic year. However, he noticed a glaring disparity in his research experience, especially since research was not a significant emphasis throughout his career and prior journey into the doctoral program. Nonetheless, the student hoped to embark on obtaining research experience vital to the goal of seeking a counselor education faculty position at a research-focused department and institution. Initially, the student felt intimidated by a prolific researcher, scholar, and writer in his department; their interests have a slight overlap in both adult development and trauma areas. Eventually, the student summoned

> enough courage and confidence to approach the specific faculty member for research mentoring. After an exciting conversation, the faculty member immediately invited the student to become the second author in the middle of a current project, although there were already two other doctoral students on the authorship. The faculty member had not consulted the entire research team before adding the doctoral student as an author. *How would you characterize the mentoring associated in this vignette? What mentoring strategies could remain useful in a likely situation? What were effective aspects in the mentoring? What mentoring aspects could have detracted from the doctoral students involved? How could cultural and social identity play a role in the mentoring process?*

Also, if you currently do not have a mentor, you can use these strategies to develop a criterion for choosing a mentor. As a mentor or potential mentor, these five mentoring strategies can help you to review, reflect, and possibly revise your mentoring strategy. Many mentors are selected for this role with little or no training or education about the mentoring experience. Few counselor education programs have developed mentoring manuals or trainings for faculty to serve as a foundation for assessing their performance. Additionally, few programs provide formal evaluation of their mentoring activities. Thus, little is known about the effectiveness, consistency, and conventions of mentors across faculty, programs, mentees, or over time (Fulton & Shannonhouse, 2014).

Considerations for Resistant Students

Identifying the connection and mentoring needs of resistant students can be a complex process, given the differences in style, personality, and cultural understandings. While the formative development of resistant students can easily present challenges to counselor education faculty members, there are multiple perspectives to consider (Shugar, 2016). Positioning students as resistant necessitates contextual interpretations about the differences in cultural meanings of resistance and discursive approaches. Although resistant students can appear challenging for some counselor educators, you can broaden their understanding and expand their mentoring competence by utilizing cultural understanding and engaging in dialogue to elicit the student's lens (Smith-Augustine, Dowden, Wiggins, & Hall, 2014). Faculty, as mentors, can better conceptualize resistant students' motivations by critically analyzing systemic factors that influence students' lives. Drawing from counseling's foundational values of humanism, strengths-based perspectives, wellness, and holistic perspectives, mentors can meaningfully adapt their language and better meet the needs of resistant students. As a mentor, you can also use motivational interviewing techniques (Miller & Rollnick, 2009, 2013) to aid resistant students to explore the pros and cons they can see in decision-making (Giordano, Clarke, & Borders, 2013; Iarussi, Tyler, Littlebear, & Hinkle, 2013; Iarussi, Vest, Booker, & Powers, 2016; Wahesh, 2016; Young & Hagedorn, 2012). Students may need time for self-reflection and can benefit from a mentor who validates their experiences and articulates what challenges may lay ahead (West-Olatunji, 2010).

Summary

Mentoring has been shown to foster relation and a sense of belonging and serves to socialize mentees into the counseling community. Additionally, mentoring is useful in improving learning for a new professional to gain self-confidence and master skills. Finally, mentoring promotes developmental progression in a mentee's career. However, ineffective mentoring, due to role confusion, dual relationships, or dysfunctional dynamics, can serve as an impediment to growth and job satisfaction for both the mentee and the mentor. We have outlined five strategies for effective mentoring that can ensure that the mentoring experience has positive outcomes that ultimately impact the counseling profession as a whole. For all levels of mentees, there is the clear challenge to further explore mentoring in counselor education. This is an area in which we know very little as it relates to our unique core assumptions in counselor education.

Useful Websites

The following websites provide additional information relating to mentoring in counselor education.

Center for Servant Leadership. https://greenleaf.org/
 This website provides information about programs that are designed to advance awareness and understanding about the practice of servant leadership by individuals and organizations.
Free Management Library. http://managementhelp.org/
 This site offers free, online articles for self-development of individuals, groups, and organizations, including over 10,000 links and 650 topics.
Center for Creative Leadership. www.ccl.org/leadership/index.aspx
 This site presents links to training programs, articles, speakers' bureaus and online learning resources, such as podcasts and webinars for individuals seeking to enhance their leadership skills.
Chi Sigma Iota (CSI). www.csi-net.org
 This website presents multiple resources on leadership development and mentoring among students in counselor education and counseling programs, given CSI's mission to advocate for counselor professional identity and counselor education.

Additional Resources

The following resources provide additional information relating to the chapter topics.

Borders, L. D., Wester, K. L., Granello, D. H., Chang, C. Y., Hays, D. G., Pepperell, J., & Spurgeon, S. L. (2012). Association for counselor education and supervision guidelines for research mentorship: Development and implementation. *Counselor Education and Supervision, 51*(3), 162–175. doi:10.1002/j.1556–6978.2012.00012.x
Maxwell, J. (2008). *Mentoring 101.* New York: Thomas Nelson;

A quick and easy read on the practices of being a mentor and choosing a mentor. It gives a brief foundation of the benefits and general history on the experience of mentoring from multiple disciplines.

Zachary, L. J. (2011). *The mentor's guide: Facilitating effective learning relationships.* Hoboken, NJ: Jossey-Bass.

A practical tool book for being an effective mentor that highlights service and support of others that will help them reach their potential.

Zachary, L. J., & Rischler, L. (2009). *The mentee's guide: Making mentoring work for you.* Hoboken, NJ: Jossey-Bass.

This book provides stories of mentoring that express what a deep and personal relationship it can provide for both sides (mentor and mentee).

References

Allen, T. D., Eby, L. T., & Lentz, E. (2006). Mentorship behaviors and mentorship quality associated with formal mentoring programs: Closing the gap between research and practice. *Journal of Applied Psychology, 91*(3), 567.

American Counseling Association. (2014). *ACA code of ethics: As approved by the ACA Governing Council, 2014.* Alexandria, VA: American Counseling Association.

Baltrinic, E. R., Jencius, M., & McGlothlin, J. (2016). Coteaching in counselor education: Preparing doctoral students for future teaching. *Counselor Education and Supervision, 55*(1), 31–45.

Baltrinic, E. C., Waugh, J. A., & Brown, S. (2013). Faculty and student perspectives on what helps counselor education doctoral students towards program completion. *Operant Subjectivity, 36*(4), 253.

Barrett, J., & Brown, H. (2014). From leaning comes meaning: Informal comentorship and the second-career academic in education. *The Qualitative Report, 19*(37), 1–15. Retrieved from http://proxygw.wrlc.org/login?url=http://search.proquest.com.proxygw.wrlc.org/docview/1565808191?accountid=11243

Black, L. L., Suarez, E. C., & Medina, S. (2004). Helping students help themselves: Strategies for successful mentoring relationships. *Counselor Education and Supervision, 44*(1), 44–55. doi:10.1002/j.1556–6978.2004.tb01859.x

Borders, L. D., Glosoff, H. L., Welfare, L. E., Hays, D. G., DeKruyf, L., Fernando, D. M., & Page, B. (2014a). Best practices in clinical supervision: Evolution of a counseling specialty. *The Clinical Supervisor, 33*(1), 26–44. doi:10.1080/07325223.2014.905225

Borders, L. D., Wester, K. L., Fickling, M. J., & Adamson, N. A. (2014b). Research training in doctoral programs accredited by the council for accreditation of counseling and related educational programs. *Counselor Education and Supervision, 53*(2), 145–160. doi:10.1002/j.1556–6978.2014.00054.x

Borders, L. D., Wester, K. L., Granello, D. H., Chang, C. Y., Hays, D. G., Pepperell, J., & Spurgeon, S. L. (2012). Association for counselor education and supervision guidelines for research mentorship: Development and implementation. *Counselor Education and Supervision, 51*(3), 162–175. doi:10.1002/j.1556–6978.2012.00012.x

Borders, L., Young, J., Wester, K., Murray, C., Villalba, J., Lewis, T., & Mobley, A. (2011). Mentoring promotion/tenure-seeking faculty: Principles of good practice within a counselor education program. *Counselor Education and Supervision, 50*(3), 171–188. doi:10.1002/j.1556–6978.2011.tb00118.x

Briggs, C. A., & Pehrsson, D. (2008). Research mentorship in counselor education. *Counselor Education and Supervision, 48*(2), 101–113. doi:10.1002/j.1556–6978.2008.tb00066.x

Boswell, J. N., Wilson, A. D., Stark, M. D., & Onwuegbuzie, A. J. (2015). The role of mentoring relationships in counseling programs. *International Journal of Mentoring and Coaching in Education, 4*(3), 168–183. Retrieved from http://proxygw.wrlc.org/login?url=http://search.proquest.com.proxygw.wrlc.org/docview/1707763152?accountid=11243

Butler, S. K., Evans, M. P., Brooks, M., Williams, C. R., & Bailey, D. F. (2013). Mentoring African American men during their postsecondary and graduate school experiences: Implications for the counseling profession. *Journal of Counseling & Development, 91*(4), 419–427. doi:10.1002/j.1556-6676.2013.00113.x

Butner, B. K., Burley, H., & Marbley, A. F. (2000). Coping with the unexpected: Black faculty at predominately white institutions. *Journal of Black Studies, 30*(3), 453–462.

Cashwell, C. S., & Barrio Minton, C. A. (2012). Leadership and advocacy in counselor education programs: Administration and culture. In C. Y. Chang, C. A. Barrio Minton, A. L. Dixon, J. E. Myers, & T. J. Sweeney (Eds.), *Professional counseling excellence through leadership and advocacy* (pp. 165–184). New York, NY: Taylor & Francis.

Casto, C., Caldwell, C., & Salazar, C. F. (2005). Creating mentoring relationships between female faculty and students in counselor education: Guidelines for potential mentees and mentors. *Journal of Counseling & Development, 83*(3), 331–336. doi:10.1002/j.1556-6678.2005.tb00351.x

Chung, R. C., Bemak, F., & Talleyrand, R. M. (2007). Mentoring within the field of counseling: A preliminary study of multicultural perspectives. *International Journal for the Advancement of Counselling, 29*(1), 21–32. doi:10.1007/s10447-006-9025-2

Clayton, J. K., Sanzo, K. L., & Myran, S. (2013). Understanding mentoring in leadership development perspectives of district administrators and aspiring leaders. *Journal of Research on Leadership Education, 8*(1), 77–96.

Council for Accreditation of Counseling and Related Educational Programs. (2015). *2016 CACREP Standards*. Alexandria, VA: Author.

Covey, S. R. (1989). *The 7 habits of highly effective people: Powerful lessons in personal change*. New York, NY: Free Press.

Dang, Y., & Sangganjanavanich, V. F. (2015). Promoting counselor professional and personal well-being through advocacy. *Journal of Counselor Leadership and Advocacy, 2*(1), 1–13. doi:10.1080/2326716X.2015.1007179

Dollarhide, C. T., Gibson, D. M., & Saginak, K. A. (2008). New counselors' leadership efforts in school counseling: Themes from a year-long qualitative study. *Professional School Counseling, 11*, 262–271. doi:10.5330/PSC.n.2010-11.262

Eby, L. T., & Allen, T. D. (2002). Further investigation of protégés' negative mentoring experiences patterns and outcomes. *Group & Organization Management, 27*(4), 456–479.

Fulton, C. L., & Shannonhouse, L. (2014). Developing servant leadership through counselor community engagement: A case example. *Journal of Counselor Leadership and Advocacy, 1*(1), 98–111. doi:10.1080/2326716X.2014.886978

Gibson, D. M., Dollarhide, C. T., & McCallum, L. J. (2010). Nontenured assistant professors as American Counseling Association division presidents: The new look of leadership in counseling. *Journal of Counseling & Development, 88*, 285–292. doi:10.1002/j.1556-6678.2010.tb00024.x

Gibson, D. M., Dollarhide, C. T., Leach, D., & Moss, J. M. (2015). Professional identity development of tenured and tenure-track counselor educations. *Journal of Counselor Leadership and Advocacy, 2*(2), 113–130. doi:10.1080/2326716X.2015.1042095

Giordano, A., Clarke, P., & Borders, L. D. (2013). Using motivational interviewing techniques to address parallel process in supervision. *Counselor Education and Supervision*, *52*(1), 15–29. doi:10.1002/j.1556-6978.2013.00025.x

Goldberg, R., Dixon, A., & Wolf, C. P. (2012). Facilitating effective triadic counseling supervision: An adapted model for an underutilized supervision approach. *The Clinical Supervisor*, *31*(1), 42–60.

Goodrich, K. M., Hrovat, A., & Luke, M. (2014). Professional identity, practice, and development of Kenyan teacher-counsellors: An ethnography. *Journal of Counselor Leadership and Advocacy*, *1*(1), 44–66, doi:10.1080/2326716X.2014.886976

Harvey, M., McIntyre, N., Thompson Heames, J., & Moeller, M. (2009). Mentoring global female managers in the global marketplace: Traditional, reverse, and reciprocal mentoring. *The International Journal of Human Resource Management*, *20*(6), 1344–1361.

Hicks, D. (2011). The practice of mentoring: Reflecting on the critical aspects for leadership development. *The Australian Library Journal*, *60*(1), 66–74.

Hill, N. R. (2004). The challenges experienced by pretenured faculty members in counselor education: A wellness perspective. *Counselor Education and Supervision*, *44*(2), 135–146. doi:10.1002/j.1556-6978.2004.tb01866.x

Hill, N. R. (2009). An empirical exploration of the occupational satisfaction of counselor educators: The influence of gender, tenure status, and minority status. *Journal of Counseling & Development*, *87*(1), 55–61. doi:10.1002/j.1556-6978.2009.tb00549.x

Hill, N. R., Leinbaugh, T., Bradley, C., & Hazler, R. (2005). Female counselor educators: Encouraging and discouraging factors in academia. *Journal of Counseling & Development*, *83*, 374–380. doi:10.1002/j.1556-6978.2005.tb00358.x

Iarussi, M. M., Vest, R., Booker, A. T., & Powers, D. F. (2016). Motivational interviewing training in correctional education. *Journal of Correctional Education*, *67*(1), 39–57. Retrieved from http://proxygw.wrlc.org/login?url=http://search.proquest.com.proxygw.wrlc.org/docview/1795922683?accountid=11243

Iarussi, M. H., Tyler, J. M., Littlebear, S., & Hinkle, M. S. (2013). Integrating motivational interviewing into a basic counseling skills course to enhance counseling self-efficacy. *The Professional Counselor*, *3*(3), 161–174. doi:10.15241/mhi.3.3.161

Jones, D., Jones, J. W., & Murk, P. J. (2012). Writing collaboratively: Priory, practice, and process. *Adult Learning*, *23*(2), 90–93. doi:10.1177/1045159512443526

Kram, K. E. (1985). Improving the mentoring process. *Training and Development Journal*, 40–43.

Kuo, P. B., Woo, H., & Bang, N. M. (2017). Advisory relationship as a moderator between research Self-Efficacy, motivation, and productivity among counselor education doctoral students. *Counselor Education and Supervision*, *56*(2), 130–144. doi:10.1002/ceas.12067

Lamar, M. R., & Helm, H. M. (2017). Understanding the researcher identity development of counselor education and supervision doctoral students. *Counselor Education and Supervisions*, *56*(1), 2–18. doi:10.1002/ceas.12056

Lambie, G. W., & Vaccaro, N. (2011). Doctoral counselor education students' levels of research self-efficacy, perceptions of the research training environment, and interest in research. *Counselor Education and Supervision*, *50*(4), 243–258. doi:10.1002/j.1556-6978.2011.tb00122.x

Lambie, G. W., Hayes, B. G., Griffith, C., Limberg, D., & Mullen, P. R. (2014). An exploratory investigation of the research self-efficacy, interest in research, and research knowledge of Ph.D. in education students. *Innovative Higher Education*, *39*(2), 139–153. doi:10.1007/s10755-013-9264-1

Letourneau, J. L. H. (2015). Infusing qualitative research experiences into core counseling curriculum courses. *International Journal for the Advancement of Counselling, 37*(4), 375–389. doi:10.1007/s10447-015-9251-6

Lonn, M. R., Tello, A. M., Duffey, T., & Haberstroh, S. (2014). Relational-cultural theory as pedagogy: Preparing doctoral student leaders for the counselor education workforce. *Journal of Counselor Leadership and Advocacy, 1*(2), 140–151.

Luke, M., & Goodrich, K. M. (2010). Chi Sigma Iota leadership and professional identity development in early career counselors. *Counselor Education & Supervision, 50*, 56–78. doi:10.1002/j.1556-6978.2010.tb00108.x

Magnuson, S., Norem, K., & Lonneman-Doroff, T. (2009). The 2000 cohort of new assistant professors of counselor education: Reflecting at the culmination of six years. *Counselor Education and Supervision, 49*(1), 54–71. doi:10.1002/j.1556-6978.2009.tb00086.x

McCloughen, A., O'Brien, L., & Jackson, D. (2009). Esteemed connection: Creating a mentoring relationship for nurse leadership. *Nursing Inquiry, 16*(4), 326–336.

McKibben, W. B. (2016). The content and process of counseling leadership: Implications for research and practice. *Journal of Counselor Leadership and Advocacy, 3*(2), 147–157. doi:10.1080/2326716X.2016.1147396

McKibben, W. B., Webber, W. B., & Wahesh, E. (2017). Exploring CSI chapter leaders' development toward leadership excellence. *Journal of Counselor Leadership and Advocacy, 4*(1), 52–65. doi:10.1080/2326716X.2017.1282332

Meany-Walen, K. K., Carnes-Holt, K., Barrio Minton, C. A., Purswell, K., & Pronchenko-Jain, Y. (2013). An exploration of counselors' professional leadership development. *Journal of Counseling & Development, 91*, 206–215. doi:10.1002/j.1556–6676.2013.00087.x

Metcalfe, S. E. (2010). Educational innovation: Collaborative mentoring for future nursing leaders. *Creative nursing, 16*(4), 167–170.

Miller, W. R., & Rollnick, S. (2009). Ten things that motivational interviewing is not. *Behavioural and Cognitive Psychotherapy, 37*(2), 129–140. doi:10.1017/S1352465809005128

Miller, W. R., & Rollnick, S. (2013). *Helping people change* (3rd ed.). New York, NY: Guilford Press.

Milsom, A., & Moran, K. (2015). From school counselor to counselor educator: A phenomenological study. *Counselor Education and Supervision, 54*(3), 203–220. doi:10.1002/ceas.12014

Myers, J. E., Trepal, H., Ivers, N., & Wester, K. L. (2016). Wellness of counselor educators: Do we practice what we preach? *Journal of Counselor Leadership and Advocacy, 3*(1), 22–30. doi:10.1080/2326716X.2016.1139479

Okech, J. E. A., Astramovich, R. L., Johnson, M. M., Hoskins, W. J., & Rubel, D. J. (2006). Doctoral research training of counselor education faculty. *Counselor Education and Supervision, 46*(2), 131–145. doi:10.1002/j.1556-6978.2006.tb00018.x

Olson, D. A., & Jackson, D. (2009). Expanding leadership diversity through formal mentoring programs. *Journal of Leadership Studies, 3*(1), 47–60.

Pente, P., & Adams, C. (2010). The slow breath to tenure: Unwinding the university. *The Journal of Educational Thought (JET)/Revue De La Pensée Éducative, 44*(1), 117–129.

Peterson, C. H., Hall, S. B., & Buser, J. K. (2016). Research training needs of Scientist-Practitioners: Implications for counselor education. *Counselor Education and Supervision, 55*(2), 80–94. doi:10.1002/ceas.12034

Quezada, R., & Louque, A. (2004). The absence of diversity in the academy: Faculty of color in educational administration programs. *Education, 125*, 213–222.

Ratts, M. J. (2011). Multiculturalism and social justice: Two sides of the same coin. *Journal of Multicultural Counseling and Development, 39*(1), 24–37. doi:10.1002/j.2161-1912.2011.tb00137.x

Sangganjanavanich, V. F., & Balkin, R. S. (2013). Burnout and job satisfaction among counselor educators. *The Journal of Humanistic Counseling, 52*(1), 67–79. doi:10.1002/j.2161-1939.2013.00033.x

Sherman, W. H. (2005). Preserving the status quo or renegotiating leadership: Women's experiences with a district-based aspiring leaders program. *Educational Administration Quarterly, 41*, 707–740.

Shugar, A. (2016). Teaching genetic counseling skills: Incorporating a genetic counseling adaptation continuum model to address psychosocial complexity. *Journal of Genetic Counseling, 26*(2), 215–223. doi:10.1007/s10897-016-0042-y

Smith-Augustine, S., Dowden, A., Wiggins, A., & Hall, L. (2014). International immersion in Belize: Fostering counseling students' cultural self-awareness. *International Journal for the Advancement of Counselling, 36*(4), 468–484.

Solomon, C., & Barden, S. M. (2016). Self-Compassion: A mentorship framework for counselor educator mothers. *Counselor Education and Supervision, 55*(2), 137–149. doi:10.1002/ceas.12038

Storlie, C. A., Shannonhouse, L. R., Brubaker, M. D., Zavadil, A. D., & King, J. H. (2016). Exploring dimensions of advocacy in service: A content analysis extending the framework of counselor community engagement activities in Chi Sigma Iota chapters. *Journal of Counseling Leadership and Advocacy, 3*(1), 52–61. doi:10.1080/2326716X.2015.1119071

Sweeney, T. J. (2012). Leadership for the counseling profession. In C. Y. Chang, C. A. Barrio Minton, A. L. Dixon, J. E. Myers, & T. J. Sweeney (Eds.), *Professional counseling excellence through leadership and advocacy* (pp. 3–20). New York, NY: Taylor & Francis

Tillman, L. C. (2001). Mentoring African American faculty in predominantly White institutions. *Research in Higher Education, 42*, 295–325.

Warnock, D. M., & Appel, S. (2012). Learning the unwritten rules: Working class students in graduate school. *Innovative Higher Education, 37*(4), 307–321. doi:10.1007/s10755-011-9204-x

Wahesh, E. (2016). Utilizing motivational interviewing to address resistant behaviors in clinical supervision. *Counselor Education and Supervision, 55*(1), 46–59. doi:10.1002/ceas.12032

Wahesh, E., & Myers, J. E. (2014). Principles and practices of leadership excellence: CSI chapter presidents' experience, perceived competence, and rankings of importance. *Journal of Counselor Leadership and Advocacy, 1*, 83–97. doi:10.1080/2326716X.2014.886977

West-Olatunji, C. (2010). If not now, when? Social justice, advocacy, and counselor education. *Professional Issues in Counseling, 42*, 1–11.

West-Olatunji, C. (2013). Fostering inclusivity in counselor education for culturally diverse women. In A. Seto & M. A. Bruce (Eds.), *Women's retreat: Sharing voices of female faculty in counselor education* (pp. 157–171). Lanham, MD: University Press of America.

West-Olatunji, C., Watson, Z., Nelson, M., Frazier, K., & St. Juste, S. (2008). Encouraging advocacy and multicultural competence among counselor trainees through service learning. *Louisiana Journal of Counseling, 15*, 1–18.

Young, T. L., & Hagedorn, W. B. (2012). The effect of a brief training in motivational interviewing on trainee skill development. *Counselor Education and Supervision, 51*(2), 82–97. doi:10.1002/j.1556-6978.2012.00006.x

12 Voices From the Classroom

The following essays are a collection of real life experiences shared by counselor educators around the United States.

You Decide

Having taught and counseled in Michigan in a K–12 background for over 20 years, there have been some distinct differences once I entered the Counselor Educator world. Those differences became evident on a cold winter night in the western corner of Michigan. I am an adjunct for Western Michigan University at the downtown Grand Rapids, Michigan, office. I work with students in the clinical setting while they are doing their practicum; I oversee the students' work with real clients. In my second semester of working at Western Michigan University, I found myself driving to work in a blistering snowstorm. Numerous times in my over two-hour commute I called the main campus (about 60 miles from our campus) to find out if our Grand Rapids campus was closed. I was ecstatic when I got word that the main campus had closed—only to find out that the main campus closing does not affect the subsidiary campuses. I white-knuckled the commute and arrived to the clinic exhausted from the treacherous trip. Brushing layers of snow off as I walked in, I exclaimed that I couldn't believe the clinic had not closed. My sweet secretary looked at me and said, "Dr. Emde, you decide if the clinic closes due to weather." These words were the greatest culmination of a long strenuous education anyone could hear. I had arrived. I called "snow days." It was a moment I will never forget.

Robin Emde, PhD, LPC

Have You Seen My Students?

Walking into my classroom, fresh from summer break, I take in the smell of freshly brewed coffee, printer toner, and pine cleaner. Adorned in a brand new tie and suit jacket, tucking a stack of freshly printed syllabi under my arm, I stride past the faculty offices and into my classroom. Although many years old, the desks gleam and reflect the fluorescent lights streaming down to the rugged industrial carpet. A presentation for the first lecture is displayed brightly on the projector, illuminating the wall with a giant "Welcome to Counseling Techniques" banner. I sit at my desk, organizing the syllabi and other handouts for the students in pristine piles. Although a few minutes early, I am surprised no one has entered the classroom yet. I often enjoy meeting my students as they stroll in, taking note of the excitement or anxiousness they present in our first meeting.

Despite not seeing students yet, I realize I am smiling at the empty classroom. It's a nice feeling. A few more minutes pass and my entire class is now three minutes late. My smile vanishes and a panicked flutter reverberates in my stomach. Feeling as if I know the error, I grab my coffee cup and check my syllabus, preparing to bolt to another room. To my surprise, I realize that I am in the right room. My brain lunges to the next possible conclusion: I must have the wrong time. Again, I am surprised to note that I am on time. This then begs the question—where are my students? Out of the corner of my eye, I see the chair for my department passing my door. I yell to her quickly: "Hi! Have you seen my students?" She smiles and chuckles a little. "No," she responds. "But I don't expect to for another week. Enjoy the rest of your summer." As she laughs quietly down the hall, I proceed to lecture to the empty room, in smiling anticipation of the students arriving one week from today.

Eric J. Perry, MA, NCC, ACS

Out of the Closet: The Decision of a Counselor Educator

As counselors, we are taught that limited self-disclosures are appropriate in order to ensure that a counseling session remains focused on the client and supports client growth. The same is true for counselor education, where as professors and practitioners we are responsible for modeling appropriate behavior for our students. As a queer counselor educator, the decision about whether or not to self-disclose sexual orientation is a complicated one that involves weighing the professional responsibilities verses the personal cost.

As a young adjunct professor at a rural college in Virginia I spent the first part of my career not referring to my wife when other professors openly talked about their heterosexual partners. As I matured as a faculty member and counselor educator, I found my voice and decided that my responsibility as a queer woman and counselor educator was to represent and disclose as appropriate. This first attempt at disclosure was one that involved stumbling, tripping, and perhaps falling flat on my face. However, over the years I have developed a solid sense of self as a queer counselor educator and am now adept at deciding when self-disclosure is appropriate and will benefit my students and create minimal risk for me.

However, there isn't always support in academia for being out and it is important to understand that your greatest obstacles may not be your students but rather fellow educators. When I transitioned into a full time tenure line position I was met with increased opposition to my mindset of self-disclosure in counselor education. My biggest obstacle was a fellow counselor educator who, while willing to admit to me that she was gay, was adamant that students view her as a "blank slate." My willingness to be out created conflict for her amongst the program which was fueled by fear that she would ultimately be outed. This difference in philosophy ultimately left me questioning my position at this university and searching for other opportunities.

Jennifer Keith, PhD, LPC, NCC

Classroom Chaos

We all know that famous anxiety nightmare. You know, the one where you're standing in front of a room, naked, and everyone is laughing at you. *That* nightmare. You wake up as relief washes over, realizing that isn't your reality. I can honestly say I lived that nightmare (minus the being naked part) in my very first class of my counselor education career. There I was, standing in front of twenty master's-level counseling students ready to begin the semester. Instead of class going how I had optimistically envisioned, everyone was talking and laughing over me; the room was complete chaos. I couldn't focus them or interrupt. The students kept asking why I wanted to be called "Dr." when I was their age. All of those doctoral discussions on pedagogy were somehow a faded, distant memory. My mind went blank; why wasn't I waking up?!

Ready for class with a PowerPoint, activities, and discussion questions, I was thrilled at the thought of realizing a professional milestone, the endless dissertation hours finally meaning something. I don't think anything could have fully prepared me for experiencing absolute vulnerability and the sudden realization that I had no idea how to manage a room full of adult learners. I spent the next sixteen weeks desperately researching and consulting on how I could engage the learning process before I lost my mind, or my job.

Five years later, I am working toward tenure. The amount of personal and professional growth that has happened for me since that first class is immeasurable. I love teaching; being in the classroom with counselors-in-training is the best part of my week. I hang onto those early memories of teaching because they have shaped me into the counselor educator I am today. I still identify with those feelings of inadequacy as they connect me to the vulnerability of our students and our clients in times of transition and stress. Ultimately, I am grateful for the opportunity to develop both necessary skills and the deep understanding that we have as much to learn from the educational process as our students.

Courtney M. Holmes, PhD, LPC, LMFT, NCC

My Dreams Came True

During my undergraduate studies in Early Childhood Education I had an influential professor that encouraged my classmates and me to care about not only the academic health of our young students but also the mental and emotional health as well. In my heart, a desire grew to one day be that influential person in someone else's life. As my undergraduate studies continued I gained additional clarity during my "Young Children with Special Needs" course where I was exposed to Play Therapy. I knew that was going to be my "Big Girl Job," and that has driven my personal and professional choices for the last 14-plus years.

After completing my bachelor's degree I taught in the elementary school setting and pursued my graduate studies in School Counseling. I had no desire to be a school counselor, and my department chair was aware of this. She allowed me to modify my course plan to include some courses in mental health counseling. During my graduate studies I learned the foundational knowledge of counseling children. I completed my master's degree, which was my first accomplishment towards earning my Registered Play Therapist (RPT) Certification. I then pursued a Graduate Certificate in Play Therapy in order to learn the skills and apply the knowledge that I would one day use with clients and teach to future children's counselors.

In order to teach the future counselors, I knew there was one more hurdle in my academic career. During my doctoral program in Counselor Education, a local institution was in need of an adjunct professor to teach their Introduction and Advanced Play Therapy courses. My dreams had come true! I have since taught the courses multiple times along with many other counselor education courses. I know that the passion for young children's mental health that was planted in me is now planting seeds into the future school, clinical, and rehabilitation counselors at my institution.

Korinne H. Babel, PhD, LPC, NCC

Getting an A Was More Important

I came to teaching in Counselor Education from my experiences working in Student Affairs. So I thought the transition to college teaching would be pretty simple. I had worked on college campuses for a number of years and had developed my skills as a trainer. I understood the student experience on a variety of levels, studied student development theory, and utilized it in my work.

One of the things I was unprepared for and surprised about was the depth of isolation that I felt as a faculty member. In Student Affairs, collaboration was the name of the game. Much of my career had been spent working on projects and developing training but always sharing input and ideas with others. As a professor, I found that others were busy doing their own things and not interested in collaboration or sharing ideas. Sometimes I felt at odds with my colleagues because of my focus on the holistic perspective of the student and my natural inclination to be student centered.

The second thing that I was unprepared for was the emotional toll of grading. As did most faculty, I liked school, studying, reading, and talking about ideas. I thought each graduate student would be just as interested and enthusiastic about her studies. I remember the first few semesters coming to the realization that the continuum of students and their expectations about professors, assignments, and grading were not the same as mine. Many of my students had grown up receiving rewards for just showing up; some looked at graduate school as a necessary evil or a barrier to the real work they wanted to do. My heart was broken the first time I discovered that some students chose to fabricate having actually participated in an experiential assignment and just wrote creative fiction. Feedback for some students was unwelcome. Getting an "A" was more important than understanding the content or fully participating in experiential lessons or assignments.

Jelane Kennedy, EdD, LMHC, LPC, NCC

It's All Downhill From Here

My first teaching experience is best described as a "trial by fire." I was given a 10-week online course with little notice and components that did not function, then found myself in charge of a second section of the course when its designer suddenly proved unable to teach. Student issues began the second week of the quarter: one missed the first two weeks of the course due to confusion over the start date, another surfaced four weeks into the term insisting on making up the first month's worth of work. She reported a compelling reason, but in an effort to remain fair to her peers, I agonizingly denied her request. When the midterm week concluded, another student realized the exam could have been taken multiple times to improve one's score. She emailed me angrily, asking me to reopen the midterm, saying, "I know that's what you said, but I didn't think that's what you meant." I had no idea how to respond, no precedent to follow, so I stuck to my guns and denied her request, but worried terribly about the decision.

As the course neared its end, student issues compounded. First, the student who missed the initial month of the term refused to drop the course despite completing almost no work. Another student was being deployed and, in an effort to accommodate their military responsibilities, I had to adjust the last three weeks of their course. Finally, I was left grading papers that I did not design—nor did I fully understood the purpose they served.

When the quarter ended and grades were entered, I left this course with more insights into teaching than I ever would have imagined. I learned it is easier to create a course than to follow someone else's template. I learned it can be excruciating to create a rubric for an assignment I did not design (especially since I was unclear about its purpose). I learned how to draw a firm line, yet still leave room for compassion and flexibility. Finally, I learned that sometimes I can only do as much as I can do. It's been all downhill from there.

Susannah Coaston, EdD, LPCC-S, CWC

Empathy

Empathy. The guiding and gentle concept in counseling that is not only essential to helping professionals, but also elusive in its essence. Instructing future counselors on empathy can be a challenge, but one in which I recently relished. The course affording me that opportunity was created to give a glimpse into the spirit of mental disorders, and to learn about the stigma and bias that accompanies it. On the syllabus was William Styron's *Darkness Visible: A Memoir of Madness* in order to illustrate deep, prolonged depression and suicidal ideation for my first semester graduate students.

I chose to take a risk by having the students write Found Poems from the text of the first chapter before we even discussed it. They had to use pieces of the prose and rearrange them into a poem form that elucidates the text in a personally meaningful way. I could not have expected what happened with the project. The students used fonts, effects, staggering lines and word shapes in an attempt to show the nature of depression. They excitedly explained their analysis to one another and how it describes what Styron states in his prose. One chose to use her poem to depict the "Mysteriously painful and elusive" feeling by making the poem actually hurt one's eyes to read it. Another chose to illuminate Styron's thought that depression is "close to being beyond description" by making the poem able to be read multiple ways, causing the reader to not be certain of its meaning. Every poem became a symbol of the horrors of depression.

The sheer pride and delight I had in the students was nothing compared to the empathy they gained when they used a non-traditional method to come to terms with a difficult concept. Sometimes being an instructor means taking a risk from the norm, and for me, this risk ended up forming one the most successful moments in teaching I have had to date.

Corey A. VanSickle, PhD Candidate in Counselor Education

My Second Home

I was preparing for my first Teaching Assistant (TA) experience as required for my doctorate program in counseling education and supervision. I was attending a CACREP accredited, blended program, which incorporated a three-day, in-house weekend. The course was Counseling Community Settings and the topic was a combination of the history, community, and foundation of counseling itself. I had prepared a PowerPoint and lecture to cover the topics I was responsible for. While this was a master's level course, it was for those in their first year. Some of the advice that my mentor shared with me prior to the weekend experience was to be myself and share some of the "stories" from my practice and that, if I did so, I would be a success. I was already a Licensed Professional Counselor (LPC) in private practice for roughly eight years. I wasn't sure exactly what he meant at the time but I was about to find out. My prepared PowerPoint and lecture turned out to be a total bomb. It was far too advanced and ambitious. Truth be told, I probably lost most of them shortly after I started. Without realizing it, I naturally started to share how I utilize the material I had presented and how it applied to actual clients in my practice. This intrigued the counseling students. As they realized I was a practicing clinician, the questions started and the stories began to flow. In turn, this confirmed for me that becoming an educator as well as a licensed clinician and supervisor was where I belonged. I felt as though I had found my second home.

Today, I am an assistant professor and practicing clinician and continue to maintain a small private practice. As we know, no two students learn the same. It is important to use a variety of teaching methods and utilize many strategies. Yet, I find one of the most powerful tools I have to offer my counseling students is the real-life examples the clients from my practice provide. They have a way of breathing life into the material!

Jean Georgiou, EdD, LPC, NCC, ACS

The Importance of Falling Off Our Bicycle: Scraped Knees and Lessons Learned

If I were to sum up graduate school in two words, they would be: not easy. I can prepare for all of the readings and effectively manage the course assignments, but there are some things I could not prepare for. No one told me about feeling incompetent at my graduate assistantship or at my internship. No one described the feeling I got in the pit of my stomach when I was unable to help someone and I had to let go. I was not prepared to come into a graduate lecture, expecting to be, well, lectured to, and instead find myself divulging the inner workings of my heart and mind with my peers, practically strangers then, making myself so vulnerable and exposed for the sake of getting over the fear of being vulnerable and exposed.

I was not prepared to be a year and a half into a program and, retrospectively, yet confidently, say "Wow, I've grown." I remember all of the times that I walked into class ready to talk about my experiences—specifically my downfalls and failures—in hopes that my professor would help me. I came in like a child who had fallen off of their bike and had tears in their eyes and two scraped knees.

I think about all of the times I processed case studies prior to class or thought about the experiences I had at my internship or assistantship. It did not matter whether I shared with my peers and professor that I had fallen. My scraped knees were still there. I would sit in class and listen to the experiences and thoughts of my peers and professor. After two and a half hours of class, something was different. My knees still hurt but I was able to put bandages on the scrapes. It hurt to fall, yes, but I knew that by listening, *really* listening, and trying to make sense of everyone else's thoughts, philosophies, and critiques, I would be able to get back on my bicycle. When I fall again—which is a part of learning how to ride a bike—there are always more bandages. In graduate school, there is always more support. Sometimes it is from my professors and sometimes it is from my peers, but all of that support makes me little bit more ready for the next scraped knee.

Andrew Melendez

As the title of this book suggests, as an educator, I strive to help students acquire necessary skills to be competent practitioners. The role I assume is often one of a coach, facilitating dialogue in an atmosphere where candid discussion of sometimes uncomfortable topics can take place. I firmly believe that institutions of higher education are teaching hospitals where students should be free to practice skills and make mistakes. Learning from these mistakes, ultimately, students gain proficiency in their craft. Utilizing Andrew's illustration, student resilience is built when they fall from their proverbial bicycles and skin their knees. Likewise, much can be learned from this example as it relates to my teaching pedagogy. My teaching is a work in progress, always changing and evolving in order to be as effective as possible. Yet, I don't always get it right. For example, myopic rigidity on curricula does not always allow for flexibility that is required in the most effective learning moments. How can I expect flexibility of students when I, myself, am unable to model the same behavior? It is in these missed opportunities that I, too, fall off my bicycle and skin my knees. I bandage my skinned knees by listening; listening to students' struggles and lived experiences. In essence, I become the student in my own classroom. There is power in listening. And when we, as educators, truly listen to our students, we create a process that enriches the understanding for both teacher and student.

Matthew R. Shupp, EdD, NCC, DCC

Learning From Non-Traditional Students

As a counselor educator, I not only have the pleasure of imparting knowledge and experiences in preparation of counseling students for future practice, but I most importantly have the great honor of encountering students from diverse backgrounds and often those who are considered "non-traditional." These non-traditional students bring with them interesting backgrounds, journeys, talents, and life experiences that the class benefits from in more profound ways than from reading the assigned textbooks.

Betty is one example of such a student who has greatly impacted my teaching experience. Betty is a 70-year-old, African American woman; a retired ESL teacher; a world traveler; a mother and grandmother; and is legally blind. Betty's life's journey, which she has shared during various reflective classroom activities, has contained tragic family losses, hurtful encounters with racism as a young girl growing up during the Jim Crow era, challenges faced with her developmental disability, and her 30 years of teaching experience. Her experiences have provided real-life examples for her fellow classmates and me, as the core aspects of counseling, such as human growth and development, grief and loss, career development, and cross-cultural issues, have been broached in the classroom. Betty's teaching skills, which are apparent during student presentations, and her many years of teaching experience have also inspired me as her instructor to adopt teaching methods that I had not previously considered.

Ria E. Baker, PhD, LPC-S

Upon entering my Counselor Education doctoral program, I developed an unmerited, misguided, and somewhat foolish sense of arrogance in underestimating the program and overestimating my abilities. The first semester of the program came and went smoothly. This was not surprising to me because I never struggled academically. "Maybe I am just that good?" I thought to myself. Boy, was I wrong!

During my second semester, I had a class in which I had to create a syllabus for a course. I decided to create a syllabus for a multicultural counseling class and I thought I had done an excellent job. In fact, I knew I had done an excellent job. In reality, I did a terrible job! The syllabus was filled with unrealistic assignments that did not correspond well with the course objectives and lacked overall coherence.

By my second semester in the program, I had developed close relationships with the majority of the faculty; the course professor was one of them. This added to her feedback, which cut like a knife. She was direct and blunt. With disappointment etched in her face, she ended her feedback by commenting on the obvious lack of effort I dedicated towards the assignment. In the moment, I was hurt, embarrassed, and offended. I wanted to defend myself and then run out of the classroom in embarrassment and shame. But I sat in my seat, swallowed, thanked her for her feedback, and waited for class to be dismissed.

Later that night, I realized I had (what my grandmother used to call) "become too big for my britches." I had overestimated my abilities and underestimated the demands and the expectations of the program. I also realized that I was approaching the program as though I were earning the degree for someone else and not taking ownership of my work. From that day forward, I never looked at the program, the degree, or the profession the same. I discovered a profound pride that transcended the previous, "Well, I guess this is the next logical step" mentality I subscribed to previously. I asked the instructor for an opportunity to re-write the syllabus. I still received a terrible grade on the assignment, but I wanted feedback on a revised syllabus that reflected my newly adopted sense of ownership, pride, and control. As for the instructor and me? The incident strengthened our relationship, and despite my graduating and beginning my career as an Assistant Professor in another state, she remains one of my most trusted mentors and a dear friend.

Maia Niguel Moore, PhD, NCC

Repositioning the Privilege of Language as a Counselor Educator

Much of my emerging career as a counselor educator starts with a commitment as a feminist, humanist, and postmodernist, where I have the opportunity to focus on two aspects: (a) the language defining narratives of my students and (b) the possibilities of socially constructing knowledge together in a collaborative manner. It is my privilege as a counselor educator to recognize the types of power I hold in the classroom with my students, which magnify a responsibility to facilitate growth, development, learning, and ethical responsibility for my students. More recently, I recalled this idea upon teaching a Counseling Interview Skills course this semester. As the child of two immigrants and a second-generation, multiethnic Asian American, I found myself in moments and experiences that challenged me to reflect on my own positionality. For instance, I had several international students in my course this year, which challenged me to think about how I was properly connecting and engaging these students through differences in the socialization of education. I critically examine the methods through which pedagogical practices continue to assist these students with their professional development and growth as counseling trainees. Utilizing a philosophy of cultural humility begins with me and how I approach my tasks, functions, and roles. I teach courses in an educational context that demonstrates my positioning with a dominant majority as my language easily attends to the majority of my students in the course. My international students often relate their challenges and frustrations about fear of opening dialogue in the class because their language is not that of the dominant majority. They also relate the challenges of reviewing materials multiple times because the materials were not oriented to their cultural reference points of education nor in their first language. It is heartbreaking to hear their experiences of disconnectedness from the classroom and community, but the experiences represent my responsibility to activate efforts of change.

Christian D. Chan, MA, NCC

Index

Note: *Italicized* page numbers indicate a figure on the corresponding page. Page numbers in **bold** indicate a table on the corresponding page.

abstract conceptualization (thinking) 79
academic integrity and conduct 135
accommodator learner 103
active experimentation (doing) 79
active processing 24
admissions gatekeeping 172–173
adult learners: andragogy and 102–103; application to counselor education students 85–86; autonomy 87; CACREP standards 79; chalk talk/gallery walk technique 90; constructivism 83–84; efficacious teaching 86; experiential learning 79, **80**; group work 88, 92; Guided Practice Example 90–91; Honey and Mumford model 79–80, **80**; introduction to 8–9, 78; isolation of 88; learning basics 79–83, **80**, **81**, **82**; learning objectives 78; limitations of 82–83; mid-quarter course evaluation 94; mind styles 81, **82**; motivation of 87; multiple intelligences 80–81, **81**; ongoing evaluation and feedback 93–94; online learning 86–88; overview of 83–85; Perry's Stages 84–85; positivist learning environment 88–94; problem-based learning 89–90; resistant students 94–95; summary of 95; syllabi excerpt 93; think-pair share 92; VAK/VARK styles 82, **82**
Advanced Group Counseling course 105–106
adversity protection in mentoring 218–220
Advocacy Competencies (ACA) 62
Age Discrimination in Employment Act (1967) 37

American Counseling Association (ACA) 43, 89
American Counseling Association (ACA) Code of Ethics (2014) 148–149, 169, 175, 190–191, 219; *see also* ethical/legal issues
American Psychological Association (APA) 106
American with Disabilities Act of 1990 (ADA) 135, 138
analytic rubrics 154
andragogy: adult learners and 102–103; influence on syllabus 129–130; introduction to 16, 17–18; learning objectives 110; methods of 103–104
assessment: case study 153, 163–164; culture of 150; defined 146; developmental approach to 151; dispositional assessment 152–153; ethical/legal issues 39–41; evaluation of student learning 146–148; knowledge-based assessment 151–152; learning in counselor education 148–150; resistant students 162–163; screening, remediating, gatekeeping 162; skills-based assessment 152; *see also* evaluation of student learning
assignment schedule in syllabus 136
assimilator learner 103
Association for Specialists in Group Work (ASGW) 68
Association for Spiritual, Ethical, and Religious Values in Counseling (ASERVIC) Competencies for Addressing Spiritual and Religious Issues in Counseling 62
Association for Supervision and Curriculum Development (ASCD) 125

Index 241

Association of Counselor Education and Supervision (ACES) 23, 138, 172
Association of Multicultural Counseling and Development (AMCD) Multicultural Counseling Competencies (Sue, Arredondo, McDavis) 61, 62
asynchronous learning opportunities 128
asynchronous technologies 202–204
attendance and participation policy 134
autonomy 1, 17, 19, 87

blogs 204–205
Bloom's Taxonomy of Educational Objectives 101, 107–109, *108*, 111–112, **112**, 122
bottom-up communication 163
brain-based teaching approaches (BBTA) 23–24

Carnegie Classifications of Institutions of Higher Learning, Research I schools 5
Case Studies in School Counseling (ACA) 89
chalk talk technique 90
Characteristics of an Effective Psychotherapist Index (CEPI) 181
characteristics of effective teachers 9–11
cheating by students 46–47
Civil Rights Act (1968) 37
clarity in syllabus 131
classism 221
classroom environments 2–8
classroom real-life experiences 231–239
class schedule in syllabus 136
clear guidance 214
clinical experience in teaching 11
clinical judgment 170
Clinical Mental Health Counseling 107
clinical supervision and gatekeeping 173–174
closing the gap group project 92
cognitive regression 85
collaborative learning 24
collaborative mentoring 217–218
collegiality mentoring 217–218
communication platforms 205–208
community mentoring 217–218
Competencies for Counseling Lesbian, Gay, Bisexual, Queer, Questioning, Intersex and Ally Individuals 111
concrete experience (feeling) 79
constructivism 18–19, 83–84
construct validity of rubrics 160
content-heavy classrooms 110
content validity of rubrics 160
converger learner 103
Cornell University Center for Teaching Excellence 132–133
Council for Accreditation of Counseling and Related Programs (CACREP): adult learners 79; counseling preparation programs 44; curriculum development 120–121; diversity/multicultural considerations 60, 64, 69, 72; ethical/legal issues 36–37; evaluation of student learning 146; gatekeeping 169; identity of counselor educator 2; knowledge/skills acquisition 101–102, 106–107, 112–113; mentoring 214; personal philosophy of teaching 15–16; role of 149–150; syllabus in curriculum development 133, 138; teaching across educational platforms 190–191
Council for Higher Education Accreditation (CHEA) 44, 147
Council for the Accreditation 106
Counseling Competencies Scale (CCS) 180
counseling preparation programs 44
Counseling Self-Estimate Inventory (COSE) 180–181
counselor educator/education: adult learners and 85–86; awareness/attitudes 61; classroom real-life experiences 231–239; gatekeeping competence 170–172; knowledge of diversity issues 61–62; mentoring role of 4; role of 4–5, 7–8; roles of 4–6; scholarship of 5–6; service by 6; skills of 62–64, *63*; supervision role of 4–5; as teacher 37–42; technology in 201–204; *see also* diversity/multicultural considerations; identity of counselor educator
Counselor Preparation Comprehensive Examination (CPCE) 151, 180
courageous conversations 70–71
course management platforms 201
course materials 123–126
creativity/response to student learning styles 10
Crisis Response Teams 6
criterion referencing 155
criterion validity of rubrics 160
critical pedagogy (CP) 19
Critical Race Theory 74
critical thinking 20, 132
Cross-cultural Counseling Competence Inventory-Revised (CCCI-R) 181
cultural awareness 220

Cultural Name Game 67–68
culture of assessment 150
curriculum and due process 174–175
curriculum development: course materials 123–126; course syllabus 128–141; delivery platforms 126–128; Guided Practice Exercise 124; introduction to 120; learning objectives 120–121; overview 121–128; summary of 141–142; *see also* syllabus in curriculum development

delivery platforms in curriculum development 126–128
developmental level of students 11
difficult dialogues 70
Discussion Boards online 191, 197
discussion forums 204–205
dispositional assessment 152–153
diverger learner 103
diversity/multicultural considerations: CACREP standards 60, 64; case study 73; counselor awareness/attitudes 61; counselor knowledge 61–62; counselor skills 62–64, *63*; ethical/legal issues 50–51; group dynamics and 68–69; Guided Practice Exercise 64–65, 69–70, 74; history and competency development 60–64, *63*; initiating courageous conversations 70–71; introduction to 59; learning objectives 59; pedagogical strategies for integrating 65–71, **66**; privilege/oppression framework 64–65; summary of 75; training with resistant students 71–75
dualistic thinking 84

effacious teaching 86
efficacious learning objectives 110
efficacious teaching 86
e-learning communities 127
email technology 202–203
empowerment 19, 62
endorsements 35, 38, 47–49, 54, 175
enjoyment from teacher 10
Equal Pay Act (1963) 37
ethical/legal issues: case study 40; cheating/plagiarism 46–47; counselor educator as teacher 37–42; endorsements and recommendations 47; establishing/following procedures 44–45; Family Educational Rights and Privacy Act 47–48; gatekeeping 45–46; Guided Practice Exercise 195; introduction to 35–36; learning objectives 36; legal requirements 42–48; malpractice insurance requirements 47; mentoring 42; multicultural considerations 50–51; orientation to program 38–39; practicum and internship 41–42; problematic student behaviors/dispositions 51–53; professor-student relationships 48–50; requiring student counseling 42; student admission 37–38; student appeals policies 45; student remediation 52–53; summary 53–54; teaching across educational platforms 194–195; teaching and assessment 39–41
Eurocentrism 221
evaluation competence to teach 40
evaluation of student learning: accrediting bodies, requirements 149–150; CACREP standards 146; evolution of assessment 146–148; introduction to 145; learning objectives 145; methods of 150–153; rubrics 153–161; summary of 164; *see also* assessment
expanded course description 134
experiential learning 24, 79, **80**, 104

face-to-face counselor training 126–127
face-to-face instruction 1, 191–192
face-to-face practicum course 126
factual knowledge 170
faculty-student communication 195–196
faculty-student ratio 4
Family Educational Rights and Privacy Act (FERPA) 47–48
feedback in teaching across educational platforms 197–198
feminist pedagogy 19
formative assessment 146–147
formative evaluation 147
full value contract 67

gallery walk technique 90
Gardner, Howard 80–81, **81**
gatekeeping: admissions gatekeeping 172–173; assessment and 162; CACREP Standards 169; case study 174, 183–184; clinical supervision 173–174; counselor competence 170–172; curriculum and due process 174–175; dispositions 171–172, 181; factual knowledge and 170; generic clinical skills 170–171; Guided Practice Exercise 172, 182–183; importance of 169; introduction to

Index 243

1, 168; knowledge measures 180; learning objectives 168; multicultural considerations in 183; objective measures of 180–181; obstacles to 181–183; opportunities for 172–176; overview of 45–46; program gatekeeping 173–175; resistant students 184; sample remediation plan 175–176; skill measures 180–181; strategies for 176–179; summary of 184; teaching across educational platforms 194–195
gate slippage 182
gender roles 19
generic clinical skills 170–171
grading policy 134–135
graduate assistants 49
graduate-level counseling programs 122
graduate writing 109
group agreements 67
group assignments 92
group leadership competence 105
group project learning 102
group work with adult learners 88

Health Advisory Boards 6
Health Information Technology for Economic and Clinical Health (HITECH) Act 201
Health Insurance Portability and Accountability Act of 1996 (HIPAA) 48, 201
heterosexism 221
higher learning platforms 191–193
Historically Black College/University (HBCU) 221
holistic rubrics 153–154
Horowitz v. Board of Curators of the University of Missouri 46
Hull, Jane 63
hybrid instruction 193

identity of counselor educator: act of teaching 8–11; adults as learners 8–9; CACREP standards 2; characteristics of effective teachers 9–11; classroom environments 2–8; guided practice exercise 3, 7, 8–9; introduction to 1; learning objectives 1; professional identity 3–4; roles of 4–6; scholarship of 5–6; service by 6; summary of 11–12; as teacher 7–8; teaching and supervision 4–5
Immigration Reform and Control Act 37
impairment and gatekeeping 176
imposter syndrome 85, 86

inclusiveness statement 136
incompetent trainee 177
Individuals with Disabilities Education Act (IDEA) 51
instructional materials 134
intergroup dialogues 70
International Counseling Case Studies Handbook (ACA) 89
Internet-based resources 125
internship ethical/legal issues 41–42
interpersonal attributes 170
inter-rater reliability of rubrics 160
intervention in mentoring 218–220
intra-rater reliability of rubrics 160
isolation of adult learners 88

Just-in-Time Teaching (JITT) 93, 201

key performance indicators (KPIs) 122
kinesthetic learner 103
Knapp, Alexander 16
knowledge-based assessment 151–152
knowledge/skills acquisition: adult learners 102–103; andragogical methods 103–104; CACREP standards 101–102; construction of learning objectives 111–115, **112**; developing effective learning objectives 109–111; Guided Practice Exercise 112–113; introduction to 101; learning objectives 101, 104–107; summary of 115; teaching methods overview 102
Knowles, Malcolm 16
Kolb, David 79, **80**
Kram, Kathy 215
KWL chart 23

learner-centered approach 20
learning objectives: adult learners 78; andragogical learning objectives 110; assessment 148–150; clinical courses and 114–115; construction of 111–115, **112**; curriculum development 120; defined 104–107; diversity/multicultural considerations 59; efficacious learning objectives 110; ethical/legal issues 36; evaluation of student learning 145; gatekeeping 168; identity of counselor educator 1; incorporation into courses 113–114; knowledge/skills acquisition 101, 104–107; mentoring 213; personal philosophy of teaching 15; teaching across educational platforms 190
legal issues *see* ethical/legal issues

lesbian, gay, bisexual, transgender, queer, intersex, and questioning (LGBTQIQ) 43, 62–63, 73, 123

male gender bias 221
malpractice insurance requirements 47
McIntosh, Peggy 64
mentoring: as aspect of leadership 215; CACREP standards 214; case study 221, 223–224; coaching to socialize 217–218; collaborative mentoring 217–218; effective strategies for 215–225; ethical/legal issues 42; increasing mentee credibility 222–224; introduction to 213; learning objectives 213; necessity of 214–215; performance challenges 220–222; protection from adversity 218–220; resistant students 224–225; role of counselor educator 4; sponsor advancement 216–217; summary 225
microaggressions 64
micro-skills 102
mind styles 81, **82**
minority stress 64
motivation of adult learners 87
Multicultural and Social Justice Competence Principles for Group (ASGW) 68
Multicultural and Social Justice Competencies (Ratts) 63
Multicultural and Social Justice Counseling Competencies 111
multicultural considerations *see* diversity/multicultural considerations
Multicultural Counseling Competencies (AMCD) 62
multicultural society 122
multiple intelligences 80–81, **81**
multiplistic thinking 84

National Counselor Exam (NCE) 151–152
Net Generation 204
neuroscience findings on teaching 23–24
Neuroscience Interest Network 23
norm referencing 154

on-demand videos 203–204
online instruction 86–88, 137, 192–193
oppression 64–65, 73, 220
orientation-specific technical skills 170

passive learning 102
personal philosophy of teaching: andragogy and 16, 17–18; CACREP standards 15–16; congruence between theory and practice 20–22, 21; constructivism 18–19; critical pedagogy 19; development of 25, 28; example of 28–30; Guided Practice Exercise 15, 25–27; introduction to 14–15; learning objectives 15; neuroscience findings on 23–24; pedagogy and 16; summary of 31; theories of 18–20; theory in action 22–23; transformative learning 20
persons with disabilities 135
plagiarism by students 46–47
pluralistic society 122
positivist learning environment 88–94
practicum ethical/legal issues 41–42
predominately White institution (PWI) 221
Pregnancy Discrimination Act 37
prevention in mentoring 218–220
Principles and Practices of Leadership Excellence of Chi Sigma Iota 214
privilege framework in diversity/multicultural considerations 64–65
problematic student behaviors/dispositions 51–53
problematic trainee 177
problem-based learning (PBL) 22–23, 89–90
problems of professional competence 176
professional identity 3–4
professor-student relationships 48–50
program gatekeeping 173–175
program level strategies 177

qualitative inquiry 5

racial/ethnic privilege 61
reflection in mentoring 218–220
reflective observation (watching) 79
Rehabilitation Act (1973) 37, 135
relationship building through syllabus 128–129
relationships in teaching across educational platforms 193–194
relativistic thinking 84
relaxed alertness 24
remediating and assessment 162
remediation 45, 52–53
repertoire of teaching strategies 5
requirements in syllabus 136
resistant students: as adult learners 94–95; assessment considerations 162–163; gatekeeping 184; mentoring 224–225; syllabus in curriculum development 130–131; training of 71–75

roles of counselor educator 4–6
rubrics: analytic rubrics 154; development of 155–157, **158–159**; Guided Practice Exercise 161; holistic rubrics 153–154; introduction to 153–155; overview of 153–161; in practice 161; reliability and validity of 160–161

scholarship of counselor educator 5–6
screening and assessment 162
self-actualization 19
self-reflection 24, 61
service by counselor educator 6
The Seven Habits of Highly Effective People (Covey) 222
sincerely held principles 43
skill deficit 176
skill difficulty 176
skills-based assessment 152
social construction 104
social identity groups 61
socialization process 214
social marginalization 220
social media 204
standardized supervision 114
student-centered learning 102, 110–111
student-faculty interactions 64, 194
student learning outcomes (SLOs) 122; *see also* evaluation of student learning
student level strategies 177–178
students: admissions 37–38; appeals policies 45; autonomy of 17, 19; problematic behaviors/dispositions 51–53; remediation of 45, 52–53; self-directedness 17
summative assessment 146–147
summative evaluation 147
supervision role of counselor educator 4–5
supportive environments while gatekeeping 10
syllabus in curriculum development: academic integrity and conduct 135; andragogy influence on 129–130; attendance and participation policy 134; building relationships through 128–129; case study 137–141, 142; clarity in 131; class schedule, assignment schedule, requirements 136; components of 132–136; expanded course description 134; grading 134–135; Guided Practice Exercise 137; inclusiveness statement 136; instructional materials 134; introduction to 128; online classes 137; persons with disabilities 135; philosophy of teaching 133–134; preparing to craft 132; resistant students 130–131; student disposition evaluations 130
synchronous learning opportunities 128
synchronous technologies 202

teacher-centered instruction 102
teacher/teaching: act of 8–11; characteristics of effective teachers 9–11; counselor educator as 37–42; efficacious teaching 86; enjoyment from 10; ethical/legal issues 39–41; evaluating effectiveness of 11; evaluation competence 40; identity of teachers 7–8; professor-student relationships 48–50; role of counselor educator 4–5, 7–8; *see also* mentoring; personal philosophy of teaching
teaching across educational platforms: asynchronous/synchronous technologies 202; CACREP standards 190–191; case study 196–197; communication platforms 205–208; course management platforms 201; discussion forums/blogs 204–205; ethical/legal issues 194–195; face-to-face instruction 1, 191–192; faculty-student communication 195–196; feedback 197–198; hybrid instruction 193; introduction to 190; learning objectives 190; online instruction 86–88, 137, 192–193; platforms of higher learning 191–193; relationships in 193–194; roles and responsibilities 193–198; technology in counselor education 201–204; technology options 198–201; wikis 205
Teaching Methodology Instrument 18
Teaching Task Force Report (ACES, 2016) 23
Technical Competencies for Counselor Education (Jencius, Poynton, Patrick) 48
technology: asynchronous technologies 202–204; in counselor education 201–204; counselor educator/education 201–204; email technology 202–203; synchronous technologies 202; teaching across educational platforms 198–201; in teaching across educational platforms 198–201

Technology Acceptance Model 202
textbook selection 123–124
think-pair share 92
transformative learning 20
transgender and gender nonconforming (TGNC) people 70

Unified Theory of Acceptance and Use of Technology 202
Universal Design (UD) principles 125
unprofessional behavior 2
U.S. Constitution 37
U.S. Department of Education (USDE) 147
U.S. Supreme Court 46

VAK/VARK learning styles 82, **82**
visual learner 103

Ward v. Wilbanks (2011) 43
well-being 19
White-Black discussions 60, 61
White privilege 64
wikis 205
William Perry's Theory of Intellectual and Ethical Development (Perry) 84
willingness to reflect 10–11
Working Alliance Inventory-Short Form (WAI-SF) 181

YouTube platform 204

Made in United States
Troutdale, OR
01/09/2024

16844212R00146